## International Trade Centre

Product and market development

UNCTAD CNUCED   WTO OMC

# *Coffee*

## *An exporter's guide*

Geneva 2002

## ABSTRACT FOR TRADE INFORMATION SERVICES

2002                                                                                          SITC 071
                                                                                              COF

INTERNATIONAL TRADE CENTRE UNCTAD/WTO
Coffee: An exporter's guide
Geneva: ITC, 2002. xxii, 310 p.

Guide on coffee – provides overview of world coffee trade, demand in importing countries, prices, statistical data; discusses niche markets, environment and social aspects; highlights organic coffee production, marketing and quality control issues; reviews contracts and deliveries, shipping, financial aspects and insurance, electronic commerce and supply chain management, dispute resolution, arbitration, futures markets, and hedging; explores commercial risk and risk related to trade credit issues; describes marketing systems; gives coffee producers' country profiles. Annexes include International Coffee Agreement 2001, list of useful web addresses.

Subject descriptors: **Coffee, Export marketing, Prices, Statistical data, Contracts, Insurance, Electronic commerce, Supply management, Quality control, Arbitration, Export credit.**

English

Palais des Nations, 1211 Geneva 10, Switzerland

*The Government of Denmark financed the preparation and publication of this guide.*

Digital image on the cover provided by: Migros-Genossenschafts-Bund, Switzerland/Ziggurat, London, United Kingdom.

ITC/P140.E/PMD/MDS/02-VIII                              ISBN 92-9137-241-2
                                                        United Nations Sales No. E.02.III.T.6

# Acknowledgements

The main contributors to this guide were:

**Hein Jan van Hilten**, coordinator and principal author of the guide (niche markets, sustainability and related issues, contracts and arbitration, logistics and insurance, electronic supply chain management, financial risk and credit, marketing systems, coffee quality and quality control issues); Independent Coffee Development Consultant; former Chairman of the Mild Coffee Trade Association of Eastern Africa, Nairobi. Email: cafeknsult@scottburgh.co.za

**Paul J. Fisher**, principal consultant and collaborating author (contracts, coffee trading, e-commerce, price risk management, futures markets, hedging, general review); Independent Coffee Consultant; former Chairman of the Board of Directors of the Green Coffee Association and Chairman of the GCA Contracts Development Committee, New York. Email: pjfisher@ix.netcom.com

**Michael A. Wheeler** (economic issues, mainstream markets, trends and statistical information); Independent Coffee Economist; former President of the Specialty Coffee Association of Europe, London. Email: wheeler@globalnet.co.uk

**Morten Scholer** (management issues); Senior Market Development Adviser, Market Development Section, International Trade Centre UNCTAD/WTO, Geneva. Email: scholer@intracen.org

This guide was made possible through the voluntary contribution of expertise, experience, insider knowledge and valuable time by the people, companies and organizations below, whose assistance is acknowledged with thanks and appreciation.

- Gerd Boschen, former Managing Partner, Nikolaus Reuter, Bremen, Germany
- Ted Davis, Director of Corporate Communications, New York Board of Trade, New York, United States of America
- Captain Reinhard Diegner, Vice President, Lampe & Schwartze Insurance, Bremen, Germany
- Dick Engelsma, General Manager, Decotrade AG, Zug, Switzerland
- Mauk Faber, Director, Global Structured Trade Finance, Rabobank International, Utrecht, the Netherlands
- Michael P. Flynn, Chairman, European Coffee Federation Contracts Committee, London, United Kingdom
- Laut Hilckmann, Immediate Past Chairman, European Coffee Federation Transport Committee, Utrecht, the Netherlands
- Patrick F. Installé, Managing Director, EFICO n.v. Green Coffee, Antwerp, Belgium
- Jasper P. van Schaik, Manager, Coffee Cocoa and Dairy Desk, Global Commodities Group, Fortis Bank, Amsterdam, the Netherlands
- Garth Smith, President, Organic Products Trading Co., Vancouver, Washington, United States
- Roel Vaessen, Secretary General, European Coffee Federation, Amsterdam, the Netherlands
- Jan van der Wyck, retired Shipping Executive, P&O Nedlloyd, Rotterdam, the Netherlands
- Paul Wilkes, Director, Complete Coffee Limited, London, United Kingdom
- The International Coffee Organization
- The European Coffee Federation
- The Green Coffee Association of New York
- The All Japan Coffee Association

- The New York Board of Trade – NYBOT
- The London International Financial Futures and Options Exchange – LIFFE
- Kraft Foods International
- Nestlé
- Sara Lee / DE

Contributions and assistance from the following are also gratefully acknowledged.

- Rainer Baechi, Institute for Marketecology, IMO, Sulgen, Switzerland
- Romeo S. Barbara, Kraft Foods International, Commodity Group Procurement KF1, Zug, Switzerland
- Sergio Beczkowski, BM&F (Brazilian Mercantile & Futures Exchange), São Paolo, Brazil
- Maurice Blanc, Nestec Ltd, Vevey, Switzerland
- Francisco van der Hoff Boersma, Col. Estación, Mexico
- Bolero.net, London, United Kingdom
- Carlos H.J. Brando, P&A Marketing International, E.S. Pinhal, Brazil
- Gabriel Cadena Gomez, National Coffee Research Center, Cenicafé-Federacafe, Chinchiná, Colombia
- Ivan Carvalho, Statistician, International Coffee Organization, London, United Kingdom
- Joris G.M.R. Claeys, Accelerate Supply Chain Solutions, Hackettstown, New Jersey, United States
- Robin Dand, London International Financial Futures and Options Exchange, United Kingdom
- Carlo Delfs, Kraft Foods International, Commodity Group Procurement KF1, Zug, Switzerland
- Frans, Norbert and Reinier Douqué, J.Th. Douqué's Koffie BV, Amstelveen, the Netherlands
- Stephen Dunn, Nestec Ltd, Vevey, Switzerland
- Gerrit van Elst, Decotrade AG, Zug, Switzerland
- John Eustace, former Managing Director, E.D. & F. Man Coffee Limited, London, United Kingdom
- Clive H. Furness, Contango Markets Ltd, East Grinstead, United Kingdom
- M.P.H. Gathaara, Coffee Research Foundation, Ruiru, Kenya
- Bernard Gaud, Walter Matter SA, Geneva, Switzerland
- Daniele Giovannucci, Agribusiness Consultant, Philadelphia, Pennsylvania, United States
- Michael C. Glenister, Amcafé Inc., New Rochelle, New York, United States
- Ward de Groote, Ahold Coffee Company BV, Zaandam, the Netherlands
- Jos Harmsen, Stichting Max Havelaar, Utrecht, the Netherlands
- Hidetaka Hayashi, Hayashi Coffee Institute, Tokyo, Japan
- Clive A. van Hilten, Information Technology Developer, London, United Kingdom
- Ernesto Illy, Illycaffè S.p.a, Trieste, Italy
- Christian A. Joerg, Société Générale de Surveillance SA, Geneva, Switzerland
- Sipke W. de Jong, Decotrade AG, Zug, Switzerland
- Rebecca L. Johnson, science writer, Sioux Falls, South Dakota, United States
- Paul Katzeff, Thanksgiving Coffee Co., Fort Bragg, California, United States
- Soren Knudsen, Knudsen Group, Santos, Brazil
- Paula A Koelemij, Simon Lévelt BV, Haarlem, the Netherlands
- Karl Kofler, Kraft Foods International, Commodity Group Procurement KF1, Zug, Switzerland
- Alf Kramer, Remarc, Independent Coffee Consultant, Horten, Norway
- Dennis Macray, Starbucks Coffee Company, Seattle, Washington, United States
- Sandy McAlpine, Coffee Association of Canada, Don Mills, Ontario, Canada
- David R. McGaw, University of the West Indies, St Augustine, Trinidad and Tobago
- Sue Mecklenburg, Starbucks Coffee Company, Seattle, Washington, United States
- Roland Meier, CTA–CFC Projects, UNOPS, Nairobi, Kenya
- Jan Meijer, J. Wolff & Company BV, Brielle, the Netherlands
- Sunalini N. Menon, CoffeeLab Private Ltd, Bangalore, India
- Malcolm Wall Morris, London International Financial Futures and Options Exchange, United Kingdom

- Kerry Muir, former Chairman, ICO Statistics Committee, London, United Kingdom
- Robert F. Nelson, National Coffee Association of USA Inc., New York, United States
- Henry Ngabirano, Uganda Coffee Development Authority, Kampala, Uganda
- Doan Trieu Nhan, Vietnam Coffee & Cocoa Association, Hanoi, Viet Nam
- Ronald J. Onzima, Interafrican Coffee Organisation, Abidjan, Côte d'Ivoire
- R. Price Peterson, Hacienda la Esmeralda, Boquete, Panama
- Alain Pittet, Nestlé Research Center, Lausanne, Switzerland
- Joost Pierrot, Organic Production and Marketing Consultant, Leiden, the Netherlands
- The Procter & Gamble Co., Cincinnati, Ohio, United States
- Gloria Inés Puerta Quintero, National Coffee Research Center, Cenicafé-Federacafe, Chinchiná, Colombia
- Paul Rice, TransFair USA, Oakland, California, United States
- Mike Ritchie, TFC Commodity Charts, North Battleford, Saskatchewan, Canada
- Aimee Russillo, Rainforest Alliance, New York, United States
- Paul Soucy, Environmental Solar Systems, Boston, Massachusetts, United States
- Susie Spindler, Cup of Excellence, Missoula, Montana, United States
- Gerrit H.D. van der Stegen, Sara Lee / DE, Utrecht, the Netherlands
- Ria Stout, Utz Kapeh Foundation, Antigua Guatemala, Guatemala
- Søren Sylvest, Estate Coffee, Copenhagen, Denmark
- Birthe Thode Jacobsen, Scanagri, Copenhagen, Denmark
- David Towler, Complete Coffee Limited, London, United Kingdom
- Panos Varangis, The World Bank, Washington, D.C., United States
- Luis Rodriquez Ventura, Consejo Salvadoreno del Café, El Salvador
- Rinantonio Viani, consultant, Corseaux, Switzerland
- Maja Wallengren, Oster DowJones Commodity News, Mexico City, Mexico
- David Wehrli, Migros-Genossenschafts-Bund, Zurich, Switzerland
- Birgit Wilhelm, Naturland-Verband, Graefelfing, Germany
- Mary Williams, Starbucks Coffee Company, Seattle, Washington, United States
- Philippe D.A. Witts, Fortis Bank, Amsterdam, the Netherlands
- Christian B. Wolthers, Blaser & Wolthers Specialty Coffee, Miami, Florida, United States
- Eric C. Wood, USGS/Eros Data Center, Sioux Falls, South Dakota, United States

Special acknowledgement is made of the valuable assistance and guidance received from the members of the editorial review board. The board comprised:

- Abba Bayer, Managing Director, J W Phyfe & Co. Inc., New York, United States
- Pablo Dubois, Head of Operations, International Coffee Organization, London, United Kingdom
- Gordon S. Gillett, Senior Vice President, Nestec Ltd, Vevey, Switzerland
- Francisco E.G. Garcez Ourique, former Secretary General of the Federação Brasileira dos Exportadores de Café (FEBEC), Andar-Centro, Brazil
- Josefa Sacko, Secretary General, Interafrican Coffee Organisation, Abidjan, Côte d'Ivoire
- Mick Wheeler, Overseas Representative, Papua New Guinea Coffee Industry Corporation, Goroka, Papua New Guinea

At ITC, contributions and assistance were offered by:

- Peter Walters, Director, Division of Product and Market Development
- Bertil Byskov, Chief of Market Development Section
- Rudy Kortbech-Olesen, Senior Market Development Adviser
- Bastiaan Bijl, Associate Market Analyst
- Alison Southby, Editorial and Publications Officer and Carmelita Endaya, Editorial and Publications Unit
- Kathryn Della Corte, Administrative Support, Market Development Section

# Contents

## CHAPTER 2
# The mainstream market                                                                             27

## CHAPTER 6

# E-commerce and supply chain management

## CHAPTER 7

# Dispute resolution – arbitration

## CHAPTER 8
# Futures markets                                                        169

# CHAPTER 9
# Hedging and other operations

## CHAPTER 10
# Risk and the relation to trade credit

## CHAPTER 11
# Coffee quality          243

**CHAPTER 12**

# Marketing systems and country profiles

# Note

Unless otherwise specified, all references to dollars ($) and cents (cts) are to United States dollars and cents. All references to tons are to metric tons. The term 'billion' denotes 1 thousand million.

The following abbreviations are used:

| | |
|---|---|
| AA | Against actuals |
| ACPC | Association of Coffee Producing Countries |
| ASP | Applications Service Provider |
| B/L | Bill of lading |
| BM&F | Brazilian Mercantile & Futures Exchange |
| CAD | Cash against documents |
| CFR | Cost and freight |
| CFTC | Commodity Futures Trading Commission (United States) |
| CFC | Common Fund for Commodities |
| CFS | Container freight station |
| CHIPS | Clearing House Interbank Payment System |
| CIF | Cost, insurance, freight |
| CM | Collateral manager |
| COFEI | Coffee Futures Exchange India Limited |
| COT | Commitment of traders |
| CSCE | Coffee, Sugar and Cocoa Exchange (New York) |
| CTF | Coffee Trade Federation (United Kingdom) |
| CY | Container yard |
| DAF | Delivered at frontier |
| eCOPS | Electronic Commodity Operations Processing System (at NYBOT) |
| ECCB | European Contract for Coffee in Bulk |
| ECF | European Coffee Federation |
| EDK | Ex dock |
| ETA | Estimated time of arrival |
| EU | European Union |
| EUREP | Euro-Retailer Produce Working Group |
| EUREPGAP | EUREP Good Agricultural Practice |
| FAO | Food and Agriculture Organization of the United Nations |
| FAQ | Fair average quality |
| FCA | Free carrier |
| FCL | Full container load |
| FCM | Futures commission merchant |
| FDA | United States Food and Drug Administration |
| FOB | Free on board |
| FOT | Free on truck/train |

| | |
|---|---|
| FLO | Fairtrade Labelling Organizations |
| GAP | Good Agricultural Practice |
| GBE | Green bean equivalent |
| GCA | Green Coffee Association (United States) |
| GIS | Geographic information system |
| GPS | Global positioning system |
| GSP | Generalized System of Preferences |
| GTC | Good till cancelled |
| HACCP | Hazard Analysis Critical Control Point |
| ICA | International Coffee Agreement |
| ICO | International Coffee Organization |
| ICS | Internal Control System (organic) |
| IFOAM | International Federation of Organic Agriculture Movements |
| ISO | International Organization for Standardization |
| ITC | International Trade Centre UNCTAD/WTO |
| JIT | Just-in-time |
| LCL | Less than container load |
| L/C | Letter of credit |
| LIFFE | London International Financial Futures and Options Exchange |
| MFN | Most favoured nation |
| NCA | National Coffee Association (United States) |
| NCAD | Net cash against documents |
| NCSE | New York Coffee, Sugar and Cocoa Exchange |
| NGO | Non-governmental organization |
| NYBOT | New York Board of Trade |
| NYCC | New York Clearing Corporation |
| NY 'C' | Coffee 'C' Contract at New York Board of Trade |
| OAMCAF | African and Malagasy Coffee Organization (Organisation africaine et malgache du café) |
| OTA | Ochratoxin A |
| PTBF | Price to be fixed |
| RTD | Ready-to-drink |
| SAS | Subject to approval of sample |
| SCAA | Specialty Coffee Association of America |
| SCAE | Specialty Coffee Association of Europe |
| SURF | Settlement Utility for Managing Risk and Finance |
| SWIFT | Society for Worldwide Interbank Financial Telecommunication |
| TGE | Tokyo Grain Exchange |
| THC | Terminal handling charges |
| UNCTAD | United Nations Conference on Trade and Development |
| USDA | United States Department of Agriculture |
| WTO | World Trade Organization |
| XML | Extensible mark-up language |

# Introduction

*Coffee: An Exporter's Guide* was first published by the International Trade Centre UNCTAD/WTO (ITC) in 1992. This was shortly after the lifting of export quotas in 1989 and in a period when many coffee producing countries were engaged in the liberalization of their coffee export trade. Numerous new exporters were also then entering the coffee trade.

During the 10 years since 1992 the landscape has again changed, significantly. Prior to 1992 world production averaged just over 92 million bags, compared to 112 million bags in 2000/01. Current production capacity in Brazil is estimated at anything from 40 million to 50 million bags, against 1990/91 output of around 24 million to 25 million bags. Viet Nam exceeded 1 million bags for the first time in 1990/91, against 14 million bags in 2000/01. In consuming countries new roasting processes achieve higher extraction rates and change some quality aspects, resulting in a notable shift in demand from arabica to robusta. Price volatility reached previously unknown levels and new instruments appeared to address this phenomenon. Trade in futures and options rose dramatically, reaching a combined turnover in 2001 equivalent to 45 million tons of green coffee or some seven times annual world consumption. E-commerce trading platforms made their entry into the world of conventional coffee trading but as yet have generally not achieved the expected impact.

Growing demand for specialty coffee deservedly raised many hopes but nevertheless coffee prices fell to an almost all-time low at the end of 2001: in absolute terms comparable to what they were over 30 years ago, and in real terms the lowest for more than 100 years. Why is this so? Primarily because annual world production exceeds demand by 5 million–10 million bags, a discrepancy that is unlikely to disappear in the immediate future.

Of course, this rather bland statement does not even begin to explain the abject misery that current low coffee prices bring to coffee growers worldwide, most of whom are smallholders and least able to cope. The object of the statistical and pricing data in this guide is to quantify the world coffee trade, but this does not mean that the authors are not aware of what these figures mean to many, many people.

Despite ongoing change in the coffee world, product knowledge, respect for quality and impeccable contract execution remain absolutely essential for today's exporters who in addition face many new challenges: commercial, technical, logistical, environmental and social. This guide addresses both conventional and new coffee trade issues, including electronic contracts and documentation. Inspiration and practical information have been drawn from many personalities in the coffee world. They and ITC share the belief that increased efficiency and better understanding of the trade will assist growers and exporters in their quest to maximize their earnings.

### Conversions

*All quantity data in this guide represent bags of 60 kg net (132.276 lb) green coffee or the equivalent thereof, i.e. GBE: green bean equivalent.*

*Green coffee means all coffee in the naked bean form before roasting.*

*To convert different types of coffee to GBE:*

**Dried cherry to green bean:** *multiply the net weight of the cherry by 0.5;*

**Parchment to green bean:** *multiply the net weight of the parchment by 0.8;*

**Roasted coffee to green bean\*:** *multiply the net weight of the roasted coffee by 1.19;*

**Soluble coffee to green bean\*:** *multiply the net weight of soluble coffee by 2.6;*

**Liquid coffee to green bean:** *multiply the net weight of the dried coffee solids contained in the liquid coffee by 2.6.*

*Alternatively, for statistical purposes:*

| 60 kg green coffee represents: | 120 kg dried cherry |
| --- | --- |
| | 75 kg parchment |
| | 50.4 kg roasted coffee |

\* *Applies equally to decaffeinated coffee.*

# CHAPTER 1

# World coffee trade – an overview

## The importance of coffee in world trade

Coffee is an important commodity in the world economy, accounting for trade worth approximately US$ 5.6 billion in 2000/01 (October–September). Like all other primary agricultural commodities, coffee suffers from sharp variations in supply that, at times, can cause wide and violent fluctuations in price. The last twenty years or so have provided a classic demonstration of the recurrent boom and bust cycle that characterizes the coffee market. Prices boomed in 1986 and 1987 in response to a perceived shortage brought about by a drought in Brazil, only to slump again in 1989 when the International Coffee Organization (ICO) quota system collapsed. Prices remained depressed for the next four years until the next boom, induced by a general reduction in overall supply and exacerbated by the 1994 frosts in Brazil. Over-supply in 1996 forced prices sharply downwards but this was relatively short-lived; prices boomed again in 1997 over fears of shortages of good quality arabicas following poor harvests because of the El Niño phenomenon. As a consequence, producing countries have seen their export revenues slump from an estimated US$ 14.3 billion in 1986/87 to US$ 5.4 billion in 1992/93, rise again to reach a high of US$ 12.4 billion in 1996/97, then dwindle back to US$ 5.6 billion in 2000/01.

| Table 1 | World coffee exports, by value and volume, 1995/96–2000/01 | | |
|---|---|---|---|
| **Coffee year** | **US$ billion** | **Million bags** | **Cts/lb (FOB)*** |
| 1995/96 | 10.1 | 70.2 | 109 |
| 1996/97 | 12.4 | 74.5 | 126 |
| 1997/98 | 12.0 | 78.4 | 116 |
| 1998/99 | 9.7 | 78.9 | 93 |
| 1999/00 | 8.6 | 89.3 | 73 |
| 2000/01 | 5.6 | 88.9 | 48 |

*Source:* ICO.

* Rounded to nearest cent.

Coffee is also a very political crop. Its importance in world trade and to the economies of many developing countries makes it so. Some 70 countries produce coffee. Of these, 45, nearly all of whom are exporting members of the International Coffee Organization (ICO), are responsible for over 97% of world output. A list of ICO exporting members is given in annex I to this chapter.

For many countries, coffee exports not only are a vital contributor to foreign exchange earnings but also account for a significant proportion of tax income and gross domestic product. For nine countries – nearly a quarter of the ICO's exporting members – the average

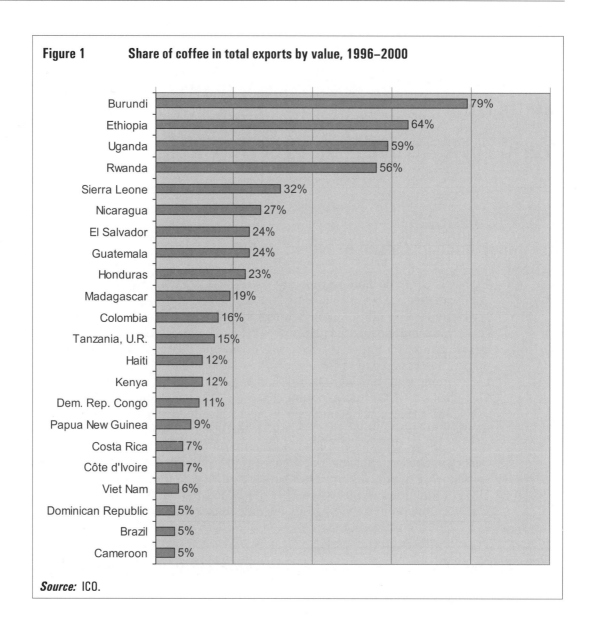

**Figure 1    Share of coffee in total exports by value, 1996–2000**

| | |
|---|---|
| Burundi | 79% |
| Ethiopia | 64% |
| Uganda | 59% |
| Rwanda | 56% |
| Sierra Leone | 32% |
| Nicaragua | 27% |
| El Salvador | 24% |
| Guatemala | 24% |
| Honduras | 23% |
| Madagascar | 19% |
| Colombia | 16% |
| Tanzania, U.R. | 15% |
| Haiti | 12% |
| Kenya | 12% |
| Dem. Rep. Congo | 11% |
| Papua New Guinea | 9% |
| Costa Rica | 7% |
| Côte d'Ivoire | 7% |
| Viet Nam | 6% |
| Dominican Republic | 5% |
| Brazil | 5% |
| Cameroon | 5% |

*Source:* ICO.

share of coffee exports in total export earnings exceeded 20% in the period 1996–2000 and for 24 – over half the producer membership – it exceeded 5% (see figure 1). The price of coffee is a political reality few governments can afford to ignore. It is hardly surprising that over the years a large number of producing country governments have wanted to participate in different attempts aimed at bringing about long term stability in the coffee market through some form of international cooperation: through cartels, such as Pancafe in the 1970s; the ICO and its quota system in the 1960s and again in the 1980s; and the largely ineffective retention plans implemented by the Association of Coffee Producing Countries (ACPC) in the 1990s.

The reason so many producing country governments have been prepared to consider such initiatives is the fact that coffee's price instability owes more to the fluctuations in its supply than to variations in its demand. World coffee production inevitably varies from year to year; this is a natural function of the production process. Coffee production is relatively, but not totally, price inelastic although the impact of current low prices (2002) remains to be seen.

Demand, on the other hand, has not demonstrated the same degree of variation as supply over the years. While relatively unresponsive to small changes in prices, demand does respond to more significant ones, especially large upward price movements.

# Supply, production, stocks and domestic consumption

## Introduction

Supply is generally defined as the sum of production in a given coffee year plus stocks carried over from the previous year. *Exportable supply*, however, is defined as supply minus domestic consumption and an amount deemed to be required for working stocks. The definition of *working stocks* is imprecise as it relates to the volume of coffee required to maintain a steady and planned flow of exports to the market. It is generally perceived as the amount of coffee in the pipeline in an exporting country at any one time. Harvesting and export patterns vary from country to country, so working stocks are not defined as a fixed percentage or proportion of a country's production or export capacity, but rather as an individual amount unique to every country. In many respects the calculation of working stocks is arbitrary, but it is generally based on historical data for each country.

Coffee is a seasonal crop. Seasons vary from country to country, starting and finishing at different times throughout the year. This makes statistics on worldwide annual production very difficult to collate: any single twelve-month period may encompass a whole crop year in one country but will also include the tail end of the previous year's crop and the beginning of the next year's crop in others. In order to compare supply aggregates as well supply with demand all data have therefore been converted from crop year to coffee year (which runs from October to September). Table 2 shows each producing country's crop year.

| Table 2 | Crop years in producing countries | | |
|---|---|---|---|
| | Benin | Ghana | Nigeria |
| | Cameroon | Guatemala | Panama |
| | Central African Republic | Guinea | Sierra Leone |
| | Colombia | Honduras | Sri Lanka |
| | Costa Rica | India | Thailand |
| | Côte d'Ivoire | Jamaica | Togo |
| 1 October–30 September | Democratic Republic of the Congo | Kenya | Trinidad and Tobago |
| | El Salvador | Liberia | Uganda |
| | Equatorial Guinea | Mexico | Venezuela |
| | Ethiopia | Nicaragua | Viet Nam |
| | Gabon | | |
| | Angola | Indonesia | Paraguay |
| | Bolivia | Madagascar | Peru |
| 1 April–31 March | Brazil | Malawi | Rwanda |
| | Burundi | Papua New Guinea | Zimbabwe |
| | Ecuador | | |
| | Congo | Haiti | United Republic of Tanzania |
| 1 July–30 June | Cuba | Philippines | Zambia |
| | Dominican Republic | | |

Using ICO and United States Department of Agriculture (USDA) data, world coffee production in coffee year 2000/01 is estimated at 111.6 million bags of 60 kg each (6.7 million tons). A further 21.6 million bags were reported to have been held in stock by producers at the beginning of the year. Consumption of coffee in producing countries is estimated at approximately 26.0 million bags, while exports totalled 88.6 million bags. The volume of stocks held by producing countries is therefore estimated to have fallen by around 3 million bags over the year, while stocks in consuming countries are likely to rise by 2.3 million bags to 19.6 million bags.

The ICO's quarterly distribution of production available for marketing is given in annex II.

## Coffee producing countries by ICO quality group

For administrative and other reasons the ICO has divided coffee production into four groups on the basis of the predominant type of coffee produced by each member country.

| *Quality group* | *Producers* |
|---|---|
| *Colombian mild arabicas* | *Colombia, Kenya, United Republic of Tanzania* |
| *Other mild arabicas* | *Bolivia, Burundi, Costa Rica, Cuba, Dominican Republic, Ecuador, El Salvador, Guatemala, Haiti, Honduras, India, Jamaica, Malawi, Mexico, Nicaragua, Panama, Papua New Guinea, Peru, Rwanda, Venezuela, Zambia, Zimbabwe* |
| *Brazilian and other natural arabicas* | *Brazil, Ethiopia, Paraguay* |
| *Robustas* | *Angola, Benin, Cameroon, Central African Republic, Congo, Côte d'Ivoire, Democratic Republic of the Congo, Equatorial Guinea, Gabon, Ghana, Guinea, Indonesia, Liberia, Madagascar, Nigeria, Philippines, Sierra Leone, Sri Lanka, Thailand, Togo, Trinidad and Tobago, Uganda, Viet Nam* |

## World production

World production of coffee from 1986/87 to 2000/01 is given in annex III, which lists all 40 members of the ICO plus the more important non-member exporting countries. There are a number of other small producers (which together account for less than 0.5% of the total) for which data is not readily available and which therefore have been excluded from this table. An overview of world production over the five-year period 1996/97–2000/01 is given in table 3.

## Geographical distribution

Coffee is indigenous to Africa, with arabica coffee reportedly originating from Ethiopia and robusta from the Atlantic Coast (Kouilou region and in and around Angola) and the Great Lakes region, and today it is widely grown throughout the tropics. The bulk of the world's coffee, however, is produced in Latin America and in particular in Brazil, which has dominated world production since 1840. Brazil is the world's largest grower and seller of coffee. Viet Nam, which expanded its production rapidly throughout the 1990s, now holds the number two position, bringing Colombia into third place and Indonesia into fourth.

Brazil began growing coffee more than 250 years ago and quickly increased production to the point where it dominated the market. The earliest available statistics indicate that in 1852 world production totalled 4.6 million bags, with production in Brazil amounting to 2.4 million bags. By the year 1900 world production totalled 15.1 million bags, Brazil's 11.3 million.

**Table 3** **Overview of world production by type, 1996/97–2000/01 (in millions of bags)**

| Coffee year | 1996/97 | 1997/98 | 1998/99 | 1999/00 | 2000/01 |
|---|---|---|---|---|---|
| **WORLD*** of which: | **99.4** | **103.6** | **104.0** | **115.0** | **111.7** |
| **Arabicas** | 64.8 | 69.5 | 73.4 | 75.4 | 68.8 |
| Brazil | 20.8 | 24.2 | 29.0 | 27.4 | 23.7 |
| Colombia | 10.9 | 12.2 | 11.1 | 9.4 | 10.5 |
| Other America | 23.0 | 23.3 | 23.3 | 27.0 | 24.2 |
| Africa | 6.5 | 5.7 | 5.8 | 7.2 | 5.9 |
| Asia and the Pacific | 3.7 | 4.1 | 4.2 | 4.5 | 4.4 |
| **Robustas** | 34.6 | 34.1 | 30.6 | 39.6 | 42.9 |
| Brazil | 4.5 | 4.4 | 4.5 | 4.8 | 6.4 |
| Other Latin America | 0.7 | 0.8 | 0.7 | 0.4 | 0.5 |
| Viet Nam | 5.7 | 6.9 | 6.9 | 11.7 | 14.8 |
| Indonesia | 7.2 | 7.3 | 5.7 | 5.5 | 5.7 |
| Other Asia and Pacific | 4.3 | 5.5 | 4.5 | 5.6 | 5.3 |
| Côte d'Ivoire | 4.5 | 3.7 | 2.0 | 5.9 | 4.0 |
| Uganda | 3.9 | 2.3 | 3.0 | 2.7 | 2.8 |
| Other Africa | 3.8 | 3.2 | 3.3 | 3.0 | 3.4 |
| **Shares (per cent)** | | | | | |
| *Arabicas* | *65.2* | *67.1* | *70.6* | *65.6* | *61.6* |
| *Robustas* | *34.8* | *32.9* | *29.4* | *34.4* | *38.4* |

***Sources:*** ICO and USDA.

* Note: Totals may not add up owing to rounding.

Six years later Brazil's production was up to 20 million bags and coffee was responsible for 70% of its foreign exchange earnings. This massive jump in production was short lived, however, and the following year production returned to 11 million bags. Brazil continued to dominate the market but by the late 1930s other origins had begun to increase their output. In the 1950s Brazil still accounted for more than 50% of the world production of coffee and in 1959 it produced a record crop of 44.1 million bags. Since that time, production of coffee in Brazil has averaged around 25 million bags although on a number of occasions it has produced crops of over 30 million bags and in 1987/88 produced a crop of just over 42.1 million bags. In 1994 two frosts and a drought devastated the Brazilian coffee industry reducing the crop from around 24 million bags to around 13.2 million bags. However the downturn was short-lived and in 2001/02 Brazil's production is estimated to be 31 million–32 million bags. Extensive planting since 1994 has given Brazil the capacity to produce significantly larger crops in the future. As an example, in mid 2002 forecasts for the 2002/03 harvest ranged from a low of 38 million bags to a high of 45 million bags or more.

Latin America's share (including Brazil) of world production is, however, declining, falling from around 70% in 1981 to 58% in 2000/01. This has been mainly due to increases in production in other regions, especially Asia and the Pacific where production has grown relatively steadily from 4% to over 27%. The largest increase has occurred in Viet Nam:

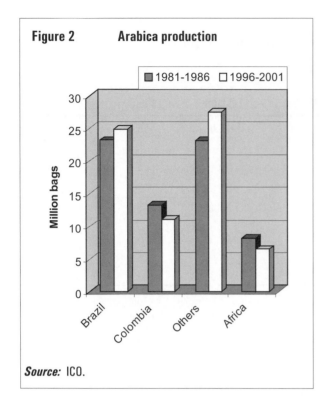

**Figure 2      Arabica production**

■ 1981-1986  □ 1996-2001

*Source:* ICO.

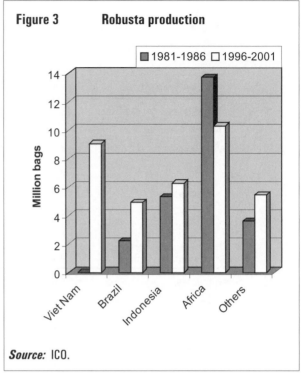

**Figure 3      Robusta production**

■ 1981-1986  □ 1996-2001

*Source:* ICO.

annual production has grown from an estimated 40,000 bags in 1981 to an estimated 14.8 million bags in 2000/01. During the same period African producers have seen their share of world production oscillate quite wildly; currently their share is around 15%.

Figures 2 and 3 demonstrate the shifts in regional shares of arabica and robusta production between the five-year average over the period 1981–1986 and the period 1996–2001.

## Exportable production

Exportable production is total annual production less domestic consumption in producing countries. Availability for export is equivalent to the carry-over stocks from the previous year plus exportable production of the current year. Any difference between exportable production and actual exports (surplus or shortfall) results in an adjustment up or down of the carry-over stocks to the following year.

World exportable production fell by 5.1 million bags during the coffee year 2000/01 from 90.5 million bags to 85.4 million bags. The bulk of this fall occurred in arabica producing countries, notably the 'other milds' group and the Brazilian and other natural arabicas. The Colombian milds group was the only arabica group to see an increase; this was due primarily to a recovery in the production of Colombia, which saw its exportable production rise from 7.9 million bags in 1999/2000 to 10.5 million bags. This is, however, still below the 16.8 million bags reached in 1991/92. The robusta group on the other hand has witnessed a dramatic rise both in the absolute volume of exportable production over the past five years and in its share of overall exportable production. In 1995/96 robusta accounted for 31% of the total, whereas by 2000/01 this had increased to 38% of exportable production. This surge is primarily attributable to the increase in production in Viet Nam but notable increases in Brazil and India have also played a significant role.

## Domestic consumption

Domestic consumption in producing countries is estimated to have risen from about 23.2 million bags in 1995/96 to about 26.0 million bags in coffee year 2000/01. The bulk of this increase is attributed to growth in the internal market in Brazil, which has increased from 10.6 million bags to 13.3 million bags in five years. Industry sources point to the growth in real disposable incomes in Brazil and a policy of using better quality coffee for the internal markets as important factors behind this growth. Elsewhere in Latin America, consumption is constrained by relatively low urban income levels although there has been some growth in Mexico over the last three years and consumption remains reasonably substantial in Colombia. Consumption in Africa is negligible with the exception of Ethiopia, where there is a long and well-established tradition of coffee drinking. In Asia, total consumption is reasonably high in India, Indonesia and the Philippines, although per capita consumption levels are relatively low.

## Exports

The world export situation from 1996/97 to 2000/01 is given in table 4.

| Table 4 | Overview of world exports by type, 1996/97–2000/01 (in thousands of bags) | | | | |
|---|---|---|---|---|---|
| **Coffee years** | **1996/97** | **1997/98** | **1998/99** | **1999/00** | **2000/01** |
| **Arabicas** of which from: | **52,643** | **49,090** | **55,070** | **54,362** | **53,451** |
| Brazil | 15,535 | 13,731 | 18,902 | 15,829 | 18,385 |
| Colombia | 10,564 | 10,251 | 9,780 | 8,430 | 8,839 |
| Other Latin America | 18,942 | 18,046 | 19,121 | 21,851 | 18,483 |
| Africa | 5,120 | 4,472 | 4,448 | 5,083 | 4,727 |
| Asia and the Pacific | 2,482 | 2,590 | 2,819 | 3,169 | 3,017 |
| **Robustas** of which from: | **24,846** | **25,205** | **24,933** | **29,887** | **30,739** |
| Brazil | 616 | 718 | 2,236 | 969 | 738 |
| Other Latin America | 480 | 511 | 395 | 271 | 199 |
| Viet Nam | 5,421 | 6,614 | 6,658 | 10,903 | 14,430 |
| Indonesia | 5,719 | 4,764 | 4,679 | 4,352 | 4,091 |
| Other Asia and Pacific | 2,486 | 3,126 | 2,816 | 3,548 | 3,047 |
| Côte d'Ivoire | 3,352 | 4,416 | 2,182 | 5,227 | 3,493 |
| Uganda | 3,779 | 2,700 | 3,266 | 2,397 | 2,616 |
| Other Africa | 2,993 | 2,356 | 2,701 | 2,220 | 2,125 |
| **Roasted coffee** | **52** | **72** | **157** | **102** | **54** |
| **Soluble** of which from: | **4,535** | **4,192** | **3,685** | **4,229** | **5,005** |
| Brazil | 2,464 | 1,883 | 1,787 | 2,006 | 2,475 |
| Other Latin America | 1,154 | 1,312 | 1,098 | 1,229 | 1,454 |
| Africa | 157 | 154 | 143 | 192 | 169 |
| Asia | 760 | 843 | 657 | 802 | 907 |
| **Shares (per cent)** | | | | | |
| *Arabicas* | *64.14* | *62.49* | *65.68* | *61.37* | *59.89* |
| *Robustas* | *30.27* | *32.08* | *29.73* | *33.74* | *34.44* |
| *Roasted* | *0.06* | *0.09* | *0.19* | *0.12* | *0.06* |
| *Soluble* | *5.53* | *5.34* | *4.40* | *4.77* | *5.61* |

*Source:* ICO.

Unsurprisingly, the data on exports confirm the rise in importance of *robusta* (and in particular Viet Nam) in the world coffee trade over recent years. Of note is the increase in total exports, which in 2000/01 reached a record 89.25 million bags. While a sizeable and probably major proportion of this increased export volume has replenished and even increased inventories held in consuming countries and free ports, there can be little doubt that a significant proportion must have gone into increased consumption.

In *arabica*, the importance of Latin America continues unabated. Brazil, although erratic, continues to dominate. Colombia's importance is declining, but is showing some signs of revival. Poor prices have obviously affected the export performance of the rest of Latin America during 2000/01. The growth in arabica output in Asia can be attributed almost entirely to that experienced in India. In Africa exports have fluctuated markedly from year to year but the trend overall has remained relatively flat.

Exports of *roasted coffee* from producing countries remain a relatively insignificant proportion of the overall trade in coffee, accounting for just 54,000 bags GBE (green bean equivalent) in 2000/01, less than 0.06% of the overall total. This figure is still preliminary but shows a marked decrease over exports of roasted coffee recorded in 1999/00.

Exports of *soluble coffee* have varied from year to year and were showing signs of decline until two years ago when there was a marked turnaround, most notably in the exports of soluble coffee from Brazil. As a result, exports of soluble coffee from producing countries in 2000/01 are the highest on record, although still only just over 5% of world coffee exports.

## Stocks in producing countries

According to the ICO, producer-held stocks at the beginning of crop year 2000/01 stood at 21.63 million bags. This, the lowest total since 1980, reflects the fact that for many years exports have exceeded exportable production. However, extreme caution must be exercised when looking at producer-held stock figures, as the numbers involved do not necessarily reflect true availability. In some cases the official estimates will underestimate the amount held as it is often impossible to record the total volume held in private hands in a country, while in other cases the figures will exaggerate the amount available. This was certainly the case in the past when stocks played an important role in determining a producing country's quota at the ICO, as it was to a country's advantage to record the highest possible stock figure. Consequently poor quality coffee, which was difficult to sell and indeed had very little value, was often included in order to inflate a country's stock figure.

Furthermore, stock verifications ceased in 1989 with the suspension of the quota system. Although the figures produced from the verification exercise were questionable, they were the product of a reasonably rigorous procedure. Since then the figures have been based on national estimates and there has been no independent verification of the accuracy or otherwise of these figures. There was some discussion of reintroducing independently conducted stock verifications under the ACPC retention plan, but this never happened.

The estimated stock levels in each producing country at the start of the crop year over the last five years are given in table 5. Brazil still holds the largest volume, at just over 10 million bags, but it is interesting to note that the robusta share of the total has increased year on year and now accounts for more than a quarter of all stocks held in producing countries.

| Table 5 | Estimated opening stocks by type, crop years 1996/97–2000/01 (in thousands of bags) | | | | |
|---|---|---|---|---|---|
| | **1996/97** | **1997/98** | **1998/99** | **1999/00** | **2000/01** |
| **WORLD** | **33,035** | **29,574** | **25,804** | **23,462** | **21,758** |
| **Arabicas** | **28,202** | **24,285** | **20,434** | **18,397** | **16,299** |
| Brazil | 14,939 | 13,791 | 10,510 | 10,279 | 8,589 |
| Colombia | 6,022 | 4,300 | 4,000 | 3,200 | 2,100 |
| Other Latin America | 2,172 | 1,421 | 2,057 | 1,629 | 2,186 |
| Africa | 4,808 | 4,551 | 3,518 | 2,798 | 3,061 |
| Asia and the Pacific | 261 | 222 | 349 | 491 | 363 |
| **Robustas** | **4,833** | **5,289** | **5,370** | **5,065** | **5,459** |
| Brazil | 611 | 564 | 1,711 | 1,536 | 1,636 |
| Other Latin America | 82 | 152 | 113 | 40 | 53 |
| Viet Nam | 167 | 200 | 250 | 283 | 667 |
| Indonesia | 723 | 253 | 412 | 1,080 | 555 |
| Other Asia and Pacific | 1,204 | 1,153 | 1,331 | 1,302 | 1,229 |
| Côte d'Ivoire | 469 | 1,373 | 438 | 115 | 552 |
| Uganda | 1,320 | 1,305 | 801 | 396 | 450 |
| Other Africa | 257 | 289 | 314 | 313 | 317 |
| **Shares (per cent)** | | | | | |
| *Arabicas* | *85.4* | *82.1* | *79.2* | *78.4* | *74.9* |
| *Robustas* | *14.6* | *17.9* | *20.8* | *21.6* | *25.1* |

***Source:*** ICO.

# Demand

Chapter 2 discusses in detail the trends in imports, re-exports and consumption of coffee worldwide. Most of the statistical material in that chapter is expressed in calendar years, which is largely how data on demand and consumption are reported and analysed by consuming countries and trade bodies. The summary data in this section are given in coffee years in order to facilitate comparisons with supply data provided earlier.

A straight comparison between data in the two chapters is not possible as time lags produce differences between the basic and aggregate figures. To complicate the issue even further, statistics on coffee consumption tend to be misleading as no single set of statistics gives the whole picture. Import statistics, for example, are not a good indicator of consumption as they do not take into account re-exports or changes in the level of stocks held in importing countries.

To overcome this the ICO publishes figures on 'disappearance' that take these factors into account, but it is still impossible to allow for changes in the level of unreported stocks held by traders, roasters and retailers. Table 6 shows consumption in the major importing countries. For countries, which are members of the ICO and for a few non-member countries where the relevant statistics exist, the figures relate to disappearance, whereas for rest of the non-member countries they relate to net imports. Strictly speaking the two sets of figures are not the same but are close enough to be incorporated in this table. All data on imports, re-exports, consumption, and disappearance are expressed in 60-kilogram bags GBE.

| Table 6 | Consumption in importing countries/areas, 1996/97–2000/01 (in thousands of bags) | | | | |
|---|---|---|---|---|---|
| **Importing countries/areas** | **1996/97** | **1997/98** | **1998/99** | **1999/00** | **2000/01\*** |
| **WORLD** | **76,606** | **76,219** | **78,949** | **77,177** | **78,936** |
| **North America** Of which: | **20,128** | **20,449** | **21,365** | **20,988** | **21,600** |
| United States | 17,847 | 18,194 | 19,057 | 18,681 | 19,164 |
| **Western Europe** Of which: | **36,382** | **35,125** | **36,652** | **34,709** | **34,924** |
| France | 5,623 | 5,317 | 5,311 | 5,316 | 5,469 |
| Germany | 9,773 | 8,990 | 10,508 | 9,456 | 9,675 |
| Italy | 4,857 | 4,843 | 4,977 | 5,122 | 5,346 |
| **Eastern Europe** | **6,461** | **7,457** | **7,057** | **7,076** | **7,600** |
| **Asia and the Pacific** Of which: | **9,951** | **9,592** | **10,292** | **10,757** | **10,985** |
| Japan | 6,369 | 5,900 | 6,261 | 6,733 | 6,743 |
| **Others** | **3,684** | **3,596** | **3,583** | **3,647** | **3,827** |

*Source:* ICO.

\* Provisional.

# Trends

It is estimated that global consumption in coffee year 2000/01 totalled 105.0 million bags. Of this total, 61.4 million bags were consumed in importing member countries and the United States of America, 17.5 million bags were consumed in non-member countries, and the remaining 26.1 million bags were consumed in producing countries.

Consumption has grown by an average of around 1.2% a year since the early 1980s. Probably the most spectacular growth has been witnessed in Japan, where consumption has grown by more than 3.5% a year over the same period; Japan is now the third largest importer of coffee in the world. Growth in Europe has been more modest, yet still above average, seeing consumption rise on average by 1.9% a year. On the other hand, other than in Eastern Europe, non-ICO member consumption appears to have remained virtually static over the past four years or so. Before this it was growing relatively strongly at around 2.5%–3.0% a year. These figures should be read with some caution though, as the data for exports and hence consumption throughout the whole of the 1980s were distorted by the imposition of quotas and therefore probably exaggerated.

The same is not true, however, for the largest importing country, the United States, where overall consumption, despite the boom in the specialty sector, has remained virtually unaltered since the early 1980s.

## Stocks in importing countries

Stocks held in importing countries are usually referred to as *inventories* in order to distinguish them from stocks held in producer countries. Inventories tend to grow when prices are low and deplete when prices are higher, although the relationship is far from linear. Consumer-held stocks were relatively stable throughout the 1980s but increased dramatically with the suspension of quotas in 1989 and the collapse in prices. They fell in response to the price hike in 1994 but began to expand again with the collapse in prices during 2000 and 2001. By September 2001 they had reached 19.6 million bags, virtually the same level as they were in 1992, equivalent to about 13 weeks of consumer demand.

Once again some caution is required when looking at these figures as much of the data on consumer-held stock either is not published or is published only sporadically. Furthermore, as for producer-held stocks, a certain proportion of this should be seen as working stock, that is, the amount of coffee in the system or pipeline at any one time. In the past most analysts worked on the basis that around 8 million bags were required as consumer-held working stock. However the adoption of the just-in-time stock management system by most of the world's major roasters, together with the improvement in logistics, has meant that the volume that probably should now be considered working stock has been reduced to maybe as low as 4 million bags. Figure 4 shows the evolution of inventories since 1990 together with the composite indicator price.

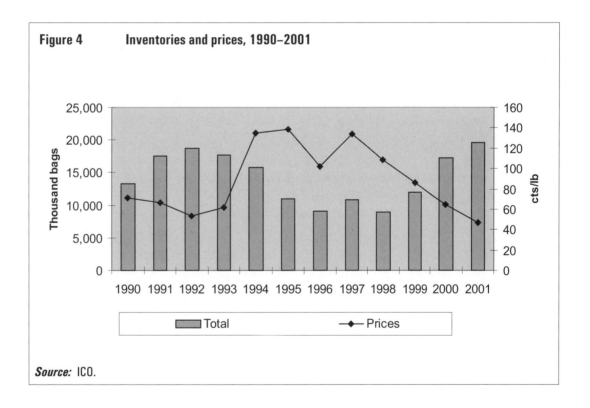

**Figure 4        Inventories and prices, 1990–2001**

*Source:* ICO.

## Prices

### ICO indicator prices and unit value of exports

The ICO has collected price quotations on various markets since 1962 and established the indicator prices system in 1965. This was designed to provide a reliable and consistent procedure for reporting prices for different types of coffee as well as an overall or composite price, which would reflect aggregated daily movements in the price of coffee. The ICO indicator price system is based on the four separate price groups (see box next page).

- Colombian mild arabicas;
- Other mild arabicas;
- Brazilian and other natural arabicas;
- Robustas.

The current composite indicator price is calculated by taking a weighted average of the indicator prices for the four separate groups, weighted according to their relative shares in international trade. This method of calculation was adopted in October 2000; before that the composite was a straight average of the other milds and robusta group indicator prices.

| *Calculation of daily ICO group and composite indicators* | |
|---|---|
| **Price basis:** *The daily arithmetical mean is taken of the ex-dock, prompt shipment prices for each growth in each market separately, then weighted as shown below.* | |
| ***Colombian mild arabicas*** | |
| *New York* | *Colombian Excelso UGQ screen size 14* |
| *Bremen/Hamburg* | *Colombian Excelso European preparation screen size 15* |
| *Weighting* | *New York 30% – Germany 70%* |
| ***Other mild arabicas*** | |
| *New York* | *Costa Rica Hard Bean, El Salvador Central Standard, Guatemala Prime Washed, Mexico Prime Washed* |
| *Bremen/Hamburg* | *Costa Rica Hard Bean, El Salvador Strictly High Grown, Guatemala Hard Bean, Nicaragua Strictly High Grown* |
| *Weighting* | *New York 40% – Germany 60%* |
| ***Brazilian and other natural arabicas (Brazilian naturals)*** | |
| *New York* | *Brasil Santos 4* |
| *Bremen/Hamburg* | *Brasil Santos 2/3 screen size 17/18* |
| *Weighting* | *New York 80% – Germany 20%* |
| ***Robustas*** | |
| *New York* | *Côte d'Ivoire Grade 2, Indonesian EK Grade 4, Uganda Standard, Viet Nam Grade 2* |
| *Le Havre/Marseilles* | *Cameroon Grade 1, Côte d'Ivoire Grade 2, Indonesia EK Grade 4, Uganda Standard, Viet Nam Grade 2* |
| *Weighting* | *New York 25% – France 75%* |
| ***ICO composite indicator*** | |
| *Composition and weighting* | *Colombian milds*     *15%* <br> *Other milds*     *30%* <br> *Brazilian naturals*     *20%* <br> *Robustas*     *35%* |
| *The weighting of each group is reviewed every two years – for full details of procedures see ICO Document EB 3776/01 Rev 1 of 28 March 2002.* | |

Figure 5 illustrates the evolution of the ICO composite indicator. The box above describes the sources of prices used to calculate the ICO indicators, the weighting given to them and the procedures used to calculate daily and 15-day moving averages.

The chart clearly shows the hike in prices in 1994 resulting from the frost in Brazil in June 1994. It is worth noting that this upward spike started a few months earlier, brought about by a change in market sentiment resulting from the introduction of the ACPC's first retention plan. Fears over the possibility of frost in Brazil, exacerbated by concerns about a possible shortage of good quality arabica coffee, caused arabica prices to spike again in 1997, but this hike proved short-lived and marked the beginning of a slow but steady decline in prices resulting from a surge in production most notably of robusta but also of arabica.

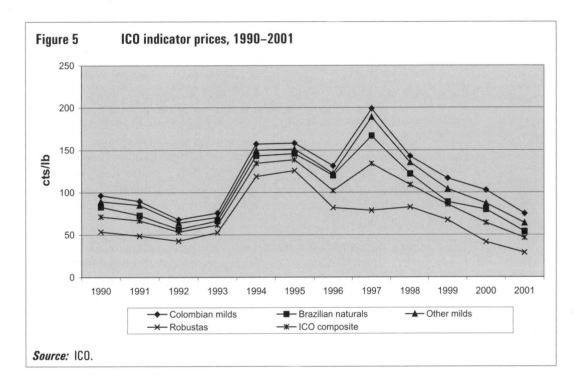

**Figure 5      ICO indicator prices, 1990–2001**

*Source:* ICO.

## The arabica/robusta differential

Figure 5 above shows that the differentials between the indicator prices of the four groups are not constant and fluctuate over time. The differential between the other milds indicator and the robusta indicator price has certainly fluctuated considerably over the last 10 years. In 1990 the differential between the indicator price of robustas and the other milds group expressed as a percentage of the other milds indicator price was 40%, yet by 1995 it had shrunk to just below 17%, only to expand again – so much so that by 2001 it had grown to 55%.

It was generally thought that this fluctuation in the size of the group differentials reflected the variations in supply of the different types of coffee on to the market. To a certain extent this is correct but it is more complicated than that. Differentials, both between different types of coffee and even between different coffees of the same type, reflect the interaction of a number of different and complex factors and functions. These can involve both supply and demand as well as seasonal quality differences.

## Physical price differentials

Coffee is not a homogeneous product; if it were then all producers would receive the same price. Each parcel of coffee is unique with regard to its characteristics, flavour and quality and hence attracts a different price. However, coffee is traditionally treated as a homogeneous commodity and priced against the level established in one of the main terminal or futures markets. Consequently the bulk of the coffee trade is conducted on what is known as a 'price differential' or 'price to be fixed' basis (see chapter 9, Hedging and other operations). This involves the buying and selling of coffee with the price expressed as a differential to the futures market, usually on an FOB basis in the country concerned. For arabica coffee the futures market is primarily New York, while for robusta it is the London market. However, not all coffees are priced initially in this way. Some, such as coffees from Kenya, have the price established via their national auction system, although in the resale market even Kenyan coffees tend to be priced on what is known as a differential basis.

There is, however, a substantial difference between the physical market for coffee and the futures market. In the physical market real parcels of coffee are traded whereas in the futures markets contracts to supply or receive coffee at some date in the future are traded. Physical and futures markets are necessarily closely linked and both play an important role in determining the price of coffee. However, prices on the futures markets reflect expectations about future events and are essentially speculative, while the prices quoted on the physical market reflect short-term availability especially of near substitutes. Futures markets are discussed in chapter 8.

Roasters are becoming increasingly sophisticated in their blending techniques and are now more prepared to substitute one coffee for another in their blends, if, for example, there are problems with supply or the price of a close substitute is more attractive. Given this ability to switch between origins, roasters tend to look for value for money, especially where close substitutes are concerned, and may not necessarily maintain the type or group composition of their blends. In addition, fierce price competition between roasters encourages them to look for the best qualities at the lowest prices, especially of near substitutes. Price differentials, both physical and group, have therefore become far more volatile today than they were in the past.

Figure 6 shows the movement in the physical price differentials for four coffees from different origins: Brazilian Santos 2/3s; Mexican Prime Washed (United States preparation); Guatemalan Hard Bean; and Papua New Guinea Y1s. These coffees are not necessarily close substitutes, but are sufficiently similar that some roasters might consider incorporating more of one of the coffees in their blends at the expense of another. It is interesting to note that while the physical price differential quotations of the different coffees do not maintain the same relationship to each other over time, they do tend to follow a similar overall pattern or direction.

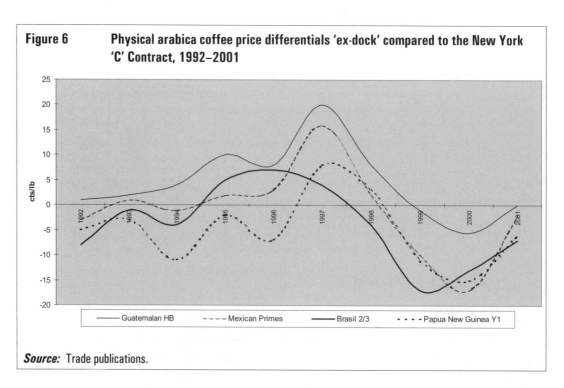

**Figure 6**     **Physical arabica coffee price differentials 'ex-dock' compared to the New York 'C' Contract, 1992–2001**

*Source:* Trade publications.

## Grading and classification

*Green coffee is graded and classified for export with the ultimate aim of producing the best cup quality and thereby securing the highest price. However, there is no universal grading and classification system – each producing country has its own which it may also use to set (minimum) standards for export.*

*Grading and classification is usually based on some of the following criteria:*

- *Altitude and/or region*
- *Botanical variety*
- *Preparation (wet or dry process = washed or natural)*
- *Bean size (screen size), sometimes also bean shape and colour*
- *Number of defects (imperfections)*
- *Roast appearance and cup quality (flavour, characteristics, cleanliness…)*
- *Density of the beans*

*Most grading and classification systems include (often very detailed) criteria, e.g. regarding permissible defects, which are not listed here. 'The Origins' Encyclopedia' at www.supremo.be is an example of a website which gives information on the export classification of coffees of most origins. Terminology on size and defects as used for classifications is also found at www.coffeeresearch.org.*

*The diversified classification terminology used in the trade is illustrated with a few examples below. It should be noted that descriptions such as 'European preparation' differ from one country to another. The examples refer primarily to the trade in mainstream coffee and do not reflect the often more detailed descriptions used for niche markets.*

| | |
|---|---|
| **Brazil** | **Santos NY 2/3**<br>*Screen 17/18, fine roast, strictly soft, fine cup.*<br><br>**Santos NY 3/4**<br>*Screen 14/16, good roast, strictly soft, good cup (often seen quoted as 'Swedish preparation').* |
| **Colombia** | **Colombia Supremo screen 17/18**<br>*High grade type of washed arabica, screen 17 with max. 5% below. Often specified with further details.* |
| **Côte d'Ivoire** | **Ivory Coast Robusta Grade 2**<br>*Grade 2; scale is from 0 (best) to 4 based on screen size and defects.* |
| **El Salvador** | **El Salvador SHG EP  max. 3/5 defects**<br>*Strictly High Grown (above 1,200 m on a scale which also includes High Grown from 900–1,200 m and Central Standard from 500–900 m). EP (European preparation) permits max. 3–5 defects per 1,000 beans according to some exporters, others indicate defects per 300 g.* |
| **Ethiopia** | **Ethiopia Jimma  5**<br>*Sun-dried (i.e. natural) arabica from the Jimma region. Type 5 refers to a grading scale based on screen, defect count and cup quality.* |
| **Guatemala** | **Guatemala SHB EP Huehuetenango**<br>*Strictly Hard Bean is from above 1,400 m. Scale includes five altitude levels from below 900 m (Prime washed) to above 1,400 m. European preparation: above screen 15, allows max. 8 defects per 300 g (American preparation: above screen 14, allows 23 defects).* |
| **India** | **India Arabica Plantation A**<br>*Washed arabica, screen 17. Classification is PB, A, B and C.  Other classifications apply to unwashed (naturals) and  robusta.* |

➡

➡

**Indonesia**          ***Indonesia Robusta Grade 4***
*The export grade scale goes from 0 (best) to 6. Grade 4 allows 45–80 defects. Region or other details are sometimes specified as quality (e.g. EK-1 and EK-Special) and processing depends on the region (island).*

**Kenya**              ***Kenya AB FAQ even roast clean cup***
*Kenya arabica grade AB, fair average quality. Internal grading system (E, AA, AB, PB, C, TT and T) is based on bean size and density, further detailed by liquor quality into 10 classifications. Top cupping coffees are mostly sold on actual sample basis.*

**Mexico**             ***Mexico Prime Washed Europrep***
*Prime Washed (prima lavado) from altitude between 600 m and 900 m, on a scale from 400 m to 1,400 m; Europrep is retained by screen 17 and allows max. 15 defects per 300 g.*

**Papua New Guinea**   ***PNG Smallholder Y1-grade***
*Y1 is one of the grades on a scale covering bean size, defect count, colour, odour, roast aspects and cup quality; AA, A, AB, B, C, PB, X, E, PSC, Y1, Y2 and T.*

**Viet Nam**           ***Viet Nam Robusta Grade 2 max. 5% blacks and broken***
*Grade 2 out of six grades: Special Grade and Grade 1 to 5, based on screen size and defects. Descriptions are often supplemented with further details on moisture content, acceptable mix of bean types, bean size, etc.*

### *Illustration of a defect count for sun-dried (natural) coffee*

| *Defect* | *Count* |
|---|---|
| *1 black bean* | *1* |
| *2 sour or rancid beans* | *1* |
| *2 beans in parchment* | *1* |
| *1 cherry* | *1* |
| *1 large husk* | *1* |
| *2–3 small husks* | *1* |
| *3 shells* | *1* |
| *1 large stone/earth clod* | *5* |
| *1 medium-sized stone/earth clod* | *2* |
| *1 small stone/earth clod* | *1* |
| *1 large stick* | *5* |
| *1 medium-sized stick* | *2* |
| *1 small stick* | *1* |
| *5 broken beans* | *1* |
| *5 green or immature beans* | *1* |
| *5 insect damaged beans* | *1* |

*Bean size, screen size and quality criteria generally are discussed further in chapter 11, Coffee quality.*

# Annex I

# The International Coffee Agreement 2001*

- **Entered into force** for six years on 1 October 2001, on expiry of the International Coffee Agreement (ICA) 1994.

- **Extension(s) of the Agreement** for up to six years now depend(s) upon a vote in the Council rather than on ratification by member country governments.

- **The Private Sector Consultative Board**, comprising eight producing and eight consuming representatives of the private sector, is now an integral part of the ICO with the power to make recommendations on matters raised for its consideration by the Council.

- **The World Coffee Conference** is also now an integral part of the ICO and will feature as an ongoing regular event. The conference is called upon to discuss matters of interest to the industry at large and to be self-financing, unless the Council decides otherwise. The first World Coffee Conference was held in May 2001.

- The ICO is authorized to **promote consumption** using resources pledged by interested parties.

- The ICO has been empowered to work towards the **sustainable management of coffee resources and processing**.

- The ICO is to consider **improving the standard of living and working conditions** of populations engaged in the coffee sector, consistent with their stage of development'.

- The ICO's headquarters is to remain in London, unless the members vote otherwise.

- The ICO's decision-making structure is virtually unaltered. The Council, which comprises all ICO members, remains the highest authority. It will continue to meet twice a year, while the 16-member Executive Board will continue to be elected annually in September.

- The ICO will continue to act as the centre for the **collection and exchange of information on coffee** and will continue to conduct studies and surveys as well maintain the system of **indicator prices**.

- **Certificates of origin** will continue to accompany all exports unless the Council deems that exceptional circumstances warrant using an alternative.

- **The preamble** acknowledges the exceptional importance of coffee to the economies of many countries and to the livelihoods of millions of people, as well as the desirability of avoiding disequilibrium between production and consumption because of the harm price fluctuations can do to both sides of the coffee industry.

- **The objectives** include providing a forum when appropriate for negotiating ways to achieve a reasonable balance between world supply and demand on a basis, which will assure adequate supplies of coffee at fair prices to consumers and markets for coffee at remunerative prices for producers and which will be conducive to long-term equilibrium between production and consumption.

---

* This list of main elements is based on F.O. Licht, *International Coffee Report*, Vol. 16 No. 3. See also *www.ico.org/aico/history.htm*.

**Key events in the history of the International Coffee Agreement (ICA)***

**1963.** First ICA comes into force at a time of low prices, regulating supplies through an export quota system.

**1972.** Export quotas suspended as prices soar.

**1980.** Export quotas restored and producers agree in return to abandon attempts to regulate the market unilaterally.

**February 1986.** Quotas suspended after a boom caused by drought losses to Brazil's crop sends prices soaring above the ceiling of the ICA's US$ 1.20–1.40 target range.

**October 1987.** Quotas reintroduced.

**4 July 1989.** Indefinite suspension of quotas after the system breaks down under the pressure of competing demands from exporters for market shares under the new ICA then being negotiated. Backed by the United States, Central American states and Mexico press for a much bigger slice of the market at the expense of Brazil (which resists this) and of African producers.

**4 September 1989.** Colombian President Virgilio Barco writes to United States President George Bush appealing for help to bring back export quotas under a new ICA and receives an encouraging response on 19 September.

**1 October 1989.** ICA extension with its economic clauses suppressed takes effect.

**February 1990.** Bush at a Latin American drugs summit in Colombia reaffirms commitment to a new ICA and a document is released setting out the administration's thinking on its possible shape.

**December 1991.** During talks with Cesar Gaviria (Colombia's new President) Brazilian President Fernando Collor de Mello (elected in March 1990), agrees in principle to back efforts to restore quotas when the local industry – given the lead role in formulating policy – can agree a common position.

**March 1992.** Brazil finally gives the go-ahead to the negotiation of a new ICA with economic clauses.

**June 1992.** First round of the negotiations.

**9 March 1993.** Bill Clinton, victor in the November 1992 United States presidential elections, writes to Gaviria supporting a new ICA, although with no sign of much enthusiasm.

**31 March 1993.** ICA negotiations collapse during the sixth round with little progress having been made and each side blaming the other for the impasse.

**September 1993.** In Brazil 29 countries sign a treaty establishing the ACPC with powers to regulate supplies and prices. Citing this as a reason, the United States pulls out of the ICO.

**September 1994.** New 'administrative' ICA without economic clauses (drafted in March) enters into force for five years.

**March 1998.** First talks open about the possibility of replacing the 1994 ICA.

**July 1999.** ICA talks break down.

---

* Based on F.O. Licht, *International Coffee Report*, Vol. 15 No. 21. See also *www.ico.org/aico/history.htm*.

**September 1999.** 1994 ICA extended for a further two years during which the first of which, it is agreed, a further attempt will be made to draw up a replacement treaty.

**September 2000.** Drafting of a new ICA completed.

**October 2001.** ICA 2001 enters into force for six years. It has no provisions for price regulation.

| Membership of the ICO* | | |
|---|---|---|
| Exporting members | | Importing members |
| Angola | Mexico | Austria |
| Bolivia | Nicaragua | Belgium/Luxembourg |
| Brazil | Nigeria | Cyprus |
| Burundi | OAMCAF: | Denmark |
| Colombia | Benin | Finland |
| Costa Rica | Cameroon | France |
| Cuba | Central African Republic | Germany |
| Democratic Republic of the Congo | Côte d'Ivoire | Greece |
| Dominican Republic | Equatorial Guinea | Ireland |
| Ecuador | Gabon | Italy |
| El Salvador | Madagascar | Japan |
| Ethiopia | Togo | Netherlands |
| Guatemala | Papua New Guinea | Norway |
| Guinea | Rwanda | Spain |
| Haiti | Thailand | Sweden |
| Honduras | Uganda | Switzerland |
| India | United Republic of Tanzania | United Kingdom |
| Indonesia | Viet Nam | |
| Jamaica | Zambia | |
| Kenya | Zimbabwe | |
| Malawi | | |

*As at 30 September 2001.

## Annex II

# Exporting countries: crop available for export by quarter, as percentage of harvest

| Members | Type | Main harvesting season | ICO coffee year | | | |
|---|---|---|---|---|---|---|
| | | | 1st quarter | 2nd quarter | 3rd quarter | 4th quarter |
| | | | Oct–Dec | Jan–March | April–June | July–Sept |
| **Crop year starting 1 April** | | | | | | |
| Angola | R | April–June | 30 | 20 | 20 | 20 |
| Bolivia | A | April–Aug | 10 | 0 | 40 | 50 |
| Brazil | A | April–Sept | 42 | 8 | 6 | 44 |
| | R | April–Sept | 5 | 20 | 55 | 20 |
| Burundi | A | April–Sept | 25 | 0 | 25 | 50 |
| Ecuador | A | June–Oct | 5 | 10 | 70 | 15 |
| | R | June–Oct | 5 | 10 | 70 | 15 |
| Indonesia | R | May–Dec | 18 | 18 | 17 | 47 |
| | A | June–Dec | 40 | 20 | 15 | 25 |
| Madagascar | R | May–Oct | 16 | 0 | 2 | 82 |
| Papua New Guinea | A | Mar–Sept* | 21 | 8 | 24 | 47 |
| | R | April–Oct | 28 | 10 | 20 | 42 |
| Paraguay | A | June–Sept | 60 | 0 | 0 | 40 |
| Peru | A | April–Oct | 30 | 13 | 19 | 38 |
| Rwanda | A | Mar–Aug | 18 | 18 | 14 | 50 |
| Zimbabwe | A | June–Sept | 56 | 11 | 1 | 32 |
| **Crop year starting 1 July** | | | | | | |
| Congo | R | Sept–Oct | 50 | 25 | 0 | 25 |
| Cuba | A | Sept–Jan | 59 | 32 | 0 | 9 |
| Dominican Republic | A | Sept–Feb | 70 | 10 | 10 | 10 |
| Haiti | A | Aug–Mar | 45 | 40 | 0 | 15 |
| Philippines | A | Dec–Mar | 42 | 51 | 4 | 3 |
| | R | Dec–May | 42 | 51 | 4 | 3 |
| United Republic of Tanzania | A | Oct–Feb | 24 | 50 | 16 | 10 |
| | R | June–Dec | 35 | 20 | 10 | 35 |
| Zambia | A | June–Oct | 0 | 0 | 0 | 100 |

| ICO coffee year | | | | | | |
|---|---|---|---|---|---|---|
| **Members** | **Type** | **Main harvesting season** | **1st quarter**<br>**Oct–Dec** | **2nd quarter**<br>**Jan–March** | **3rd quarter**<br>**April–June** | **4th quarter**<br>**July–Sept** |
| **Crop year starting 1 October** | | | | | | |
| Benin | R | Nov–Feb | 25 | 50 | 25 | 0 |
| Cameroon | R | Nov–Jan | 30 | 20 | 30 | 20 |
| | A | Oct–Dec | 35 | 25 | 25 | 15 |
| Central African Republic | R | Nov–Mar | 10 | 52 | 20 | 18 |
| Colombia | A | Oct–Mar* | 25 | 25 | 25 | 25 |
| Costa Rica | A | Sept–Feb | 24 | 44 | 17 | 15 |
| Côte d'Ivoire | R | Nov–April | 3 | 65 | 32 | 0 |
| Democratic Republic of the Congo | R | Oct–Mar* | 0 | 7 | 61 | 32 |
| | A | Dec–May | 42 | 51 | 4 | 3 |
| El Salvador | A | Nov–Mar | 31 | 67 | 2 | 0 |
| Equatorial Guinea | R | Mar–May | 50 | 50 | 0 | 0 |
| Ethiopia | A | Oct–Dec | 13 | 36 | 39 | 12 |
| Gabon | R | May–Sept | 50 | 25 | 0 | 25 |
| Ghana | R | Oct–Mar | 25 | 50 | 25 | 0 |
| Guatemala | A | Aug–Mar | 35 | 40 | 20 | 5 |
| | R | Aug–Mar | 30 | 45 | 20 | 5 |
| Guinea | R | Nov–Mar | 25 | 50 | 0 | 25 |
| Honduras | A | Oct–Mar | 20 | 40 | 20 | 20 |
| India | A | Oct–Feb | 5 | 28 | 60 | 7 |
| | R | Nov–Mar | 5 | 20 | 65 | 10 |
| Jamaica | A | Aug–Sept | 20 | 30 | 30 | 20 |
| Kenya | A | Oct–Mar | 11 | 32 | 38 | 19 |
| Liberia | R | Nov–Mar | 5 | 54 | 26 | 15 |
| Mexico | A | Oct–Mar | 34 | 60 | 6 | 0 |
| Nicaragua | A | Nov–Feb | 11 | 44 | 28 | 17 |
| Nigeria | R | Nov–Mar | 25 | 25 | 25 | 25 |
| Panama | A | Oct–Dec | 40 | 38 | 18 | 4 |
| Sierra Leone | R | Dec–Feb | 25 | 50 | 25 | 0 |
| Sri Lanka | R | Sept–Jan | 25 | 25 | 25 | 25 |
| Thailand | R | Oct–April | 3 | 77 | 20 | 0 |
| Togo | R | Nov–Feb | 0 | 56 | 34 | 10 |
| Trinidad and Tobago | R | Nov–Feb | 25 | 50 | 25 | 0 |
| Uganda | R | Nov–Feb* | 17 | 34 | 30 | 19 |
| | A | Oct–Jan | 25 | 30 | 30 | 15 |
| Venezuela | A | Oct–Jan | 18 | 20 | 34 | 28 |
| Viet Nam | R | Oct–April | 15 | 20 | 45 | 20 |

***Sources:*** ICO and information gathered by the authors.

* Peak season but harvesting occurs throughout the year.

A = arabica; R = robusta

# Annex III

# World production by coffee year, 1986/87–2000/01

(in thousands of bags)

| | Average | | | Coffee years | | | | |
|---|---|---|---|---|---|---|---|---|
| | 1986/87 1990/91 | 1991/92 1995/96 | 1996/97 2000/01 | 1996/97 | 1997/98 | 1998/99 | 1999/00 | 2000/01 |
| **TOTAL** | 95,596 | 91,261 | 106,627 | 99,408 | 103,602 | 103,991 | 114,954 | 111,643 |
| *Arabica group* | *68,207* | *64,152* | *70,757* | *64,801* | *69,478* | *73,385* | *75,408* | *68,773* |
| **North America** | 17,617 | 18,145 | 20,034 | 19,182 | 19,707 | 19,160 | 23,160 | 19,910 |
| Costa Rica | 2,416 | 2,657 | 2,347 | 2,126 | 2,500 | 2,350 | 2,404 | 2,246 |
| Cuba | 456 | 337 | 306 | 360 | 298 | 283 | 317 | 300 |
| Dominican Republic | 894 | 690 | 641 | 561 | 890 | 449 | 692 | 702 |
| El Salvador | 2,341 | 2,544 | 2,241 | 2,534 | 2,175 | 2,056 | 2,835 | 1,717 |
| Guatemala | 3,141 | 3,657 | 4,653 | 4,521 | 4,205 | 4,889 | 5,197 | 4,688 |
| Haiti | 445 | 510 | 433 | 424 | 450 | 430 | 402 | 416 |
| Honduras | 1,617 | 2,017 | 2,379 | 2,004 | 2,564 | 2,195 | 2,985 | 2,667 |
| Jamaica | 23 | 36 | 42 | 54 | 46 | 29 | 39 | 39 |
| Mexico | 5,197 | 4,477 | 5,472 | 5,324 | 5,045 | 5,051 | 6,442 | 5,125 |
| Nicaragua | 642 | 809 | 1,127 | 793 | 1,084 | 1,073 | 1,535 | 1,641 |
| Panama | 183 | 184 | 190 | 211 | 218 | 192 | 161 | 170 |
| United States | 262 | 227 | 203 | 270 | 232 | 163 | 151 | 199 |
| **South America** | 39,942 | 36,141 | 40,117 | 35,461 | 39,974 | 44,193 | 40,623 | 38,555 |
| Bolivia | 160 | 178 | 170 | 151 | 150 | 181 | 179 | 189 |
| Brazil | 23,674 | 18,466 | 25,074 | 20,759 | 24,208 | 28,981 | 27,359 | 23,700 |
| Colombia | 12,241 | 13,742 | 11,102 | 10,876 | 12,211 | 11,088 | 9,398 | 10,532 |
| Ecuador | 1,236 | 1,182 | 539 | 572 | 444 | 597 | 510 | 571 |
| Paraguay | 264 | 73 | 30 | 38 | 34 | 31 | 29 | 33 |
| Peru | 1,238 | 1,264 | 2,203 | 1,865 | 1,941 | 2,324 | 2,431 | 2,455 |
| Venezuela | 1,129 | 1,236 | 999 | 1,200 | 986 | 991 | 717 | 1,075 |
| **Africa** | 7,728 | 6,712 | 6,538 | 6,454 | 5,683 | 5,859 | 7,174 | 5,892 |
| Burundi | 567 | 534 | 363 | 318 | 340 | 463 | 379 | 317 |
| Cameroon | 272 | 94 | 88 | 49 | 78 | 43 | 104 | 153 |
| Dem. Rep. of the Congo | 271 | 150 | 133 | 99 | 195 | 56 | 41 | 70 |
| Ethiopia | 2,981 | 2,876 | 3,224 | 3,270 | 2,916 | 2,745 | 3,505 | 2,768 |

| | Average | | | Coffee years | | | | |
|---|---|---|---|---|---|---|---|---|
| | 1986/87 1990/91 | 1991/92 1995/96 | 1996/97 2000/01 | 1996/97 | 1997/98 | 1998/99 | 1999/00 | 2000/01 |
| Kenya | 1,759 | 1,616 | 1,297 | 1,246 | 882 | 1,172 | 1,502 | 1,021 |
| Malawi | 96 | 86 | 64 | 58 | 63 | 60 | 62 | 64 |
| Madagascar | 56 | 59 | 44 | 33 | 71 | 42 | 22 | 48 |
| Rwanda | 635 | 345 | 261 | 230 | 242 | 285 | 306 | 232 |
| Uganda | 166 | 240 | 340 | 408 | 264 | 280 | 427 | 400 |
| United Rep. of Tanzania | 692 | 595 | 525 | 544 | 439 | 503 | 629 | 669 |
| Zambia | 17 | 29 | 52 | 40 | 56 | 65 | 83 | 55 |
| Zimbabwe | 216 | 88 | 147 | 159 | 137 | 145 | 114 | 95 |
| **Asia and Pacific** | **2,920** | **3,154** | **4,068** | **3,704** | **4,114** | **4,173** | **4,451** | **4,416** |
| India | 1,329 | 1,383 | 1,855 | 1,689 | 1,801 | 1,728 | 2,298 | 2,328 |
| Indonesia | 499 | 580 | 790 | 759 | 866 | 797 | 761 | 720 |
| Lao People's Dem. Rep. | 0 | 50 | 145 | 100 | 100 | 153 | 173 | 200 |
| Papua New Guinea | 983 | 1,018 | 1,138 | 1,021 | 1,206 | 1,319 | 1,086 | 1,056 |
| Philippines | 39 | 52 | 54 | 57 | 57 | 79 | 37 | 38 |
| Sri Lanka | 8 | 6 | 7 | 8 | 9 | 7 | 6 | 4 |
| Yemen | 62 | 65 | 79 | 70 | 75 | 90 | 90 | 70 |
| ***Robusta group*** | *27,389* | *27,109* | *35,870* | *34,607* | *34,124* | *30,606* | *39,546* | *42,870* |
| **America** | **4,755** | **5,691** | **5,574** | **5,215** | **5,246** | **5,135** | **5,286** | **6,871** |
| Brazil | 3,974 | 4,907 | 4,924 | 4,450 | 4,443 | 4,464 | 4,812 | 6,368 |
| Ecuador | 749 | 747 | 610 | 739 | 759 | 641 | 443 | 467 |
| Guatemala | 4 | 14 | 14 | 3 | 14 | 3 | 4 | 12 |
| Guyana | 5 | 6 | 9 | 5 | 10 | 10 | 10 | 10 |
| Trinidad and Tobago | 23 | 17 | 17 | 18 | 20 | 17 | 17 | 14 |
| **Africa** | **11,800** | **8,692** | **10,344** | **12,170** | **9,193** | **8,301** | **11,642** | **10,207** |
| Angola | 173 | 59 | 59 | 68 | 71 | 73 | 58 | 30 |
| Benin | 19 | 7 | 0 | 0 | 0 | 0 | 0 | 1 |
| Burundi | 8 | 21 | 2 | 5 | 1 | 2 | 0 | 2 |
| Cameroon | 1,563 | 802 | 1,174 | 1,383 | 811 | 1,071 | 1,266 | 1,285 |
| Central African Republic | 272 | 262 | 191 | 208 | 115 | 214 | 241 | 128 |
| Congo | 21 | 10 | 5 | 10 | 3 | 3 | 3 | 4 |
| Côte d'Ivoire | 3,936 | 2,822 | 3,864 | 4,528 | 3,682 | 2,042 | 5,899 | 3,974 |
| Dem. Rep. of the Congo | 1,655 | 1,008 | 666 | 695 | 605 | 594 | 416 | 344 |
| Equatorial Guinea | 5 | 3 | 2 | 2 | 2 | 1 | 0 | 5 |
| Gabon | 17 | 3 | 3 | 2 | 3 | 4 | 2 | 1 |
| Ghana | 17 | 71 | 39 | 32 | 28 | 45 | 45 | 36 |
| Guinea | 113 | 117 | 139 | 148 | 172 | 140 | 112 | 102 |
| Liberia | 50 | 5 | 5 | 5 | 5 | 5 | 5 | 5 |
| Madagascar | 1,050 | 661 | 644 | 626 | 862 | 476 | 332 | 904 |

| | Average | | | Coffee years | | | | |
|---|---|---|---|---|---|---|---|---|
| | **1986/87 1990/91** | **1991/92 1995/96** | **1996/97 2000/01** | **1996/97** | **1997/98** | **1998/99** | **1999/00** | **2000/01** |
| Nigeria | 28 | 56 | 52 | 46 | 45 | 46 | 57 | 45 |
| Sierra Leone | 150 | 47 | 45 | 41 | 50 | 24 | 76 | 35 |
| Togo | 240 | 210 | 286 | 290 | 222 | 321 | 263 | 334 |
| Uganda | 2,338 | 2,338 | 2,949 | 3,889 | 2,288 | 3,018 | 2,670 | 2,805 |
| United Rep. of Tanzania | 145 | 190 | 219 | 192 | 228 | 222 | 197 | 167 |
| **Asia and Pacific** | **10,814** | **12,726** | **19,952** | **17,222** | **19,685** | **17,170** | **22,618** | **25,792** |
| India | 1,379 | 1,596 | 2,756 | 1,780 | 2,932 | 2,644 | 3,159 | 2,525 |
| Indonesia | 6,486 | 6,266 | 6,286 | 7,194 | 7,342 | 5,723 | 5,493 | 5,698 |
| Lao People's Dem. Rep. | 0 | 25 | 73 | 50 | 50 | 77 | 87 | 100 |
| Malaysia | 77 | 115 | 160 | 160 | 160 | 160 | 160 | 160 |
| New Caledonia | 6 | 6 | 9 | 5 | 10 | 10 | 10 | 10 |
| Papua New Guinea | 25 | 38 | 59 | 61 | 63 | 58 | 55 | 58 |
| Philippines | 1,023 | 862 | 746 | 835 | 871 | 607 | 703 | 737 |
| Sri Lanka | 66 | 46 | 35 | 29 | 49 | 28 | 32 | 38 |
| Thailand | 810 | 1,267 | 1,252 | 1,403 | 1,293 | 916 | 1,271 | 1,691 |
| Viet Nam | 942 | 2,505 | 8,576 | 5,705 | 6,915 | 6,947 | 11,648 | 14,775 |

*Sources:* ICO and USDA.

# CHAPTER 2

# The mainstream market

## The coffee trade in importing countries

### Overview

The ICO estimated that total disappearance in importing countries in 2001 amounted to 78.7 million bags. This represents a 1.9% increase over the total recorded for 2000, although it is still 0.5% lower than the total recorded in 1999 despite the significant reduction in prices that has taken place since then. Over the longer term the overall trend has been steadily upwards with consumption rising on average by just over 1.2% a year over the past twenty years. In 2001 just over three-quarters of the total was consumed in importing members of the ICO which, together with the United States of America[1], accounted for 61.0 million bags.

The structure of the coffee trade in North America, most of Western Europe and Japan is very similar. Coffee is generally purchased from the exporting countries by international trade houses, dealers and traders. The very largest roasters in Europe also maintain their own in-house buying companies, which deal directly with origin. In the main, however, roasters tend to buy their coffee from international trade houses or from specialized import agents who represent specific exporters in producing countries. The international trade plays a vital role in the worldwide marketing and distribution of coffee. Coffee is generally sold FOB (free on board) but many roasters, especially in the United States, prefer to buy on an ex-dock basis, and small roasters often prefer to buy in small lots on a delivered-in-store or ex-store basis. This allows plenty of scope for the various middlemen involved in the trade to operate and perform useful functions, although the increasing concentration at the roasting end of the industry has led to a substantial reduction in their number.

Essentially the coffee trade assists the flow of coffee from the exporting country to the roaster. Traders and dealers take responsibility for discharging the coffee from the incoming vessel and make all the necessary arrangements to have the coffee delivered to the roaster. Using the futures market either for hedging or as a price guide, traders offer and provide roasters spreads of physical coffee for shipment 1 month to 18 months in the future. Many of these sales, especially for later shipment positions, are short sales: the seller will source the required green coffee at a later date.

Such positions are more often than not sold at a premium or a discount (the differential) against the price of the appropriate delivery month on the London or New York futures markets (selling 'price to be fixed' – PTBF). This gives the roaster the right to fix the price for each individual shipping position at their option, usually up to the first delivery day of the relevant month. Some roasters might want a separate contract for each position, while others might have a single contract for six shipping positions, for example July through December. Trading in futures and PTBF sales are discussed further in chapters 8 and 9.

---

1    At the time of writing, mid 2002, the United States was not a member of the ICO.

Obviously selling so far ahead carries considerable risk. In some cases the coffee may not even have been harvested yet. To reduce their exposure, traders therefore sometimes offer such forward positions as deliveries of a basket of acceptable coffees rather than committing to a single growth. This is becoming less common today than it was in the past but it remains a significant feature of the trade in many parts of the world. Typical examples of such baskets are given below.

- Guatemala Prime Washed, and/or El Salvador Central Standard, and/or Costa Rica Hard Bean, versus the appropriate delivery months of the New York futures market.

- Uganda Standard Grade, and/or Côte d'Ivoire Grade 2, and/or Indian Robusta AB/PB/EPB Grades, versus the appropriate delivery months of the London futures market.

These baskets represent coffees that are acceptable for the same purpose in many blends of roasted coffee; traders can fulfil their delivery obligations by providing one of the specified growths. Any shipment would however still be subject to the roaster's final approval of the quality.

Not all coffee is always immediately sold to a roaster. Before arrival an individual parcel of coffee may be traded several times before it is eventually sold to a roaster. This trading in physical coffee should not be confused with trading coffee contracts on the futures exchanges and terminal markets. Given the variability of supply, the coffee market is inherently unstable and is characterized by wide fluctuations in price. The futures market therefore plays an important role in the coffee trade, as it does with other commodities, by acting as the institution that transfers the risk of price movements to speculators and helps to establish price levels. These markets do not handle significant quantities of physical coffee, although dealers do occasionally deliver coffee or take delivery of coffee in respect of contracts that have not been closed out. Participants in the industry use the futures markets primarily for hedging.

Traditionally traders and dealers operated in the ports to which the coffee was delivered. Hence in Europe Hamburg, London, Amsterdam, Rotterdam, Le Havre, Marseilles, Antwerp, Trieste and Genoa have all become important coffee trading centres. However, the world's biggest single market for coffee is in the United States and so New York dominates the world coffee market. For futures trading the New York Coffee, Sugar and Cocoa Exchange[2] is the focal point for arabica coffee, while the London LIFFE market is the main robusta coffee futures market.[3] There are also coffee futures trading operations in Tokyo (Japan), São Paulo (Brazil) and Bangalore (India) but the volumes traded are much lower than in New York or London (see chapter 8, Futures markets).

The structure of the trade in other importing countries is broadly similar although naturally there are variations. In some countries, such as the Nordic countries, there are no main traders or importers as such but rather just roasters and brokers/agents. In others, such as in Eastern Europe, importers either import directly or increasingly via the international trade houses based in the main coffee centres of Hamburg, Rotterdam, Le Havre, Marseilles and Trieste.

## Structure of the retail market

Retail sales of coffee (both roasted and instant) in the main importing countries are channelled through a combination of retail shops owned by the roasters themselves, their own direct sales force supplying supermarkets and hypermarkets, and wholesalers and food brokers. Supermarkets today play a much larger role in the retailing of coffee than they ever did before and supermarket own brands now account for a sizeable proportion of retail

---

2    Owned by the New York Board of Trade or NYBOT.
3    The London International Financial Futures and Options Exchange, since early 2002 part of the Euronext Group.

coffee sales. Roasted coffee is sold in ground form or as whole bean and is packaged in various types and sizes of cans and packets. Soluble coffee is generally sold in jars, although sachets are becoming increasingly popular especially in emerging markets and in particular for the '3-in-1' products where instant coffee is pre-mixed with sugar and a creamer. There is also a strongly growing, although still small, market for ready-to-drink (RTD) liquid coffee beverages sold in cans or bottles.

Roasters have two distinct market segments:

- The retail (grocery) market, where coffee is purchased largely but not exclusively for consumption in the home;

- The institutional (catering) market, where coffee is destined for the out-of-home market e.g. restaurants, coffee shops and bars, hospitals, offices, and vending machines.

The percentage share of each segment varies from country to country, but in most retail sales for in-home consumption generally account for 70%–80% of the overall market. There are exceptions, especially in countries such as Greece, Italy and Spain, where there is a well established catering trade and eating out is part of the country's traditions.

Each segment accepts a wide range of products, the quality and taste of which depend largely upon the coffee growths that make up the blends, the degree of roast, the type of grind, and so on. Most small roasters tend to specialize in one segment, while larger and in particular multinational roasters usually service both. The major part of the retail market is, however, controlled by a handful of huge multinational roasters and the degree of concentration is increasing. Although this trend was temporarily halted by the growth in the specialty trade, it is once again accelerating with the rapid acquisition of small specialty roasters by the multinationals.

## Market concentration

Since the 1970s concentration has increased in all aspects of the trade on the importing side. On the roasting side, for example, most roasters then tended to operate within national markets, rather than multinationally, yet today a significant proportion of the world's roasting and processing industry is dominated by just a small number of multinational companies. In France, it is estimated that there were more than 2,500 roasters operating in 1970, yet by 2000 the top four roasters shared approximately 75% of the market. The same trend can also be detected in Italy where the number of small, independent roasters has been in rapid decline, although this trend seems to have levelled off somewhat over the last ten years or so. Despite this, however, the number of roasters has fallen from an estimated 4,000 in 1970 to around 1,000 in 2000; the top five account for over 70% of the Italian coffee market.

Globally the top ten roasters accounted for an estimated 63% of all processed coffee sales (roasted and soluble). The situation in the soluble coffee sector is even more exaggerated. This sector has always been dominated by a few large multinational companies, such as Nestlé and Kraft Foods, although smaller manufacturers have been able to secure a reasonable foothold in their own national markets. Figure 7 shows the percentage share of the top five roasters in some selected markets.

The same can be observed in the international trade in green coffee, although to a lesser extent. Competition in the sector has shrunk to a point where in 2000 it is estimated that five leading green coffee trading companies accounted for over 40% of the total volume of green coffee imports worldwide. A similar trend can also be seen in the retail sector, with growing domination by the large supermarket chains as the number of smaller independent food outlets shrinks day by day. The world's top 30 grocery retailers account for 10% of the global retail market. In Europe, the top 10 supermarket chains account for 23% of the total grocery trade.

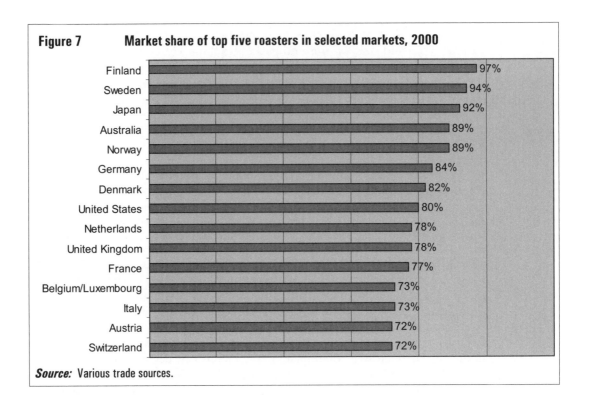

**Figure 7          Market share of top five roasters in selected markets, 2000**

| | |
|---|---|
| Finland | 97% |
| Sweden | 94% |
| Japan | 92% |
| Australia | 89% |
| Norway | 89% |
| Germany | 84% |
| Denmark | 82% |
| United States | 80% |
| Netherlands | 78% |
| United Kingdom | 78% |
| France | 77% |
| Belgium/Luxembourg | 73% |
| Italy | 73% |
| Austria | 72% |
| Switzerland | 72% |

*Source:* Various trade sources.

The highest degree of concentration in the retail grocery sector is found in Germany, France, Switzerland, Scandinavia and the United Kingdom. In all of these countries the top five supermarket chains account for more than 60% of retail food and grocery sales. A similar trend is evident in the United States where the top four food retailers account for 28% of food sales and the top 20 account for 52%.[4] The small traditional non–self-service grocery shops still retain the largest proportion of the retail food market in Spain, Portugal and Italy, but their share is diminishing.

As often happens, there has been a backlash against this dominating trend. The recent growth of the gourmet or specialty coffee sector has certainly slowed, although by no means halted, this increase in market concentration in all sectors of the coffee business. The growth of the specialty sector has definitely increased again the number of small roasters and retailers operating worldwide, although this has not not had any real impact on the reducing number of active traders and importers. Why has there been such an increase in concentration? There are probably several answers, one of them being the growing domination of the large retail groups and the resulting increase in specification buying (where the retailer rather than the roaster determines the specifications of the coffee). This has caused the roasters and manufacturers to actively seek to become larger in an effort to maintain their end of the balance of power in the food industry.

Another possible answer is that this concentration is a natural phenomenon resulting from the inevitable globalization of all businesses seeking economies of scale. There is little doubt that the sheer size of the larger groups enhances their negotiating power.

Either way there has been a noticeable reduction in the number of importers, roasters and coffee retailers and the trend looks set to continue.

---

**4**    Various industry sources including *Coffee International File 2000*, Euro Monitor, USDA and trade press.

# Demand

## Overview

Coffee is one of the world's most popular beverages. Gross imports of all types of coffee have increased by 266% from 27.6 million bags in 1947 to 101.2 million bags in 2001. However, statistics on gross imports are a poor indicator of demand as they ignore re-exports. In 2001 re-exports accounted for some 21.4 million bags, although in the past they were not as important as they are today. Data on re-exports are not available prior to 1964 but figure 8 shows the growth in gross exports since 1947 and in total net imports since 1964. Net imports are what is actually consumed in the country of importation plus any surplus that goes into inventories.

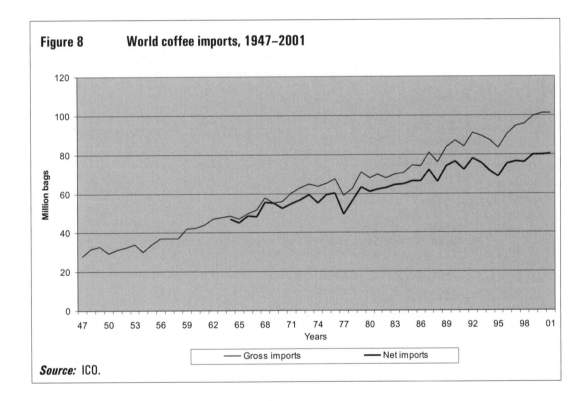

**Figure 8    World coffee imports, 1947–2001**

*Source:* ICO.

A more accurate indicator of consumption is provided by statistics on disappearance which take into account re-exports and changes in the level of stocks held in importing countries. Table 7 shows world gross imports, net imports, disappearance and inventories by form of coffee over the period 1995–2001.

Table 7 shows that green coffee accounted for 82.7% of gross imports in the year 2001, while roasted and soluble coffee accounted for 6.6% and 10.7% respectively, with the import of processed coffee growing faster than that of green coffee.

Gross imports of roasted coffee, although relatively flat for many years, have started to show signs of significant growth. However, only a very small proportion of this total is from producing countries. Overall annual gross imports of roasted coffee have grown on average by just under 7% a year over the past five years – more than twice the rate of growth in gross imports overall – but there appears to have been a slight downturn in 2001. Imports of soluble coffee have also grown at much faster rate adding 8% a year, while gross imports of green beans have increased only by just under 1.5% a year.

| Table 7 | World gross and net imports, disappearance and inventories by form of coffee, 1995–2001 (in millions of bags) | | | | | | |
|---|---|---|---|---|---|---|---|
|  | **1995** | **1996** | **1997** | **1998** | **1999** | **2000** | **2001\*** |
| **A. Gross imports** | **83.3** | **90.1** | **94.5** | **95.6** | **99.4** | **101.1** | **101.2** |
| Green | 71.5 | 78.0 | 80.1 | 81.2 | 83.5 | 83.9 | 83.7 |
| Roasted | 4.6 | 4.9 | 5.2 | 5.6 | 6.4 | 6.8 | 6.7 |
| Soluble | 7.2 | 7.2 | 9.2 | 9.8 | 9.5 | 10.4 | 10.8 |
| **B. Gross re-exports** | **14.6** | **15.8** | **18.1** | **19.6** | **19.7** | **21.4** | **21.1** |
| Green | 7.2 | 6.7 | 8.2 | 9.7 | 8.8 | 9.0 | 8.6 |
| Roasted | 4.1 | 4.9 | 5.2 | 5.1 | 5.6 | 5.8 | 5.7 |
| Soluble | 3.3 | 4.2 | 4.7 | 4.8 | 5.3 | 6.6 | 6.8 |
| **C. Net imports** | **68.7** | **75.3** | **76.4** | **76.0** | **79.7** | **79.7** | **80.1** |
| Green | 64.3 | 71.3 | 71.9 | 71.5 | 74.7 | 74.9 | 75.1 |
| Roasted | 0.5 | 0.0 | 0.0 | 0.5 | 0.8 | 1.0 | 1.0 |
| Soluble | 3.9 | 3.0 | 4.5 | 5.0 | 4.2 | 3.8 | 4.0 |
| **D. Disappearance** | **73.3** | **76.1** | **77.2** | **77.9** | **78.7** | **76.7** | **78.8** |
| **E. Inventories as at 31 December\*\*** | **9.4** | **7.8** | **8.5** | **8.3** | **10.7** | **16.3** | **18.8\*** |

*Source:* ICO.

\*   Provisional.

\*\* Comprises all stocks in consuming countries, including stocks in free ports.


## Roast and ground

Estimates suggest that some 81 million bags or 77% of all coffee consumed in the world are roast and ground. In importing countries, about 75% of consumption is roast and ground, and of this about 88% is roasted in-country. The remainder is imported from producing countries or from other consuming countries.

In some regions the cross-border trade in coffee roasted by consumers themselves is growing strongly. The European Union dominates this trade, and in 2000 had 60% of world exports of roasted coffee. Producing countries accounted for just 12% of this trade in roasted coffee, the United States and other countries made up the remaining 28%.

The market for roast and ground coffee is dominated by large multinationals (Kraft Foods, Sara Lee/DE and Nestlé), despite the fact that in many countries there has been a resurgence in small, locally based roasters. The bulk of roast and ground coffee consumed in importing countries is blended (usually before roasting), in order to ensure a certain uniformity in the finished product. Blending increases the roasters' flexibility, making them less dependent on one source of supply. It also allows them to compensate for changes in the taste of the coffee bean and to switch to other coffees if there are any problems with availability or price. Roasting develops the coffee's flavour and fragrancy; the higher the roast the more the flavour is developed. Lightly roasted beans produce a thin, straw-coloured liquid with little flavour except perhaps acidity, although the weight loss is less. A darker roast will give a dark liquid which may have lost acidity but has gained body and stronger flavour, although the weight loss will be higher. The darker the roast the greater the cell destruction. This facilitates the extraction of solubles, but too dark a roast merely leaves a burnt flavour.

Roast and ground coffee has a shorter shelf life than soluble coffee. It loses quality the longer it is exposed to air, so it is frequently packed in vacuum or gas-flushed packs.

## Soluble coffee

The term *soluble coffee* encompasses spray-dried powder, freeze-dried powder and liquefied forms of coffee such as liquid concentrates. All of these methods of processing involve dehydrating brewed roasted and ground coffee. The freeze-dried method produces a superior but more expensive product.

Figure 9 shows that world consumption of soluble coffee has remained relatively stable since 1994, with a small upturn in global consumption to 24.6 million bags GBE in the year 2000.

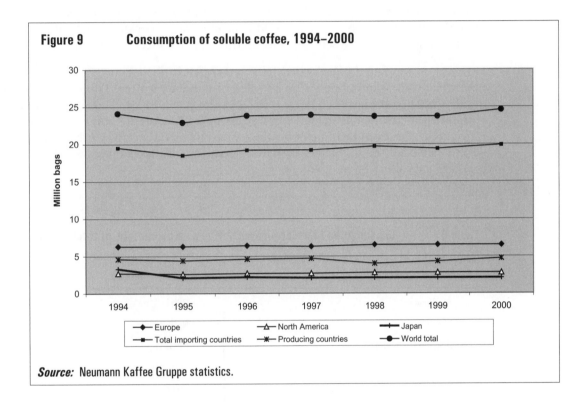

**Figure 9    Consumption of soluble coffee, 1994–2000**

*Source:* Neumann Kaffee Gruppe statistics.

In Europe growth in demand has been relatively modest at around 0.5% a year in recent years, which is slower than the overall growth in consumption for all types of coffee. In the United Kingdom, where soluble coffee accounts for around 80% of total consumption, demand is stagnating. Elsewhere in Europe, however, it has been making small inroads in a number of traditional roast and ground markets, such as Germany, where new specialty instant coffee products (such as instant cappuccino) are growing in popularity. The Deutscher Kaffee-Verband estimates that the instant coffee share of demand in Germany grew from 6.2% to 6.7% between 1998 and 2000.

Much of the recent growth in soluble coffee consumption can be attributed to a rise in demand in Eastern Europe, notably the Russian Federation, and the Far East – both regions where soluble coffee enjoys a high market share. In the Far East there has been a tremendous growth in the demand for the product known as '3-in-1', a beverage which combines the convenience of soluble coffee with a non-dairy creamer and sugar, usually in single-serve sachets that often can be bought one at a time.

In 2000, 83% of the soluble coffee consumed in importing countries was processed into soluble coffee in those countries. The corresponding figure in 1989 was 81%. This suggests that producing countries may be seeing a decline in their share of the soluble coffee market in importing countries. Imports of soluble coffee are often referred to as *offshore powder.* Consumption of instant coffee in producing countries varies considerably. In the Philippines and Thailand instant coffee accounts for around 95% of coffee consumption whereas in Brazil, the largest exporter of soluble coffee, domestic consumption of instant coffee is less than 5% of overall coffee consumption. In India most soluble coffee is also exported although it does account for around 30% of local consumption. In Mexico the figure is about 60%.

Globally Nestlé and Kraft Foods account for around 75% of the world market, with Nestlé alone supplying over half the world demand for instant coffee.

### Decaffeinated

Decaffeinated coffee was developed in Europe but achieved its first broad market in the United States during the 1950s. World consumption of decaffeinated coffee is difficult to gauge owing to the lack of separate data on this type of coffee in many importing countries.

However, in the United States decaffeinated coffee is estimated to account for 8%–9% of mainstream sales and about 20% of sales of specialty coffee. Globally, consumption of decaffeinated coffee has been fairly static over the last decade, although this situation is not entirely clear-cut in that in many countries new low-caffeine coffee products have been introduced. These products are not caffeine free but are either a mixture of regular coffee and decaffeinated coffee or blends of coffees with a naturally low caffeine content. These products are sold as 'light' coffee.

| **Table 8** | **Consumption of decaffeinated coffee as a percentage of total consumption, 2000** | | | |
|---|---|---|---|---|
| **Country** | **%** | **Country** | **%** |
| Australia | 7 | Italy | 3 |
| Austria | 12 | Netherlands | 12 |
| Belgium/Luxembourg | 12–13 | Norway | Low |
| Canada | 7-8 | Portugal | Low |
| Denmark | Low | Spain | 10 |
| Finland | 1 | Sweden | Low |
| France | 9 | Switzerland | 5 |
| Germany | 11 | United Kingdom | 13 |
| Greece | Low | United States | 9 |

***Source:*** Various trade publications and estimates.

## Demand by geographical area

### North America

#### United States of America

Coffee consumption in the United States, the largest single national market for coffee in the world, is now showing some rather hesitant signs of recovery after almost two decades of decline.

**The United States market in a nutshell**

*Population: 282 million.*

*The United States accounted for 21% of world gross imports in 2001; the equivalent figure was 69% in 1947, 44% in 1968 and 18% in 1994.*

*2001 green bean imports were 19.29 million bags; gross imports of all forms of coffee were 21.45 million bags GBE.*

*Main green bean suppliers were: Colombia 17%, Viet Nam 15%, Brazil 15%, Guatemala 11% and Mexico 10%. Between them, Costa Rica, Ecuador, El Salvador, Honduras, Nicaragua and Peru provided a further 17%. India, Indonesia, Papua New Guinea and Thailand 9%, and Africa just under 3%.*

*675,000 bags of green coffee were also imported from countries in Europe, mainly from Germany.*

*Estimated shares in 2001 green bean imports from producing countries were: arabica 76%; robusta 24%.*

*Imports of processed coffee were 2,156,000 bags, of which approximately 27% were from Canada and 14% from Mexico. Exports of processed coffee were 1,530,000 bags, of which an estimated 65% went to Canada.*

*Consumption per head in 2001: 4.07 kg, marginally up from 3.98 kg in 1995.*

*Estimates of the combined market share of Kraft Foods, Sara Lee / DE, Procter & Gamble, Starbucks and Nestlé range from 75% to over 80%.*

*9% of consumption is decaffeinated, down from 25% in 1987.*

***Roast and ground.*** Two-thirds of all coffee sales are of roast and ground coffee sold through supermarkets. Over 70% of the coffee sold for home consumption (where 75% of total consumption takes place) is roast and ground coffee sold in a can or vacuum pack. It is for this reason that the United States was, possibly unfairly, frequently referred to as a high volume market in which more attention is paid to price than to quality. However, in recent years, there has been a dramatic turnaround resulting from the surge in the expansion of the specialty sector, which has transformed and improved the image of coffee in the eyes of the American consumer. In 1991 it was estimated that there were just 500 gourmet or specialty coffeehouses, yet by 2001 this had grown to an estimated 8,500. This number excludes other coffee venues such as coffee carts, kiosks, vending machines and cafés in bookstores, sporting arenas and transportation facilities, which have also seen an explosion in numbers.

***Specialty coffee.*** Consumption of specialty coffee has grown from approximately 7 million drinkers daily in 1997 to approximately 29 million drinkers daily in 2001. At the same time occasional consumption of specialty coffee has surged, increasing from 35% of the adult population to 62%, or from 80 million drinkers to 127 million drinkers. Despite this, roasted or regular coffee remains the most popular type of coffee consumed in America today, accounting for 73 out of every 100 cups of coffee consumed. Soluble coffee accounts for around 8, while the other 19 cups per 100 consist of gourmet or specialty coffee beverages.

***Consumption per head.*** In the two years since the National Coffee Association of USA, Inc. (NCA) started collecting detailed information on gourmet or specialty coffee, consumption in this segment has grown by over 65%, from 11.6 cups out of every 100 in 1999 to 19.2 cups in 2001. Nevertheless, consumption per head in the United States is still considerably below that of the early 1970s. In 1975, individual consumption was 5.62 kg per head or approximately 2.2 cups per person per day. Consumption reached a low of 3.98 kg per head in 1995, or 1.67 cups per person per day, a fall of over 29%. By 2001 it was still only just marginally higher at 4.07 kg per head, or 1.72 cups per person per day. Figure 10 shows the evolution of consumption on the basis of cups consumed daily by people aged 10 years or older over the period 1971–2001.

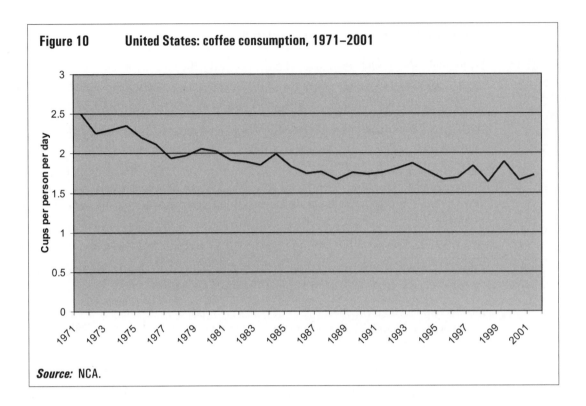

**Figure 10        United States: coffee consumption, 1971–2001**

*Source:* NCA.

***Decaffeinated*** coffee (all forms) showed a huge but short-lived increase in popularity during the 1980s. In 1987, 25 cups out of every 100 consumed were decaffeinated, compared to 14 in 1975. But by 2001 consumption was down again to just 9 cups out of every 100 consumed.

**Table 9        United States: beverage consumption, 1975–2001**

| Percentage of the population drinking: | 1975 | 1990 | 1999 | 2000 | 2001 |
|---|---|---|---|---|---|
| Coffee | 62 | 54 | 54 | 54 | 52 |
| Tea | 27 | 30 | 31 | 30 | 31 |
| Milk | 51 | 47 | 34 | 31 | 33 |
| Soft drinks | 47 | 65 | 61 | 60 | 58 |
| Juices | 44 | 46 | 38 | 38 | 43 |

*Source:* NCA.

The consumption and popularity of different beverages have remained relatively stable over the last three years although there have been some significant changes over the longer term. Tea and soft drinks are both more popular today than they were in 1975, while milk and coffee are less popular. Soft drinks, which overtook coffee in the 1980s to become the most popular form of beverage, have maintained that lead although they appear to have suffered a small downturn in their popularity over the past three years.

Green coffee makes up the bulk of imports into the United States, although almost 6% of gross imports were of soluble coffee, the main suppliers of which are Brazil, Mexico and the Netherlands. Rather surprisingly given the growth in specialty coffee consumption in the

United States, the origin mix of its green coffee imports has not altered greatly over the last 10 years or so. In 1990, 61% of United States imports of green coffee from producing countries came from the Colombian milds and other milds groups, while in 2001 this was slightly down to 60%. However, imports of Brazilian arabicas have fallen from 22% to 16%, while imports of robusta coffee have risen from 13% to 24%. This greater use of robusta may reflect the greater consumption of espresso blends containing robusta coffee or, on the other hand, it may reflect the greater use of cheaper coffee in the blends of the mainstream roasters, suggesting competition is on price more than on quality.

## Canada

*Population: 31 million.*

*Gross imports in 2001: 3,337,000 bags (GBE).*

*Consumption per head in 2000: 4.7 kg; minor growth is registered.*

*20% of gross imports in all forms are from the United States.*

*The largest green bean suppliers are Colombia 21%; Brazil 17%, Guatemala 12% and Viet Nam 10%.*

*Kraft Foods and Nestlé are the largest roasters but domestic roasters are gaining market share.*

*Soluble coffee covers 9% of consumption.*

## Western Europe

Consumption of coffee in the European Union (EU)[5] plus Switzerland and Norway has been relatively flat over the past five or six years both on an aggregate level and per head. The ICO estimates that, overall, the 15 countries that make up the EU consumed 33.6 million bags in 2001 or almost 43% of the consumption in all importing countries. This compares with the 1995 total of 33 million bags. Within the EU Germany continues to be the largest consumer of coffee, accounting for approximately 9.7 million bags but this is almost 5% lower than the 10.2 million bags it consumed in 1999. France comes second with consumption estimated at around 5.4 million bags, roughly the same as the year before but 3.5% down on the 1997 figure, while Italy is third, consuming 5.3 million bags in 2001, the highest figure ever recorded for Italy.

**Intra-EU trade.** Strictly speaking there is no intra-EU import or export since the creation of the single market, only movement of goods. This is more than just terminology. It means in practice that the vast majority of imports are declared at the point of entry into the EU and not at the point of destination. This tends to increase gross import figures for those countries with the major points of importation (in essence, the major ports). At the same time, the single market means that the earlier documentary requirements for cross-border traffic no longer exist. Operators are required to report cross-border traffic to the statistical bodies, but only above a certain value and/or volume. Eurostat, the EU statistical office, has developed models to extrapolate total intra-EU movement of goods on the basis of the reported data, but these have their limitations.

For these reasons data on the movement of green as well as finished coffee within the EU have inevitably become less accurate. As far as green coffee is concerned, the European Coffee Federation estimates (on the basis of Eurostat data) the intra-EU movement to have been 1.9 million bags in 2001. However, not only do many of the statistics for individual EU country coffee imports produced by both the EU authorities and the ICO not always present the total picture, but there are also differences between them. Most individual EU member country statistics must, therefore, be treated with some caution.

---

5    Members of the EU as at 1 September 2002: Austria, Belgium, Denmark, Finland, France, Germany, Greece, Ireland, Italy, Luxembourg, the Netherlands, Portugal, Spain, Sweden and the United Kingdom.

But, clearly, over the past ten years or so there has been a noticeable rise in the cross-border trade in processed coffee between European countries. Indeed, the markets and coffee industries of the EU member countries have become even more closely related following the creation of the single market in 1992. Many believe that this has made it much more difficult to distinguish between individual country markets. Germany, for example, has seen its re-exports of processed coffee (both roasted and soluble) rise from just over 45,000 bags GBE in 1964 to 1.9 million bags GBE in 2001, of which much went to EU destinations. The country also exported 1.6 million bags of decaffeinated green bean. Likewise, Italy has seen its re-exports of processed coffee rise from around 20,000 bags to just over 1 million bags while Belgium/Luxembourg has seen a yet more spectacular increase.

Below are summary details on the green coffee imports, that is, excluding processed coffee, of individual countries in Western Europe. In this context green coffee means not decaffeinated and from all sources, so also from other European countries. Green bean imports are identified by country of origin but not all were necessarily imported directly from origin.[6]

## Austria

*Population: 8 million; member of the EU.*

*2001 green bean imports: 1.06 million bags; Brazil led with 40%.*

*Brazil, Colombia, Viet Nam, Guatemala and Indonesia represented 73% of green bean imports.*

*Exports of processed coffee were around 380,000 bags in 2001. No import data were readily available but the amount was thought to be equally substantial.*

*Consumption per head in 2001: 8.2 kg, up from 7.5 kg in 1995, despite an increase from 10% to 20% on value added tax on coffee in 2000.*

## Belgium/Luxembourg

*Population: 11 million; member of the EU.*

*2001 green bean imports: 2.51 million bags; Brazil led with 21%.*

*Brazil, Colombia, Viet Nam, Guatemala and Uganda represented 57% of green bean imports.*

*Imports of roasted coffee were 220,000 bags; exports were 740,000 bags, mostly within Western Europe.*

*Consumption per head in 2001: 5.0 kg; down from 6.4 kg in 1995. Sources of information on consumption differ and the drop from 1995 to 2001 may well have been smaller than indicated.*

*One roaster, Sara Lee / DE, accounts for around half of the market but Belgium also has many small roasters, particularly in the specialty sector.*

## Denmark

*Population: 5 million; member of the EU.*

*2001 green bean imports: 989,000 bags; Brazil led with 43%.*

*Brazil, Colombia, Peru, Uganda and Honduras represented 71% of green bean imports. Estimated shares: arabica 82%, robusta 13%, not specified 5%.*

*Imports of processed coffee were 64,000 bags; exports were 185,000 bags.*

*Consumption per head in 2001: 9.8 kg, 12% higher than in 1995.*

*Four roasters account for 80% of the market, six account for 90%.*

---

6    Source for most import/export data for all EU countries, Norway and Switzerland: The European Coffee Federation's *European Coffee Report 2001*, which itself draws on data provided by Eurostat and member associations. Other data come from ICO and other trade statistics. Figures for imports/exports of processed coffee are expressed as GBE. All figures have been rounded.

## Finland

Population: 5 million; member of the EU.

2001 green bean imports: 1 million bags; Brazil led with 41%.

Brazil, Colombia, Guatemala, Costa Rica and Honduras represented 78% of total green bean imports. Estimated shares: arabica 98%, robusta 2%.

94% of imports reportedly come direct from origin. Imports of processed coffee were 54,000 bags; exports were 112,000 bags.

Consumption per head in 2001: 9.6 kg; up from 8.6 kg in 1995.

Four roasters account for 97% of the market.

## France

Population: 59 million; member of the EU.

2001 green bean imports: 5.1 million bags; Brazil led with 22%.

Brazil, Viet Nam, Colombia, Côte d'Ivoire and Cameroon represented 66% of total green bean imports. Estimated shares: arabica 51%, robusta 49%.

Imports of roasted coffee were 980,000 bags; exports (excluding soluble coffee) were 627,000 bags, of which 474,000 bags were decaffeinated green bean.

Consumption per head in 2001: 5.5 kg, same as in 1995.

Kraft Foods and Sara Lee / DE account for 60% or more of the roast and ground market by volume. Nestlé accounts for almost two-thirds of the soluble market.

## Germany

Population: 82 million; member of the EU.

2001 green bean imports: 13.9 million bags; Brazil led with 25%.

Brazil, Viet Nam, Colombia, Indonesia and Peru represented 63% of total green bean imports. Estimated shares: arabica 76%, robusta 24% (up from 14% in 1990).

Processed coffee imports were 714,000 bags; exports were 3.46 million bags of which 1.61 million bags were decaffeinated green bean.

Consumption per head in 2001: 6.7 kg; down from 7.4 kg in 1995, but the same as in 2000. Espresso coffee gaining popularity, mostly imported from Italy. Decaffeinated coffee holds 11% of the market.

Two roasters, Kraft Foods and Tchibo, account for 55% of the market.

## Greece

Population: 11 million; member of the EU.

2001 green bean imports: 457,000 bags; Brazil led with 78%. However, Greece is also a very large importer of soluble coffee and total 2001 imports are estimated (by the ICO) at 830,000 bags GBE.

Brazil, India, Viet Nam, Uganda and Colombia represented 95% of total green bean imports.

Soluble coffee accounts for 45% of the market, and 82% comes from Côte d'Ivoire, the single largest supplier of coffee to Greece. Overall robusta makes up around 40% of imports. Data on processed coffee trade were not available.

Consumption per head in 2001: 4.9 kg, a significant increase from 2.2 kg in 1995.

## Ireland

*Population: 4 million; member of the EU.*

*Imports of all forms in 2001: 211,000 bags GBE (ICO estimate).*

*36% of green coffee imports are sourced from the United Kingdom.*

*More than half of imports are processed coffee, mainly from the United Kingdom. Soluble coffee accounts for about 75% of total consumption.*

*Consumption per head in 2001: just 2.3 kg but growing.*

## Italy

*Population: 58 million; member of the EU.*

*2001 green bean imports: 6.08 million bags; Brazil led with 29%.*

*Brazil, Viet Nam, Cameroon, India and Côte d'Ivoire represented 69% of total green bean imports. Estimated shares: arabica 56%, robusta 44%.*

*Imports of processed coffee were 352,000 bags; exports were 1 million bags of which 97% was roasted coffee. It is estimated that Germany buys 30% of Italian exports of roasted coffee and Greece 17%.*

*Consumption per head in 2001: 5.4 kg, up from 4.8 kg in 1995.*

*Five roasters, of which Lavazza is the largest, account for more than 70% of the market.*

## Netherlands

*Population: 16 million; member of the EU.*

*2001 green bean imports: 2.28 million bags – net figure, excluding re-exports, based on coffee roasted in the Netherlands; Brazil led with 24%.*

*Brazil, Uganda, Colombia, Viet Nam and Kenya represented 66% of total green bean imports (of which Kenya 6%). Estimated shares: arabica 69%, robusta 30%, not specified 1%.*

*Imports of roasted coffee were 351,000 bags; exports were 89,000 bags.*

*Consumption per head in 2001: 6.6 kg (est.); down from 7.2 kg in 2000 and 8.9 kg in 1995.*

*Sara Lee / DE dominates with more than two-thirds of all coffee sales.*

## Norway

*Population: 4 million.*

*2001 green bean imports: 624,000 bags; Brazil led with 41%.*

*Brazil, Colombia, Guatemala, Mexico and Peru represented 86% of total green bean imports. Estimated shares: arabica 98%, robusta 1%, not specified 1%.*

*Imports of processed coffee were 52,000 bags; exports were just 2,500 bags.*

*Consumption per head in 2001: 9.3 kg; slowly declining since mid 1990s.*

*90% of the market is shared by four roasters who are also importers.*

## Portugal

*Population: 10 million; member of the EU.*

*2001 green bean imports: 688,000 bags; Brazil led with 14%.*

*Brazil, Viet Nam, Côte d'Ivoire, Uganda and India represented 46% of total green bean imports. Estimated shares: arabica 41%, robusta 38%, not specified 21%. A further 115,000 bags or so were imported in processed form, mostly from Spain, and total 2001 imports are estimated at approximately 800,000 bags GBE.*

*Consumption per head in 2001: 4.3 kg, up from 3.4 kg in 1995.*

*Nestlé's market share is 33%; around 70 roasters cover the balance, many operating in small, local niche markets.*

## Spain

*Population: 39 million; member of the EU.*

*2001 green bean imports: 3.73 million bags (est.); Viet Nam led with 30%.*

*Viet Nam, Brazil, Uganda, Côte d'Ivoire and Colombia represented 72% of all green bean imports (of which Colombia 6%). Estimated shares: arabica 44%, robusta 55%, not specified 1%.*

*Imports of processed coffee were 201,000 bags; exports were 422,000 bags.*

*Consumption per head in 2001: 4.5 kg, up from 4.2 kg in 1995.*

*Mezclas, blends of torrefacto and regular coffee, account for about half the market. Torrefacto itself is made from roasting regular coffee with sugar.*

*The top three roasters control 60% of the market. Some 300 smaller roasters cover 40% and dominate the out-of-home market where espresso is in high demand.*

## Sweden

*Population: 9 million; member of the EU.*

*2001 green bean imports: 1.4 million bags; Brazil led with 43%.*

*Brazil, Colombia, Peru, Kenya and Guatemala represented 86% of total green bean imports. Estimated shares: arabica 99%, robusta 1%.*

*Imports of processed coffee were 126,000 bags; exports were 147,000 bags of which close to 25% goes to the United States.*

*Consumption per head in 2001: 8.7 kg; down from 11.8 kg in 1990.*

*Dominating roasters are Kraft Foods with about 50% of the market and Löfbergs Lila with more than 15%. About eight roasters share the balance.*

## Switzerland

*Population: 7 million.*

*2001 green bean imports: 1.1 million bags; Brazil led with 14%.*

*Brazil, Colombia, India, Guatemala and Mexico represented 45% of total green bean imports. Estimated shares: arabica 72%, robusta 20%, not specified 8%.*

*Imports of processed coffee were 88,000 bags; exports were 182,000 bags.*

*Consumption per head in 2001: 8 kg, about the same as in 1995.*

*The main roaster, Migros, accounts for 45% of the market. The re-export of processed coffee is growing, in particular of soluble.*

### United Kingdom

*Population: 60 million; member of the EU.*

*2001 green bean imports: 2 million bags; Viet Nam led with 33%.*

*Viet Nam, Brazil, Colombia, Indonesia and Mexico represented 70% of total green bean imports, of which 53% was arabica, 46% was robusta and 1% was not specified. However, a further 1.1 million bags GBE of processed coffee were imported as well, almost half from Germany, and gross total 2001 imports were estimated at just over 3.1 million bags GBE. Re-exports were just over 600,000 bags GBE.*

*Consumption per head in 2001: 2.3 kg, the same as in 1995.*

*Soluble coffee accounts for 87% of the market by value with roast and ground at just 13%. The United Kingdom hot beverage market continues to be dominated by tea.*

*Nestlé accounts for around 50% of the market, Kraft Foods just over 20%.*

The blends, methods of preparation and overall usage of coffee in Western Europe vary from country to country depending on such factors as habits, tradition, taste and historical ties. Up until the mid 1970s robusta coffee, primarily from African origins, constituted the major component in most coffee blends available in Belgium/Luxembourg, France, Portugal and the United Kingdom, whereas the majority of blends available in the Scandinavian countries, Austria, Switzerland, Germany, Italy and Spain generally incorporated a much higher proportion of arabica coffees. Today, however, while former traditional links are still fairly important, the import statistics suggest that in the majority of EU countries, coffee roasters now reflect the growing consumer preference for mild arabica coffee in their blends. However, with the increasing availability of cheap robustas there has been a noticeable rise in recent years in the inclusion of these coffees in many of the major blends.

Even so, there can be little doubt that these regional variations are becoming less pronounced and that coffee blends are becoming more universal throughout Europe.

## Eastern and Central Europe

The opening up of many of the markets of Eastern Europe coincided with the collapse in world coffee prices in 1989/90 and this certainly had a major effect on consumption in these countries. Imports of green coffee did not increase substantially but imports of roasted and soluble coffee did. Even so, official statistics in general tend to underestimate, sometimes significantly so, the amount of coffee being imported into these countries, not least because the border controls where such imports were originally recorded no longer exist or are bypassed.

Many of the larger Western European roasters, conscious of the opportunities that existed, were keen to establish themselves in these new markets. Initially Western European brands of coffee, both roast and ground and soluble, were heavily promoted in many of these countries; subsequently many of these roasters began to establish a more permanent set-up in these markets by taking over existing capacity or installing their own roasting plants. However there has been a downside to this success in many Eastern European countries where counterfeiting provides serious problems for many of the major roasters. In the Russian Federation the formation of the Coffee Manufacturers Association in 2000 can be attributed to the wish of many of these larger companies to have a collective voice with which to talk to the government about controlling counterfeiting.

Liberalization has also brought changes in the way the coffee trade in Eastern and Central Europe operates. In the past state controlled agencies tended to buy direct from origin, usually by barter deal or other long-term arrangement, but now most roasters in these countries buy through external trade houses which are able to supply a much wider range of origins than was available in the past. Some do import directly but the number is relatively small.

**Consumption of coffee** per head remains relatively low in all of the countries of Eastern and Central Europe, where tea tends to be the more popular beverage, but it does appear to be rising. The highest individual consumption of coffee is in Hungary at an estimated 4.3 kg per head; in the Czech Republic it is estimated to be around 3.6 kg per head and in Poland 2.8 kg. In the Russian Federation it is only around 0.6 kg per head. Roast and ground coffees tend to be the more popular in countries like Hungary and Poland, but soluble coffee is gaining in popularity in nearly all the countries of Eastern Europe. The lower price of soluble coffee together with its western 'luxury' image makes it more attractive to new coffee consumers.

**Table 10      Eastern Europe: imports by type for selected countries, 1995–2000 (in thousands of bags)**

|  | 1995 | 1996 | 1997 | 1998 | 1999 | 2000 |
|---|---|---|---|---|---|---|
| **TOTAL** | **6,838** | **6,565** | **8,366** | **8,181** | **8,191** | **9,057** |
| **Bulgaria** | **515** | **272** | **294** | **306** | **359** | **271** |
| Colombian milds | 0 | 1 | 0 | 0 | 2 | 0 |
| Other milds | 8 | 5 | 4 | 6 | 7 | 5 |
| Brazilian naturals | 123 | 13 | 7 | 0 | 8 | 19 |
| Robustas | 287 | 212 | 254 | 262 | 290 | 206 |
| Unspecified | 105 | 41 | 29 | 36 | 52 | 41 |
| **Croatia** | **320** | **322** | **385** | **339** | **352** | **344** |
| Colombian milds | 37 | 32 | 40 | 20 | 22 | 18 |
| Other milds | 68 | 84 | 83 | 79 | 80 | 76 |
| Brazilian naturals | 184 | 177 | 209 | 173 | 182 | 177 |
| Robustas | 11 | 8 | 20 | 25 | 19 | 22 |
| Unspecified | 20 | 21 | 33 | 52 | 49 | 51 |
| **Czech Republic** | **553** | **525** | **560** | **765** | **798** | **798** |
| Colombian milds | 36 | 35 | 31 | 33 | 18 | 80 |
| Other milds | 197 | 262 | 116 | 106 | 113 | 92 |
| Brazilian naturals | 58 | 31 | 78 | 42 | 57 | 118 |
| Robustas | 117 | 142 | 262 | 265 | 231 | 282 |
| Unspecified | 145 | 55 | 73 | 319 | 379 | 226 |
| **Hungary** | **520** | **603** | **675** | **716** | **835** | **895** |
| Colombian milds | 40 | 46 | 37 | 45 | 29 | 30 |
| Other milds | 83 | 103 | 60 | 29 | 91 | 151 |
| Brazilian naturals | 35 | 14 | 41 | 39 | 53 | 45 |
| Robustas | 292 | 341 | 397 | 448 | 458 | 441 |
| Unspecified | 70 | 99 | 127 | 155 | 204 | 228 |

**Table 10** (cont'd)

| | 1995 | 1996 | 1997 | 1998 | 1999 | 2000 |
|---|---|---|---|---|---|---|
| **Poland** | **1,771** | **1,939** | **2,274** | **2,305** | **2,414** | **2,578** |
| Colombian milds | 98 | 175 | 132 | 86 | 80 | 112 |
| Other milds | 402 | 449 | 209 | 191 | 350 | 369 |
| Brazilian naturals | 13 | 17 | 79 | 62 | 30 | 71 |
| Robustas | 983 | 965 | 1,353 | 1,469 | 1,377 | 1,626 |
| Unspecified | 275 | 333 | 491 | 498 | 577 | 400 |
| **Romania** | **551** | **687** | **631** | **595** | **511** | **552** |
| Colombian milds | 2 | 5 | 9 | 9 | 14 | 15 |
| Other milds | 13 | 55 | 7 | 9 | 25 | 47 |
| Brazilian naturals | 111 | 113 | 56 | 28 | 49 | 48 |
| Robustas | 64 | 236 | 326 | 318 | 271 | 315 |
| Unspecified | 361 | 278 | 228 | 230 | 152 | 127 |
| **Russian Federation** | **1,728** | **1,128** | **2,145** | **1,603** | **1,290** | **1,786** |
| Colombian milds | 0 | 0 | 9 | 11 | 6 | n.a |
| Other milds | 0 | 0 | 34 | 24 | 62 | n.a |
| Brazilian naturals | 0 | 0 | 123 | 11 | 3 | n.a |
| Robustas | 0 | 0 | 18 | 5 | 30 | n.a |
| Unspecified | 1,728 | 1,128 | 1,962 | 1,552 | 1,189 | n.a |
| **Others** | **880** | **1,089** | **1,402** | **1,552** | **1,632** | **1,833** |

*Source:* ICO.

Below are summary data on selected Eastern and Central European countries.

## Czech Republic

*Population: 10 million.*

*Gross imports in 2000: 798,000 bags (GBE).*

*Consumption per head in 2000: 3.6 kg (est.), up from 2.9 kg in 1995.*

*Three foreign roasters, Tchibo, Balírny Douwe Egberts and Kraft Foods, each account for around 30% of the market. Nestlé covers almost 50% of the soluble market.*

*Green beans are imported mainly through trade houses elsewhere in Europe.*

*Largest suppliers of green beans are Viet Nam 20%, Indonesia 16% and India 14%.*

*28% of imports are as roasted or instant.*

## Hungary

*Population: 10 million.*

*Gross imports in 1999: 895,000 bags (GBE).*

*Consumption per head in 2000: 4.5 kg (est.), up from 2.8 kg in 1995.*

*Growth in consumption per head partly caused by reduction in tax applicable to coffee; there are some indications that earlier statistics might have underestimated consumption.*

*Robusta, half of which is imported from Uganda, accounts for 70% of green coffee imports; other main suppliers are Viet Nam and Brazil.*

*Two roasters, Sara Lee / DE and Tchibo, accounted for around three-quarters of the market in the late 1990s.*

*Processed coffee accounts for 12% of gross imports.*

## Poland

*Population: 39 million.*

*Gross imports in 2000: 2,578,000 bags (GBE).*

*Consumption per head in 2000: 2.8 kg (est.); stable for several years.*

*Re-exports are increasing and reached 27% of gross imports in 1999; markets are mainly in Eastern Europe.*

*Robusta accounts for three-quarters of imports; largest suppliers are Indonesia 26%, Viet Nam 15%, Uganda 13%, Côte d'Ivoire 12% and India 10%.*

*Instant coffee gains importance and covered 30% of the market in 1999.*

*23% of gross imports are as roasted or instant.*

## Russian Federation

*Population: 146 million.*

*Gross imports in 2000: 1,786,000 bags (GBE).*

*Per capita consumption is around 0.5–0.6 kg per year (est.).*

*Green coffee accounts for under 10% of gross imports; largest suppliers are Viet Nam and India.*

*Instant coffee accounts for more than 80%, with largest supply from India 42%, Brazil 24% and Germany 15%.*

# Asia

## China

China (population 1,262 million) is a producer as well as a consumer. Detailed statistics on the internal consumption of coffee are not readily available but all the indicators suggest that it has grown very rapidly over the past ten years or so. Gross imports in 1999 reported by the ICO totalled 240,000 bags, although the true figure is probably much higher as not all the imports of coffee from neighbouring countries such as Viet Nam are always recorded. Of the gross import total, 48% comprised processed coffee. Re-exports totaled 157,000 bags leaving approximately 83,000 bags as net imports. This, together with internal production and unreported imports, suggests that consumption might have been as high as 300,000 bags in 1999. Furthermore the ICO suggests that consumption may have been growing by as much as 20% a year since 1998, in which case total consumption could easily have been around 400,000 bags in 2001. This would tally with the reported strong growth in arabica production to about 215,000 bags in 2001 (USDA estimate), primarily in the Yunnan

Province. Production was expected to approach 250,000 bags (15,000 tons) in 2002. A substantial amount is exported, and China arabica is becoming fairly well known abroad, certainly in Europe.

Nestlé, which is the market leader and accounts for more than 80% of all soluble coffee sales in China, has been active in promoting internal production and obtains as much of its raw material requirements from local sources as it can. It has achieved very good market penetration and its Nescafé brand, including ready-to-serve coffee mixes, is widely available throughout China.

However, over the last five years there has also been an explosion in the number of new American-style coffee bars opening up in all the major cities. Starbucks alone has opened at least 30 new shops in Beijing and Shanghai since 1999 and other similar companies have also been expanding at the same rate. As a result coffee is acquiring a more modern image and is becoming a very popular beverage with the young.

Most of China's coffee imports originate from countries in the region. Viet Nam is the top supplier, accounting for around 40% of gross imports of green coffee, Indonesia is second and Colombia, which has also invested heavily in promoting its coffee in China, is third.

## Japan

*Population: 127 million.*

*2001 green bean imports were 6.36 million bags. Imports of roasted and soluble were 659,000 bags GBE; total imports were 7.02 million bags. Re-exports of processed coffee were 166,000 bags GBE.*

*Main suppliers: Brazil 26%, Colombia 17%, Indonesia 16%, Guatemala and Viet Nam each 7%, Ethiopia 6%.*

*Estimated shares: arabica 73%, robusta 26%, not specified 1%.*

*Consumption per head in 2001: 3.2 kg, up from 2.8 kg in 1995 and still growing.*

*Instant coffee covers 29% of the market, the balance being split between 40% roast coffee and 31% canned (ready-to-drink) as well as liquid coffee.*

*Leading roasters (all forms of coffee) are Nestlé, Ajinomoto General Foods (AGF), KEY, UCC and ART, with the instant market entirely dominated by Nestlé and AGF.*

Almost half of the consumption takes place out of home, a significantly higher portion than in other consuming countries.

Japanese demand has been growing at an average rate of close to 2% a year for the last decade. That is approximately double the pace of growth seen in the other major importing countries over the same period and has secured coffee's place as the number two beverage behind tea.

Japanese coffee consumers now drink on average 11.0 cups per week, up from 7.4 cups per week in 1980. Roast coffee is becoming more popular whereas instant coffee, which has been in serious decline for many years, appears to have bottomed out. Consumption of canned coffee fell back slightly in 2000 and 2001 but remains the most popular form of consumption among the young.

The instant coffee market is dominated by two processors, Nestlé and AGF, who between them account for approximately 99% of domestic production. Excluding the industrial market, Nescafé is the top brand, accounting for 72% of the branded instant coffee market. Ranked second are the brands Blendy and Maxim from AGF with 20%. About 11%–12% of the overall instant coffee market is for industrial use in such products as canned and liquid coffee.

| Table 11 | Japan: gross imports of all forms of coffee, 1995–2001 (in thousands of bags GBE) | | | | | | |
|---|---|---|---|---|---|---|---|
| **Type** | **1995** | **1996** | **1997** | **1998** | **1999** | **2000** | **2001** |
| **TOTAL** of which: | **5,537** | **6,026** | **5,977** | **6,055** | **6,576** | **6,935** | **7,022** |
| Green | 5,010 | 5,449 | 5,421 | 5,540 | 6,057 | 6,370 | 6,363 |
| Roasted | 42 | 66 | 35 | 31 | 37 | 55 | 72 |
| Soluble | 272 | 262 | 258 | 300 | 285 | 311 | 363 |
| Others | 213 | 249 | 263 | 184 | 197 | 199 | 224 |

*Source:* All Japan Coffee Association.

Imported soluble coffee of all forms accounts for around 8% of gross imports, with Brazil as the major supplier followed by Colombia, EU, Ecuador and Malaysia. A significant proportion of this is coffee extract with or without sugar.

| Table 12 | Japan: imports of soluble coffee and coffee extract, 1990–2001 (in thousands of bags GBE) | | | |
|---|---|---|---|---|
| | **Instant** | **Extract with sugar** | **Extract without sugar** | **TOTAL** |
| 1990 | 247 | 82 | 177 | 506 |
| 1995 | 272 | 48 | 165 | 485 |
| 2000 | 311 | 26 | 173 | 510 |
| 2001 | 348 | 26 | 181 | 555 |

*Source:* All Japan Coffee Association.

## Other regions and countries

### Brazil

Brazil (population 170 million), the world's largest coffee producer, is also the world's second-largest consumer, drinking an estimated 13.5 million bags of coffee in 2001. The structure of the internal industry is relatively diverse, characterized by a large number of small to medium-sized roasters, possibly as many as 1,400. Sara Lee / DE has become the major player in the market following a string of acquisitions since 1998 and now controls an estimated 22% of the market. Melitta from Germany and the Israeli group Strauss-Elite each have 4%–5%. Roast and ground coffee dominates the market and although the country is a large exporter of soluble coffee, instant coffee accounts for only approximately 5% of the overall domestic market in Brazil.

Domestic consumption in Brazil amounts to just under 4.0 kg per person; almost the same as the United States and only 11% lower than the average of all of the main importing countries. However this is lower than the consumption recorded in 1965: per head consumption fell to its lowest level in 1985 at 2.3 kg and stagnated around this level until steps were taken in 1989 to improve the quality of coffee available on the domestic market. In particular the industry introduced what became known as the Purity Seal (*Selo de Pureza*) which, together with an active marketing policy aimed at encouraging consumption by providing more information on the product, formed the basis of a successful push to increase consumption. This and the entry of the multinational roasters raised the quality of domestic coffee overall and as a result consumption has increased steadily.

A café culture is also beginning to emerge in the major cities, attracting the younger generation into coffee, but it is still very much in the early stages of development. Although the industry failed to achieve its aim of 15 million bags by the year 2000, there is every chance that it will achieve this ambitious target relatively soon.

| Table 13 | Brazil: domestic consumption of coffee, 1965–2001 | |
|---|---|---|
| **Year** | **Million bags** | **Kg per head** |
| 1965 | 8.1 | 4.72 |
| 1975 | 7.1 | 3.18 |
| 1985 | 6.4 | 2.27 |
| 1995 | 10.1 | 3.11 |
| 1996 | 11.0 | 3.34 |
| 1997 | 11.5 | 3.45 |
| 1998 | 12.1 | 3.63 |
| 1999 | 12.8 | 3.82 |
| 2000 | 13.0 | 3.86 |
| 2001 | 13.5 | 3.99 |

*Sources:* Brazilian Coffee Industry Association (ABIC) and ICO.

## Australia

*Population: 19 million.*

*Gross imports in 2000: 832,000 bags (GBE).*

*Consumption per head in 2000: 2.8 kg (est.), up from 2.3 kg in 1995.*

*Re-exports are around 27% of gross imports.*

*Robusta contributes 44% of gross imports; largest suppliers are Viet Nam 35% and Papua New Guinea 26%.*

*Almost 90% of consumption is as soluble coffee.*

*Nestlé is the largest roaster, covering around 60% of the market.*

Freeze-dried premium coffees account for about 25% of the soluble market and are growing; agglomerated instant coffees are around 45% and lower-priced spray-dried instant coffees now are at less than 25%.

## Other countries

Most other countries import only modest amounts of coffee. As a group they import about 9.3 million bags a year as shown in table 14.

| Table 14 | Other non-ICO member coffee imports, 1990 and 2000 (in millions of bags) | |
|---|---|---|
| | **1990** | **2000** |
| **Total** of which: | **5.3** | **9.3** |
| Algeria | 1.4 | 1.8 |
| Republic of Korea | 0.8 | 1.3 |
| Argentina | 0.6 | 0.6 |
| Morocco | 0.3 | 0.6 |
| Malaysia | 0.1 | 0.5 |
| Saudi Arabia | 0.4 | 0.4 |
| Israel | 0.3 | 0.4 |
| South Africa | 0.3 | 0.4 |
| Taiwan Province (China) | 0.1 | 0.4 |
| Lebanon | 0.2 | 0.3 |
| Syrian Arab Republic | 0.1 | 0.3 |
| New Zealand | 0.1 | 0.2 |
| Turkey | 0.1 | 0.2 |
| Egypt | 0.2 | 0.1 |
| Others | 0.3 | 1.8 |

*Source:* ICO.

### Algeria

*Population: 30 million.*

*2000 imports: 1,778,000 bags; virtually no re-exports.*

*Per head consumption in 2000: 3.3 kg (est.).*

*Main suppliers: Côte d'Ivoire, India, Viet Nam, Indonesia and Cameroon.*

### Republic of Korea

*Population: 47 million.*

*2000 imports: 1,316,000 bags; re-exports 71,000 bags.*

*Per head consumption in 2000: 1.6 kg (est.).*

*Main suppliers: Viet Nam, Indonesia, Honduras, Brazil, Colombia.*

## Factors influencing demand

Why people drink coffee and how much coffee they consume are topics that are more complex than might at first appear. As an example, figure 11 shows the response of United States consumers to movements in price from 1990 to 2000.

Studies have shown that different countries react in a different way and although it is clear that all consumers do react to large price movements, small variations in price from year to year do not have the same effect, which suggests that other factors are also important.

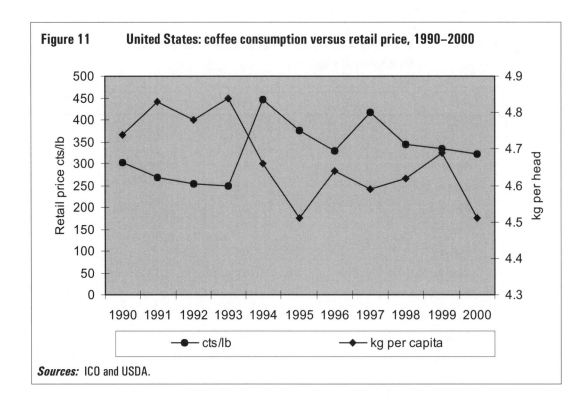

**Figure 11    United States: coffee consumption versus retail price, 1990–2000**

*Sources:* ICO and USDA.

## Income

Income is an important factor affecting the demand for coffee. In many ways this is not surprising especially as coffee is still perceived by many to be a luxury item, especially in low income countries. There is clear evidence that consumption is highly dependent not only on absolute income levels but also, and probably more importantly, on changes in real income levels.

In countries that have a history of drinking coffee, there seems to be a direct correlation between the level of income and the level of consumption. For example, the highest consumption per head is found in Scandinavia, the Netherlands and Austria, all countries which have a history of drinking coffee and which also enjoy a relatively high income per head. Clearly habit and tradition play a significant role in determining the overall level of consumption in a country, but it is noticeable that countries that also have a tradition of drinking coffee but have a much lower income per head, such as Spain, Portugal and Greece, have a considerably lower rate of consumption.

Given that coffee is still considered to be a luxury item in many consuming countries, it is not surprising that, as a general rule, changes in real incomes have a greater effect on consumption in low income countries than they do in high income countries. For example, Spain has witnessed a relatively fast rate of growth in the consumption of coffee per head over the past ten years and has also experienced a fairly impressive rate of growth in its overall level of real disposable income per head, whereas in many Scandinavian countries consumption has either remained static or fallen although real income levels have continued to rise.

## Lifestyle, diet and competition from other beverages

While price and incomes obviously part a major role in determining the demand for coffee, it is difficult to ignore the effect other factors, such as competition from alternative beverages, adverse publicity as a result of various health studies, advertising, or lifestyle, may have had on overall consumption. Coffee, apart from its traditionally recognized role as an everyday beverage that is frequently seen as a stimulant and an aid to alertness, is also seen as a social lubricant fulfilling a very necessary function enabling people to socialize. 'Let's have a coffee' is a phrase often used to cover a general request for an informal get-together regardless of whether coffee is to be drunk or not. It is interesting to note that coffee is more likely to be consumed at breakfast, lunch or dinner if these are taken as family meals rather than eaten alone. However as meals are becoming less formal and structured in many countries, more coffee is being consumed out of home, although the home remains the most popular place to consume coffee. The type of food consumers prefer may also have an effect on the amount of coffee they drink. Either through habit or taste, coffee seems to complement some foods more than others. This might explain why coffee is generally less popular in restaurants serving oriental foods than in those serving traditional Western European cuisine.

Competition from other beverages has also been an important factor affecting the demand for coffee. Over the last thirty years or so, soft drinks have become more popular, invariably at the expense of coffee, especially among young people. However, the situation is far from static and the new American-style coffee bars appear to be reversing this trend, although the situation varies from country to country. Consumption of soft drinks in the United States has shown rapid growth since the mid 1960s: the percentage of the population drinking soft drinks grew from 47% in 1975 to 58% in 2001. It does appear to have reached a plateau, as very little growth has been achieved over the last four years, and may even be showing evidence of decline. In Germany, on the other hand, coffee remains the most popular beverage and although the consumption of herbal teas, fruit juices and mineral water is rising, it does not appear to be doing so at the expense of coffee. In Japan coffee is gaining ground at the expense of other beverages, but more slowly than in the early 1980s.

Price may be a major factor in the change to alternative beverages, but health worries and advertising also provide strong motives to switch to other beverages. Over the years a number of studies have suggested that coffee – in fact invariably caffeine, but the stigma attaches to coffee rather than to all beverages containing caffeine – is linked in some way to some cancers (although a report from the International Agency for Research on Cancer[7] stated that no causal effect could be identified between coffee consumption and cancer), to fibrocystic breast disease and to an increase in the risk of suffering from a heart attack and other related conditions.

There can be little doubt that the publicity given to the findings of these studies has contributed significantly to the decline in the consumption of coffee in some developed markets. A number of the cola drinks currently on the market contain high levels of caffeine (but not as high as most coffees), and more and more studies have found that coffee may have some beneficial health effects, (such as helping to relieve stress and inhibiting the viruses that cause cold sores, measles and polio), is beneficial in preventing some types of cancer and may delay the onset of Parkinson's disease. But this positive information does not gain wide publicity and does not yet appear to counteract the effects of the adverse publicity. The ICO is however highlighting some of these benefits of coffee through its Positive Communication on Coffee Programme.

Fruit juices, on the other hand, are perceived to be healthy beverages and with the trend towards greater health consciousness it is not surprising that consumption of fruit juices has shown rapid growth. In addition, soft drinks, especially cola drinks, receive considerably more advertising than coffee.

### Tariffs and taxes

It has long been recognized that tariffs and taxes influence coffee consumption. The coffee community considers tariffs and taxes to be part of a broader group of legal, political and administrative barriers to coffee consumption (as mentioned for example in Article 33 of the 2001 International Coffee Agreement).

---

7    *IARC Monograph*, Volume 51, 1991.

Significant progress in reducing tariffs and taxes on coffee imports into consuming countries has been made both through the various rounds of the General Agreement on Tariffs and Trade (GATT) and more recently through negotiations under the auspices of the World Trade Organization (WTO). However, while most tariff barriers have been removed for green coffee, there remain a number of tariffs imposed on processed coffee that continue to act as an effective barrier to importation into consuming countries. In addition there are also a number of non-tariff barriers still in place, such as quantitative restrictions and internal taxes, that continue to inhibit consumption.

# Value added

## Overview

Downstream processing is often seen as a way of adding value to a raw product at origin. Unfortunately this is not as straightforward as it at first appears: if it were, there would be a far greater trade in processed coffee products from origin than there is today. In 2000/01 just 5.4% of all coffee exports from producing countries were processed coffee. This is slightly higher than 10 years ago, but virtually identical to the proportion achieved 20 years ago. Producer exports of processed coffee have not exceeded 6.5% of world exports in any year since 1980, and the bulk of this is instant coffee. Roasted coffee exports have never exceeded 0.2% of total coffee exports from producing countries.

The consuming market for coffee is dominated by a few very large companies, mainly multinationals, which sell their product by promoting their brand name and image through large-scale advertising. Normally advertising expenditure is equivalent to between 3% and 6% of sales revenue. Most coffee is sold through supermarket chains, which, in general, stock a relatively limited range of brands that meet their criteria for sales per unit of shelf space. In that environment it is difficult and costly for new brands and new suppliers to penetrate the market, but it is not impossible as there are always some openings for new suppliers.

Smaller packers and roasters however have managed to secure a place in practically every consuming country to a greater or lesser degree, often either selling coffee under their own brand names or providing supermarket chains with own label (also known as private label) coffee to be sold under the brand name of the supermarket. Own label or secondary brands generally sell at a substantial discount and are not usually advertised in the press or television. Instead they are promoted in store.

In the past such brands were usually considered to be inferior in quality, but that is not the case any more and as a result own label coffees have been able to capture a significant share of the market. The own label area offers the best opportunity for coffees processed at origin because such coffees cannot afford large advertising expenditure. But with increasing concentration at the retail level the scope for new entrants is becoming more limited, and furthermore the own label market is fiercely price competitive. Soluble coffee packed for supermarkets retails at a discount of 10%–30% (in some cases even more) on the price of the leading comparable brands. For spray-dried soluble coffee the retail market is not only oversupplied but is also shrinking as consumers switch to better quality freeze-dried and agglomerated soluble coffees.

### Soluble coffee

The soluble coffee market is dominated by two multinational firms: Nestlé and Kraft Foods. One or the other or both have a presence in every main consumer market and indeed probably in many producing country markets as well. In addition there is often a third large supplier in each main market. For example, in the United States Procter & Gamble enjoys a reasonably large share of the market while the Ueshima Coffee Company (UCC) is of some significance in Japan. The larger companies manufacture soluble coffee in their own plants and rarely obtain soluble coffee from outside suppliers.

Nestlé also operates a small number of soluble processing plants in producing countries, primarily aimed at supplying the domestic market there, but also nearby regional markets.

The scope for outside manufacturers lies in supplying product for:

- Secondary (own label) brands that have no manufacturing facilities (although this market tends to be rather sluggish); and

- Specialist packers of own label coffee in consuming countries.

Most supermarket chains prefer to buy from a specialist packer rather than direct from origin, and usually insist that bulk supplies are repacked in retail jars. For all practical purposes, an origin supplier seeking to enter the own label market would be best advised to trade through a specialist packer in a consuming country, especially as in most cases the finished retail product is a blend of coffee from several sources.

There are several specialist packers of soluble coffee for own label product in consuming countries. Some operate their own processing plants, but also often purchase soluble coffee for blending from other sources to fulfil contracts that are beyond their capacity, or when imported soluble is cheaper than their own product. Other specialist packers have no processing capacity of their own and merely blend and repack product from other sources.

The retail market for soluble coffee has three general segments:

- **Premium brands of freeze-dried soluble.** Nestlé and Kraft Foods dominate in this segment, but there is some significant participation by other brands, particularly supermarkets' own labels. Both Brazil and Colombia supply freeze-dried soluble coffee to this market, which is still growing. Although not the most popular form of soluble coffee, in general freeze-dried coffee is gaining market share in every consuming country at the expense of other types of soluble coffee. It has obtained just under 40% of the soluble coffee market in Japan and the United States, a little over 30% in Spain and the United Kingdom and around 20% in Australia. Extra premium blends of freeze-dried coffee composed solely or mainly of arabica and sometimes from a single origin are also marketed in this sector.

- **Standard brands of spray-dried soluble.** These generally consist of coffee that has been agglomerated. Agglomeration is a process that not only improves solubility but also transforms the coffee powder into more attractive granules. Agglomerated coffee is the most popular form of soluble coffee. It accounts for more than half the sales in the majority of consuming markets, although it is losing market share to freeze-dried.

- **Cheap blends of spray-dried powder.** This is often soluble coffee that has been imported from origin and repacked. Considerable excess manufacturing capacity has resulted in extreme price competition and although this is by far the cheapest type of soluble coffee available in many markets, it is losing market share to all other types of instant coffee. It does, however, constitute the larger share of the market in the Russian Federation and many other Eastern European and Asian markets as well as in producing country markets.

The total market for soluble coffee has been relatively flat over the past decade. Estimated consumption in countries that do not produce coffee was just over 20 million bags GBE, of which 17% was manufactured in producing countries.

The bulk of the soluble coffee exported from producing countries is spray-dried powder. Brazil accounts for just under half of all soluble coffee exports. Intense price competition coupled with diminishing demand has led to a marked reduction in the spray-dried powder manufacturing capacity in many consuming countries, although a significant proportion of that reduced capacity has been transferred to other, usually emerging, markets. It does not appear, therefore, that there is a very secure future for new entrants planning to supply spray-dried powder.

Freeze-dried soluble continues to make significant progress, although processing is comparatively expensive and the product quality demands a high proportion of the more expensive arabica. The process is therefore unsuitable for countries that produce only robusta. The market has primarily been developed by Nestlé and Kraft Foods, although a number of other companies are actively involved in the sector, particularly those producing own labels. Brazil and Colombia are important suppliers and while the market for freeze-dried coffees is growing there are concerns that there is already quite some manufacturing overcapacity in both Brazil and a number of consuming countries such as Germany. Freeze-dried coffee accounts for around 30% of all sales of soluble coffee. Trade opinion suggests that the market for soluble coffee as a whole is likely to grow only slowly over the next ten years; by contrast the market for freeze-dried coffee is expected to continue growing at a much faster rate.

The opportunity for new suppliers must be weighed against current excess manufacturing capacity, which is probably sufficient to cover most, if not all, the anticipated increase in demand for a number of years. Although most exports of soluble coffee are as finished product (in primary, not retail, packaging), some sales are made as frozen concentrate for finishing in the country of destination. Exports of soluble coffee by coffee producing countries for the period 1995–2000 are shown in table 15. Most of the coffee exported was produced in the country of shipment. Soluble coffee is also produced in Malaysia for use in regional markets and in the Philippines, where it is used for domestic consumption.

**Table 15        ICO exporting member countries: exports of soluble coffee, 1995–2000 (in bags GBE)**

|  | 1995 | 1996 | 1997 | 1998 | 1999 | 2000 |
|---|---|---|---|---|---|---|
| **TOTAL** | **4,505,898** | **4,506,824** | **4,510,533** | **3,928,301** | **3,892,763** | **4,339,055** |
| **Colombian milds** | **492,056** | **591,438** | **635,620** | **649,812** | **527,228** | **607,794** |
| Colombia | 485,528 | 584,610 | 625,513 | 641,608 | 520,707 | 599,374 |
| Tanzania, United Rep. of | 6,528 | 6,828 | 9,107 | 8,204 | 6,521 | 8,420 |
| **Other milds** | **1,163,398** | **954,807** | **1,137,278** | **1,248,810** | **1,060,235** | **1,300,481** |
| Ecuador | 457,582 | 328,072 | 330,074 | 406,158 | 308,233 | 342,103 |
| El Salvador | 7,278 | 4,471 | 4,322 | 7,796 | 6,139 | 7,092 |
| Guatemala | 317 | 117 | 0 | 0 | 0 | 0 |
| India | 424,753 | 396,120 | 561,343 | 595,695 | 485,634 | 699,644 |
| Jamaica | 453 | 529 | 357 | 365 | 401 | 319 |
| Mexico | 264,929 | 203,251 | 220,843 | 205,615 | 213,369 | 292,834 |
| Nicaragua | 8,086 | 22,247 | 20,271 | 23,968 | 31,408 | 37,352 |
| Venezuela | 0 | 0 | 68 | 9,213 | 15,051 | 11,137 |
| **Brazilian naturals** | **2,566,967** | **2,578,188** | **2,376,833** | **1,676,690** | **1,962,413** | **2,066,047** |
| Brazil | 2,557,665 | 2,568,719 | 2,374,150 | 1,678,034 | 1,962,413 | 2,066,047 |
| Paraguay | 9,302 | 9,469 | 2,683 | 1,656 | 0 | 0 |

**Table 15** (cont'd)

| | 1995 | 1996 | 1997 | 1998 | 1999 | 2000 |
|---|---|---|---|---|---|---|
| **Robustas** | **283,477** | **382,391** | **360,802** | **349,989** | **342,887** | **274,733** |
| Côte d'Ivoire | 217,065 | 299,575 | 165,039 | 164,695 | 142,066 | 173,414 |
| Guinea | 1 | 0 | 0 | 0 | 0 | 0 |
| Indonesia | 42,392 | 55,316 | 158,829 | 163,380 | 181,205 | 86,829 |
| Nigeria | 1,006 | 0 | 0 | 0 | 0 | 0 |
| Philippines | 15,213 | 18,270 | 22,470 | 8,266 | 5,488 | 267 |
| Sierra Leone | 0 | 0 | 4 | 0 | 0 | 0 |
| Thailand | 4,519 | 5,556 | 10,954 | 7,267 | 4,223 | 3,129 |
| Trinidad and Tobago | 3,281 | 2,850 | 3,025 | 4,345 | 2,314 | 1,278 |
| Viet Nam | 0 | 824 | 481 | 2,036 | 7,160 | 9,178 |

*Source:* ICO.

## Soluble coffee

**Extraction.** Optimum extraction of soluble coffee solids depends on the temperature of the extraction water and its rate of flow through roasted, ground coffee. In practice incoming water can be approaching 200°C under high pressure. Extraction requires a row of interconnecting percolators or cells, using a continuous reverse flow principle. Each cell is filled in turn with fresh coffee. Incoming hot water is introduced into the cell containing the least fresh, most extracted coffee, where it collects those soluble solids that are vulnerable to the high temperature and carries these to the next cell in the cycle, and so on. In each cell the coffee liquor collects more soluble solids. By the time the sixth cell in a cycle has been reached the liquor's temperature has been reduced and so inflicts minimum damage on the delicate flavour constituents of the freshest roast coffee that are essential to the final quality. The liquor is then drawn off and cooled. It now consists of approximately 85% water and 15% soluble coffee. Meanwhile the first cell in the cycle (which underwent extraction with the hottest water), is emptied of the spent grounds and is recharged with fresh coffee to start the cycle again. Thus there is always one cell outside the process, which requires seven cells altogether.

**Evaporation** is necessary to reduce the liquor's water content to 50%. But first the liquor is centrifuged to remove non-soluble particles. To evaporate liquor at normal pressure would require very high temperatures that would cause the liquor to acquire off flavours and lose valuable coffee aromas as well. Consequently evaporation takes place under low vacuum and low temperature conditions.

**Spray drying** requires a large cylindrical tower with a conical base. The concentrated liquor is introduced into the top under pressure, with a jet of hot air. The falling droplets dry into a fine powder that cools as it descends. These particles may then be agglomerated into granules by wetting them in low-pressure steam, allowing them to stick together. The wet granules are then dried as they descend through a second tower and are sifted to provide a uniform final granule size.

**Freeze drying** consists of freezing the coffee liquor into a ¼ inch (about 6 mm) thick cake on a moving conveyor at a temperature of −45°C. The frozen cake is then broken into small particles and the ice crystals are removed under very high vacuums, being converted directly to water vapour by a process known as sublimation. Freeze drying is more energy expensive but is gentler on the product as less heat is applied to evaporate the water content. Consequently, freeze drying is used for the finer tasting and more expensive blends of instant coffee.

Trade sources suggest that the cost of manufacturing plants for soluble coffee is considerable, ranging from around US$ 10 million for an annual capacity of around 1,800 tons of spray-dried or 600 tons of freeze-dried coffee, to around US$ 20 million for an annual capacity of 8,500 tons of spray-dried or 1,500 tons of freeze-dried coffee. By far the greatest proportion in the investment would be taken in foreign exchange. Without an assured year-round production programme, operating costs would be excessive.

## Decaffeinated coffee

The decaffeination process is applicable to both soluble coffee (spray-dried and freeze-dried) and roasted coffee. Decaffeinated coffee enjoyed a considerable rise in popularity during the 1980s, especially in the United States, but its performance in the market during the 1990s has not been very strong. Decaffeinated coffee is seen as having to compete with other specialty coffees and although consumers of decaffeinated coffee tend to be very loyal to the product, caffeine no longer appears to be an issue that most consumers are particularly concerned about. Despite technological improvements in the decaffeination process over the last fifteen years, and in particular the development of what many see as better processes which use water and carbon dioxide rather than methyl chloride, the product is losing market share. It is estimated that decaffeinated coffee currently accounts for around 10% of all coffee sales. Usually, it commands only a small premium over non-decaffeinated coffee and frequently is sold for the same price: consequently the economics of the decaffeination are tight. In early 2002, trade sources estimated that the cost of the process ranged from US$ 0.50–0.60 per kg of green bean, for the cheapest process using methylene chloride, to about double that for the more expensive methods. Incidentally, there is a substantial market for extracted crude caffeine in industries such as pharmaceuticals and soft drinks.

### Decaffeination

*Arabica coffee beans contain 1%–1.5% caffeine, whereas robusta contains more than 2%. Caffeine is an alkaloid with stimulant properties that are pleasing to the majority of coffee drinkers, but not to all. Decaffeination caters for those who for whatever reason do not want the stimulant effect of caffeine.*

*The caffeine in the green coffee beans has to be extracted. Different processes are used. The solvents are water, organic extraction agents or carbonic acid. The processing steps are vaporization, decaffeination and drying. All these steps are carried out using the green coffee bean.*

*First the green coffee is treated with vapour and water to open up the bean surface and the cell structure to access the crystalline caffeine taken up on the cell walls. The second step is the extraction of the caffeine by an extraction agent which has to possess the ability to extract only the caffeine. The caffeine extraction is not a chemical process but a physical one. No chemical changes take place. Instead differences in the characteristics of the extraction agent, which has to absorb the caffeine, and the beans containing the caffeine, are used. The extraction agent absorbs the caffeine selectively. Once the extraction agent is saturated with caffeine the next processing step removes the caffeine and the extraction agent can be used again. This cycle is repeated until practically all the caffeine is removed from the coffee bean. Then the wet coffee, from which the caffeine has been removed, is dried until once again it reaches its normal moisture content. It can then be roasted as usual.*

*The following decaffeination agents are allowed in the European Union: methylene chloride, ethyl acetate, carbon dioxide, and watery coffee extract from which the caffeine is removed by active carbon. All conventional decaffeination methods have undergone intensive scientific examination and are considered safe. In the European Union the absolute caffeine content in roasted, decaffeinated coffee may not exceed 0.1%, or 0.3% in soluble coffee. In the United States, the caffeine is to be reduced to less than 3% of the coffee's original content.*

## Roasted coffee

The market for roasted coffee is somewhat less concentrated than that for soluble coffee. Although market concentration in the roast and ground sector increased significantly, particularly during the 1980s and in the late 1990s, the development of the specialty sector has slowed the trend and the number of small roasters operating worldwide did increase significantly for a while. Small roasters rarely buy direct from origin, but make their purchases through importers who are able to offer some security of supply and cost savings for small lots. In many cases importing direct from origin involves buying a full container load of around 300 bags (18 tons), which is simply too large an order for most small roasters.

As a result of the development of the specialty and gourmet sectors in many countries single origin roasted coffees are now widely available. However, blends of roasted coffee from different origins remain the most predominant roasted coffee product in the overall market today and this makes it difficult for producers to enter the retail market on their own. The trade in roasted coffee from origin is limited: in 2000 only 118,000 bags were exported from origin in roasted form compared to 4.3 million bags GBE of soluble and 84.4 million bags of green coffee. In total, roasted coffee accounted for just 0.13% of all coffee exports. Somewhat surprisingly, perhaps, the Dominican Republic was the largest exporter of roasted coffee, accounting for more than 44% of all exports of roasted coffee from producing countries. Over 93% of its roasted coffee exports go to Puerto Rico, however. Mexico held second position, supplying the neighbouring United States, while Costa Rica and Brazil were joint third.

There are several obstacles to exporting roasted coffee from origin. None of them are insurmountable but together they form a significant barrier to this trade. Roasted coffee rapidly loses its flavour unless it is vacuum packed or gas flushed. A supplier wishing to export must therefore install an appropriate packing facility.

Furthermore, consumers are becoming increasingly sophisticated and demand high quality packaging that requires a significant level of investment. Additionally, legislation in importing countries frequently insists that packs are marked with a 'sell by' or 'use by' date. Transporting the product to market from origin can take a considerable amount of time and this puts the exporter at a disadvantage compared to a more local roaster who is able to offer the retailer a product with a longer shelf life. Exporters of roasted coffee therefore need to develop speedy distribution systems in order to minimize this disadvantage. This usually requires the active collaboration of agents or specialized importers or roasters in the target market(s).

## Ready-to-drink and extracts or concentrates

Canned, ready-to-drink (RTD) coffee was originally developed by the Ueshima Coffee Company. By 2001 it accounted for 17% of total consumption in Japan, where it is sold mainly through vending machines, and accounts for more than a third of all soft drink sales. RTD coffee in plastic bottles, cartons and other packs is becoming increasingly popular and is generally sold in supermarkets. Canned coffee products are also finding a good market in many emerging markets in Asia, particularly in China, although the success of the product depends very much on its availability in vending machines. RTD coffee products are particularly suitable for iced coffee drinks, and as such are beginning to make inroads in the North American and Western European markets. Originally the obvious requirement for success was access to vending machines and vending sites and as a result soft drink manufacturers currently dominate this sector of the market. But the major roasters are now pushing hard as well, not least because market sources consider the prospects for RTD coffee excellent because of its convenience. Sales of shelf-stable (i.e. not refrigerated or frozen) iced coffee products are the most likely area of growth because such products can be sold off supermarket shelves like any other dry goods. Another potential winner could be concentrated liquid coffee. The frozen concentrate is designed for commercial and out-of-home consumers such as hotels, restaurants and offices for whom, it is reported, it will produce a 'fresh' cup of coffee in a few seconds.

How much these developments do for coffee consumption or indeed coffee quality is debatable – the coffee content is usually not very high and the coffee taste is often masked by flavouring. Nevertheless, it is a new and growing niche market. Brazil and Colombia are the main manufacturers of concentrate at origin. Unfortunately, it is difficult to see how smaller producers without a substantial home market to support a manufacturing capability can participate.

## Trade prices and tariffs

### *Imports and prices*

Average imports of roasted and soluble coffee of the seven leading importers and the origin of those imports are shown in figures 12 and 13.

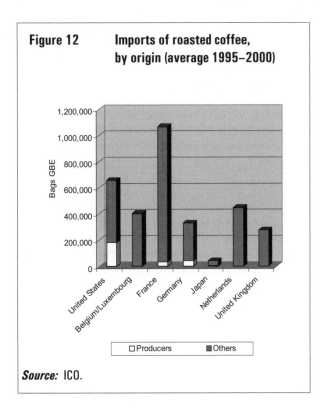

**Figure 12  Imports of roasted coffee, by origin (average 1995–2000)**

*Source:* ICO.

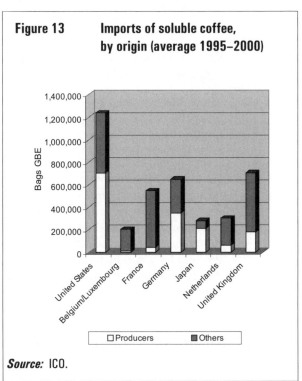

**Figure 13  Imports of soluble coffee, by origin (average 1995–2000)**

*Source:* ICO.

These seven countries account for the bulk of the imports of both roasted and soluble coffee. And as can be seen, with the exception of the United States, imports of roasted coffee from ICO producing country members barely register on the chart. Imports of roasted coffee into the United States have been increasing significantly over the last five years, with a noticeable increase in imports of roasted coffee from Costa Rica and the Dominican Republic. Imports of roasted coffee from Colombia appear to be in decline although traditionally the total does vary significantly from year to year. Imports of soluble coffee from ICO producing country members are clearly more significant and form a larger share of the trade in the United States, Germany, Japan and the United Kingdom.

The average price paid for soluble coffee by the seven countries is compared with the ICO composite indicator in figure 14. The import price is expressed as the price of the green bean equivalent to facilitate comparison. Generally the import price tracks the indicator, sometimes at a lower level and at other times at a premium. However, because of intense competition the value added, on an FOB basis, is less than popularly supposed.

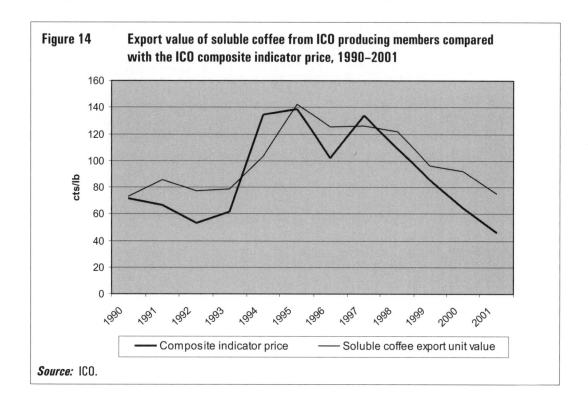

**Figure 14    Export value of soluble coffee from ICO producing members compared with the ICO composite indicator price, 1990–2001**

*Source:* ICO.

In the calculation, the volume of soluble coffee has been transformed into the green bean equivalent by applying the ratio of 1:2.6 (soluble coffee: GBE).

Export unit value statistics show that the prices of Brazilian soluble are lower than both the New York market prices for Brazilian green coffee and, at times, the London market prices for robustas. Colombian prices correspond more closely with New York prices, although the unit value of exports of Colombian soluble (an aggregate of spray-dried and freeze-dried) remains for the most part just slightly above the quoted green coffee price. One of the reasons for producing countries to continue with this is that coffee which is transformed in the country of origin does not have to possess all quality characteristics of coffee which can be exported in green form. The transformation into soluble may therefore allow the use of lower grades. Nevertheless the value added by the manufacture of soluble at origin is likely to be, at best, marginal and a run of low prices may not allow the speedy recovery of costs of new installations.

Roasted coffee (figure 15) sells at a premium over both the ICO composite indicator and the New York market for other milds, but this trade is more specialized and export prices may include the provision of retail packs. Nevertheless, the trade remains negligible.

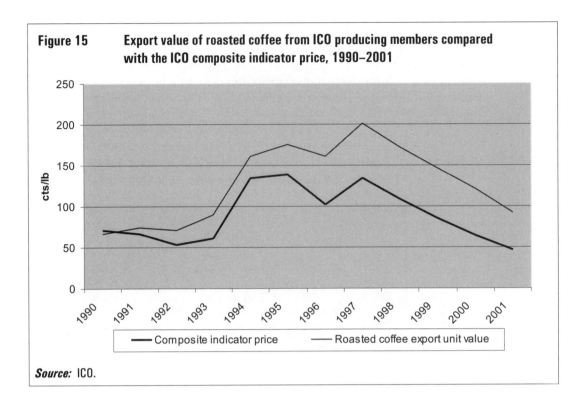

**Figure 15    Export value of roasted coffee from ICO producing members compared with the ICO composite indicator price, 1990–2001**

*Source:* ICO.

## Tariff barriers

Import tariffs on green coffee are becoming lower and rarer. However, as a rule, progressive tariffs are levied on coffee that has been processed. The information in table 16 summarizes the available information but the compilation is not exhaustive and readers are advised to check for any changes in the rates that are levied.

**Table 16    World tariffs on processed coffee**

| Country/area | Roasted | Decaffeinated, roasted | Soluble |
|---|---|---|---|
| United States | 0 | 0 | 0 |
| European Union | 7.5% MFN | 9.0% MFN | 9.0% MFN |
| | 2.6% GSP | 3.1% GSP | 3.1% GSP |
| Canada | 4.15 cts/kg MFN | 4.15 cts/kg MFN | 14.32 cts/kg MFN |
| | 0 GSP | 0 GSP | 0 GSP |
| Japan | 20% general | 20% general | 12.3% general |
| | 16% WTO | 16% WTO | 13.2% WTO |
| | 10% GSP | 10% GSP | 9.0% GSP |
| Switzerland | 0.69 CHF/kg MFN | 0.69 CHF/kg MFN | 2.13 CHF/kg MFN |
| | 0.69 CHF/kg GSP | 0.69 CHF/kg GSP | 2.13 CHF/kg GSP |

*Sources:* Various publications and national authorities.

The difference between the normal tariff rates (MFN rates – most favoured nation) and the preferential tariff rates (GSP rates – generalized system of preferences) is often sufficient to provide some benefit. In addition, African, Caribbean and Pacific Group of States (ACP) countries which have acceded to the Cotonou Agreement (replacing the Lomé Convention) with the European Union are exempt from EU import tariffs. This exemption is also granted to some developing countries outside the ACP group. Of interest to coffee are Bolivia, Colombia, Costa Rica, Dominican Republic, Ecuador, El Salvador, Guatemala, Haiti, Honduras, the Lao People's Democratic Republic, Nicaragua, Panama, Peru, Venezuela and Yemen.

---

### Classification of coffee products traded internationally

*Among the trade-related product nomenclatures, the following three are of particular interest to coffee:*

**HS – Harmonized System.** *The Harmonized Commodity Description and Coding System (Harmonized System) is the system for classification of goods in international trade and for customs tariffs. It has been developed under the auspices of the World Customs Organization. HS assigns a six-digit code to general categories. In most countries, these codes are broken down to a more detailed level referred to as the tariff line. Details at www.wcoomd.org.*

**CN – Combined Nomenclature** *– is the European Union's eight-digit coding system. It is based on the HS. Details at www.europa.eu.int.*

**SITC – Standard Industrial Trade Classification** *– was developed by the United Nations. It is commonly used for trade statistics and by trade analysts. The current version is Revision 3.*

|  | *HS code* | *CN code* | *SITC Rev.3* |
|---|---|---|---|
| *Coffee in green form (not roasted)* | *0901.10* | *0901 10 00* | *07110* |
| *Not decaffeinated* | *0901.11* | *0901 11 00* | *07111* |
| *Not decaffeinated, arabica* | | *0901 11 10* | |
| *Not decaffeinated, robusta* | | *0901 11 20* | |
| *Not decaffeinated, other* | | *0901 11 90* | |
| *Decaffeinated* | *0901.12* | *0901 12 00* | *07112* |
| *Decaffeinated, arabica* | | *0901 12 10* | |
| *Decaffeinated, robusta* | | *0901 12 20* | |
| *Decaffeinated, other* | | *0901 12 90* | |
| *Roasted coffee* | *0901.20* | *0901 20 00* | *07120* |
| *Not decaffeinated* | *0901.21* | *0901 21 00* | |
| *Decaffeinated* | *0901.22* | *0901 22 00* | |
| *Coffee husks and skins* | *0901.90* | *0901 90 00* | *07113* |
| *Coffee substitutes containing coffee* | *0901.90* | *0901 90 00* | *07132* |
| *Extracts, essences and concentrates of coffee* (Various CN codes for a range of sub-products) | *2101.11* | *2101 11 xx* | *07131* |
| *Preparations with a basis of these extracts, essences or concentrates or with a basis of coffee* (Various CN codes for a range of sub-products) | *2101.12* | *2101 12 xx* | *07131* |

## Coffee promotion

The promotion of coffee consumption world wide is vital. Competition from other beverages is intense and the total amount of money spent on advertising soft drinks, for example, far exceeds the amount spent on coffee. Well coordinated national and international generic (general) campaigns are necessary not only to encourage people, particularly in emerging markets, to take up coffee drinking, but also to retain the loyalty of existing consumers. This is not to ignore the fact that roasters worldwide invest tens of millions of dollars in brand promotion, the costs of which are estimated to be between 3% and 6% of total sales. Although such promotion is not generic, it does encourage consumption of coffee in general. Nevertheless there is a distinct need for the entire industry to engage in generic promotion of the type as undertaken by the ICO, most recently in the Russian Federation and China.

### *Generic versus brand (or type) promotion*

There are several methods of categorizing promotional activities depending upon the ultimate objective. Promotion conducted with respect to a basic product such as coffee for the purpose of enlarging the total market for the product is termed *generic promotion*. For example the ICO campaigns in China and the Russian Federation did not focus on any one brand or indeed type of coffee but promoted all types and brands of coffee simultaneously. This helps the entire industry rather than just one segment or company.

*Brand promotion* on the other hand is conducted with the objective of gaining a larger market share for a particular brand of coffee, rather than enlarging the market for every brand. Even if the promotion results in an overall increase in the market as a whole it still represents brand rather than generic promotion, as this was not the original intention. When individual producing countries use promotion to encourage demand for their own coffee, this cannot be considered generic either as it is merely attempting to influence decisions within the existing market about the composition of supply rather than attempting to enlarge the market for all producers.

### *Necessity for generic promotion*

At first glance, it may seem that generic promotion of coffee is unnecessary. The widespread consumption of coffee suggests that demand for the product is practically guaranteed. But there is a real need to educate potential consumers in emerging markets. Demand for coffee can decline as has been witnessed in the United States and in some parts of Europe.

Sporadic fragmented attempts at generic coffee promotion in the United States, for example, were unable to prevent the decline in daily consumption per head. It was only once the spotlight was turned back on coffee, thanks primarily to the specialty movement, that there was any real improvement in the situation. Although not entirely generic, a significant proportion of the advertising content promoting specialty coffee to date has been informative, educational and outwardly unbiased towards brands, so much so that it has been essentially generic. However there is now a very real danger that as the initial enthusiasm for specialty wears off, and with the growing corporatization of the specialty sector, the generic content of any promotion will diminish quite rapidly. There is therefore a need to replace this with an ongoing generic campaign in order to ensure that any gains are not only held on to but are also built upon.

In most countries coffee faces immense competitive pressures from the strong and ingenious generic promotional efforts of such beverages as tea and milk as well as from the many well-financed campaigns promoting various brands of soft drink and juice. These industries would like to convince coffee drinkers to switch to their products. Coffee drinkers need reassurance that coffee is the right drink for them. In addition new potential consumers need very basic information about coffee to allay any fears they might have about coffee and to learn the best ways of preparing the beverage. This is best achieved through generic promotion.

### *The role of market research in promotion*

Promotion campaigns cannot be successful without market research. Such research usually has four broad aims:

- To determine demographic and psychological characteristics of current consumers and non-consumers of coffee, together with insights into why they consume coffee or why they do not.

- To estimate the size of both the total market for coffee and its individual components, and to set objectives for the overall campaign.

- To test the proposed promotional message or messages to ensure effectiveness before conducting the full campaign.

- To monitor the results of the campaign after it is under way and also to assess its impact after the campaign has finished.

**Who are the customers**  It is helpful in developing a generic promotion campaign to understand the primary characteristics of the people who drink coffee as well as to discover what benefits they derive from coffee consumption. With this information, promotional messages are more likely to be relevant and believable.

One purpose of generic promotion is to keep existing customers satisfied and perhaps to encourage them to consume more coffee. The other purpose of generic promotion is to encourage people who do not drink coffee to try the product and also to create a positive attitude towards coffee in order to improve the chances of their liking their first tastes of the beverage. To that end, promoters should know why non-drinkers do not drink coffee. This was very important in the campaigns run by the ICO in China. Market research had determined that many potential Chinese consumers saw coffee as bad for the stomach and something more akin to a medicine. This enabled the organizers of the campaign to tailor the message so that it directly tackled these issues.

People have different reasons for choosing to drink or not to drink coffee. It may therefore be necessary to divide the total potential market into broad segments, called target markets, each requiring a different promotional message or even a differentiated product or distribution channel.

**How large is the potential market**  With a reasonably accurate idea of how many people drink coffee and how much they currently consume, it can be estimated how much more (if any) they can be induced to consume. Before investing in a full-blown campaign it is essential to test the promotional message to make certain that it will convince the consumers to take some type of action or to change their attitude in line with the message's objectives. The promotion is therefore tested on a sample number of people and if a sufficient proportion is favourably influenced, a full campaign is initiated.

**What is progress like**  If the campaign is continued, results must be monitored. Techniques exist to determine whether adequate progress is being made. Note that if no clearly defined goals are set, it will be difficult to assess whether progress warrants continuation. The annual *United States Winter Coffee Drinking Study* is a good example of a survey on coffee consumption – go to *www.ncausa.org* for details.

# CHAPTER 3

# Niche markets, environment and social aspects

## The specialty market

It is often neither viable nor possible to add value to green coffee by processing at origin. Many coffees are suitable only for blending or processing into neutral or anonymous end products. For such coffees it is not possible to add monetary value as prices are determined solely by market conditions. However, reliable and consistent grading procedures, strict compliance with contractual obligations, and regular delivery will add value in the sense that the product will be preferred by primary buyers over those from less consistent origins. Certain growths of coffee may be highly prized for their flavour characteristics and attract a suitable premium. Examples include Jamaican Blue Mountain, Hawaii Kona, Top Kenya AA and Guatemalan Antiguas.

Some of these growths attract extremely high premiums. Jamaican Blue Mountain attracts such a large premium that the unit value of coffee exported from Jamaica in 2001 was over 13 times higher than the average of all 'other milds' producers and more than 16 times higher than the average achieved by all origins. The top Kenyan grades regularly achieve prices more than double that achieved by other growths. Colombia has adopted an active marketing and publicity policy which has resulted in many brands throughout the world being labelled as 100% Colombian. Besides the promotional effort, the availability, reliable quality, regular delivery of Colombian green coffee, and on occasion price guarantees have assisted sales, as has consumer acceptance of its taste characteristics. Other potential suppliers could adopt strategies such as those below.

- If the coffee is of outstanding flavour or quality, sales should be directed to roasters who buy direct from origin (or through a suitable agent) and who retail single origin coffee either in their shops or through other retail outlets. It should be noted that sales of roasted coffee by producing countries direct to foreign retail outlets are generally expensive and difficult.

- If the coffee is of satisfactory quality, but unsuitable either for drinking unblended or for marketing in the premium or gourmet market, sales should be directed to roasters who buy direct from origin or agents. Producers should try to ensure that the label of the blend containing their coffee carries a reference to the composition of the blend. Unfortunately, very few roasters are actually willing to do this. In any case, a roaster who markets such a blend will need to be assured of consistent quality and regular delivery.

Consumer awareness of the origins they drink does lead to product loyalty and the development of a brand image. This results in some (albeit limited) protection from the vagaries of the market. If roasters are unable to obtain regular supplies from one exporter, they will of course be encouraged to seek alternative sources.

## The meaning of specialty

The term 'specialty coffee' originated in the United States. It was initially used to describe the range of coffee products sold in dedicated coffee shops, in order to differentiate these coffees from coffee generally available through supermarkets and other retail outlets. The term 'gourmet' is also used but is now applied to so many products that it has lost all relevance.

Specialty today refers both to whole bean sales and to coffee beverages sold in coffee bars and cafés (as opposed to restaurants and other catering establishments). The range includes higher quality coffees, both single origin and blends, unconventional coffees such as flavoured coffees and coffees with an unusual background or story behind them. However, with the rapid growth in the number of specialty coffee retail outlets and more particularly the expansion of the specialty coffee product range into more mainstream outlets such as supermarkets, the term has become much looser. It is fair to say that 'specialty coffee' has become a generic label covering a range of different coffees, which either command a premium price over other coffees or are perceived by consumers as being different from the widely available mainstream brands of coffee. The term has become so broad that there is no universally accepted definition of what constitutes 'specialty coffee', and it frequently means different things to different people.

Given this lack of precision in definition it is extremely difficult to describe the market in a global way. The best approach appears to be to look at the specialty market from different country or regional viewpoints. However, the very notion 'gourmet' or 'specialty' suggests some degree of exclusivity. It is unlikely that one could market thousands of tons of a particular coffee and still call it 'exclusive'.

*The first lesson to be learned therefore is that one should not 'overdo it'.* It is, and always has been, a mistake to consider specialty coffee a different industry from the rest of the coffee business. Supply and demand will not only determine the general level of coffee prices, but will also determine the premium paid for 'quality'.

*The second lesson is that producers need to target any special coffee very carefully* because the term 'specialty' covers a large and growing number of different products, each of which has its own niche.

## Niche markets

A niche combines a set of conditions that enable a single species or a single product to thrive within the greater ecological or commercial environment. While much of global coffee production consists of mainstream type coffees, there are many other coffees, often of limited availability, with greatly varying taste characteristics that appeal to different groups of consumers, and which sell at a premium over mainstream coffees. Simply put, where the producers or exporters of such a coffee and such a group of consumers get together, a niche market is created.

Two main factors determine whether a coffee can find a niche market: **quality** and **availability**. 'Availability' is easily understood, but 'quality' is a subjective term which means different things to different people. (See chapter 11, Coffee quality.)

### Quality segmentation of coffees

Broadly speaking, coffees can be divided into three commercial categories.

- *Exemplary quality* coffees have a high intrinsic value with a fine or unique cup. Usually of quite limited availability. Mostly retailed under straight estate or origin names. Usually very well presented washed coffees, including some superior washed robustas, but also includes some naturals (Ethiopian Harar, Yemeni Mochas, some Indonesian Arabicas), top organic coffees. True niche products. Usually, but not always, roasted by comparatively small firms and marketed through fairly exclusive outlets e.g. retail coffee shops or bars and upmarket delicatessens.

- **High quality or premium brands**, good cupping coffees, well presented, but not necessarily visually perfect. Retailed both as straight origins and as blends. Includes good quality, well prepared organic coffees, and washed as well as superior quality natural robustas. The market for this quality band is much broader and includes a good percentage of today's specialty coffee. Also produced by leading multinational coffee companies and marketed through normal retail outlets such as supermarkets.

- **Mainstream quality**, average quality, reasonably well presented but certainly not visually perfect. Will offer a decent, clean but not necessarily impressive cup.

In today's specialty market all three types of coffee are represented: exemplary and high quality coffees either as stand-alone or as a named blend component, and mainstream quality in many of the ready-to-drink and flavoured drinks that are sold alongside filter coffee and espresso.

Obviously, for smaller exporters of top quality coffee the exemplary segment initially offers more promise. However producers or exporters of good quality coffee have three basic options open to them.

- Sell to the leading roasters (through the usual trade channels), if volume sales are required and the coffee sold lacks the flavour characteristics necessary to be marketed on its own;

- Sell to specialty roasters either direct or through importers or agents. The latter in most cases is the more realistic option as these importers or agents have a wide coverage of the small roasters and other retail outlets which are too small to import direct;

- Focus on specialty coffee retailers either by selling direct (for roasting in store) through specialty wholesalers or by selling through specialty roasters. The number of specialty coffee retailers importing direct is extremely small, however.

Premiums for specialty coffee can be considerable at the retail level but the premiums available for producers are inevitably much lower, although they can still be significant. It is sobering to realize that mainstream qualities, including robusta, account for an estimated 85%–90% of world coffee consumption, while the share of exemplary and high quality coffee is no more than 10% or perhaps 15% of the world market. This suggests that for many producers it would be inadvisable to ignore the mainstream market altogether. Instead they should concentrate on both: specialty for their top quality and mainstream for the remainder of their production.

A further point to note is that sales to small roasters are mostly on extended credit terms, something only an importer can easily afford. Inventory costs, late payment costs and even the risk of payment defaults are therefore part of the cost equation. Also, most roasters purchase subject to approval of the quality on delivery which means the importer will be left with any coffee that does not meet the roaster's expectations. In other words, the premium for specialty coffee at the wholesale level includes many more factors than just the quality.

**The United States specialty market** has seen strong development over the past ten years or so, which has helped to arrest the fall in United States consumption. Much of this has been driven by the Specialty Coffee Association of America (SCAA) (*www.scaa.org*). Part of the industry now appears to be moving from past insistence on straight quality and exclusivity towards more manipulated products (flavourings, for example) in which the quality of the underlying coffee sometimes takes second place. Increasing sales of espresso-type drinks also mean growing demand for low-acid coffees such as Brazils and robustas at the expense of traditional specialty mild arabicas.

Note here also that espresso drinks generate higher profit margins than do traditional cups of coffee. And furthermore, on the roaster/retailer side – coffee bars and shops ranging in size from international chains at one extreme to firms with just a few stores at the other – the trend has been to follow the example of the Starbucks operation. Not only to get bigger, mostly through merger or acquisition, but also to 'commoditize' and simplify business. This can mean eliminating or reducing the number of 'straight' origin coffees that are carried, and as a result increasing dependence on blends because higher sales mean larger and more centralized buying requirements. This makes it increasingly cumbersome to deal with many small suppliers. So-called signature blends are often used in the branding strategy of larger companies.

At the same time, mainstream roasters have been upgrading their image by offering 'quality' coffees but many have very different perceptions of what this means. Some of the large United States mega-discount stores have installed 30-pound capacity computerized coffee roasters and are selling freshly roasted 'specialty' coffee at much lower prices than the traditional specialty stores. The quality may not always be there, but the coffee is fresh. Some such chains have also started importing roasted beans direct from some producing countries in partnership with roasters at origin.

Given this strong industry growth and the accompanying proliferation of specialty coffee products, the SCAA is in the process of establishing a standard for Certified Specialty coffee. The aim is to provide producers, exporters, importers, roasters and retailers of specialty coffee with the means to have the quality and authenticity of their product independently certified. The programme builds on the existing SCAA Green Coffee Classification System and Grading Chart; see *www.scaa.org/standards.cfm*.

**The Japanese specialty market** is not dissimilar to the United States, and it too has distinctive segments:

- Almost mythical name coffee: Blue Mountain, Hawaiian Kona etc.;

- Good quality, straight origin estate or area coffees;

- Decent standard qualities;

- Branded blends.

There are no dedicated specialty importers but most importers handle at least some specialty coffees and increasingly service smaller downstream buyers directly although there is also a network of coffee dealers and wholesalers. Interestingly, larger roasters maintain their own coffee outlets within large department stores – in so doing they of course achieve widespread exposure.

The Japanese market basically offers producers the same sales prospects as does the United States with the exception that it is very difficult to gain recognition for new individual coffees. This is because creating a stand-alone brand image for an individual coffee would be enormously expensive and without guarantee of success. Disclosure of origin at retail level is provided for in consumer legislation but as the composition of blends is flexible and they are sold under the roasters' own brand names, usually only the main components are identified by country of origin (and never by individual grower or producer). As a result price resistance in Japan, other than for a few stand-alone top coffees, is probably greater than in the United States specialty market.

Other emerging specialty markets in Asia would appear to be strongly influenced by trends in the United States. United States operators have opened or franchised specialty stores in Australia, Hong Kong (China), Singapore and elsewhere.

**The Northern European specialty market** is part of the world's largest market for coffee. Europe's total imports are double those of the United States. But the great concentration of buying power in the hands of very few roasters has not made it easy for small producers to add value through improved quality, or through promotion in Europe. This is mainly because their production is deemed insufficient to be considered for sale as straight origin coffee, but also because specialty coffee in Europe is a true niche market in a continent where much good quality coffee is already readily available. The true specialty target segment consists mostly of real enthusiasts searching for something different, rather than large numbers of people who are disappointed in their daily cup of coffee as was the case in the United States.

The entry of Europe's mega-roasters into this field demonstrates that they appreciate its potential. Competition between them and smaller specialty roasters will probably limit the latter's potential market more than has been the case in the United States, where until fairly recently the large roasters did not have any 'quality' to offer. In many European countries the opposite applies and both sides are therefore targeting more or less the same niche market, with large operators benefiting from economies of scale the smaller ones cannot match. The establishment in 1999 of the Specialty Coffee Association of Europe *(www.scae.com)* must therefore be seen as extremely positive in this somewhat uneven playing field. Exporters should note that the area to be covered is vast, with hugely varying quality preferences. Smaller producers in particular will almost certainly have to depend on specialty importers or agents to access the European market efficiently.

**The Southern European specialty market**, mainly Italy, is entirely different from that of most other European countries. Italy is a gateway into a number of Eastern European markets and many Italian importers and roasters traditionally supply ready-made specialty blends (green or roasted, for roast and ground or for espresso) to nearby countries in Eastern Europe as well as the many small roasters that operate in Italy itself. The Italian market counts over 1,500 individual roasters: there is a substantial mainstream segment but many small specialty roasters exist and flourish. Many of these buy ready-made, ready-to-roast green coffee blends from the specialty importers, especially for the strong espresso segment. Larger specialty roasters such as Lavazza and Illy export substantial quantities of Italian espresso blends all over Europe and the United States, so the sales opportunities for specialty type coffee that meets the quality requirements for the espresso trade are quite substantial. For a review of those requirements and how they differ from traditional specialty coffee see 'Traditional versus espresso' at the end of chapter 11, Coffee quality.

# Organic coffee

## Introduction

Organic products have come a long way since small groups of consumers started buying organic food directly from farms or from small health food shops, where quality was secondary as long as the products were organic. In the early 1990s supermarket chains started paying systematic attention to organic food. Year after year they have taken over market share from the specialized shops, to the point where growth in the market share of organic food today is mostly driven by them. In some countries supermarkets now account for more than 50% of organic food sales, and organic products are on offer in all Western countries. Increasing numbers of farmers in developed countries have entered organic farming. It is estimated that 2% of all agricultural land in Europe is cultivated organically. In Austria, by 2001 more than 8% of the entire agricultural area was already under organic cultivation.

The market share for organic products in Western countries ranges between 0.5% and 3% for food generally, but varies widely for different product groups. For instance, baby food in Germany and Denmark is reportedly more than 50% organic, and organic dairy products are best-sellers as well, sometimes with a market share of 25%. Western annual growth rates for organic products as a whole range from 10% to as high as 40%. This means that within five years, the market share in some countries might reach 10%.

Several European Union member states have introduced programmes to promote organic agriculture. France for example has targeted 1 million hectares of agricultural land to be converted by 2005 (5% of its total), and has established a budget for subsidies for farmers converting to organic production and for generic promotion of organic products. However, the rather optimistic growth figures forecast by the organic industry for the last 10 or 15 years have not always been realized, or have often been realized much later than originally predicted.

Certainly the market for organic coffee is difficult to estimate: facts are difficult to come by and aspiring producers must also be careful not to confuse growing insistence on ISO (International Organization for Standardization) and GAP (Good Agricultural Practice) certification, with demand for pure organic coffee as such.

Of course the large supermarket chains all carry their own range of organic products nowadays. In so doing they are undoubtedly raising both the profile and the market share of organics, but not necessarily at the sort of premiums that producers may believe exist, because most large chains do not hesitate to use their buying power to cap prices. Nevertheless, the growing presence of organic coffee on supermarket shelves is prompting large roasters to evaluate the market potential with at least one organic brand in some countries. However, for the time being organic coffee lies mostly within the domain of specialized, smaller roasters and a few large supermarket chains.

## What are organic products?

Organic agriculture means holistic production management systems that promote and enhance agro-ecosystem health, including biodiversity, biological cycles, and soil biological activity (holistic means handling or dealing with an entity or activity in its entirety or wholeness rather than with emphasis on its parts or various aspects). Organic production systems are based on specific and precise production, processing and handling standards. They aim to achieve optimal agro-ecosystems that are socially, ecologically and economically sustainable. Terms such as 'biological' and 'ecological' are also used in an effort to describe the organic production system more clearly. Requirements for organically produced foods differ from those for other agricultural products in that the production procedures, and not just the product by itself, are an intrinsic part of the identification and labelling of, and status claims for, such products.[8]

Advocates of organic agriculture believe that conventional agriculture, with its use of chemical inputs, will not be sustainable in the long run as it leads to soil degradation and pollution of the environment, and poses health risks for both consumers and producers. Therefore, organic agriculture replaces manufactured inputs (fertilizers, pesticides, herbicides, etc.) by natural compost and vermiculture[9], biological pest controls and the growing of legumes and shade trees.

The International Federation of Organic Agriculture Movements (IFOAM; founded 1972) has formulated basic standards for organic products.[10] These standards are at the base of the legislation that has been introduced in the European Union (1992), the United States (2000), Japan (2001), and a number of other countries (including Argentina, Bolivia, India and Mexico) that have created national legislation to regulate the market for organic products.

---

8   From the FAO/WHO Codex Alimentarius Commission Guidelines for the Production, Processing, Labelling and Marketing of Organically Produced Foods (1999) – go to *www.codexalimentarius.net.*

9   Vermiculture is the raising of earthworms to aerate soil and/or produce vermicast: the nutrient-rich by-product of earthworms, used as a soil conditioner.

10   To view these in full go to *www.ifoam.org.* For more on regulation issues see later in this chapter.

## What is organic coffee and why grow or buy it?

### *Definition*

Organic coffee is grown as part of an intensive, holistic agricultural production management system that includes the composting of organic materials, mulching, shade regulation and biological pest control. Such a system is based on the principle that a value corresponding to that harvested should be returned to the soil. It excludes the use of agro-chemicals. For the product to be marketed as organic, it must be certified as such by a third party. Variants on this basic theme, such as shade grown, are discussed later in this chapter.

Western countries have developed extensive legislation for organic products. The conditions that must be met before coffee may be marketed as organic are both comprehensive and well defined. No coffee may be brought to the marketplace and labelled organic unless it is proved to conform to the regulations. In other words, coffee can be marketed as organic only when it is certified as such by a recognized organization or certifier, based on regular inspection of all stages of production, processing, transporting and roasting of the coffee.

The first organic coffee cultivation was recorded at the Finca Irlanda in Chiapas, Mexico (1967), and the first organic coffee to be imported into Europe from a small farmers' cooperative came from the UCIRI cooperative in Oaxaca, Mexico (1985). The cooperative converted and marketed its coffee with the help of a joint venture formed by a Netherlands commercial roaster, Simon Lévelt/Haarlem, and GEPA (Gesellschaft für Partnerschaft mit der Dritten Welt), a German NGO (non-governmental organization) specializing in alternative trade.

### *Why do consumers choose organic coffee?*

**Health considerations.** Many consumers are increasingly concerned with the content of their daily intake of food and beverages: organic foods are perceived as healthier. This motive is less important for coffee than it is for some other crops in that roasted coffee hardly ever contains harmful residues. But there is also a growing body of consumers whose health worries extend to the workers who have to work with the chemicals that are used in the traditional production system.

**Demand for specialty coffee.** This is growing and organic coffees are perceived as belonging to this category. Although the quality of organic coffee is not necessarily better than that of conventional coffees, the market for organic coffee is increasingly demanding higher quality, which is why organic coffees are often positioned in the specialty segment. The first organic coffees to appear on the market in the 1980s were good quality arabicas from Mexico, but nowadays lower grades of organic arabica as well as organic robusta are also available. Some quality estates or exporters have their coffees certified as organic to underline their quality, hoping it will be perceived as truly special.

**Environmental concerns.** Other consumers are concerned about the negative impact of agro-chemicals on the environment. They are not necessarily concerned only about health issues but primarily want to be sure that the products they buy are produced in an environmentally friendly way in order to prevent pollution, erosion and soil degradation.

### *Why produce organic coffee?*

In principle producers are motivated by the same concerns as consumers, but in addition they want to secure their social and cultural future by realizing the premium that certified organic coffee obtains. This benefit depends on the demand for organic coffee, which in turn determines the amount of the premium that can be obtained, and the extra costs involved in organic production. See later in this chapter for more on this.

### Growing organic coffee

Growing any organic product, including organic coffee, is more than just leaving out fertilizers and other agro-chemicals. Coffee produced in this way should instead be called 'natural' coffee and, to the surprise of many, the industry looks upon this as *non-sustainable production*. This is because, in the long run, the soil will be depleted by natural production, which is often referred to also as 'passive cultivation' or 'organic by default'.

To achieve ***sustainable production*** it is necessary to make active use of various organic agriculture techniques including the composting of organic material, mulching of the soil under the trees with organic material, use of biological pest control, and investing in shade regulation. The principle of sustainable agriculture is that a value corresponding to that harvested should be returned to the soil. All possible methods have to be used to enhance the fertility of the soil. This is why passive production of coffee, even when no chemicals are used, is viewed as non-sustainable and not as organic.

According to European Union regulations these standards must be followed:

● Cultivation of legumes, green manures, or deep-rooting plants in an appropriate multi-annual rotation programme.

● Incorporation in the soil of organic material, organic livestock manure and vermicompost.

● Pests, diseases and weeds to be controlled by using appropriate varieties, rotation programmes, biological pest control, mechanical practices and flame weeding.

● Seeds and propagation materials organically produced.

● Use of non-organic fertilizers, pesticides and biological pest control methods is limited.

(Minimum standards according to and adapted from EU-2092/91. See Annex II of EU-2092/91 for further specifications of approved inputs: *www.europa.eu.int*.)

CERTIMEX, a leading organic certifying organization from Mexico, has formulated standards specifically for coffee.

● Biodiversity should be promoted; therefore cultivation must be done under diversified shade.

● Varieties should be adapted to the local climate and be resistant to local plagues and diseases.

● Nurseries should be organic and seeds should come from organic coffee fields.

● Coffee bushes may not be planted too densely.

● Erosion should be controlled by: mulching and growing of soil covers; planting on contours and/or terraces; shade trees with a lot of foliage leaf; and construction of barriers.

● Techniques to promote organic content of the soil should be used: growing of legumes, incorporation of organic fertilizers and other organic material such as leaves and branches of shade trees.

● Correction of pH-value with permitted inputs, e.g. lime, is allowed.

● Coffee pulp is recycled.

● Processing is done only with mechanical and physical means; attention should be given to reduction of energy use and cleaning of water that has been used to wash the coffee.

(Adapted from CERTIMEX: Normas para la producción de café orgánico/01.2001.)

Usually, a producer may simultaneously grow both conventional and organic coffee, although this is not recommended. There must be a clear separation between the two types and adequate barriers to prevent contamination with agro-chemicals from neighbouring fields.

Coffee may normally be sold as organic only once organic cultivation has been practised for at least three years before the first marketable harvest. This also means three years of inspection. These years are called the *conversion period*.

In specific cases, depending on previous agricultural practices, this conversion period may be reduced, but only after approval of the certifying organization, which in turn has to report such a decision to the authority granting the import permit in the European Union member State concerned. For a producer who can prove that no agro-chemicals have been used in the past, it is important to try to reduce the conversion period. If a producer can document that no agro-chemicals have recently been used, it is certainly worthwhile discussing the possibility with the certifier.

## Processing and marketing organic coffee – the audit trail

Not only coffee cultivation, but all subsequent steps in the production chain have to be certified. On-farm processing, storage, transport, export processing, shipping, export, import, roasting, packaging, distribution and retailing all have to be certified organic. Contact with conventionally produced coffee must be excluded and so there has to be a separation in space and/or time. Spraying or fumigation with toxic agents is never permitted and special measures must be taken to prevent contact with areas where fumigation has taken place. Adequate records are to be kept of incoming and outgoing coffee so that the entire product flow can be documented and accounted for, often referred to as traceability. All the steps in the chain should therefore be documented and administered in a way that makes it possible to trace back the origin of the product from one step to the next (track and trace), ensuring that no contamination with conventional coffee has occurred. This traceability minimizes the risk of fraud at all stages and is a very important part of the inspection process by certifying organizations.

The flavouring of roasted coffee is permitted when natural flavouring substances or preparations are used. For packaging roasted coffee, flushing with nitrogen or carbon dioxide is permitted. For the decaffeination of coffee, chemical solvents (e.g. methylene chloride) are not permitted, but the water method or the supercritical carbon dioxide method (the $CO_2$ method) may be used.

## Certification and import

As already indicated, the importation and sale as organic of both green and processed coffee must comply with the legal regulations of the consuming countries. This compliance needs to be verified by a third party; the procedure is called *certification*. It is important to realize that *different rules apply in different countries*.

The certification procedure includes a number of steps. Note that there is a clear distinction between the certification of an operator to produce organic coffee, and the certification of an export shipment to be imported as organic coffee.

- **Registration**. The producer selects a certification organization (certifier for short) and signs a contract. The producer provides information on their farm/processing facilities and is registered.

- **Inspection.** At least once a year the certifier inspects the production and processing facilities.

- **Certification.** The inspection report is the basis for deciding whether a *master certificate* can be granted or not.

- **Control certificate** (formerly called transaction certificate). This must be issued for every export shipment, indicating the exact quantity and organic origin, after which the goods may be exported/imported as organic.

The certification process includes an assessment of the grower's production and export capacity against which the authenticity of future export transactions will be tested. This is to ensure that sellers of organic products do not exceed their registered capacity. Also, organic products can be labelled as such only once the entire production and handling chain, from the grower through to the importer, has been inspected and certified.

## Organic regulations

In the initial development stages there was no legal definition of organic food and so farmers' organizations and others formulated their own standards, and issued certificates and seals to offer consumer guarantees. The next phase was when IFOAM united these different standards into its 'Basic standards for organic production and processing'. These standards provide a framework for certification bodies and standard-setting organizations worldwide to develop their own certification standards. In an effort to harmonize standards and certification, and also to provide a universal quality seal for organic products, IFOAM also has a programme for accrediting certification organizations.[11] In the third phase, different countries or states (e.g. Germany, California) developed laws on organic agriculture and processing, which were incorporated in formal European Union or United States regulations in the last phase. A review of import regulations in major consuming markets follows.

## Europe

**Regulation.** In the European Union, the market for organic food is regulated by Council Regulation EU 2092/91 of 24 June 1991 and subsequent amendments.[12] All major European certifying organizations operate according to this regulation, although some organizations have stricter standards in some respects, such as Naturland in Germany.

However, and most unfortunately, the practical application by individual member states of this legislation can differ considerably, particularly where products imported from countries outside the European Union are concerned. The main problem is that whereas regulations for organic certification are based on equivalence (equal values), they are not always interpreted in this way. Some therefore consider such differences as non-tariff barriers leading to unjust treatment of developing country exporters.

**Accreditation of certification organizations.** The European Union standard known as EN 45011 and the international ISO 65 equivalent both stipulate that certification organizations should be accredited by a recognized accreditation body. But the so-called third option (at the time of writing valid until end of 2002) permits competent authorities in individual European Union member states to declare that a certification organization is judged to be operating in accordance with the requirements of regulation EU 2092/91.[13]

---

11   See *www.ifoam.org* for more information on this accreditation programme and for links to other publications, e.g. on the differences between European Union and United States regulations for organic agriculture.

12   A consolidated version, compiled by UKROFs (United Kingdom Register of Organic Food Standards), is to be found at *www.defra.gov.uk/farm/organic/import/import.htm*. Alternatively go to *www.europa.eu.int*.

13   In the context of this chapter the terms 'certifying or certification organization', 'certifying or certification body' and 'certifier' all have the same meaning.

For example, the competent authority for organic agriculture for the Union State of Hamburg in Germany may declare that products certified by certifier X comply with the requirements of EU 2092/91. In this case, organic products certified by X are accepted in Hamburg and therefore should also be accepted in other European Union member states, even though the certifying body lacks direct EN/ISO accreditation.

In practice, however, not all national authorities accept such declarations. Either they require additional information or they simply do not allow such products to be imported as 'organic'. Therefore, aspiring exporters of organic coffee to the European Union should verify whether:

- The proposed certifying organization has an EN 45011/ISO 65 accreditation (which they should be able to submit on request) or is accepted on the basis of the escape clause as in the example above (but again, they should be able to submit proof).[14]

- The proposed importer is fully aware of and follows the required European Union customs documentation, i.e. is certified and has an import permit.

The second point has gained considerable importance since, as a consequence of instances of fraud, the rules governing the importation of organic products into the European Union were considerably strengthened with effect from 1 July 2002. Now organic products can only be imported if:

- The importer submits an *import permit* for the organic coffee in question, issued by the competent authority in the member state, giving details of the exporter or producer, the certifying body, and the importer into the European Union. (These import permits were always necessary but, in practice, could be applied for at the importer's risk and after the import had already taken place. This is now impossible and *European Union importers require an import permit for each individual exporter they intend dealing with.*)

- An *original control certificate*, formerly called transaction certificate, is submitted to customs for verification and endorsement. This is issued by the certifying body and this is where the earlier inspection of production capacity comes in, i.e. the *master certificate* that was issued by the certifier to confirm the seller's authenticity and capacity. At the end of a year it can then be seen whether the total exports for which control certificates were issued correspond with the production capacity stated in the master certificate.

*Without this documentation European Union customs will not clear a shipment as organic but only as conventional coffee.*

Once cleared through European Union customs the organic product enjoys free movement to other member states. But when all or part of a consignment is to be re-exported as organic to a destination outside the European Union, then the original European Union importer has to obtain a new inspection certificate from a competent European Union certifying organization.

Producers of organic coffee should be aware that the reality of the trade in organic products is quite different from the normal trade in coffee: logistics require importers to trade mainly in full container loads (see chapter 5, Logistics), but selling full container loads to small roasters in a single European Union market is not easy and so the loads must be split on arrival. This presents major administrative problems and is very time consuming and costly. It is completely different from what happens in the conventional coffee trade, not least because each European Union member state has its own competent authority and recognized certifying organization: some are government agencies; in other countries they are private organizations, sometimes even more than one.

---

14   The European Union does not recognize certifiers whose agronomic stipulations do not conform to EU specifications. For example, the use of sodium nitrate is permitted by some non-EU certifiers but is prohibited under EU stipulations.

**Label confusion.** Most certifying bodies have their own quality labels and as a result many different labels exist in the European Union for the designation of organic products. Efforts to come up with a single European label have not been successful yet – the increasing trade within the European Union in roasted coffee therefore forces roasters to display several labels on their retail packets, an arrangement that does not provide the clarity one would expect. As food scares increase general awareness of health issues and thereby the profile of the organics trade as well, these labelling issues will surely have to be resolved eventually.

## United States

As required by the Organic Foods Production Act (OFPA), the National Organic Standards (part of the National Organic Program, NOP) became effective on 21 October 2002. OFPA itself was adopted in 1990 to establish national standards for the production and handling of foods labelled as 'organic'.

Although private and state agencies certified organic practices, national certification requirements did not exist and therefore there were no guarantees that 'organic' meant the same thing from state to state, or even locally from certifier to certifier. Consumers and producers of organic products jointly sought to establish national standards to clear up confusion in the marketplace, and to protect the trade against mislabelling or fraud. Organizations that are fully NOP-compliant (certified) may label their products or ingredients as organic, and may use the 'USDA Organic Seal' on organic products in the United States, irrespective of whether they are produced domestically or are imported. As a result of NOP there will therefore be a *single national label* in the United States to designate organic products, thereby avoiding the label confusion that exists in Europe. A list of accredited certifying agents can be found on the USDA (NOP) website *www.ams.usda.gov/nop* and on *www.ioia.net* – Independent Organic Inspectors Association.

The North American market for organic coffee is served mainly by importers who handle conventional products as well, although some specialize in organics entirely. As with the trade in specialty coffee generally, it is often difficult to convince an importer to take a container load of an unknown coffee and the introduction of new coffees can therefore be a lengthy and tedious process.

## Japan

Coffee consumption has been growing strongly in Japan, from 5.6 million bags in 1995 to 6.7 million bags in 2001, mostly of good quality coffee. Official statistics on the amount of organic coffee imported are not readily available but trade estimates put the market share of organic coffee in 2002 at not more than 0.5% or 35,000 bags. Despite coffee's undoubted popularity there is relatively little consumer awareness of conditions in coffee producing countries, or the role that coffee cultivation can play in sustaining the environment there. Nevertheless, the reputation for better quality and flavour of organic fresh produce items has kindled a positive interest in organically grown coffee. Against this stands a certain disappointment in that in Japan the cup quality of organic coffee generally does not live up to the expectations created by the high asking prices.

To illustrate, in early 2002 average quality coffee retailed in Japanese supermarkets at 400 yen per 200 g compared, for example, to Starbucks Gold Coast Blend at 863 yen per 200 g. For most organic coffees the retail price stood at over 900 yen per 200 g, without necessarily offering the cup quality that this suggests. Part of the pricing problem is related to the limited turnover and high overheads of the cooperatives and other bodies that market most of the organic coffee in Japan. In addition to the effects of high prices, the sustainability aspect of the organics label has not yet affected consumers in quite the same way as it has in some other consuming countries, thus limiting growth still further. Industry sources suggest that current prices inhibit growth and put a realistic premium expectation at the FOB level at around 15–20 cts/lb over average quality conventional coffee.

The Japan Agricultural Standard (JAS) for Organic Agricultural Products entered into force in April 2002. JAS operates under the auspices of the Ministry of Agriculture, Forestry and Fisheries and regulates the production and labelling of organic food items produced in Japan. Although coffee is not grown in Japan, JAS nevertheless also covers organic coffee (and tea) under 'organic agricultural products'.

Only JAS-accredited certifying bodies may issue organic certification for coffee to be imported into Japan. See the box on page 80 for names and website addresses of some of the certifying bodies known to be active in coffee in Japan in 2002.

It is expected that once an accreditation protocol is concluded between the governments of the United States and Japan, upon application all certifying bodies authorized under United States law will also be accredited by Japan. In addition, interested certifying bodies in producing countries may also apply for accreditation under JAS. Subject to meeting the JAS standard for their products, set by the Agriculture Ministry, suppliers of organic coffee and tea may display the JAS mark, giving Japan also a single organic label for the entire Japanese market.

# World market for organic coffee

Different trade sources have varying views on the growth prospects for organic coffee sales. Table 17 is therefore simply a projection of the levels consumption could be expected to reach in the near term.

In 2001/02 trade sources estimated world production of organic coffee at some 48,000 tons or 800,000 bags, a total that therefore exceeds estimated current consumption. As long as the major coffee roasters in Europe and the United States do not include organic coffee in their range of major brands (and by mid 2002 they did not yet), it is unlikely that any substantial increase in supply can be readily absorbed.

# Organic coffee and small producers

Numerous grower organizations and smallholders are aware of the market for organic coffee. Because many of them do not use, or use a minimum of agro-chemicals, conversion seems a logical option especially when coffee prices are low. As well as the problem of possible oversupply, potential producers should also carefully consider the costs of certification. They have to assure themselves not only that their future output will be in accordance with the rules of organic production, but also that the proposed inspection system is in accordance with the regulations in the import markets that are to be targeted.

To assist in this regard the organic sector has developed an internal control system (ICS) that provides a practical and cost-effective inspection option. Generally, if a grower group has more than 30 members then it qualifies for an ICS. Although an ICS can be quite burdensome, it is a means to reduce the costs of inspection. Otherwise each individual member must be inspected every year, which is extremely expensive, especially for larger groups with a geographically far-flung membership. With a proper internal control system, only a random sample of the total number of producers has to be inspected by an independent certifying organization. Major elements of an ICS include:

- Internal regulation, including sanctions;

- Personnel;

- Infrastructure;

**Table 17** **Estimated consumption of organic coffee in 2002/03 in major consumer countries**

| Country | Bags | Market share organic coffee (%) |
|---|---|---|
| United States | 200,000 | 1.1 |
| Canada | 27,000 | 1.1 |
| Japan | 33,000 | 0.5 |
| Germany | 110,000 | 1.2 |
| France | 49,000 | 0.9 |
| Italy | 48,000 | 0.9 |
| United Kingdom | 23,000 | 1.0 |
| Denmark | 22,000 | 2.8 |
| Spain | 22,000 | 0.7 |
| Switzerland | 18,000 | 2.3 |
| Austria | 15,000 | 2.0 |
| Netherlands | 15,000 | 0.8 |
| Sweden | 12,000 | 1.0 |
| Finland | 9,000 | 0.8 |
| Belgium/Luxembourg | 7,000 | 0.9 |
| Norway | 7,000 | 0.9 |
| Other Europe* | 33,000 | 0.4 |
| Unspecified | 20,000 | – |
| Brazil | 30,000 | 0.2 |
| **Total** | **700,000** | – |

*Source:* Various trade estimates.

* Including Eastern Europe.

- Training and information;
- A 100% internal farm control at least once a year;
- Monitoring of product flow.

The magnitude of the random sample to be taken by the external inspection body under an ICS system is a major item of debate within the European Union. Most competent authorities require a sample of 10% of producers to be inspected annually, but some officials consider this number much too small to offer the required consumer guarantees and want significant larger samples. Others consider 10% far too high, especially for grower organizations with large memberships and where access to the actual growing areas may be difficult. By mid 2002 the issue had not been resolved, but most competent authorities require proof that the external certification has been based on a sample of *at least* 10%. (Note that some roasters submit random coffee samples for chemical analysis to verify the accuracy of the inspection and certification process.)

> *In September 2002 there were producers of certified organic coffee in the following countries: Bolivia, Brazil, Colombia, Costa Rica, Cuba, Dominican Republic, East Timor, Ecuador, El Salvador, Ethiopia, Guatemala, Honduras, India, Indonesia, Kenya, Madagascar, Malawi, Mexico, Papua New Guinea, Peru, Uganda and United Republic of Tanzania.*

# Certification costs and viability

## Production and export

It is impossible to give a precise indication of the cost of certification. It depends on the time needed for preparation, travel, inspection, reporting and certification, and the fees the certification organization charges. Not only the agricultural production of the coffee but also the wet and dry processing as well as the storage and export process have to be inspected and certified. Fee structures vary considerably and it is therefore advisable to review in detail which inspection and certification organization offers the best service at the lowest price. Some charge a fee per hectare, others a percentage of the export value. As a norm, the cost of inspection and certification should not exceed 3%–4% of the sales value of the green coffee, although it should be noted that some grower organizations pay more than this.

Local certifiers (i.e. those established in the same producing country or region) are usually but not always cheaper than the international agencies. However, local certificates are not necessarily or easily recognized by importing countries, so their validity has to be carefully checked. A number of international certifiers have branch offices in producing countries and locally employed staff carry out inspections at lower expense than external personnel could. Another option for international certifiers is to use a recognized local inspection body with which they have a cooperation agreement (e.g. IMO (Switzerland/Germany) and KRAV (Sweden) cooperate with CERTIMEX in Mexico).

Also to be taken into account are increased production costs and sometimes a fall in the yield per hectare. These costs are extremely difficult to assess because they depend entirely on the nature and intensity of the conventional cultivation practices before the conversion to organic agriculture.

A further cost and a real problem for the producer is the conversion period from conventional to full organic production: during this time the coffee cannot be sold as organic and so does not realize any premium. Meanwhile, not only does the producer have to bear the inspection and certification costs, but production might also fall, at least for a couple of years. Some sources suggest yields may fall by some 20%.

Inspection costs tend to be higher in the initial phase as the certifiers need time to get to know the producer and to register his fields and facilities. Note that in order to overcome the start-up problems during the conversion period, coffee growers in a number of countries can have access to funds to finance the costs of certification. Nevertheless, if the average annual inspection and certification cost for example comes to US$ 5,000 or more then there is little financial point in converting to certified organic if the annual exportable production amounts to only two or three containers.

*Premiums for organic coffee* are difficult to indicate because they depend on the quality of the coffee and on the market situation at a given moment. As a rule of thumb however, the potential producer premium (FOB) for the organic version of a particular coffee compared to the equivalent non-organic quality could in 2002 be put at 10%–15%. This compares with consumers generally accepting to pay retail prices of around 20% more for organic coffee than they do for conventional coffee. Some exceptional coffees realize higher premiums but there is a strong feeling in trade circles that, realistically, this is the maximum that should be expected. Consumer interest tails off rapidly if premiums go beyond this unless the coffee's quality is absolutely outstanding.

The high of 15% is an indication only. Actual producer premiums fluctuate alongside coffee prices as a whole: high coffee prices probably reducing the premium percentage and, conversely, low coffee prices probably encouraging somewhat higher premium percentages. Fairtrade offers a fixed US$ 15 cts/lb premium for organic coffee over its minimum guaranteed price for conventional coffee that meets Fairtrade criteria.

Contrary to popular belief the liquor of organic coffee is not necessarily better than that of its conventional equivalent. Where it is not, the premium over conventional coffee has to be justified purely by the organic aspect and is therefore strictly limited by supply and demand unless and until the quality is such that the organic coffee in question can achieve a true stand-alone position in the market – its own niche. Then the premium potential becomes entirely demand driven, just as is the case for some well known conventional specialty or gourmet coffees, and such organic brands indeed achieve premiums of 25% or even higher over conventional coffee.

But as the supply of organic coffee grows, so growers should be more cautious when venturing into this field. Just as producers of conventional specialty coffee have experienced, it is equally difficult to launch new stand-alone brands of organic coffee. Organic coffees that do not offer quality as such, or that are available in large quantities, will sell at much lower premiums over their conventional equivalent, perhaps as low as 5% because, just like any other standard type coffee, they end up as bulk blenders. Chapter 11, Coffee quality, makes it clear that to produce good quality coffee of any kind takes much work and strict management. Organic certification will always complement such efforts but cannot replace good, honest hard work and integrity.

Remember:

● Check which certifier is the most acceptable and the most appropriate for the target export market. If possible, determine which certifier the prospective buyer(s) may prefer. Make sure the preferred certifier is accredited and approved in the target market. See the box overleaf for a listing of some major certifiers relevant for the coffee sector.

● Obtain quotations from various certifiers and ask for clear conditions (especially how many days will be charged) and timelines. Conditions are usually negotiable. Remember certifiers are offering a service, not favours, and should serve their clients, not the other way around.

● Ensure your potential export production warrants the conversion cost, i.e. calculate the opportunity cost of converting to organic production.

Information on costs and current sales prices for comparable coffees is available on many websites and can relatively easily be compared.

## Importing, roasting and retailing

The green coffee importer and the coffee roaster also have to be inspected and certified. Inspection costs in the European Union vary from US$ 500 to US$ 750 per year per import/production location. In addition, the importer (who does not process the coffee, but only trades it) pays a licence fee of 0.1%–0.7% of the sales value or US$ 0.20–0.50 per kilogram, depending on turnover. Roasters pay a licence fee of 0.1%–1.5% of the sales value of the roasted coffee, depending on turnover. And, as already mentioned, every European Union importer of organic coffee must apply for an individual import permit for each of their suppliers and for each consignment.

### Some major certifiers relevant for the coffee sector

| Company | Country | Website |
|---|---|---|
| ACT Organic Agriculture Certification Thailand | Thailand | |
| AIAB Associazione Italiana per l'Agricoltura Biologica | Italy | www.aiab.it |
| AIMCOPOP | Costa Rica | |
| Argencert | Argentina | www.argencert.com.ar |
| BCS Öko-Garantie GmbH | Germany | www.bcs-oeko.de |
| Bio.inspecta | Switzerland | www.bio-inspecta.ch |
| Biolatina | Peru | www.biolatina.org |
| BioAgriCert | Italy | www.bioagricert.org |
| Bio-Gro New Zealand | New Zealand | www.biogro.co.nz |
| Bolicert | Bolivia | |
| CCOF California Certified Organic Farmers | United States | www.ccof.org |
| CCPB Consorzio per il Controllo dei Prodotti Biologici | Italy | www.ccpb.it |
| CERTIMEX | Mexico | |
| ECOCERT | France | www.ecocert.fr |
| Ecológica | Costa Rica | |
| IBD Instituto Biodinâmico | Brazil | www.ibd.com.br |
| ICS International Certification Services, Inc. also seen as Farm Verified Organic (FVO) | United States | www.ics-intl.com |
| ICS Japan, Inc. | Japan | www.pure-foods.co.jp/index2.html |
| IMC Instituto Mediterraneo di Certificazione | Italy | www.imcdotcom.com |
| IMO Institut für Marktökologie | Switzerland | www.imo.ch |
| IMO Institut für Marktökologie GmbH | Germany | www.imo.ch/imo/imo-frame.htm |
| INAC GmbH | Germany | www.inac-certification.com |
| JONA Japan Organic & Natural Foods Association | Japan | www.jona.organic.co.jp |
| KRAV Ekonomisk Förening | Sweden | www.krav.se |
| Lacon GmbH | Germany | www.lacon-institut.com |
| NASAA | Australia | www.nasaa.com.au |
| Naturland e.V. | Germany | www.naturland.de |
| OCIA Organic Crop Improvement Association | United States | www.ocia.org |
| OCIA Japan | Japan | www.ocia.org |
| OCPRO | Canada | www.ocpro-certcanada.com |
| OIA Organización Internacional Agropecuaria | Argentina | www.oia.com.ar |
| OFG Organic Farmers & Growers | United Kingdom | www.organicfarmers.uk.com |
| OMIC Overseas Merchandise Inspection Co. Ltd | Japan | www.omicnet.com |
| OTCO Oregon Tilth Certified Organic | United States | www.tilth.org |
| Qualité-France | France | www.qualite-france.com |
| QAI Quality Assurance International | United States | www.qai-inc.com |
| QAI Japan | Japan | www.qai-inc.com |
| QC&I GmbH | Germany | www.qci.de |
| SGS Nederland | Netherlands | www.sgs.nl |
| SKAL | Netherlands | www.skal.com |
| Soil Association | United Kingdom | www.soilassociation.org |

# Mapping technology in coffee marketing: GPS and GIS

Not only can authoritative information about where or how a coffee is grown contribute to making it a successful specialty or organic coffee, but it can also help prevent misrepresentation. Modern technology enables one to show on a map where a coffee is grown and the special characteristics of that area such as altitude, soils, vegetation type, slope, rainfall and special environmental attributes. By demonstrating this information in maps or graphics producers can show why their coffee is unique, or at least different from the majority of other coffees in their country or region. If in addition a producer seeks an authorized, enforceable 'appellation' for their coffee then they also need the spatial information necessary to legally or formally define the extent of the appellation zone and thus lead to the authentication of the appellation and the coffee in question. Technologies are now available and being applied in the field to help producers' and farmers' organizations address these issues and many more.

**Example.** The United States Agency for International Development (USAID) has funded a project with over 6,000 coffee producers in Peru that is using the following approach to address these issues.

- Data are being collected on how producers grow their coffee including varieties, altitude, application of pesticides, and other details that may be important for marketing or certifying. Extension agents collect data on practices and quality and whatever else defines the 'uniqueness' of the coffee at the farm, farmers group, or 'appellation zone' levels.

- The physical location of each farm is recorded by project extension agents using a *global positioning system* (GPS) unit.

- This information (production and location) is entered into a spatial database known as a *geographic information system* (GIS). This works like a more traditional database, but includes location information for each record.

- Maps are created showing not only where the farms are located, but also whatever characteristics are of interest about each farm and the coffee produced on that farm.

- The system is available on the Internet (*www.perucoffee.com*). Any user can look at the maps, zoom in and out to see details, or even ask to see all of the farms meeting some criteria (e.g. 'show me all farms in this zone growing arabica at an altitude over 1,000 m').

The system leads to better overall production management. At the same time, it provides information about the coffee to potential buyers, thereby assisting the marketing effort. Although individual farmers' need for such systems is limited, it can be useful for estates using specific estate logos or appellations.

## Some tools

The following list is not exhaustive.

- GPS – to get locations.
  - Inexpensive handhelds, e.g. Garmin, Magellan.
  - US$ 300 with antenna.
  - Easily learned; typically half a day for an extension agent.

- GIS – for creating a spatial database and mapping. Mapping software is optional. Could use regular database or even paper files to store data.
  - US$ 600–1,000 for the software, e.g. ArcView by ESRI. More likely used by cooperative, group of cooperatives, or large estate producer.
  - More rigorous training required.

- Internet – for staging maps on the Internet.
  - Static maps easily put into website.
  - Interactive maps (move around, zoom in and out, query based on particular characteristics of interest, etc.) require special software and training. Again, more likely used by cooperatives, groups of cooperatives or large estates.

## Outlook

New technologies are being developed to aid in data collection. Handheld devices already exist that combine spatial data (GPS locations) and traditional data collection (specific non-spatial information). These data are entered into the device and downloaded into the database at the end of each day or week. In the area of authentication – proving that a coffee actually comes from a specific area or source – technologies such as *smart tags* are also being developed. These tiny computerized tags, attached to each bag, can contain any set of information required to meet the authentification requirements, and could even be tracked by satellite if such control was necessary.

# Trade marking

A registered trademark or logo can help protect a successful product from being fraudulently duplicated. The Colombian Juan Valdez trademark needs no explanation or description: it is virtually known worldwide and is protected against fraudulent use because it is registered in all the main import markets. But the cost of developing and registering a trademark can be high and prospective applicants may even find that their favourite choice is already in use, or is too close to an existing registration to be accepted. The first step in the process is therefore to pay a firm of attorneys to conduct a search of existing registrations. Note also that the degree of protection offered by trademark legislation varies from country to country. Taken together these considerations suggest that trademarking should be considered only where the product warrants it, and where the degree of protection is such as to make the effort and cost worthwhile. But certainly, where a producer goes to the trouble and cost to create an appellation for their coffee and backs it up with registration in a GIS database, then trademarking of the name will complete the safeguarding process.

For more information on trademarking go to:

- European Union: *www.oami.eu.int*
- United States: *www.uspto.gov*
- Japan: *www.jpo.go.jp*

# Environment, sustainability, codes of conduct and social issues

Coffee has always been connected with emotions and opinions; therefore the debate about socio-economic aspects of coffee production is decades old already. One regular topic, especially in times when coffee prices are low or when there is political turmoil in coffee producing areas, is the working and living conditions of coffee farmers and workers on coffee plantations.

Advocacy groups and NGOs lobby for improved livelihoods and fair treatment of coffee growers and plantation workers. Some consumer activists wanted to change the system from within and started constructing alternatives to the dominant free market coffee economy. They began to import coffee, tea and other commodities from small producer organizations which they sold through so-called Third World shops.

Another step was the initiative in the Netherlands to develop a certification system and a label for coffee of such producers in order to create sales potential for these products in supermarket chains under the Fairtrade label (see later in this chapter). These systems engage the producers, who then rely on the market to pay a premium. But as a percentage of the total world trade in coffee these various initiatives still represent less than 1%.

**Rainforest Alliance Certification**, formerly known as ECO-OK, is another example. The certification effort of the Sustainable Agriculture Network in Central and South America, coordinated by the Rainforest Alliance, is based on the forestry certification model. Under this system a rigorous set of mutually agreed international standards are used to verify best management practices, leading to an operation that is sustainably managed. The conservation of natural resources, protection of biodiversity, respect for workers' rights and the commercial success of the farms are central themes. The standards for sustainable coffee farms include: a minimum number of native forest trees per hectare; no replacement of virgin forest with coffee plantings; preservation of watersheds; minimal use of agro-chemicals; promotion of biological controls; soil conservation; and protection of wildlife and natural resources. The Sustainable Agriculture Network's programme also emphasizes decent working conditions, adequate pay, access to proper housing and sanitation, and respect and fair treatment for workers. Details at *www.rainforest-alliance.org*.

**Biodynamic coffee.** This is usually high quality arabica at high premiums with a low market share. A well-known example is coffee from the Finca Irlanda (Chiapas, Mexico) where organic cultivation began in the 1960s. Biodynamic products are organic and can be marketed as such, but they meet even higher production standards and represent a true niche market. For more see *www.demeter-usa.org*.

**Shade grown coffee.** Especially in the United States and Canada, there is a market for so-called bird-friendly or shade grown coffee. Limited use of agro-chemicals is permitted and the emphasis is put on the conservation of shade trees on plantations in order to preserve bird life and biodiversity. Shade grown coffee is not the same as organic coffee but there are specific standards and a certification system has been developed by the Smithsonian Migratory Bird Center (see *www.natzoo.si.edu.smbc*) and other institutions and NGOs in Canada, the United States and Mexico. Shade grown represents a step along the way towards environmentally sustainable coffee. So far the market for such coffees is small and limited to North America.

A more general development is that the mainstream coffee industry is increasingly accepting responsibility for the conditions under which the coffee is produced. Coupled with growing interest in and support for environmental causes in importing countries generally this has led to the introduction of terms such as environment-friendly or environmentally sustainable coffee. (For a good introduction to the subject go to *www.consumerscouncil.org*. and look for the Conservation Principles for Coffee Production.)

## Sustainability

Sustainability has been defined by some as 'meeting the needs of the present generation without compromising the ability of future generations to meet their needs'. It can then be further defined in social, ethical and environmental dimensions with biodiversity perhaps as the key measure of environmental sustainability in the natural world. This concept appeals to coffee growers and consumers who are not necessarily interested in, or who see no rationale to the production of organic coffee as such, perhaps because they believe that low yields coupled with increasing availability of organic coffee will always prevent small growers from generating the high incomes that some proponents of organic coffee production believe can be achieved. Others do not see the market potential as sufficiently large, and still others simply believe that it is possible to achieve more or less the same objectives without going the organic way, which for mainstream producers would be very difficult if not entirely impossible to do.

This is not the place to pronounce for or against any of these arguments but, if a production process maintains biodiversity then, presumably, one may consider that it sustains rather than harms the environment. If so, and when linked with consideration for social and ethical issues, this concept presents a broad alternative for the more directly focused objectives of individual labels that may appeal to pure niche markets, traditionally not available for mainstream coffees, and that will encompass the more complete global coffee industry at large: growers, roasters and consumers alike.

## Integrated farming systems

Integrated farming systems are one such approach and might in the end be the most promising: minimize the use and negative effects of agro-chemicals. Basically this means that in all phases of production and processing one tries to minimize the impact on the environment. This approach does not exclude the use of agro-chemicals, but rather attempts to reduce their use to a minimum. Moreover, more attention is given to the reduction of energy consumption, packaging materials, and so on. Documentation and certification can be achieved within the framework of the ISO 14001 system, with the producer or processor documenting where and how in each step of the production and processing system they are reducing the environmental impact (see *www.iso.org*).

## The European Retail Protocol for Good Agricultural Practice

The European Retail Protocol for Good Agricultural Practice (Eurepgap: see *www.eurep.org*) was originally introduced by European retail chains for sourcing their fresh produce purchases. Work is underway to bring their coffee supply under the same scheme, more appropriately called a *code of conduct* or a *code of practice*, and this is expected to happen in 2003.

Eurepgap forms the basis of this code. The protocol was established by over 30 leading European retailers working together in the European Retailers Produce Working Group (EUREP) to harmonize their agricultural standards for fruits and vegetables. The protocol is now an established part of their sourcing strategy and enjoys wide acceptance. It is consumer-driven and provides an assurance of basic good agricultural practices and social conditions.

## Codes of conduct

Codes of conduct or codes of practice such as Eurepgap are a good example of how purchasing power translates into change at the producing end. The retailer demands certain assurances of the roaster who in turn requires their suppliers to conform. This is not to say that all this has come about entirely spontaneously: the 1990s saw a number of food scares that have undoubtedly focused consumer attention on the how and what of the food and drink they consume. But even so, as in some other industries, one can probably mark the 1990s as a turning point for the policies of the larger roasters with respect to social responsibility. Pressure through lobbying and campaigns may have contributed to this attitude change. At the same time, the market share for roasted coffee under the Transfair and Fairtrade seals reached 10,000 tons for the first time in 1995. As an example, since Starbucks introduced Transfair coffee to the United States market in 1999, about another 70 coffee retailers in the United States have become licensed to sell Fairtrade (as at early 2002).

An increasing number of individual companies and associations such as the Specialty Coffee Associations of America and of Europe are engaged in a variety of activities related to what may broadly be called codes of conduct. Some of these are listed here by way of example; this listing is by no means exhaustive.

1.    A campaign by the Guatemala Labour Education Project (US-GLEP, now US-LEAP) led the United States-based Starbucks coffee company to create a company code of conduct in 1995. In 1998 Starbucks began its '98-99 Framework for Action', under which it launched different programmes aimed at community building and improving conditions in coffee

producing regions. Since then **Starbucks** has also introduced its **Preferred Supplier pilot programme** (late 2001), which provides financial incentives for producers of high quality coffee that meet important social, environmental and economic criteria. Producers meeting all criteria are awarded Preferred Supplier status. For details of these sourcing guidelines in English and Spanish go to *www.starbucks.com*.

2.  In late 1998, the Fairtrade movement and other groups, through widespread publicity, urged action to improve the social conditions of workers on coffee plantations. This eventually resulted in the formation of an informal working group on ethical sourcing within the European Coffee Federation (ECF). The subject was also introduced in the ICO's Private Sector Consultative Board.

3.  The coffee division of Ahold, one of the largest retail chains in the world and headquartered in the Netherlands, initiated work on a system of independent supplier certification as early as 1997 through a pilot project that aimed to develop a 'guarantee that coffee was produced responsibly in terms of social, environmental and food safety issues'. This was done by adapting the Eurepgap fresh produce protocol to coffee production, linked to an independent certification capability. This was followed by the establishment in Latin America and the Netherlands of the **Utz Kapeh Foundation.** The Ahold company relinquished ownership of the project to the foundation and informed all its coffee suppliers that it was moving towards purchasing only Utz Kapeh certified coffee.

**Utz Kapeh certification** is now available to any interested parties, roasters and growers alike. The foundation authorizes third party certifiers who in turn must have Eurepgap accreditation. Interested growers (individuals or groups) receive technical assistance to help them implement the changes necessary to achieve accreditation. By mid 2002 certified coffee was available from Bolivia, Brazil, Colombia, Costa Rica, Guatemala, Honduras, Indonesia, Peru and Viet Nam. Go to *www.utzkapeh.org*.

What appears to distinguish this still relatively under-publicized initiative from all others is that it offers a way forward towards some form of market-driven recognition that is open to all who can qualify, is available to both mainstream and specialty coffee, and precludes no one from participating. Other retail chains, for example Carrefour of France, are taking in the organic standards of IFOAM and the social criteria of the Fairtrade movement.

4.  In early 2002 the United States firm of Procter & Gamble, owner of the Folgers and Millstone coffee companies, announced a long-term US$ 1.5 million alliance with the international non-profit organization **TechnoServe** to boost the competitiveness of small-scale producers in selected Latin American coffee producing countries and, where appropriate, to explore alternatives to coffee production. TechnoServe itself, founded in 1968, has been involved with providing small-scale growers with coffee production, processing and marketing assistance for a number of years. It is active in El Salvador, Honduras, Nicaragua, Peru, Ghana, Kenya, Mozambique, South Africa, Uganda and the United Republic of Tanzania. For more information go to *www.technoserve.org*.

5.  There are also other, smaller but more directly focused programmes, such as the well-known **Coffee Kids** initiative in the United States (*www.coffeekids.org*), that also work successfully to improve the lives of coffee growers, their workers and their families.

Unfortunately, space does not permit more such individual initiatives to be reviewed here.

The European Coffee Federation is now producing guidelines, to be adopted by its members and to be endorsed by relevant NGOs. The mainstream industry welcomes this initiative since internationally recognized standards that take on board ILO principles, for example, will ensure a level playing field while avoiding label and perception confusion among consumers. The significant change here is that whereas previously such initiatives originated from producing countries (with NGO support), they are now increasingly being generated by the mainstream industry in consuming countries where food retail chains demand more and more guarantees from their suppliers that the goods they provide are responsibly produced. This suggests that, eventually, proof of compliance with a generally accepted code of conduct is likely to become a pre-condition for unrestricted market access.

For further information on social accountability issues (SA8000 framework) see *www.cepaa.org*, the website of the Council on Economic Priorities Accreditation Agency.

## Fairtrade

As a consequence of growing awareness of differences in development between North and South, small groups of consumers organized so-called Third World shops, which sold products from developing countries that were purchased under just conditions from small producers. Initially, such shops were simply a table in the church after Sunday service but gradually they have evolved and, as in the case of the Fairtrade movement, have become professional franchise organizations with turnovers of several million United States dollars. Coffee typically constitutes up to 50% of their sales as they usually supply a lot of coffee to institutional markets and caterers.

Originally consumer coffees from such alternative trade organizations were sold only through their own outlets or by mail order operated by volunteers. Usually they reached only the people who were prepared to make a detour to buy their coffee in a Third World shop instead of in their normal supermarket.

Therefore, at the request of small growers in Mexico (UCIRI), in 1988 a Netherlands NGO, Solidaridad, took the initiative to start the Max Havelaar certification system for *Fairtrade coffee* (and subsequently also for other products) with the goal of bringing these coffees into conventional supermarket channels.

### *Objectives*

The Fairtrade initiative aims to enable smallholder producers of coffee (and cocoa, tea, honey, bananas, orange juice and sugar) to improve their conditions of trade, resulting in more equitable and more stable prices.[15] Coffee prices are by nature unstable, especially since the disappearance of the old ICO price support agreements, and during the closing decades of the twentieth century extremely low, sub-economical coffee and cocoa prices caused serious economic and social problems. Many growers could not even recoup their production costs, let alone make a decent living. The Max Havelaar Foundation was established in the Netherlands in 1988, and since then another 16 countries have followed suit (see table 18 below). In 1997 the different national institutions established an umbrella organization known as FLO (Fairtrade Labelling Organizations International) with offices in Bonn, Germany. FLO, together with its member organizations, works towards improvement in the unequal distribution of wealth between North and South.

The objective is to assist without patronizing anyone by providing the instruments necessary to enable small growers to take their development into their own hands, as independent producers and not as recipients of occasional gestures of largesse. This is achieved by incorporating in the producer price not only the cost of production but also the cost of providing basic necessities such as running water, health care and education, and the cost of environmentally friendly farming systems. Consumer support for more equitable North–South trading conditions is then linked to participating growers through the by now well-known Fairtrade labels on retail packaging in consuming countries. Simply put, the higher prices consumers pay for Fairtrade products reach the grower through a combination of guaranteed minimum prices and premiums.

---

15    Currently, Fairtrade efforts in coffee and cocoa are concentrated on smallholder producers only. Conversely, in tea, bananas and sugar the emphasis is mainly on estates (improving conditions for the labour force).

| Table 18 | Sales of Fairtrade roasted coffee, 1999–2001 (in kilograms) | | |
|---|---|---|---|
| **Market** | **1999** | **2000** | **2001** |
| **TOTAL** | **11,816,363** | **12,817,973** | **14,396,353** |
| Austria | 283,843 | 299,484 | 332,261 |
| Belgium | 477,236 | 547,853 | 582,203 |
| Canada | 77,600 | 154,224 | 258,124 |
| Denmark | 695,361 | 742,437 | 697,070 |
| Finland | 35,600 | 90,648 | 97,000 |
| France | 270,300 | 495,425 | 945,000 |
| Germany | 3,332,237 | 3,098,440 | 3,127,650 |
| Ireland | 40,490 | 55,000 | 62,000 |
| Italy | 353,347 | 398,511 | 457,000 |
| Japan | 6,200 | 6,600 | 6,569 |
| Luxembourg | 69,316 | 64,129 | 77,320 |
| Netherlands | 3,185,513 | 3,101,923 | 3,104,681 |
| Norway | 54,700 | 125,313 | 178,851 |
| Sweden | 218,005 | 216,886 | 253,569 |
| Switzerland | 1,424,584 | 1,381,860 | 1,306,415 |
| United Kingdom | 1,237,060 | 1,332,240 | 1,647,640 |
| United States | 54,971 | 707,000 | 1,263,000 |

*Source:* Max Havelaar.
Note: In addition there may be sales (of green coffee) not necessarily reflected in the above.

The FLO role in this is to:

• Promote Fairtrade coffee in consumer markets.

• Identify and assist eligible groups of small growers to become inscribed in the FLO coffee producers' register, i.e. to obtain FLO certification.

• Verify adherence by all concerned to the Fairtrade principles, thus guaranteeing the label's integrity.

The Fairtrade labels aim to make the initiative and the growers behind it *visible* and therefore *marketable* on a sustained basis. The labels enable FLO and others to provide sustained publicity and support where it counts most – in the consuming countries – for example by building a public image of quality, reliability and respect for socio-economic and environmental concerns that consumers recognize and appreciate. Fairtrade does not aim to replace anyone in the traditional marketing cycle and works on the basis that there is a place for each provided all accept the Fairtrade goal of selling the largest possible volume of smallholder coffee at a fair price: fair for growers and consumers alike. The labels guarantee for the consumer adherence to this principle while leaving production, purchasing, processing, marketing and distribution where it belongs, in the coffee industry.

Fairtrade is a certification programme that all smallholders and roasters who satisfy the criteria can join. But in the end success in the retail market depends on consumer support. By end 2001 some 200 groups were inscribed, representing approximately 500,000 smallholders. As yet much of this production cannot be absorbed by the Fairtrade labels;

some groups manage to sell perhaps 50% of their output but others only about 10% so the supply potential exceeds the demand. Despite these limitations the label is well established in a number of markets and additional growth can be expected, not only in consuming countries but also in producing countries with a substantial home market (for example, Mexico). Accelerating sales growth is expected especially in the United States market but for aspiring grower organizations to share in Fairtrade growth in any import market they will first have to achieve FLO certification – see details on page 89.

## Using Fairtrade labels

Coffee to be sold under a Fairtrade label must be purchased directly from groups inscribed in the FLO Coffee Producers' Register. The purchase price must be set in accordance with Fairtrade conditions of which the following are the most significant:

- **Arabicas:** the New York 'C' market (NYKC) shall be the basis plus or minus the prevailing differential for the relevant quality, FOB origin, net shipped weight. The price shall be established in United States dollars per pound.

- **Robustas:** the London Terminal market (LIFFE) shall be the basis plus or minus the prevailing differential for the relevant quality, basis FOB origin, net shipped weight. The price shall be established in United States dollars per metric ton.

- These prices shall then be increased by a fixed premium of 5 cts/lb.

- For certified organic coffee with officially recognized certification, that will be sold as such, a further premium of 15 cts/lb per pound green coffee will be due.

- Guaranteed minimum prices have been set as per table 19, differentiated according to the type and origin of the coffee.

| Table 19 | Guaranteed minimum Fairtrade coffee prices, in cents per pound | | | |
|---|---|---|---|---|
| **Type of coffee** | **Regular** | | **Certified organic** | |
| | **Central America, Mexico, Africa, Asia** | **South America, Caribbean area** | **Central America, Mexico, Africa, Asia** | **South America, Caribbean area** |
| Washed arabica | 126 | 124 | 141 | 139 |
| Unwashed arabica | 120 | 120 | 135 | 135 |
| Washed robusta | 110 | 110 | 125 | 125 |
| Unwashed robusta | 106 | 106 | 121 | 121 |

**Note:** Prices are FOB port of origin, net shipped weight.

In addition, if the producer so requests, the roaster or buyer undertakes to facilitate the coffee producer's access to credit facilities at the beginning of the harvest season, for up to 60% of the value of the contracted coffee at Fairtrade conditions, at regular international interest rates. The credit will be reimbursed through shipment of the coffee. Given the need on all sides for continuity and reliability roasters and buyers will as much as possible encourage long-term relationships. Finally, roasters and buyers have to accept and facilitate external control on their compliance with FLO conditions.

**Minimum tonnage**

Mention has already been made of the difficulty of shipping small lots that do not fill an entire container. FLO itself does not impose minimum volumes on grower organizations but for practical reasons shipments must be in container size lots, meaning a minimum exportable production of about 18 tons.

In practice, small producer groups in some countries do manage to combine shipments so as to fill a container, for example by establishing an umbrella organization to coordinate this and other activities to achieve the necessary economies of scale. FLO's start-up requirement also serves a developmental objective: taking into account membership and other characteristics, producer groups should at least have the potential to reach a volume of business that will achieve sustainable development impact.

**Applying for FLO certification**

FLO certification provides access (*www.fairtrade.net*) to all FLO member organizations. Participating organizations of small coffee growers must meet criteria consisting of requirements against which the producers will actually be monitored. (Look for Generic Fairtrade Standards for Small Farmers' Organizations on the same website.) Criteria include:

- Minimum entry requirements which all must meet when joining Fairtrade, or within a specified period.

- Progress requirements, i.e. show improvement over the longer term.

**Application procedure.** The applying organization directs its request to FLO International. The certification unit of FLO sends an application pack to the applicant, containing general information on FLO and the Fairtrade market, FLO standards, detailed information on the initial certification process and the application form. If the first evaluation, based on the application form, is positive, the applying organization will be visited by an FLO inspector who will examine the organization on the basis of the minimum requirements of FLO. All relevant information is then presented to the FLO Certification Committee charged with the certification of new producer groups. Once approved the certification will be formalized by means of a signed producer agreement with FLO and a certificate indicating the duration of validity of the certification (to be renewed every two years).

## CHAPTER 4

# Contracts – concluding and executing

International trade in coffee would not be possible without general agreement on the basic conditions of sale. To this end the coffee trade has developed standard forms of contract of which the most frequently used are those issued by the European Coffee Federation (ECF) and the Green Coffee Association (GCA) of New York. Although many details must be still agreed before a contract is concluded, the basic conditions of sale can be covered simply by stipulating the applicable standard form of contract. Even so, an offer to sell (or a bid to buy) must stipulate the quality, quantity and price, the shipment period, the conditions of sale, the period during which the offer or bid is firm (valid), and so on.

The first part of this chapter deals with what one must know and do before any contracts can be concluded; the second part deals with the standard forms of contract themselves.

## Commercial or 'front office' aspects

### The quality

Quality can be specified in any one of a number of ways.

**On description.** The quality will usually correspond to a known set of parameters relating to country of origin, green appearance and liquor quality. Most of the descriptive parameters are open to varying interpretations.

For example, in the description 'Country XYZ arabica grade one, fair average quality, crop 2002, even roast, clean cup', the only real specifics are that the coffee must be of the 2002 crop in country XYZ and that the bean size and defect count should correspond to what country XYZ stipulates for grade one arabica.

**Fair average quality (FAQ)** essentially means that the coffee will be representative of the average quality of the crop, but there is no defined standard for this.

**Even roast** implies that the roasted coffee will not contain too many pales (yellow beans) and will be of reasonably even appearance.

**Clean cup** indicates that the liquor should not present any unclean taste or off-flavour, but otherwise says nothing about the cup 'quality'. Nevertheless, buyers know roughly what the cup quality ought to be and, for example, if the cup were to be completely flat or lifeless, they would argue that this was not consistent with fair average quality for country XYZ.

The trade in robusta is largely based on descriptions. These convey the quality being sold fairly well because the liquor quality of robusta does not normally fluctuate as widely as that of arabica. Descriptions greatly facilitate the trade in coffee but it should never be forgotten that the roaster (the end-user) will always consider the liquor quality when assessing the overall quality of a coffee.

The 'quality' represented by FAQ will vary from season to season. 'FAQ of the season' means the quality must be comparable to the average quality shipped during that crop year; arbitrators will judge any claims on that basis. If quality tends to vary widely within a country and a season, the seller may go further and stipulate 'FAQ of the season at the time and place of shipment'.

Because descriptions provide a minimum of detail concerning quality they are seldom if ever used for the trade in high quality coffee. In addition, buyers know that different sellers have their own interpretation of FAQ and so prefer to deal with shippers whose interpretation is acceptable to them. However, a trader wishing to short-sell XYZ arabica grade one FAQ forward does not necessarily know in advance which shipper or exporter he will later buy from. In this case the term 'first class shipper' can be added to the description, thereby implying that a reputable exporter will ship the coffee. But the term 'first class' is open to interpretation as well and so the contract may instead stipulate the names of exporters of whom the buyer approves, one of whom must eventually ship the coffee. Large roasters are quite flexible about the origin of standard or commercial grade coffee, and to widen their purchasing options often leave the seller free to deliver an agreed quality from one of a number of specified origins and shippers.

***Subject to approval of sample (SAS).*** This is one way to eliminate most of the quality risk inherent in buying unseen coffee from unknown shippers, as buyers are not obliged to accept any shipment that they have not first approved. SAS obliges the exporter to provide an approval sample before shipment. There are three generally recognized possibilities.

- **SAS, no approval–no sale.** If the sample is not approved the contract is automatically cancelled.

- **SAS, repeat basis.** If the first sample is rejected, a second or even a third sample may be sent. Sometimes the contract will mention how many subsequent samples can be submitted. This option provides maximum quality security without immediately jeopardizing the contract, and works well in long-standing relationships.

- **SAS, two or three samples for buyer's choice.** When the buyer's quality requirements are very specific, and in order to save time, multiple samples may be submitted at the same time. To avoid confusion such contracts should stipulate whether repeat samples may be sent or whether no approval means no sale.

Theoretically, an exporter who feels aggrieved by what seems to be an unreasonable (intentional) rejection and cancellation could declare a dispute and proceed to arbitration. The chance of success would however be extremely slim if not non-existent, not least because an arbitration panel might rule it has no jurisdiction over what was in essence a purely conditional contract that never became binding (because the buyer did not approve a sample). Exporters should therefore be fairly selective when agreeing to sell subject to approval of sample.

***Stock-lot sample.*** Selling on stock-lot sample avoids potential approval problems. The sample represents a parcel that is already in stock so there should be no discrepancy between the sample and the shipment, including the screen size (even if the screen size was not stipulated). Day-to-day business would become too cumbersome if one insisted on stock-lot samples for all deals, but for newly established exporters or for those wishing to break into a niche market or to trade top quality coffees, stock-lots usually are the best route.

Once a satisfactory delivery has been made, an exporter may wish to sell a similar quality again. Rather than send new samples, the exporter may offer 'quality equal to stock-lot X'; this guarantees that the coffee is of comparable quality, suitable for the same end-use as the original purchase. The words 'equal to' must be used because the sample was not drawn from the new lot of coffee. If the exporter feels that the quality is very similar but that a little latitude is needed as to the coffee's bean size or green appearance, they may say 'quality about equal to stock-lot X'. Usually, such business is only between parties in a long-standing relationship who know each other well.

*Type.* Once a few transactions have been satisfactorily concluded, buyer and seller may decide to make the quality in question into a type. Both parties are now confident that the quality will be respected and business can proceed without samples (although some roasters will still insist on pre-shipment samples). Usually the quality of a type (like a recipe) is kept confidential between shipper and buyer. Top or exemplary coffees are mostly sold on sample or type basis whereas medium and standard qualities are more often traded on description.

## The shipping period

The most often encountered trade terminology includes:

*Date of shipment:* the 'on board' or 'shipped' date of the bill of lading. Contracts should always stipulate from which port(s) shipment is to be made.

*Spot goods* have already arrived overseas, e.g. available ex warehouse Hamburg.

*Afloat:* coffee that is en route, i.e. on board a vessel that has sailed but has not yet arrived.

*Named vessel (or substitute):* shipment must be made on a specified vessel. Adding 'or substitute' ensures that shipment can also be made if the shipping line cancels the named vessel or replaces it with another. Many contracts simply stipulate the shipping line that shall carry the goods.

*Immediate shipment:* shipment within 15 calendar days counted from the date of contract.

*Prompt shipment:* shipment within 30 calendar days counted from the date of contract.

*Shipment February* (or any other month): shipment is to be made on any day of that month (single month); *February/March seller's option* means shipment will be made on any day within those two months (double month).

The shorter the shipping period, the shorter the roaster's exposure to market fluctuations and the more precise physical and financial planning can be. Buyers generally look for less exposure, and double months are not popular. After all, shipment March/April means that shipment can be made at any time during a 61-day period, which does not go well with the increasingly prevalent just-in-time (JIT) philosophy (see chapter 5, Logistics, for more on this). Sellers in landlocked countries or those with inefficient shipping connections are often forced to sell on double months. By contrast, countries as Brazil and Colombia can guarantee coffee to be available in Europe within 21 days from the date of sale (10 days or so for the United States). Inability to offer precise shipping options (named vessel, immediate or prompt shipment, first half of a month) is a marketing handicap.

## Delivery commitment

Offers and contracts must stipulate the point at which the exporter will have fulfilled their commitment to deliver, that is, the point at which risk and responsibility are transferred to the buyer.

*Free on board (FOB):* the goods will be loaded at the seller's expense onto a vessel at the location stipulated in the contract, e.g. FOB Santos. The seller's responsibilities and risk end when the goods cross the ship's rail, and from then on the buyer bears all charges and risk. (Under an ECC (European Contract for Coffee) FOB contract the buyer is responsible for insuring the goods from the last place of storage ahead of loading on board, e.g. the port warehouse, but this is not the case under the GCA FOB contract.) Most coffee contracts are FOB.

***Free on truck (FOT)*** or ***free on rail (FOR):*** in landlocked countries the sale is often FOT or FOR, with buyers themselves arranging transport to the nearest ocean port and onward carriage by sea. International transporters, usually linked with shipping lines, often offer one-stop services, taking the goods in hand in Kampala, Uganda, and delivering them to Hamburg, Germany, for instance, using a single document known as a combined bill of lading covering both inland and maritime transportation.[16] The exporter provides the customs clearance documentation.

***Free carrier (FCA):*** risk of loss is transferred when the coffee is delivered to the freight carrier at the place of embarkation. All freight charges, including loading onto an ocean vessel, railcar, trailer or truck (combined bill of lading), are payable by the buyer. The exporter provides the customs clearance documentation.

***Cost and freight (C&F*** or ***CFR):*** the seller is responsible for paying costs and freight (but not insurance) to the agreed destination.

***Cost, insurance, freight (CIF):*** the seller is also responsible for taking out and paying the marine insurance up to the agreed point of discharge. Very rarely if ever used nowadays.

In all cases it is the seller's responsibility to deliver the shipping documents to the buyer. When a parcel is loaded on board ship, a mate's receipt is issued to the ship's agent. This is the legal basis for the bill of lading (B/L), which should be prepared and issued immediately. Shippers are entitled to the B/L as soon as the goods have been loaded. Some agents release them only once the vessel has sailed, but this is incorrect and causes unnecessary cost.

The International Chamber of Commerce's *Guide to Incoterms* (2000) contains a more detailed description of these and other shipping terms. However, the standard contracts used in the coffee trade all state or imply that under an FOB sale too the seller is responsible for booking freight space, arranging shipment and producing a full set of shipping documents. *These stipulations in standard coffee contracts differ from, and supersede, the Incoterms definition of FOB.*

## Ocean freight

Most coffee contracts are FOB – the receivers pay the freight. Receivers prefer this because they can negotiate rates of freight which individual exporters or producing countries may be unable to obtain. For this reason bills of lading do not always indicate the freight charge, or simply state 'freight as per agreement'.

As they are liable to pay the freight, receivers consider that they should also negotiate the rates (and argue, indirectly, that they are in fact better placed to do so). This may be so, but whenever the freight from a particular port increases buyers adjust their cost calculation for the origin in question as they calculate the cost of all coffee on the basis *landed port* or *roasting plant of destination*. If the freight rate from a particular country increases, the prices bid for coffee from that origin (the differential) will eventually compensate for this if freights from comparable origins have not also risen. This because the market compares like with like, that is, the landed cost. Ultimately therefore it is the producers who pay the freight charges. However, without the present arrangements some freight rates would likely be higher. (See also chapter 5, Logistics.)

---

16    Unless special arrangements have been made with the carrier, such shipments must be re-stuffed at the port of shipment if an LCL bill of lading is required.

*Terminal handling charges (THC)* are an important part of container transport costs and can vary considerably between shipping lines, sometimes to the point where an apparently attractive rate of freight is in fact not attractive at all. Shippers should keep themselves informed of the THC raised directly or indirectly by individual shipping lines at the ports they load from as they can face unexpected costs if buyers specify a line whose freight is low (buyer's advantage) but whose THC are high (shipper's disadvantage).

## Weights

Most standard forms of contract stipulate that natural loss in weight exceeding a certain percentage is to be refunded by the sellers. This is known as the weight franchise. Coffee is hygroscopic, which means that it attracts or loses moisture depending on climatic conditions. It may therefore lose a little weight during storage and transport. To counter this weight loss, a number of exporters have traditionally packed a little more per bag than they invoice. This helps to ensure that arrival weights are as close to the agreed shipping weight as possible. Buyers know from experience what losses in weight to expect from most origins and take this into account when calculating the cost landed destination or roasting plant. However, shipping in bulk has greatly reduced weight losses and such a franchise is no longer necessary.

*Net shipped weights:* the weights established at the time of shipment are final, subject of course to the stipulations of the underlying standard form of contract.

*Net delivered weights* or *net landed weights:* the goods will be reweighed upon arrival and final payment will be made on the basis of the weights then established.

If buyers are suspicious about the accuracy of the shipping weights they may require an independent weigher to supervise the weighing. Sellers may stipulate the same when selling basis net delivered weights or when weights are disputed and reweighing is ordered.

## Conditions of payment

Usually, and advisedly so, the conditions of payment will have been agreed on in advance and will therefore already be known to both parties, especially if the business relationship has existed for some time. But when offering to a new buyer the payment conditions must be specified. (See also chapter 6, E-commerce and supply chain management.)

*Payment against letter of credit (L/C)* requires the buyer to establish an L/C before shipment is effected. A letter of credit is an undertaking from the buyer's bank to the exporter's bank that payment will be made against certain documents such as the invoice, certificate of origin, weight note, certificate of quality and bill of lading (for sea transport) or waybill (for road or rail transport). The exporter should check that the documents specified in the letter of credit are obtainable. Sometimes buyers require verification of documents by an embassy or consulate not located in the exporter's country, or they may include documents which the exporter is not contractually required to provide.

The timing of letters of credit is very important. The L/C must be available for the exporter's use from day one of the agreed shipping period, and it must remain valid for negotiation for 21 calendar days after the last date that shipment is permitted to be made. Watch the timing very carefully indeed: once the expiry date has passed, the letter of credit is only as good as the buyer's willingness to extend it.

If the terms and conditions of an L/C are not met, the exporter's bank will not pay the exporter until the buyer has confirmed that all is in order. This may involve sending the documents abroad without payment. If at that stage the buyer refuses to make payment, the exporter may be left with an unpaid shipment in some foreign port. The importance of conforming to all the conditions in a letter of credit cannot be stressed enough. Exporters should always consult their bankers before they assume that a letter of credit is acceptable.

*An ordinary or unconfirmed letter of credit is nothing more than an uncertain promise to pay if certain documentation is submitted.*

An ***irrevocable letter of credit*** cannot be cancelled once established. The exporter can be certain that funds will be available if valid documents are presented. Even so, the exporter's bank may pay the exporter only when it has received the funds from the bank that established the letter of credit. This can create problems if for example the buyer argues that the documents are not correct or the buyer's bank is slow in making payment.

Under a ***confirmed and irrevocable letter of credit*** the exporter's bank confirms that payment will be effected upon the timely presentation of valid documents without reference to the establishing bank. By adding its confirmation, the exporter's bank therefore guarantees payment. If the negotiating bank discovers a minor discrepancy in the documents such as a spelling error, it may still negotiate them providing the exporter signs a guarantee that in case of refusal by the buyer, the exporter will refund the payment received until the matter is settled.

Whenever exporters feel that letters of credit are required, they should insist that they are confirmed and irrevocable. Even then, extreme care must always be taken to ensure that all details are respected, even to the spelling of words and shipping marks.

***Payment net cash against documents (NCAD or CAD) on first presentation:*** the buyer is expected to make payment when the documents are first presented. Exporters will agree to this method of payment if they know their buyers well and have confidence in their financial strength and integrity. An exporter can submit the documents through the intermediary of its own bank, which then asks a correspondent bank abroad to present them to the buyer, collect the payment and remit the funds, less all collection costs, to the instructing bank for the account of the exporter. (This includes the (reasonable) charges raised by the buyer's bank because that bank is now acting on the instructions of the seller's bank and, therefore, the seller. See ECC Article 19(d) and the relevant section in the GCA contract.) In this way the documents remain within the banking system until payment has been received, thus ensuring that the exporter does not lose control of the goods. If the exporter is in need of prompt payment they can ask their own bank to advance them all or part of the invoice value. This is known as negotiation of documents. The exporter remains responsible for the transaction, of course: if the buyer does not pay, the exporter's bank will demand its money back.

***Documents in trust.*** Assuming the exporter's bank does not object, documents may also be sent direct to the buyer with the request to make payment upon receipt of the documents. This is known as sending documents in trust. As the term implies, the decision to do this depends entirely on the trust the two parties place in each other.

In ***payment net cash against documents upon arrival,*** payment falls due when the goods arrive at the port of destination. When selling on this basis an exporter should always stipulate that payment must be made after expiry of a certain period, whether the goods have arrived or not. Otherwise there will clearly be problems if for some reason the goods arrive six months late or do not arrive at all because the vessel has been lost. Contracts should therefore *always* stipulate 'payment net cash against shipping documents upon arrival of the goods at [destination] but not later than 30 [or 60] days after date of bill of lading'.

## Payment and credit policy

Exporters must decide for themselves which payment conditions to accept. They must assess the financial status of their buyers and act accordingly. Some information can be obtained from bank references which indicate a client's creditworthiness. Although such reports are useful, they cannot provide all the desired information nor do they place any responsibility on the bank that issues them. Exporters using borrowed working capital are usually subject to stringent conditions concerning the buyers they can sell to, and on what payment conditions.

When entering into contracts and deciding on payment terms, sellers should investigate the identity of their buyers. International trading groups often work through foreign and local subsidiaries whose commitments are not necessarily guaranteed by the parent firm, even though they may trade under the same or similar names. When in doubt a seller can demand a guarantee from the parent firm that it accepts responsibility for the contracts with a given subsidiary.

In some countries the monetary authorities dictate payment policy for exports, for instance by insisting that all exports must be covered by letters of credit to avoid possible loss of foreign exchange. This kind of blanket regulation results in some of the world's largest corporations with impeccable credentials being asked to establish L/Cs. Many buyers simply refuse to establish letters of credit, and those that do establish them calculate the cost and inconvenience involved. Ultimately therefore it is the grower who pays for such bureaucratic attitudes.

## Scope and validity of an offer (or bid)

The scope and validity of an offer (or bid) must be specified – when does acceptance constitute a firm commitment for both parties?

An exporter wishing only to publicize a potential availability at an approximate price uses terminology such as *price idea* or *we offer/quote subject to availability* or *subject unsold*. To the buyer this suggests there is a good chance of obtaining the coffee in question if the indicated price is agreed to. Although the exporter is not bound to sell, the buyer has some reason to be annoyed if the exporter refuses to do so for no obvious reason (e.g. was simply fishing for price information).

A *firm offer*, however, does commit the seller if the buyer accepts the offer within a reasonable time. 'Reasonable' is open to interpretation, so sellers must stipulate a time after which the offer lapses. The same applies to bids from buyers: these too must be specific. *Subject to immediate reply* says that the reply should be immediate, but even 'immediate' is not precise. It is always better to say, for example, 'subject to reply here by 3 p.m. our time'. The choice of time limit depends on the situation of the exporter and the type of buyer to whom the offer is addressed. An exporter who is keen to sell may wish to try various markets at the same time. If they have only limited stocks of the coffee in question they cannot make multiple firm offers and will instead offer subject to availability or subject unsold. Alternatively, they can make firm offers for short periods to individual buyers by telephone or, increasingly, by email. Conversely, they can give a buyer or, more probably, an agent an entire day to work an offer, but the exact time at which the offer expires should always be stated.

Modern communications offer almost instantaneous exchanges, especially through email and electronic commerce, enabling exporters to contact many potential buyers within short periods of time. It is not only the face of trade that is changing, but also the methodology and terminology. (See chapter 6, E-commerce and supply chain management.) *But what will not change is that acceptance, verbal or otherwise, within the time limit of a firm offer or bid constitutes a firm and binding contract.* Disputes can be submitted to arbitration but the best approach is to ensure that the wording of offers or bids is clear and precise. For example: 'We offer firm for reply here today by 5 p.m. our time 1,000 bags XYZ arabica grade one as per sample 101 at United States cents 100/lb, FOB [port], NSW (net shipping weight), shipment November/December 2002 our option, payment NCAD first presentation'. This assumes that the applicable standard form of contract has previously been agreed; for a new buyer the contract should therefore be mentioned as well.

*Counter offers:* if a buyer counter bids a lower price against a firm offer this automatically releases the seller. The offer is no longer binding, because the buyer has *rejected* it by counter offering. If the seller rejects the counter offer the buyer cannot subsequently revert to the original offer: when they countered, that firm offer lapsed unless of course the seller agrees to reinstate it.

## Using intermediaries

*Agents.* Modern communications, especially email, permit regular contact with many more clients than was the case just ten years ago and the traditional agency function is increasingly making way for direct trade. Even so, it is not always feasible to deal directly with individual buyers in more than just a few markets, especially when time differences come into play, and many exporters still use agents.

A local agent is on the spot, speaks the language, knows the buyers and usually can discuss more than just the one origin most exporters represent. This makes an agent an interesting conversation partner who is more likely to get a buyer's attention. And for exporters, agents provide a two-way information flow because they know local conditions and often gain insight into the activities of competitors.

Agency agreements must make it clear what each party is permitted and expected to do. If an agent is given exclusivity in a given market (sole agency) then the exporter can demand that the agent does not market also for any of the exporter's direct competitors. Larger agency firms sometimes represent a 'stable' of exporters, including some from the same origin, and smaller exporters may have to accept this because they cannot generate sufficient business to make a sole agency worthwhile for the agent. Such firms who do not work under an actual agency contract really function more as preferred sales channels than as true 'agents'.

*Brokers* work within a given geographical area, bringing local buyers and sellers together. Like agents they declare the name of both the buyer and the seller, and receive a commission but do not represent a party. *Traders* buy or sell in their own name and for their own account. Agents or brokers who do not declare the buyer's name operate as traders because they 'take the coffee over their own name'.

*Importers* and *traders.* Growing interest in niche products and markets, accompanied by the reappearance of small roasters (e.g. in the United States), has revitalized many importers who are once again increasingly fulfilling the traditional function of sourcing specific types of coffee (specialty, organic, but also mainstream qualities) in producing countries and bringing these to market. Today many importers represent single estates and individual exporters under agreements where, in exchange for exclusivity of supply, they undertake to stock and promote particular types of coffee. This potentially attractive alternative to the commission agency option mentioned above is discussed further in chapter 3, Niche markets. Their ability to carry stocks is of great importance, as it also enables less widely traded coffees to be immediately available in the main import markets.

Larger, more vertically integrated trade houses usually handle more easily traded coffees, standard qualities which are relatively widely bought and sold. Some of the very large houses at times almost operate as 'market makers' in that their pricing becomes a reference point, even for origin, as shown below.

*First and second hand.* Coffee sold direct from origin is *first hand* (there were no intermediate holders). If the foreign buyer then re-offers that same coffee for sale, the market will know it as *second hand.* But international traders also offer certain coffees for sale independent of origin: in so doing they are going short in the expectation of buying in later at a profit. To achieve such sales they may actually compete with origin by quoting lower prices than the producers – market reports then refer to *second hand offers* or simply the *second hand*. Traders can buy and sell matching contracts many times, causing a single shipment to pass through a number of hands before reaching the end-user – a roaster. Such interlinked contracts are known as *string contracts*.

## When things go wrong

There will always be problems and mistakes, delays and even disasters, both avoidable and unavoidable. The most important rule is: Keep the buyer informed! If a problem is advised in time the buyer may be able to re-position the contract and resolve the problem. If buyers are not promptly informed it becomes impossible for them to protect themselves and, indirectly, often the exporter as well. If it is clear the quality is not quite what it ought to be, do not hope to get away with it but tell your buyer. If a shipment will be delayed, do not wait to announce this but tell the buyer immediately – Article 11(v) of the European Contract for Coffee specifically requires that the buyer be kept informed without delay. If a claim is reasonable, settle it, promptly and efficiently. The buyer is not an enemy but a partner, and should be treated as such.

Arbitration always dents reputations and usually spells the end of a business relationship, but correctly settled claims can help to cement relationships. Bear in mind that many buyers will not bother to lodge smallish claims or pursue them through to arbitration – their time is too expensive. Instead they will simply strike the name of the offending party off their list of acceptable counterparts, often without saying so.

## Mitigation of loss

When loss is likely, both the seller and the buyer are required to 'mitigate' the loss as much as possible: that is, they must keep the loss to a minimum. Regardless of who is liable to pay, both parties are responsible to keep the loss to a minimum. A good example is when documents are lost. Yes, it is the responsibility of the seller to trace and present them as soon as possible. Yet the buyer cannot just let the coffee sit on the dock building late penalties (demurrage, container charges, etc.). The buyer is required to take all reasonable action necessary to keep the late charges to a minimum and when claiming damages has to prove both the reasonableness of the claim *and* that all possible action was taken to keep the loss to the unavoidable minimum.

# Documentation or 'back office' aspects

International coffee transactions are executed by transfer of title rather than by the physical handing over of coffee. Title to goods shipped under contract by sea from one country to another is represented by the bill of lading, accompanied by a set of additional documents, together known as 'the shipping documents'. The document of title for goods already stored in the port or place of delivery under a spot contract can be a warehouse receipt or storage warrant issued by a recognized public warehouseman. The only difference between the traditional chain of paper documents and *electronic* documentation is that the paper is largely eliminated. This is why electronic documentation is sometimes also called paperless trading. Using electronic documentation does not change the contractual responsibility of the seller or the buyer: the only differences are in how and when documents are issued, and how and when they are made available to the buyer.

Shipping documents must always comply in all respects with the conditions of the contract between the parties. If they do not, a seller may not be paid on time, or, in extreme circumstances, may lose the money altogether. The shipping documents must therefore show or state (i) that they represent the contracted and shipped coffee, (ii) that a known series of shipping rules has been complied with, and (iii) that they conform in all respects to the sales contract between the parties and to the standard form of contract on which that sales contract is based. Shipping documents must also be presented on time. Nothing is more annoying than *late documents*.

## Letters of credit

Where payment against a letter of credit is stipulated then the seller should obtain full details of the buyer's letter of credit as soon as possible. This is to ensure that the required documentation is in fact obtainable, that there will be sufficient time to obtain such documentation, and that there are suitable shipping opportunities to the named port of destination within the stipulated period of shipment. The European Contract for Coffee only requires a full and complete letter of credit to be available for use from the first day of the contractual period for shipment, even though the letter of credit may well contain stipulations on what must be done before loading. Therefore it may be wise to provide specifically in the contract for earlier receipt of the full and complete letter of credit. Sellers should also ensure that the letter of credit remains valid for the negotiation of documents for at least 21 days after the date of shipment.

Both ECC and GCA stipulate this. If the length of validity is not carefully checked one could fulfil all the L/C conditions only to find it has lapsed.

Buyers calculate all costs (from FOB through to delivery at final destination) to arrive at the final cost *price landed roasting plant*, taking into account any extra costs. For example, an origin that habitually delivers documents late (i.e. after the vessel has arrived) is penalized as the buyer will provide for this eventuality in the calculation to 'landed plant'. In fact the importer actually saves money by not having to finance the goods for the expected period of time, but should the goods arrive before the documents then serious trouble will arise. If a letter of credit is demanded, the bid price will be lowered correspondingly to cover the costs. Such a bid would also be lower than that for similar coffees from other origins that do not require a letter of credit.

## Destinations, shipment and shipping advices

*If the port of destination is not known* it is not easy for the seller to organize shipment. For forward shipment contracts the ECC therefore sets a time limit of 14 calendar days (GCA 15) before the first day of the contractual shipping period for communicating this information to the seller. Otherwise it might not be possible to complete the processes required for shipment within the agreed period. For immediate and prompt shipment contracts the destination must be declared at the latest on the first calendar day following the date of sale (and at the time of contract by GCA).

*Shipment must be made during a vessel's last call at the agreed port of loading* during that particular voyage. This rule is intended to exclude vessels that trade up and down the coast of a country with several ocean ports until enough cargo has been accumulated to make the main journey more profitable.

*The coffee must be shipped on a port to port or a combined transport bill of lading* issued by a regular or Conference shipping line which, using one or more vessels, will carry the goods throughout the voyage without further intervention by seller or buyer. The line issues a B/L at the port of origin to cover the entire voyage, enabling the buyer to see the details of shipment on the first vessel and to claim the coffee at final destination from a subsequent vessel. (See also chapter 5, Logistics.)

*Transshipment:* the first vessel discharges at an intermediate port and the goods are reloaded onto another vessel to the final destination. This is increasingly frequent as shipping companies rationalize operations. In particular, the use of containers has encouraged the development of shipping hubs: larger or more central ports that are fed containers from outlying ports by smaller vessels for loading onto large container vessels.

*Shipping advice:* as soon as the required information is available, the seller must advise certain specific details of the shipment.

For a shipment on terms other than CIF (which the seller insures), the shipping advice enables the buyer to insure the shipment and either to make the necessary arrangements to receive it at the port of destination or (where the bill of lading allows such a choice) to declare an optional port of destination in time for the shipping company to arrange discharge there. A series of time-limits in ECC are designed to ensure that these objectives are met, and to give the buyer the freedom to procure a replacement parcel elsewhere if no shipment is forthcoming.

The details to be included in the advice of shipment are listed in ECC. The buyer is entitled to receive such an advice, or an advice of delayed shipment, or an advice of *force majeure*. Failure to receive an advice theoretically entitles the buyer to take the drastic step of cancelling the contract and claiming recompense for any loss suffered.

## Delayed shipments

The seller must advise the buyer of delayed shipment as soon as, for example, they become aware that a vessel may not load within the contracted period due to problems connected with the operations of the vessel itself such as a delay on the inbound voyage. The seller must also show, using independent documentary proof, that a late shipment is not their fault.

If a problem of a much wider scope and of a more serious nature arises that prevents the seller, as well as other shippers, from shipping within the contracted period then, in addition to sending the notification of delayed shipment immediately this becomes evident, under certain circumstances the seller may be able to claim *force majeure*. Under ECC the effect of both an advice of delayed shipment and an advice of *force majeure* (see page 111) is initially to extend the period allowed for shipment. Cancellation of the contract follows if the problem continues after that period (although cancellation would be rather unusual). GCA on the other hand does not specify any extension and explicitly excludes events taking place before arrival of the goods at port of shipment.

Experienced exporters know that quick and frank admission of shipping problems usually helps them to reach an amicable settlement with their buyers. Failure to ship is bad enough, but failure to keep buyers informed is even worse as it prevents them from making alternative arrangements in time.

## The bill of lading

The bill of lading (B/L) usually contains:

- The name of the seller at origin (*the shipper*); the name of the buyer (*the consignee*); and, specified by the buyer, the name of the party to whom delivery is to be made and who is to be notified of the arrival of the shipment (*the notify address*).

- The bill of lading's unique number, the name of the vessel, the port of loading, the destination, and the number of originals that have been issued.

- Details of the cargo and whether shipped LCL/LCL or FCL/FCL, together with the container and seal numbers, where shipment is in containers.

- A statement that the coffee is *on board* or *shipped*, i.e. not simply received by the shipping company for shipment, and that there is no record of damage to the coffee (*a clean* B/L), and the date of onboard shipment. A 'received for shipment' LCL B/L may be acceptable if this has previously been agreed by the buyer.

Bills of lading are issued in sets of identical originals, normally two or three, with a variable number of non-negotiable copies for record purposes only. Each original can be used independently to claim the coffee shipped, although not everyone holding an original bill of lading will automatically be handed the goods by the shipping company at destination. Who is allowed to claim the goods depends on how the bills are made out.

## Title to and endorsement of a bill of lading

When bills of lading are made out, or endorsed, to a named consignee, then only that consignee can take delivery of the shipment. A B/L made out to a named consignee can be endorsed only by that consignee, not the shipper. Once a consignee has been named the original shipper no longer has any power to alter the B/L in connection with title to the shipment.

If the consignee is not known at the time the shipper instructs shipment on a particular vessel then the bills of lading may also be made out 'to order'. In this case, only the party to whom they are endorsed with the words 'deliver to …' or 'deliver to the order of …' can take delivery. This endorsement is made by the shipper who is named on the B/L. Occasionally buyers stipulate in their shipping instructions that the goods be consigned to order.

A bill of lading is a negotiable instrument and can be passed from a shipper through any number of parties, each party endorsing it to assign title to the next party. The only condition is that title can be assigned only by the party shown on the bill as having title at the time. Any failure to respect this condition breaks what is known as the chain of title; all purported assignments of title after such a break are invalid. Before paying for documents a buyer will therefore carefully examine the bill of lading to see that they are named on it as consignee, either on the face or on the reverse in an endorsement. In the latter case, the buyer will also make sure that the endorsements show an unbroken chain of title through to them.

There is one exception to the general rule that a consignee must be named on a bill of lading to take delivery of a shipment. This is when the bill is a bearer bill. In this case, anyone holding (or bearing) the bills (or one bill of the set) can take delivery. Bills are considered bearer bills when the word 'bearer' is entered in the space marked 'consignee' when the bills are first made out. Alternatively a title-holder endorses the bills with the words 'deliver to bearer', or a named title-holder endorses the bills 'in blank', i.e. by stamping and signing them without naming any other party in his endorsement. Although this may be simple and convenient, it means that anyone who obtains all or any of the originals (including a thief or a buyer who has not yet made payment) can take delivery of the shipment. *Bills of lading are therefore usually made out to or endorsed to a named consignee.*

The greatest security of all is afforded by issuing or endorsing a bill to a buyer's nominated bank with an instruction to the bank to endorse and hand the bill over to the buyer when, and only when, payment has been made.

## Dispatching bills of lading

Because in theory each original B/L in a set can be used to claim the goods at destination, a buyer will want to be in possession of all the originals in a set before making payment. Documents are often sent in two dispatches with the bills of lading split between them, simply to minimize the risks of all of them being lost or delayed. Only when the buyer has received both dispatches will payment be made, unless the first contains a bank guarantee for any missing B/L. Many exporters use courier services however and send all documents at once.

## Certificates

### ICO certificates of origin

ICO certificates of origin are issued for every international shipment of coffee from producers to consumers (whether the importing country is an ICO member or not), and are used to monitor the movement of coffee worldwide.

The forms contain details of identity, size, origin, destination and time of shipment of the parcels in question. ICO certificates were particularly important when ICO export quotas were in force as they were also used to enforce the quota limits for individual exporting countries. The certificates are now less important (and some consumer countries no longer insist on them) but it is in the interest of exporting countries to comply with ICO regulations on certificates of origin as they enable the ICO to monitor coffee movements and produce accurate statistics on each country's exports.

Moreover, from 1 October 2002 all ICO exporting members are required to ensure that all coffee issued with certificates of origin complies with the minimum quality standards indicated by ICO resolution 407 (see chapter 11, Coffee quality).

### *Preferential entry certificates*

Countries that levy duties or taxes on coffee imports sometimes grant duty exemptions to certain exporting countries. Entitlement to remission of duty or tax is obtained by submitting an official certificate of exemption (EUR1, GSP and others). Individual sales contracts often state that an exemption certificate must be provided where appropriate. This certificate must accompany the shipping documents, failing which the buyer is entitled to deduct the duty difference from the invoice and pay only the balance. The seller will be able to obtain refund of the shortfall by submitting the required certificate retroactively *but only if* the buyer in turn is able to obtain this within the applicable time limit from the authorities in the country of importation. Sellers who are in doubt about whether such a certificate is required should ask their local chamber of commerce or trade authority. Note also that under ECC a buyer may stipulate a country of importation other than that of the port of destination.

### *Insurance certificates*

Under a CIF contract the seller must provide an insurance certificate, issued by a first-class insurance company, showing that insurance has been effected in accordance with the terms of the sales contract. The certificate must enable the buyer to claim any losses direct from the insurance company. The certificate entitles the holder to the rights and privileges of a known and stipulated master marine insurance policy that may cover a number of shipments. The certificate therefore represents the policy and is transferable with all its benefits by endorsement in the same manner as bills of lading.

### *Other certificates*

There are an increasing number of other certificates available for special contractual requirements. Some, such as weight and quality certificates, are supplied by recognized public or private organizations in the country of origin, and have various formats. Others, such as health, phytosanitary and non-radiation certificates, are often supplied on application by government bodies, in a set format prescribed by local law and regulations. The variety of formats available for special purpose certificates is so great that it is not practical or useful to discuss them here.

Shippers should be familiar with the format of local certificates and should investigate their availability and cost before entering into any contractual obligation; otherwise they may be unable to supply a document at all or may require a price increase to cover costs.

## Missing and incorrect documents

ECC states that, provided the missing document does not prevent the importation of the coffee into the country of destination, a European bank guarantee shall be accepted for the missing document(s). Sellers under the GCA contract must provide a guarantee issued by a bank in the United States. Exporters who have not arranged with a bank in Europe or the United States to issue such guarantees should consider specifying in all their contracts that guarantees issued by a first-class international bank will be accepted.

In principle a set of shipping documents made up of some documents and some guarantees can be acceptable, and it is possible for payment to be made and delivery to a buyer to take place even though no original documents – only guarantees – have passed between seller and buyer. But when the absence of documents prevents the importation of a shipment, buyers will not make payment on the basis of a guarantee as they will be unable to gain access to the shipment.

While bank guarantees from seller to buyer are generally acceptable for missing contractual documents, guarantees for missing bills of lading must be made out to the shipping company and forwarded to the buyer for use. Shipping companies provide their own pre-printed guarantee forms for this purpose.

A buyer may also accept the seller's personal guarantee for missing documents without a bank's involvement. The seller may take steps to rectify errors in documents, especially when the documents relate to prompt landing and importation of a shipment (e.g. bills of lading) and when the time saved by amending them on the spot either benefits the buyer or prevents charges to the seller. The buyer can give the bills of lading to the shipping company's agent at destination who will amend them on receipt of authority from the seller via the shipping company's agent at the port of shipment.

Occasionally an entire set of documents is lost or destroyed in transit. The shipping company can then be requested to issue duplicate bills in return for an unlimited bank guarantee as indemnity against possible future liability to a holder of the supposedly lost documents.

As far as incorrect documents are concerned, obvious clerical errors that do not materially affect a document do not entitle a buyer to delay or refuse payment under ECC. If mistakes invalidate a document or affect its reliability, the document is regarded as a missing document and a guarantee can be submitted in its place. The document itself is then returned for re-issue or amendment by the seller.

## Standard forms of contract

The standard forms of contract set out generally accepted rules, practices and conditions in the international trade in coffee for which the terminology and precise meaning have been standardized under the aegis of leading coffee trade bodies (for Europe the European Coffee Federation (ECF), and for the United States the Green Coffee Association of New York (GCA)). Both associations publish a number of contracts dealing with different types of transactions.[17] Most coffee is traded using these standard contracts. Others exist (AFNIC/Dutch) but are rarely used.

All ECF and GCA contracts state expressly that no contract shall be contingent on any other and that each contract is to be settled between buyers and sellers without reference to any other contracts covering the same parcel. Although intended to cover string contracts this also means exporters cannot claim inability to ship because someone else, say an interior

---

**17**  Both the ECF and the GCA contracts were updated in 2002 with the GCA also publishing an electronic or XML (extensible mark-up language) version together with a price fix letter, a price fix rolling letter and a destination declaration letter. For more on using the GCA XML documents exporters should contact their United States buyers or agents. The data files are available, free of charge, from the GCA.

supplier, let them down. (Traders sometimes buy and sell matching contracts many times, causing a single shipment to pass through a number of hands before reaching an end-user. Such contracts are called string contracts.)

Details on the two associations at *www.ecf-coffee.org* and *www.green-coffee-assoc.org*.

## The European Coffee Federation contracts

There are three ECF contracts in all, of which the ECC (European Contract for Coffee) is relevant for exporters as it covers coffee to be shipped from origin. The other two contracts deal with the trade in coffee that has already been landed in an import market: the ECSC (European Contract for Spot Coffee) and the EDCC (European Delivery Contract for Coffee). While important for importers and traders they are of little direct interest to exporters.

The 2002 edition of the ECC is effective from 1 January 2003. It now covers both coffee shipped in bags and coffee shipped in bulk using lined containers (the old ECCB). Note that although hardly any bagged coffee is still shipped without the use of containers, ECC does not stipulate that containers must be used. It allows it, provided the bill of lading states that the shipping company is responsible for the number of bags. Parties wishing to conclude individual transactions on a different basis must therefore ensure that the sales contract stipulates on what basis containerization shall be permitted. (In the green coffee trade a container is always a 'twenty footer'.)

**Incoterms.** Both ECF and GCA contracts make no reference to these, not because of any disqualification or disagreement, but because Incoterms are a *general* (i.e. not coffee specific) set of international trade conditions. The exclusion is purely to safeguard the 'stand-alone' status and clarity of the ECF and GCA contracts that have been written by and for the trade in coffee. See Exclusions on page 112.

The main implication of this exclusion is that, as for CFR or CIF contracts, under an FOB contract the seller is acquitted of responsibility only once the goods pass the ship's rail.[18] This is the same for GCA contracts. Under ECC the stipulation means that any buyer wishing to impose the use of a particular shipping line or vessel must make this known at the time of concluding the contract. But under GCA this has already been formalized in that the standard GCA conditions state that for FCA and FOB sales (see below) the buyer reserves the right to nominate the carrier.

## The Green Coffee Association (of New York) contracts

Many North American roasters purchase coffee 'ex dock': the importer/trade house deals with all the formalities of shipment and landing, including customs clearance and passing the obligatory sanitation check of the Food and Drug Administration (FDA). This latter check is particular to the United States and all contracts for importation into the United States carry the stamp-over clause 'no pass no sale'. This means that if any or all of the coffee is not admitted at port of destination in its original condition by reason of failure to meet the requirements of governmental laws or acts, the contract shall be deemed null and void as to that portion of the coffee which is not admitted in its original condition at point of discharge. And further that any payment made for any coffee denied entry shall be refunded within 10 calendar days of denial of entry. (For more on this go to *www.cfsan.fda.gov* or apply for the information booklet 'Health and Safety in the Importation of Green Coffee into the United States' from the National Coffee Association of the United States.) If coffee is

---

18   Under International Chamber of Commerce rules an FOB seller's responsibility ends upon delivery into the port. Some exporters do incorporate Incoterms in their contracts; at the time of writing discussions were ongoing between producers and consumers on a possible Free Carrier Contract (FCA) that might accommodate this within the context of a new ECF contract.

refused entry under a contract that does not bear this over-stamp, in addition to having to refund payment as above the seller may also be required to make a replacement delivery within 30 days.

There are nine GCA contracts. Four of them deal with coffee that is sold outside of the country of destination, four deal with coffee sold inside the country of destination, and one deals with coffee delivered at the border or frontier. The main distinction between the contract types is based on how cost and risk are allocated between the parties.

**Free carrier (FCA).** Risk of loss is transferred when the coffee is delivered to the freight carrier at place of embarkation. All freight charges, including loading onto an ocean vessel, railcar or trailer, are payable by the buyer.

**Free on board (FOB).** Risk of loss is transferred when the coffee crosses over the ship's rail. Terminal handling costs at the place of loading are for account of the shipper. Free on railcar (FOR) and free on truck or trailer (FOT) are variations of FOB, the only difference being the type of conveyance. The buyer pays the freight charges.

**Cost and freight (CFR).** As for FOB except that freight is included in the price and paid by the seller.

**Cost insurance and freight (CIF).** As for CFR but the seller also pays marine insurance and provides a certificate of insurance.

**Delivered at frontier (DAF).** Under DAF contracts, risk of loss is transferred when the coffee is delivered to a named point at the frontier. Delivery takes place on arriving means of transport (trailer, truck, rail car), cleared for export but not cleared for import.

**Ex dock (EDK).** When coffee is sold ex dock, risk of loss transfer takes place on the dock at port of destination, after all ocean freight and terminal handling charges are paid, and customs entry and all government regulations have been satisfied.

**Ex warehouse (EWH), delivered (DLD) and spot (SPT)** contracts are outside the scope of normal export business and not discussed here.

**Price to be fixed (PTBF).** This does not feature in ECC but GCA stipulates that such contracts shall specify the differential (value) that is added to or subtracted from an agreed price basis. When applicable the number of lots of coffee futures should also be mentioned, as well as whether buyer or seller has the right to execute the fixation. If there is margin payable between time of fixation and time of shipment/delivery, it must be determined at time of contract. Finally, the earliest and the latest fixation date shall be specified at time of contract. Any changes are to be by mutual agreement and in writing.

## Most important articles in ECF and GCA contracts

The first section of this chapter reviewed what is to be done and agreed before a contract is concluded. What follows is a brief review of the ECC and the GCA's FCA and FOB contracts, which exporters are most likely to use.

### Quantity

*Tolerance to ship 3% more or less than the contracted weight.* Applicable to both ECF and GCA. The intention is not to frustrate shipment if on arrival in port five bags are missing out of five hundred. But the tolerance applies only if the cause is beyond the seller's control. If buyers suspect deliberate manipulation they may lodge a claim.

## Weights at shipment

*Weight franchise of 0.5% on coffee sold 'net shipped weight' in ECC.* Any weight loss on arrival in excess of 0.5% is to be refunded by the seller. Until the end of 1997 the tolerance was 1%. The present figure is a direct consequence of the growth in bulk shipments, in the sense that there should hardly be any weight variation if coffee is correctly shipped in lined and sealed containers. Shippers of bagged coffee often include a small tolerance (excess weight) per bag to avoid claims. GCA standard contracts make no provision for a weight franchise unless this is specifically agreed at the time of concluding the transaction, in which case it must be explicitly stated in the contract.

*Independent evidence of weight.* The shipping weight shall be established at the time and place of shipment, or at the time and place of stuffing if the coffee is stuffed into the shipment containers at an inland location. *In either case, sellers shall provide independent evidence of weight.* This ECC stipulation provides buyers with some independent evidence that a container for which the bill of lading or waybill states 'said to contain' in fact does hold a certain amount of coffee. This does not alter the shipper's responsibility in any way unless the parties agree that shipping weights shall be final (together with the procedure and conditions that shall apply). GCA does not make this stipulation. The requirement to provide independent evidence of shipping weights applies equally to coffee sold 'delivered weights'.

*Supervision by buyers' representatives (independent weighers).* Buyers can demand this under both ECC and GCA provided they give due notice and pay the costs. The seller is obliged to provide the certificate together with the shipping documents but the buyer cannot withhold payment if the seller does not provide it. It is after all possible that the supervising weigher failed to hand the certificate to the exporter, or omitted to attend the weighing when asked to do so.

## Weights on arrival (landed weights)

*Establishment of arrival weights.* ECC requires that weighing (and sampling) take place no later than 14 calendar days (15 for GCA) after discharge at the final port of destination or, in case of unforeseen complications, from the date the goods become available for weighing. Under both ECC and GCA shippers have the right to appoint supervisors at their expense.

ECC stipulates that on arrival containers (bagged and bulk) may be *on-carried to an inland destination* and weighed there provided they are on-carried not later than 14 calendar days from the date of final discharge at the port of destination, and provided weighing (and sampling) take place under independent supervision, at buyers' expense, not later than 7 calendar days after arrival at the inland destination. The point of containerization is to minimize handling and the object of this clause is to permit receivers to bring the coffee without unnecessary handling as near to its final destination as possible, for example a roasting plant. (If coffee is weighed at a roasting plant then such weights may also be called 'factory weights'.) GCA provides that coffee in bags is to be weighed either within 15 days of availability at port of destination (landed weights), or within 15 days of date of tender at buyer's plant (plant weights). Coffee in bulk is to be weighed during unloading within 21 days of availability at final destination, or 21 days after all United States Government clearances have been received (silo weights).

But the GCA approach is quite different from that of ECC in that it requires that the actual transaction contract state when, where, how and by whom, coffee is to be weighed for settlement purposes, that is, weighing responsibilities including liability for costs must be specified at the time of contract. If coffee is removed from the stipulated place of weighing or the time limits expire before the weighing takes place, then the net shipped weight will stand.

## Packing

*ECC states that the coffee shall be packed in sound uniform natural fibre bags suitable for export* and in conformity with the legal requirements for food packaging materials and waste management within the European Union valid at the time of conclusion of the contract. This is important and exporters must know what types and quality of bags are acceptable, not only in the European Union but also in other countries. Be careful not to confuse port of destination with country of destination as the two may not always be the same. To read the EU Packaging and Packaging Waste Disposal Directive go to *www.europa.eu.int* (official publications, EUR-Lex). See also the Draft Code of Hygienic Practice for the Transport of Foodstuffs of the Codex Alimentarius Commission at *www.codexalimentarius.net*, and the text under Quality control issues in chapter 11, Coffee quality.)

GCA stipulates that coffee bags shall be made of sisal, henequen, jute, burlap or similar woven material, without any inner lining or outer covering. Bulk coffee shall be in a bulk container liner. Depending on the contract so-called supersacks (jumbo bags) made of synthetic fibre may also be used. Soluble coffee is commonly shipped in cardboard cartons with a plastic liner. All forms of packaging must conform to food grade packaging standards at the country of destination.

## Quality

The quality of the coffee must be strictly as per contract. If there is a difference and the resultant claim cannot be settled amicably then it will go to arbitration, but a buyer cannot lodge any formal claim before paying for the shipping documents. Claims are usually settled by granting an allowance that the seller must pay, together with the buyer's costs and expenses. But if the coffee is unsound or the quality is radically different from that specified then the buyer may seek to have the contract discharged by invoicing back the coffee. In awarding invoicing back the arbitrators shall establish the price bearing in mind all the circumstances concerned. Basically this means they may order the contract cancelled and instruct the sellers to refund the entire cost of the coffee plus any relevant damages. *Note that an excessive moisture level is one factor towards declaring a coffee unsound.* (See chapter 5, Logistics, and chapter 11, Coffee quality.)

Under GCA all quality issues FCA, FOB, CFR, CIF and DAF are settled by allowance, except gross negligence and fraud. In the latter case the arbitration will be a technical arbitration that might convene a quality panel to verify negligence or fraud.

## Freight

Where coffee is sold CFR/CIF the costs of bringing the goods to the port of destination are for account of the seller.

If the rate of freight increases between the time of sale and the time of shipment then the increase is for the seller's account. Only increases that enter into force after the shipment took place shall be for the buyer's account. This is indicative of the trade's wish to control freights and shipping through the use of FOB contracts. Exporters who have to use national flag carriers therefore also have to accept they are potentially liable to pay for such freight increases.

*Place of embarkation.* ECC does not speak of this but GCA states that for FOB, CFR and CIF contracts this shall be defined as the named seaport of the country of origin; for FCA contracts it is defined as the place where custody of the coffee is turned over to the carrier for transport. The place of embarkation must always be clearly noted on the bill of lading.

*Port of destination.* If this is not advised when the contract is concluded, the buyer must declare it at the latest by the deadline stipulated by either ECC or GCA. Otherwise a buyer could simply refuse to declare a port of destination and so frustrate the execution of a contract (for example, if the price had become unfavourable due to change in the market).

Note that the ECC text states that the deadline is met when the declaration is made at the buyer's place of business, i.e. all the buyer has to do is send the declaration by cable, fax, email, telex or other means of written electronic communication. The shipper cannot declare the buyer in default simply because no declaration has been received; if a declaration is overdue, the shipper should make inquiries rather than just let events unfold. GCA does not say this but clearly the same principle of due diligence applies. However, whereas ECC sets a clear deadline for lodging a technical claim, GCA sets a limit of one year from the date the issue arises. Note also that ECC Article 27 states that communication by fax, email or other means of written electronic communication is at the parties' own risk (basically because proof of dispatch and receipt is not automatic).

Sometimes by the time the declaration (of destination) falls due the coffee has not yet been sold on and the buyer may not be in any position to declare a final destination. In the past the buyer would then declare a range of ports (e.g. Rotterdam, option Bremen/Hamburg), called options or optional ports. Then the goods would be stowed on board in such a way as to make discharge possible at any of the named ports, with the cost or *option fees* for buyer's account.

But on modern container vessels such stowage is difficult if not impossible and exporters should satisfy themselves therefore that the shipping line will in fact accept such cargo before they agree to ship to optional ports. Transshipment is a much more frequently used option but current transshipment practices often make it difficult to confirm the final vessel. Shipping advices against FOB contracts, and indeed bills of lading, can only mention the vessel that first loads the goods, leaving tracking of the goods to the buyer. Note also that bills of lading may stipulate the place of delivery as CFS (a container freight station) at or associated with the port of destination, regardless of the port of discharge.

## Shipment

*Shipment must be made at the vessel's last scheduled call at the port of shipment before commencing the final voyage.* This is reminiscent of when traditional break bulk vessels used to discharge and load cargo at a range of ports in the same region and in so doing might call at the same port on the way in and on the way out. Modern container vessels rarely if ever do so but the stipulation is nevertheless a valid one and applies to both ECC and GCA.

*Shipment must be made by conference line or other acceptable vessel (ECF), or metal-hulled, self propelled vessels which are not over 20 years of age and not less than 1,000 net registered tons, classed A1 American Record or equivalent, operating in their regular trade (GCA).* This prevents shippers from using any old tramp vessel that happens to be available. (Tramp vessels make irregular port calls to discharge and look for new cargo, i.e. the exact opposite of liner vessels.) Note also that at some future stage European Union authorities may introduce legislation covering the type, class, condition and age of ships that may enter European Union ports.

*Shippers will pass on to the shipping line all relevant instructions received from buyers.*

These apply equally to shipment in bags in containers, and to shipments in bulk.

## Shipment in bags

Shipment in containers, suitable for the transport of coffee, shall be permitted under LCL/FCL conditions, whereby *the shipping company is responsible for the number of bags and the condition and suitability of the containers.*

However, *shipping lines increasingly discourage LCL/FCL (or LCL/LCL)* and in future shippers may not always be able to satisfy buyers' wishes in this regard. In this case their only option will be to effect weighing and stuffing under independent supervision at their expense since all other shipments in containers shall require agreement of the parties. Again, GCA leaves the matter of the shipment basis to the parties to the contract.

LCL, or less than container load: *the shipping line accepts responsibility for the number of bags*. FCL, or full container load: *the line accepts responsibility only for the container, not for the contents*, by stating for example, 'STC (said to contain) 300 bags of coffee' on the bill of lading. See also chapter 5, Logistics.

## Shipment in bulk

*Unless otherwise agreed, shipment shall be made under FCL/FCL conditions.* This reflects the move from break bulk to almost universal containerization. The 1991 edition of the ECC still stipulated that only LCL/LCL was acceptable and that shipment in bulk required prior agreement. Unless otherwise stated, FCL/FCL is now the norm. This means that bulk is increasingly, if not always, loaded and weighed under independent supervision, but shippers still have to pass on to the shipping line all relevant instructions received from buyers, and in case of damage may be asked to provide proof of having done so. GCA leaves the matter entirely to the parties, who must stipulate the agreed shipping basis in the contract.

## Delay in shipment

*Sellers shall not be held responsible if they are able to prove their case.* The most important point this article makes is that the buyer must be kept informed at all times without undue delay. This is absolutely essential. Delays in shipment usually affect buyers adversely and they must be enabled to take measures to protect themselves. Failing to respect this clause not only is entirely unprofessional but can also result in unforeseen consequences, possibly even cancellation of the contract.

## On-carriage of containers

*Buyers may discharge containers at inland destinations.* The point of containerization is to minimize handling and the only object of this clause is to permit receivers to bring the coffee without unnecessary handling as near to its final destination as possible, for example a roasting plant. In case of weight claims buyers have to prove weighing took place under independent supervision. GCA permits the same. In addition it defines the port of entry as all dock and warehouse facilities within a 50-mile radius of ships berth that are used for the discharge of ships cargo (or all freight facilities within a 50-mile radius of a border crossing).

## Advice of shipment

*Both ECC and GCA require that advice of shipment must be transmitted as soon as known.* In practice only gross negligence could explain why one would not advise buyers as soon as possible, which only leaves the question of whether or not the advice actually reaches them promptly. But ECC and GCA approach this question very differently. ECC considers it may not be within the seller's control and so, in theory, it suffices if buyers receive the notice before the vessel arrives at the port of destination. Only someone with no interest in good business relationships would consider this normal practice, however.

There is an important provision in this article. If a shipping advice is not received by noon on the fourteenth calendar day after the expiry of the contractual shipping period, and if there has been no notification of a delay in shipment and no *force majeure* has been pleaded, then damages may be claimed or the buyer may cancel the contract altogether. This could leave a forgetful exporter with an unsold and most likely uninsured shipment on the water. See Article 13(d) of the ECC for full details.

GCA on the other hand states that for FCA, FOB, CFR, CIF and EDK contracts, written advice with all details must be transmitted not just as soon as known, but not later than on the day of arrival of the vessel at destination and/or five business days from bill of lading date, whichever is later. The advice may be given verbally with email or fax confirmation to be sent the same day. This is included because of the close proximity of many Latin American producing countries to the United States, but it applies to all contracts.

## Shipping documents

*Sellers must provide shipping documents in good time* (including a full set of 'clean on board' bills of lading, i.e. bills stating that the goods were received on board ship in apparent good order), enabling the buyer to clear the goods upon arrival. Failure to provide documents in time will incur demurrage and other costs, and could even lead to cancellation of the contract under both ECC and GCA. ECC Article 18 stipulates the documents buyers are entitled to receive and those they are entitled to request.

## Insurance

The vast majority of the trade in coffee today is on FOB terms. In this regard the relevant ECC clause contains three extremely important stipulations.

*In the case of CFR and FOB contracts the buyers have to cover the insurance ahead of the contractual shipment period.* Without this stipulation the coffee might be loaded without any insurance cover in place, leaving the exporter at risk. In case of doubt an exporter should insist on proof of insurance.

*The insurance shall commence from the time the coffee leaves the ultimate warehouse or other place of storage at the port of shipment.* This is because it can be extremely difficult to determine at what point the marine insurer became liable for any damage or loss incurred once the goods have left the ultimate place of storage. If after leaving the ultimate place of storage but before crossing the ship's rail the goods were destroyed by fire, or fell into the water, then the seller might receive no bill of lading at all and would be unable to submit shipping documents for the buyer to pay. This is why ECC also states that the sellers have the right to the benefit of the policy *until the documents are paid for.*

In the above example the buyer would have to claim the loss or damage under their insurance cover on the seller's behalf. But even if a vessel sinks immediately after loading the seller will receive a bill of lading and the buyer will have to pay for it. Until payment is made, the benefit of the insurance cover remains contractually vested in the sellers.

GCA on the other hand relies instead on the transfer of risk stipulation that applies for each contract: shippers and buyers must cover insurance accordingly.

## Export licences

Under both ECC and GCA the exporter is not only responsible for obtaining export licences but also for the consequences if such a licence is later cancelled or revoked. Similarly, buyers are responsible for obtaining any import licences required.

## Duties, fees and taxes

Both ECC and GCA stipulate that all and any such costs in the country of export are always for the account of the exporter, irrespective of whether they already existed at the time of concluding the contract or were imposed afterwards. At the import end such costs, if any, are for account of the buyer unless the seller is in breach by not supplying required documentation (see below).

## Certification of preferential entry

Certificates entitling the coffee to completely or partially duty-free entry into the stated country of destination (which may be different from that of the port of destination) must accompany the shipping documents. If they are not available the buyers are entitled to deduct the duty difference from the payment to the seller. They will only be obliged to refund this (less any expenses) if the subsequent submission of the certificate is accepted by the customs authorities in the country of import. (The United States and Canada do not levy import duties or taxes on green coffee.)

## Payment

*The coffee remains the property of the sellers until it has been paid for in full.* No third party can lay claim to any coffee that has not been paid for. This is important when documents are sent in trust. (See Conditions of payment earlier in this chapter.) If a buyer is declared insolvent after the documents are received but before they have been paid, then the judicial authorities (or liquidators) have no claim to the goods, although in some countries national insolvency law takes precedence over individual contract stipulations. How far sellers can enforce this clause in European Union and other importing countries therefore depends on local law.

In the United States there are no doubts in this respect. When invoked, bankruptcy law (11 USC365 (e)1) overrides all GCA terms and conditions. Most coffee is sold on payment terms in the United States and Canada and the risks are great. Selling 'net 30 days from delivery' means the seller is granting the buyer possession 30 days before payment. If the buyer goes bankrupt, the seller may lose the value of the coffee.

There can even be problems with payments that are made within the 90 days prior to a bankruptcy. This is called the preference period and if the liquidator or trustee can show that the payments were not normal (i.e. extraordinarily late or extraordinarily early), then a supplier might even be forced to return the payments to the bankruptcy pool.

ECC and GCA both state that *letters of credit* must conform exactly to the contract, must be available for use from day one of the agreed shipping period, and must remain valid for negotiation for 21 calendar days after the last date shipment can be made. This allows time for the seller to obtain all the required documents and possible consular visas.

## *Force majeure*

*Partial performance, non-performance or delayed performance of a contract can be justified only as a result of unforeseeable and insurmountable occurrences,* but only if these arise after the conclusion of the contract and before the expiry of the performance period allowed by the contract. And furthermore only if the seller informs the buyer as soon as the impediment arises, provides evidence and keeps the buyer fully informed of developments. In other words, make sure your buyer knows what you know yourself. Under ECC a successful plea of *force majeure* can extend the performance time limit by up to a maximum of 45 calendar days, after which the contract lapses. Disputes have to be settled by arbitration.

GCA follows the same principle but does not specify any extension. It also states that in no case shall the seller be excused by any such causes intervening before arrival of the affected portion of the coffee at the point of embarkation of the original shipment. Thus, delays within producing countries do not constitute *force majeure*. Disputes dealing with *force majeure* will by nature be technical and as such are subject to a one year filing time limit (see below).

## Submission of claims – ECC

*Quality claims.* Not later than 21 calendar days from the final date of discharge at the port of destination.

*All other claims (technical claims).* Not later than 45 calendar days from:

- The final date of discharge at the port of destination, provided all the documents are available to the buyer, (i.e. the coffee has been shipped); or

- The last day of the contractual shipping period if the coffee has not been shipped.

These limits may be extended if the arbitral body at the place of arbitration (mentioned in the contract) considers that one or other of the parties will suffer undue hardship.

## Submission of claims – GCA

Under GCA rules time limits are based instead on the filing of a demand for arbitration, not on when the defending party is notified.

*Quality claims.* A demand for arbitration must be filed with the GCA within 15 calendar days from date of discharge or after all government clearances have been received, whichever is later.

*Other claims (technical claims).* The only time limit is that a demand for arbitration must be filed with the GCA not later than one year from the date the dispute first arose. Usually one would expect to see a number of exchanges between the parties to the contract before this but there is no contractual obligation on either of the parties to do anything but file a demand for arbitration within the year. (Depending on the type of contract dispute, the United States legal system allows three to seven years for the filing of judgement. Quality claims are subject to a 15-day limit because quality deteriorates over time.)

## Default

*One of the parties does not execute its part of the contract.* After declaring the offending party to be in default the injured party can claim discharge of the contract with or without damages (but excluding any consequential, i.e. indirect, damages). If the offender fails to pay these or disputes them then the matter shall be decided by arbitration.

The default clause is stipulated separately in ECC, mainly because the notion of a claim assumes an incorrectly executed contract. Default on the other hand deals with the cost and damage to the injured party of the total and possibly wilful non-execution of a contract. As in the case of invoicing goods back for a radical difference in quality, there are no fixed rules for determining default damages. In the European Union the process depends on the arbitral body under whose jurisdiction the arbitration is held. The GCA contract provides for arbitration in New York with the arbitrators setting the damages if any are awarded.

## Arbitration

*Any dispute that cannot be resolved amicably shall be resolved through arbitration at the place stated in the contract.* The GCA contract automatically places arbitration in New York, to be held in accordance with the law of New York State. However, the ECF is the umbrella body for a number of national coffee associations in sovereign countries, quite a few of which have their own arbitral bodies, rules and legal systems.

In this context the most important are the United Kingdom (London), Germany (Hamburg) and France (Le Havre), followed by Italy (Trieste), Belgium (Antwerp) and the Netherlands (Amsterdam). All ECF contracts provide that disputes shall be resolved by arbitration but the actual commercial contract must state where this shall take place. If not then arbitration will be delayed while the ECF Contracts Committee determines where it will be held and the defending party may find itself having to deal with arbitration proceedings in a location it is not familiar with. (See chapter 7, Arbitration.)

## Exclusions

The following laws and conventions do *not* apply to ECF standard forms of contract:

- The Uniform Law on Sales and the Uniform Law on Formation to which effect is given by the Uniform Laws on International Sales Act 1967;

- The United Nations Convention on Contracts for the International Sale of Goods of 1980; and

- The United Nations Convention on Prescription (Limitation) in the International Sale of Goods Act 1974 and the amending protocol of 1980.

GCA's Legal Framework and Contract Rulings simply state that 'The UN Convention on Contracts for the International Sale of Goods shall not apply to this contract'.

## Communications

Article 27 of ECC lists the notices that must be given by cable, facsimile (fax), telex or other means of written electronic communication. The same article also states that where the parties agree to communicate by fax, email or other means of written electronic communication they do so at their own risk.

GCA allows fax and email or equivalent electronic message.

## Variations to standard forms of contract

Commercial contracts can be and often are concluded with conditions other than those of the standard forms of contract, as long as these are well understood and are clearly set out in unambiguous language (leaving no room for differing interpretations). For example, one might agree to change the shipment quantity tolerance in Article 2 of the ECC from 3% to 5%. In this case the contract should then include a paragraph to the effect that 'Article 2 of ECC is amended for this contract by mutual agreement to read a tolerance of 5%'.

If a modification to an existing contract is agreed it should be confirmed in writing, preferably countersigned by both parties. Adding the words 'without prejudice to the original terms and conditions of the contract' ensures that the modification does not result in unintended or unforeseen change to the original contract. If a modification is not confirmed in writing then one of the parties could subsequently repudiate or dispute it. Human memory is fallible and there is nothing offensive in ensuring that all matters of record are on record.

The same applies to business under GCA contracts. Some North American roasters have small booklets containing their proprietary terms and conditions, which all suppliers must sign on to before they become approved vendors. In the new GCA XML contract there is a huge field (350 characters) entitled 'exceptions'.

# CHAPTER 5

# Logistics and insurance

## Logistics

### Shipping

#### *Liner services*

Liner services are regular, scheduled shipping services between fixed groups of ports that operate regardless of cargo availability. Tramping vessels on the other hand make irregular, opportunistic calls at ports when cargo is available. In theory vessels can also be chartered for larger tonnages but chartering is a complex business and conditions for each charter must be negotiated individually. Shipment on chartered vessels is usually arranged by importers. For a while in the early 1990s for cost reasons, chartering to the United States became extremely popular, especially for shipments from Brazil but also for coffee from Central America. Chartering became so popular, in fact, that the Green Coffee Association established a Charter Party Agreement for Coffee. It is a very good document but ironically, by the time it was approved by the GCA Board and adopted by the membership, liner freight rates had come down enough to make chartering unattractive. The document still exists, but it has yet to be used by the industry.

*Unless specifically stated to the contrary, all coffee contracts automatically stipulate that shipment will be by liner vessel, operated under a regular, scheduled service.*

#### *Conferences*

Conferences are groups of ship owners who offer regular sailings by guaranteeing the number of vessels that will be available during the year between different ports and the schedules that will be maintained. Most scheduled ocean liners probably operate under liner conferences (known simply as conferences). Conferences schedule and guarantee sailings to and from an agreed range of ports, thereby eliminating duplication among their members. The system benefits both sellers and buyers because freight rates are fairly stable, schedules are published well in advance, and regular and dependable services are provided. Conference vessels are usually of good quality and the operators normally have ample experience of carrying coffee.

Vessels belonging to non-member shipping lines are called *non-conference vessels*. Such vessels may nevertheless also operate on pre-arranged schedules. On some routes they provide the only regular competition to the conferences.

Liner rates usually respond more slowly to the open market than do charter or tramp rates. Remember though that conferences also maintain the agreed schedules, irrespective of whether cargo is abundant or not. Collective pressure by sellers or buyers can however be a significant factor in determining freight rates.

## Vessel sharing arrangements

Vessel sharing arrangements (VSA) or alliances are taking away from the former dominance of the traditional conferences. In VSA, several carriers offer a joint service by agreeing a frequency and capacity from and to certain ports. The lines share the vessels each contributes but each carrier markets and sells freight space on an individual basis. Individual freight contracts can still be negotiated with each line and depending on the space available receivers can also nominate a choice of carriers for the goods. (For most shipments, the receiver rather than the shipper is the freight payer and negotiator.) The advantage for the shipping lines is better cost-control and increased efficiency; for receivers there is more flexibility in that they can negotiate rates and in a sense 'play the market'. But the number of sailings is not necessarily guaranteed and may be varied, for example to stabilize freight rates.

## Ocean freight, surcharges and terminal handling charges

Ocean freight is nowadays usually quoted as a lump sum per container, regardless of the payload or contents. Bulk containers are usually shipped under FCL/FCL conditions (loading and discharge costs are not included in the freight rate), whereas bagged coffee in containers is shipped LCL/FCL (loading supervised by the shipping line and cost included in the freight rate) or FCL/FCL. The cost of loading and discharging containers varies between container terminals and between shipping lines, sometimes considerably.

Ocean freight includes variable elements beyond the control of shipping companies. The most important are the cost of fuel and exchange rate fluctuations. If a European conference agrees a freight rate expressed in United States dollars, movement in the rate of exchange of the dollar against the euro will be reflected in its income. To avoid having to speculate on potential fluctuations in fuel prices or currencies, conference contracts instead allow for price adjustments whenever notable changes occur.

*Surcharges* due to adjustment of fuel costs are called ***bunker surcharge*** (BS) or ***bunker adjustment factor*** (BAF). They are usually applied as a sum per container. A surcharge due to currency fluctuations is called ***currency adjustment factor*** (CAF), expressed as a percentage of the freight sum. BS or BAF is applied to the basic freight rate, and CAF to the resulting sum. Contracts may also provide for surcharges when other costs change, such as port usage charges or tolls on seaways and canals. Conferences may also levy special increases on freight from or to ports where congestion causes excessive delays to vessels. 'All in' rates of freight are also available, particularly to large shippers and receivers. These remain fixed for specific periods during which no BAF or CAF surcharges can be applied.

***War risk*** came to the fore again in 2001 as a potential cause for surcharging freights; ship owners pass on higher insurance premiums for vessels operating on difficult or dangerous trade routes. Such unforeseen costs are a result of *force majeure* and may be passed on to shippers or receivers, usually at a flat rate per container.

Freight charges are of great importance to producing countries, because for the roaster the real cost of coffee is the price 'landed roasting plant'. If coffees bought from country A and from country B are used for the same purpose, the two qualities are substitutional and should therefore be priced the same. If freight from country A is 1 ct/lb higher than freight from B, then A's asking price must be 1 ct/lb lower to match the landed cost. And if freight rates from country B decrease then the FOB price or differential for that coffee will eventually rise accordingly.

Freight rates fluctuate all the time, and are also negotiable. It is very likely that different companies will apply different rates during the same time period, making it pointless to list actual rates in this guide. It is much more important to have a good grasp of the general principles governing freights. Freight rates are often governed by factors more numerous and complex than, for example, the distances involved.

The European Coffee Federation's Transport Committee meets on a regular basis with conference lines, and occasionally through seminars with all coffee-oriented shipping lines (conferences and non-conference alike) to review technical and physical issues (such as hygiene) relating to the transportation of coffee and levels of service. Conference lines provide the ECF with freight rates that can be used as a benchmark to assist smaller shippers. However, it is common practice for shippers and receivers to negotiate individual freight agreements with shipping lines, sometimes on a worldwide basis. Thus, even if on a given route shippers, receivers and a conference did negotiate a contract (increasingly unusual nowadays), the actual freight rate for many receivers would still not be general knowledge; many bills of lading simply state 'freight as per agreement' or 'freight payable at destination'.

***Freight portals on the Internet*** are also coming into use. These match available cargo with available space, and vice versa. Trucking and freight rates can be sought and offered so large shippers and receivers can relatively easily ask transporters and shipping lines to tender for certain land and sea cargoes (for an example go to *www.inttra.com*). These are fast moving developments that enable large users of sea and land transportation to strike competitive deals. Any impact on the way the shipping of coffee is arranged remains to be seen though.

***Terminal handling charges*** (THC) and post terminal charges are important components of the cost of transporting containerized coffee. (THC cover the loading and discharge of containers, not charges for inland transportation etc.) A freight quotation by itself may be attractive, but the cost of bringing a container on board or getting it to the roasting plant after discharge may well be higher than the norm and so offset any perceived advantage. Receivers keep a close watch on terminal charges; these charges are an important part of their evaluation of the competitiveness of individual carriers.

Remember that unless stated otherwise in the contract, under an FOB contract the shipper is liable for THC at origin and the receiver is liable at destination. If a receiver negotiates a lower rate of freight but at the same time the terminal handling costs at origin increase, the outcome is that freight costs are being moved around the supply chain – in this case to the detriment of the exporter. (Under an FCA contract the receiver is liable for *both* sets of THC so this is not an issue.)

***Break bulk*** means coffee is stowed in the ship's hold in bags – the cargo is loose. Sometimes the bags are left in the loading slings to speed up discharge at destination, at the expense though of less freight capacity per cubic metre. The disadvantages of break bulk shipping are numerous: the goods can be exposed to the weather during loading and discharge; the bags can be torn; there is a risk of contamination from other cargo during the voyage; and bags may be lost or mixed with other shipments. Marine insurance is usually higher for break bulk cargo.

***Containerized cargo*** (both in bags and in bulk) remains in the container throughout the journey, often to the final inland destination. Most if not nearly all coffee today travels in containers. As a result, shipping small (less than container load) parcels has become a problem (discussed later in this chapter).

Container transit is faster, more efficient and more secure than break bulk. Modern container vessels spend only short periods in port as all cargo is assembled before arrival, and container handling can proceed irrespective of weather conditions. Strict schedules can be maintained, and turnaround times are shorter. Ro-ro (roll-on roll-off) vessels carry containers on trailers which are simply driven on and off the ships. This does away with the need for gantry cranes. Ro-ro vessels are mostly used between smaller ports, for example in Europe.

### Shipping hubs

Shipping hubs and container feeder vessels are becoming increasingly important as the shipping industry evolves to meet the demands of globalization and the proportion of bigger vessels in world fleets is growing. Already some vessels can carry as many as 8,000 TEU (twenty-foot equivalent units) and forecasts are that vessels with a capacity of 10,000 to 12,000 TEU will become operational in the foreseeable future.

Such mega-vessels call only at ports with the required deep water offering both the cargo and the mechanized capability to handle it quickly and efficiently. Smaller ports will increasingly feed cargo to the nearest regional hub, in rather the same way as airlines have been doing for years. In some origins (e.g. Viet Nam, Indonesia) this practice is already well established but elsewhere it is creating some problems for the industry.

It is not uncommon for receivers of coffee to have proper advice of shipment, within contract terms, but still not know the name of the vessel that will deliver at the final port of discharge because the name of the transshipment vessel is not always known at time of loading.

In the United States the Green Coffee Association is working to remedy this problem. Internet-based track and trace services also offer solutions provided the shipping advice includes the container numbers (which shippers are obliged to provide in the shipment advice). Larger receivers working on the just-in-time supply system require carriers to inform them direct by email, within a given time limit, of all transshipment arrangements including the name of the mainline vessel and its estimated time of arrival (ETA) at destination.

## Bills of lading and waybills

A bill of lading is firstly a receipt: the carrier acknowledges that the goods have been received for carriage. But it is also evidence of the contract of carriage. The contract commences at the time the freight space is booked. The subsequent issue of the bill of lading confirms this and provides evidence of the contract, even though it is signed by only one party: the carrier or its agents.

A bill of lading is also a transferable document of title. Goods can be delivered by handing over a bill of lading provided the shipment was consigned 'to order' and all the subsequent endorsements are in order. (See chapter 4, Contracts.)

If a bill of lading is lost, or does not arrive in time for the receiver to take delivery, for example when transit times are short, then the carrier will usually be able to assist by delivering the goods against receipt of a guarantee. The guarantee safeguards the carrier in case the claimant is not the rightful owner of the goods. Wrongful delivery would constitute a breach of contract and the carrier will therefore insist on a letter of indemnity (LOI) from the receiver backed by a bank guarantee whose wording meets the carrier's specifications, usually for an amount of 150% to 200% of the actual CIF value of the goods, valid for one to two years. Although there is no express time limit beyond which the holder of a bill of lading can no longer claim the goods, a guarantee good for one or possibly two years should adequately cover the carrier's obligations.

However, carriers are not obliged to deliver goods against guarantees. That decision is entirely at their discretion and the receiver may have to negotiate the terms with the carrier, who may wish to consult the original shipper. Note that ECF contracts clearly state that buyers are under no obligation to take delivery under their guarantee and if 28 calendar days after arrival the bill of lading is not available then the buyer may declare the seller to be in default. The remedy here would be for the exporter to provide the guarantee instead. GCA does not specifically refer to missing documents and leaves settlement of any unresolved claim or dispute in this regard entirely to arbitration.

### Different types of bills of lading

The carrier's responsibility commences on the physical acceptance of the goods for carriage. If this occurs at an inland point a *combined transport bill of lading* will be issued. If the handover is in a port then a *port to port bill of lading* will be issued.

The term '*through bill of lading*' should not be used, as it means that the issuing carrier acts as principal only during the carriage on its own vessel(s) and acts as an agent at all other times. This implies that the responsibilities and liabilities may be spread over more than one carrier under different (possibly unknown) conditions at different stages of the transport chain.

Under a combined transport bill of lading the carrier accepts responsibility, subject to the normal stipulations in the bill of lading, for the whole carriage, inland and marine: from door to door, or from door to container yard or container station. The carrier arranges both the marine and the inland transport, but it should be noted that marine and overland transport are governed by different international conventions. This can have an effect on the settlement of claims – the financial liability of the carrier for inland carriage is not necessarily the same as it is for the marine voyage (on board ship, i.e. 'from tackle to tackle'). Usually the carrier will assist in any claims procedure initiated by the receiver and/or insurance company, but will not necessarily accept responsibility for settlement if the damage occurred during the overland stage. For example, a truck is stopped at gunpoint and the driver is asked to 'disappear': no liability. Or an accident occurs because of driver negligence: liability may exist depending on local jurisprudence.

Obviously, large receivers will find it easier to solve such matters than will smaller companies. Note that for contracts 'free on truck' it is the buyer's responsibility to lodge the necessary claims under their insurance policy, and insurance cover should therefore commence at the inland point of loading.

Whether a bill of lading is of port to port or combined transport depends on whether the box 'place of receipt' (or 'place of delivery') has been filled in.

### Waybills

Like a bill of lading a waybill is a receipt and evidence of a contract of carriage. But a waybill is not a document of title. Unlike bills of lading, waybills cannot be issued 'to order' and they cannot be endorsed. The advantage of a waybill is that there is no need to transmit paper documentation to the point of destination to secure delivery because delivery is made, automatically and only, to the named consignee. Waybills can be used when payment does not depend on the submission of documents, for example because the shipment is between associated companies or because payment has been made in advance. Thus waybills can facilitate paperless transactions. (See chapter 6, E-commerce and supply chain management.)

## Contract of carriage

*The coffee trade uses three basic contract conditions: FOB, CIF (or CFR) and FOT, of which the first two are most common. In the United States, FCA contracts are also used.*

*FOB – free on board.* The seller's obligations are fulfilled when the goods have passed over the ship's rail at the port of shipment. For contracts FOT (free on truck) and FOR (free on rail) this occurs when the goods have passed over the truck's tailgate or the railcar's loading gate.

Under present-day FOB contracts it is nearly always the buyer who arranges the contract of carriage and who is liable for all costs and risk from that point onwards. Nevertheless ECC clearly states that an FOB contract is in fact to be considered as an ill-defined cost and freight contract, with the freight being for account of the buyers. The exporter's contractual responsibility ends only when the coffee crosses the ship's rail. But ECC also states that the buyer is responsible for insuring the goods from the time the goods leave the ultimate warehouse or other place of storage at the port of shipment. This is important because it is increasingly difficult to establish the precise time a container leaves the stack on the quayside and is transferred across the ship's rail. Under GCA contracts the risk of loss transfers upon crossing of the ship's rail and exporters must insure accordingly. See 'Insurance' in this chapter for more on this.

*CIF – cost, insurance and freight (or CFR – cost and freight).* Here the shipper arranges and pays the contract of carriage but otherwise the transfer of risk is as under FOB.

***FCA – free carrier.*** Here the seller's obligations are fulfilled when the goods, cleared for export, are handed to the carrier or the carrier's official agent(s) at the named place or point of handing over. (Sometimes also called free in container or free in warehouse.) The buyer's responsibility starts here and they are liable to pay all and any inland transportation costs as well as the cost of loading at the port of shipment.

The total freight cost takes all this into account. Not everyone is willing to purchase basis FCA though, especially if the goods are not handed over at the carrier's own premises or at a recognized container filling station. Remember that inland and marine transports are covered by different international conventions and even though a shipping line may arrange for the inland transport it will not necessarily accept liability for events occurring before the goods reach the port of shipment or cross the ship's rail.

### Cost distribution between sellers (S) and buyers (B)

|  | FOB | CIF/CFR | FOT |
|---|---|---|---|
| Loading at sellers' premises | S | S | S |
| Inland transport (from the named place) | S | S | B |
| Trade documentation at origin | S | S | S |
| Customs clearance at origin | S | S | S |
| Export charges | S | S | S |
| Loading terminal handling charges (THC) | S | S | B |
| Ocean freight | B | S | B |
| Unloading terminal handling charges (THC) | B | B | B |

The term FCA is not generally used in the European coffee trade because it is part of the more *general* set of international trade conditions usually referred to as Incoterms. The current ECF contracts exclude all reference to Incoterms, not because of any disqualification or disagreement but simply to highlight the *stand-alone status* of the ECF contracts that have been specifically written for the trade in coffee. For more on Incoterms go to *www.iccwbo.org/incoterms/understanding.asp*. A number of producing countries are interested in selling on FCA terms. During the second half of 2002 the ECF contracts committee and producer representatives were considering the matter.

In the United States a considerable amount of business is transacted either FOT or FCA because of the coffee imported from Mexico through the land border between the two countries (around 2 million bags a year). Seller and buyer may not always be clear on the difference between the two terms. Basically, in the case of FOT or FOR the risk of loss transfers to the buyer when the goods are placed on the truck or railcar, whilst in the case of FCA that risk transfers to the buyer the moment the goods are received by the carrier, whether for overland or maritime transport.

### FCL or CY, versus LCL or CFS

***FCL – full container load*** simply means the seller/shipper was responsible for stuffing the container and the cost thereof. But the contents of a sealed container cannot be verified from the outside.

The FCL bill of lading simply states 'received on board one container STC [said to contain] X number of bags [or for bulk: kg] of coffee, shipper stow and count'. In other words, in an FCL bill of lading the shipping line acknowledges receipt of the container, undertakes to transport it from A to B without losing or damaging it, but does not commit itself as regards the contents. (See also chapter 10, Risk.)

There is no connection between FCL or LCL and Incoterms. The terms FCL and LCL are common in most coffee producing countries but do not always have exactly the same meaning. Combining FCL with the term CY (container yard: container is received), and LCL with CFS (container freight station: goods are received), removes any room for confusion.

***LCL – less than container load*** means that the carrier is responsible for the suitability and condition of the container, and the stuffing thereof. The carrier pays for this and then charges an LCL service charge. The bill of lading will state 'received in apparent good order and condition X number of bags said to weigh X kg'. Now the carrier accepts responsibility for the number of bags but still not for the contents of the bags, nor for the weight.

In the interests of service to clients, although not in all coffee producing countries, shipping lines will agree to carry coffee as LCL provided the containers are filled or stuffed on the carrier's premises, ideally at a container freight station (CFS). It has become accepted practice in some countries for containers to be stuffed at the seller's premises at their expense, under the supervision of the carrier or the carrier's appointed agent.

A higher rate of freight will still apply than for an FCL shipment but this arrangement is nevertheless of great value to smaller shippers or to those who are still relatively unknown. Importers and their bankers increasingly check on the credibility of exporters, including the documentation they supply, and do not accept FCL bills of lading from just anyone. For some exporters and origins, the stuffing and weighing of containers 'under independent supervision' is now the order of the day, not only for LCL shipments but also for FCL in order to satisfy the legitimate security concerns of all involved in the coffee trade. Such services are often provided by collateral managers who verify correct procedure in an exporter's operations on behalf of the bank that finances the business, sometimes right through to delivery at the receiving end. (See also chapter 10, Risk.)

Claims on shipping lines have dropped as a result of this, suggesting that past discrepancies in containerized cargo were at least partly the result of inadequate supervision during stuffing. The main cause of claims on containerized coffee in bags has however always been condensation damage, which is much less likely to occur when coffee is shipped in bulk.

The term LCL is something of a misnomer in that containers are nearly always full and freight is charged per container, not by weight. The reason the term is often used is that it permits marine insurers and/or receivers to lodge insurance claims directly on shipping lines.

But just as roasters argue that roasting and distribution is their core business, not the transporting, storing and financing of green coffee stocks, so shipping companies consider their business is to carry sealed containers safely and efficiently from A to B, and not to be concerned with the contents. The wish of shipping lines is to eliminate the LCL bill of lading entirely, in time. This in turn will see increased use of independent weighers and supervisors although the reliability of such services will still vary from port to port, and from country to country. If after such inspections weight or quality claims still arise there will be serious differences of opinion between shipper and receiver. This is mainly because it is not always understood that providing a certificate of weight or quality does not absolve the shipper from contractual obligations.

Some international cargo supervisors therefore go a step further by offering receivers 'full out-turn guarantees' under which the supervisor accepts responsibility for any loss in weight or shortage on discharge. There is a cost to such services, but they represent a very positive development that assists smaller exporters and origins to remain in business, and to compete on equal terms when it comes to contract execution – but only if they have enough coffee to ship a full container load.

### *Small lot logistics*

It is well known that exporters and buyers of small lots that are *less than a container load* face both logistical and cost constraints. Indeed, importers will not consider anything less than a container load, which effectively bars many potential small producers of specialty or organic coffee from direct participation in the overseas market.

Many small pockets of quality or exemplary coffee in producing countries go unrecognized, simply because they vanish in the mainstream of a country's total exports. Improved and simplified processing technology today allows even very small grower groups to produce quality coffee. But if this cannot be marketed successfully, then what is the point? For such coffees to gain individual recognition there must be at least 18 to 20 tons per shipment – but there are producing countries, for example in Africa, where 20 tons may represent the total production of 100 individual growers.

As not all their output will qualify, those 20 tons of exemplary coffee might represent just the top 10%: then 1,000 growers would be needed to produce one container of exemplary coffee. The added value of one such container can appear impressive but the accompanying administrative and organizational problems may render this meaningless in terms of returns to individual growers.

The logistics of getting small lots from A to B are daunting. Few if any carriers today will even quote freight rates per ton, let alone accept mini-lots. Finding compatible combination cargo to fill a standard container at least close to capacity is very difficult, and still means having to wait until a full load is assembled. Organic coffee may not be shipped in the same container as other cargo at all because of the risk of contamination. Mini-containers within a single, large container could be a solution but these would probably have to be disposable because of the difficulty of attracting suitable return cargo. This is where flexible intermediate bulk containers (FIBCs or bulk bags, super bags, jumbo bags) can play a role. Alternatively, if a small lot of expensive 'exemplary' coffee can bear the cost of paying freight for a full container then it may sometimes be just as cost effective to use airfreight instead. Another option, depending on the buyer, is to combine a small parcel with a parcel of easily sold, cheaper quality, for example 50 bags exemplary and 250 bags of a generally traded, run-of-the-mill coffee, together in one container shipped as FCL. In some countries (Nicaragua for example) producer associations help growers of certified exemplary coffee to create full container loads by combining different shipments for specific markets.

## Using containers

Bagged coffee in 20-foot 'dry containers' is a major improvement over the old break bulk method but still involves extensive handling and does not fully exploit a container's carrying capacity. This is important as transport and freight costs are charged per container, rather than by weight. The cost of handling bagged cargo is also escalating continuously, especially in importing countries.

When correctly lined with cardboard or sufficiently strong kraft paper, and if properly stuffed, standard 20-foot dry containers are suitable for transporting bagged coffee. This is not to suggest they are suitable for prolonged storage of coffee, because they are not. Some receivers do specify ventilated containers for shipments from certain areas. These provide ventilation over their entire length, usually top and bottom, but not all shipping lines offer them. They are expensive, and at the same time more and more coffee is shipped in bulk instead.

Bulk shipments were first experimented with in the early 1980s. After a period of exhaustive trials, mostly on coffees from Brazil and Colombia, the conclusion was that standard containers are perfectly suitable for the transportation of coffee in bulk. But they must be fitted with appropriate liners (usually made of polypropylene) and the coffee's moisture content must not exceed the accepted standard for the coffee in question.

## Bagged coffee in containers

### *Condensation*

Condensation occurs because moisture is always present in the air and hygroscopic (water-attracting) materials such as coffee normally contain a certain amount of moisture as well. Coffee with a moisture content in excess of 12.5% (ISO 6673) should *never* be shipped, whether in containers or bagged, as beyond this point the risk of condensation and therefore fungi growth occurring becomes unacceptably high. The only exceptions could be specialty coffees that traditionally have a high moisture content, such as Indian monsooned coffees.

This is not to suggest that a moisture content of 12.5% is commercially acceptable for all coffee – for certain coffees, certain origins and certain buyers it is definitely not. The figure of 12.5% simply represents a known technical point at which the risk of damage from condensation and growth of mould during storage and transport becomes unacceptably high. *Shippers who normally ship their coffee at moisture percentages below 12.5% should definitely continue to do so.*

An increasing number of buyers now include a maximum permissible arrival moisture content in purchasing contracts. Increasing preoccupations with food health and hygiene in consuming countries suggest strongly that exporters will be well advised therefore to acquaint themselves with their buyers' requirements in this regard.

Coffee is often loaded in tropical or otherwise warm areas for discharge at places where the temperatures are very much lower. Warm air holds more water vapour than cold air; when warm, moist air cools down to dew point, then condensation occurs. Dew point is the temperature at which a sample of saturated air will condense. For more on this and containerization generally go to e.g. *www.ponl.com* – P&O Nedlloyd or *www.tis-gdv.de* – Transport Information Service of the German Insurance Association.

During transit the temperature outside the container gradually cools down and the steel container allows the chill to conduct from the outside of the panels through to the inside. On arrival the container has cool roof and side panels, and moist warm air in the space above the cargo and within the stow. Most of the moisture will have been given up by the coffee beans themselves.

When the temperature of the panels falls below the dew point of the air inside the container, condensation starts and will continue until the dew point of the interior air falls to that of the air outside. Apart from making sure that the coffee has an acceptable moisture content, condensation cannot really be avoided and all one can do is try to prevent the condensation falling onto the coffee as droplets. If temperature changes are gradual and enough time passes then the coffee beans will absorb the excess moisture from the air within the container and the container will again be 'dry'. But temperature differences of 8 to 10 or more degrees over short periods of time almost inevitably will result in condensation taking place. In severe cases water droplets, mostly consisting of dislocated moisture from the coffee itself, form on the interior roof and side panels, and then drip on to the cargo causing water damage and mould.

In summary, differences in temperature plus the time factor and the speed of events combine to release moisture from the coffee. Given enough time the coffee surface will reabsorb the moisture. If events unfold too fast or there is too much moisture, then the coffee cannot reabsorb what it gave up and condensation will continue as long as the temperature difference between the steel of the container and the air inside it is greater than 8 degrees. A simple demonstration: a glass of cold beer 'sweats' because its temperature is below the dew point of the surrounding air. The moisture on the outside of the glass comes from the surrounding air, not from the beer or the glass itself. When the glass warms up, its temperature eventually reaches that dew point, which causes the moisture on the outside to dry again: it evaporates back into the surrounding air.

In producing countries condensation occurs when containers are stuffed at high altitude locations with high temperatures during the day that fall rapidly at night, leading to the same scenario. The risk is increased if full containers are left outside in the radiant heat of the sun, so containers should not be stuffed too far ahead of the actual time of shipment.

### Preventing damage from condensation

When ordering a container from the carrier, specify in writing that the container must be suitable for the carriage of coffee beans, i.e. foodstuffs, that you reserve the right to reject any container you detect to be unfit, and that you will claim compensation for losses resulting from unsuitable containers. This is no guaranteed protection, but it will alert the carrier. Even so, you remain liable for the selection of a suitable container, so firmly reject any suspect container.

Use a container approval form like the example on the next page – this will serve as a guideline for the personnel in charge of loading and will also remind them to pay the necessary attention. A copy could be left inside the container to demonstrate that you did pay the necessary attention.

The basic premise is that condensation cannot always be avoided but it *is* possible to avoid the condensed water vapour coming back into the coffee.

- Containers must be technically impeccable: watertight; free of holes and free of corrosion on the roof and sides; intact door locks, rubber packings and sealing devices. They must always be swept clean and must be dry and odourless, with no water or chemical stains or spots on the floor.

- When stuffing takes place at the shipper's premises the shipper must inspect the containers. An inspector should go inside the container and close the doors. If *any* daylight is visible the container must be rejected immediately. Also check that all rubber door seals are whole and tight.

- If possible check the moisture content of the floor. At least insist on a dry container that has not been washed recently. Note that it takes a long time for the floor to dry out and that without an instrument you have no reliable means of checking the floor's moisture content, which should not exceed 12% to 14%.

- The inspector should also particularly check for obnoxious smells by remaining inside the closed container for at least two to three minutes. There are occasional incidents of coffees arriving with a strong phenolic smell which renders them unfit for use. A phenolic smell or taste is reminiscent of disinfectant or an industrial cleaning agent such as carbolic acid. Inspectors should reject containers that show evidence of a prior load of chemical cargo or that have an IMCO/IMO dangerous cargo sticker or label affixed. For more information on the International Maritime Dangerous Goods Code (IMDG) and dangerous cargo labels go to *www.imo.org*, the website of the International Maritime Organization. Note that coffees tainted by chemical contamination or smell will show claims on arrival ranging from 50% to 100%, to which must be added the costs of destruction.

- The actual stuffing of the container should take place under cover, just in case there is a rain shower. Bags should be sound: no leaking, slack or torn bags; no wet bags; no stained bags.

- The container should never be filled to absolute capacity in terms of space. Always leave enough room above the stow to avoid contact with the sometimes hot steel roof. (This applies equally to bulk cargo.)

- Best practice is to line the container with cardboard or two layers of kraft paper, preferably corrugated with the corrugation facing the steel structure, so that no bag comes in contact with the metal of the container. When stuffing is complete a double layer of kraft paper should be fitted on top of the bags all the way to the floor in the

## Container approval form

| **Type** | ☐ 20' | ☐ Steelbox | ☐ Normal ventilated |
|---|---|---|---|
| | ☐ 40' | ☐ Plywood | ☐ Mini-vents |

| **Condition** | ☐ New | | **Rust** |
|---|---|---|---|
| | ☐ Used | | ☐ None |
| | ☐ Normal wear and tear | | ☐ A little |
| | ☐ Severe wear and tear | | ☐ Some |
| | ☐ Unacceptable | | ☐ Unacceptable |

| **Watertightness** | Checked from inside/doors closed | ☐ Yes |
|---|---|---|
| | | ☐ No (why) _____ |

**Doors**

| Closing devices | | Left side | | Right side | |
|---|---|---|---|---|---|
| | Top | ☐ OK | ☐ Defect | ☐ OK | ☐ Defect |
| | Middle | ☐ OK | ☐ Defect | ☐ OK | ☐ Defect |
| | Bottom | ☐ OK | ☐ Defect | ☐ OK | ☐ Defect |
| Door sealing | | Left side | | Right side | |
| | Top | ☐ OK | ☐ Defect | ☐ OK | ☐ Defect |
| | Middle | ☐ OK | ☐ Defect | ☐ OK | ☐ Defect |
| | Bottom | ☐ OK | ☐ Defect | ☐ OK | ☐ Defect |
| Ventilation | | ☐ Open | ☐ Taped | ☐ Other _____ | |

| **Cleanliness** | ☐ Front wall panel | ☐ Right side wall panel | ☐ Roof panel |
|---|---|---|---|
| | ☐ Doors | ☐ Left side wall panel | ☐ Floor |
| Humidity of floor checked | ☐ No | ☐ Yes _____ % | |
| Odour | ☐ Odour free | ☐ Foreign smell like _____ | |

Container number: _____

Container approved by: _____

|  Date and venue  |  Name in capital letters  |  Signature  |

doorway. This will ensure that the paper will at least partly absorb any condensation from the roof. In a fully lined container there will be cardboard or kraft paper also between the bags and the corner posts, in the junction between the upright walls and the floor, at the back of the container and at the doors, and covering the top of the stow as well. Cardboard is stronger and preferable to kraft paper. Dry bags are meant to absorb moisture during the voyage but should only be used with the express prior permission of the receiver. Many receivers do not permit their use under any circumstances.

### Stuffing bagged coffee

Stow the bags length-wise rather than across, and *cradle* the second layer into the nests of the first one. In this way fewer bags will be exposed to condensation and the lower height offers some protection against consequences of heat radiation.

Coffee is hygroscopic and contains water. When out in the open the container roof heats up during the day and cools down at night. If there is relatively free air circulation then the warm, humid air released from the coffee rises to the cooler steel plates, where condensation can be severe. The effect of this *thermal flow* is serious when coffee is stowed in bags because there are air channels within the stow, simply because of the shape of the bags. Those air channels are even larger when stowing is across as shown in the left of the picture below. Using the *saddle stow* blocks these air channels to quite an extent, and also reduces the height of the stow, thereby defusing the impact of the hottest areas within the container. This helps to explain why bulk containers have far less trouble with condensation than containers with bagged coffee.

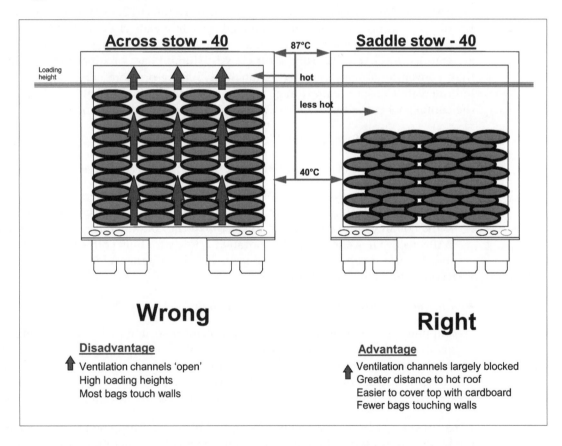

- *Transit time.* Experience shows that most of the condensation problems encountered during maritime transport are caused at origin (containers are stuffed too early ahead of actual shipment, or not properly lined), or immediately after offloading (particularly for containers arriving in winter). It is therefore of the utmost importance to limit transit times (by using dedicated sailing/routings) and the dwell periods and land legs of the transit as much as possible.

- **Storage position.** When making a booking with the carrier always give the instruction 'stow away from heat, cool stow and sun/weather protected' or 'stow in protected places only/away from heat and radiation', i.e. no outer or top position. 'Stow under deck' or 'under waterline' is not appropriate with modern container vessels, since the fuel tanks are often situated in the hull and can radiate heat.

Note however that without knowing the exact stowage position of a container it is very difficult to prove that the cause of damage was wrong positioning of the container on board ship. The damage might already have happened on shore, before loading. In any event, improper stuffing of a container (bags touching the roof, or bulk coffee not levelled) can never be compensated for by demanding special care from the carrier.

## Bulk coffee in containers

Recent years have seen a substantial increase in the movement of coffee in bulk, using normal dry containers fitted with a liner. Exact data are not readily available but informed shipping sources suggest that for a number of large producing countries most shipments, other than to the United States, are now 'in bulk'.

Shippers save on the cost of bags (and there is no need to dispose of them at the receiving end), minus of course the cost of the liner. Also, a container can hold about 21 tons of coffee in bulk compared to only about 18 tons in bags. This payload increase of almost 17% represents a freight saving of about 15% per container (basis US$ 1,000 per container). And at the receiving end the inland transport of say 50,000 tons green coffee in bulk a year for a large roaster is reduced from 2,777 movements of 18 tons to 2,380 movements of 21 tons. In Brazil, for instance, 2 million bags shipped in bulk means close to 1,000 fewer individual containers! Other obvious advantages are time and labour savings because bulk containers are emptied mechanically, using a tilt chassis. (Jumbo bags or super sacks are much larger than conventional bags, holding as much as 500 kg or more. They are mostly used for intermediate transport cum storage and must not be confused with liners that make use of the container's entire load capacity which jumbo/super sacks cannot.)

But there are other advantages, which are not always immediately apparent.

- *Coffee in bulk arrives in a better condition than coffee in bags when shipped under similar conditions.*

  Air in-between the beans and in-between the bags is called interstitial air. Interstitial air in a bulk load hardly moves since the individual beans are obstructing the free flow of air, so the hot air cannot easily move to the top of the container. As a result the temperature of the inside air at the top of the container is lower for bulk coffee than for coffee in bags, and the risk of condensation is reduced. This is why the saddle stow (previous page) is recommended for bagged coffee.

- *There are far fewer claims on coffee shipped in bulk.*

  Shipping in bulk avoids most of the problems associated with bagged cargo: no baggy smells any more, no weight losses due to handling, generally better preservation of quality. When correct liners and procedures are used, and the coffee is shipped at the correct moisture content, there are far fewer claims on coffee shipped in bulk than there are on coffee shipped in bags – according to some, claims are reduced by up to two-thirds.

In recent years, a few of the originators of the bulk coffee shipping process have patented in the United States some of the more ingenious parts of the bulk liner. The patents are on the strapping and bulkhead systems that hold the liner in place when the container doors are opened. All major importers and roasters in the United States have been cautioned to use only licensed liners for coffee shipments. As no one has contested the patent claims, the United States coffee industry has more or less agreed to use only licensed liners for coffee shipments. Shippers should therefore check with their United States buyers what brands of liners are licensed under present patents.

### Using bulk containers

The same inspection procedure must be carried out as for bagged coffee (page 123): a container is either suitable or it is not.

### Fixing the liner

The inner polypropylene liner must fit snugly against the walls, roof and floor when full – improper placing of the inlet could cause tearing – and the load must be as evenly levelled as possible. The liner's roof must not sag but must be tight so at no time will the inlet or roof rest on the coffee after loading.

Ideally, built-in reinforced straps in the liner's front panel (bulkhead) will prevent bulging when the container is full, thus allowing for easy closing of the doors. (Strapping ropes can also be used.) There should not be any pressure on the doors when closed after loading. The liner must be properly fastened to the container's interior, also at the far end: at the point of discharge the container is tilted to enable the coffee to slide out of the liner, rather than the filled liner sliding out of the container.

### Filling the container

Containers can be filled in two ways. One method is to take the coffee from the silo with the aid of a blower, or to empty individual bags into the blower's reception hopper. Blowing air into the liner makes it align itself with the walls, roof and floor of the container. Once the liner fits correctly inside the container, the blower then spews the coffee into the now fully lined container. During this process the displaced air must be able to escape.

Do not blow a heap into the centre, leaving space at the rear and the doors, but fill the liner evenly. To ensure the coffee stays away from the hot container roof, avoid as much as possible contact between the stow and the liner's roof panel, preferably by a margin of about 70 cm. Some receivers stipulate that there *must* be space between the liner's roof panel and the top of the coffee load.

Another way is to fill the container using a telescopic conveyor belt that extends into the lined box. This eliminates the need for air pressure and therefore the risk of damage to the beans.

## At the receiving end

### Inland container stations

Unlike bagged coffee in containers, bulk coffee in lined containers can be transported and stored outside for limited periods fairly safely (see Condensation, page 122). Under ECC rules containers may therefore be weighed and sampled at inland stations provided they were on-carried within 14 calendar days of arrival at the seaport and were weighed and sampled within 7 calendar days of arriving at the inland station. (Whether or not carriers raise any extra charges for such extra time is between them and the receiver.) This permits large receivers to take delivery at inland terminals. They then call the containers forward *just in time* for direct discharge at the roasting plant.

The objective of the just-in-time (JIT) supply line principle is to carry only the immediately necessary physical stocks, with *planned* arrivals to make up for draw-down. Large trade houses have the capacity to supply JIT direct from their own stocks but cannot supply all a roaster's requirements, also because roasters do not want JIT to limit their purchasing options. The alternative is to buy from smaller exporters and origins 'basis named vessel' where the buyer dictates the shipping line and the vessel to be used.

Receivers too are expected to take all reasonable measures to avoid condensation occurring, especially in winter. If the goods are not required for some time then they will be discharged in a port silo complex for call-up when required. Many ports now offer dedicated silo storage facilities or 'silo parks' which receive and store bulk. Services include blending and cleaning/sorting on demand. Deliveries to roasting plants are then made in bulk trucks that discharge by tilting, or in bulk bags. Some bulk trucks are compartmentalized and can hold different qualities, which are discharged separately by a conveyor belt that runs below the compartments.

Coffee in bags now increasingly goes to a silo installation for transformation into bulk, obviously at a cost.

## Discharge

Technology and mechanization are constantly improving supply chain management and an increasing number of bulk containers go directly from the quay or container station to the roasting plant. Here they are discharged, automatically and by a single person (sometimes the driver of the vehicle).

At the roasting plant or silo storage facility the container truck is backed onto a reception pit where the seals are checked and cut. The doors are opened, the liner is cut and the container is then gradually angled upwards by the lorry's tilt-chassis, causing the coffee to pour out. The tilting mechanism is plugged into the computerized reception mechanism, which then controls the rate of tilt and hence the rate of pour. Once the discharge is complete the liner is removed and put away for dispatch to a recycling plant. This is a far cry from when bags had to be unloaded, cut open and tipped out manually.

## Quality and sampling

Chapter 11, Coffee quality, makes it clear that to receive the wrong quality of coffee creates huge problems for any roaster. If anything this has been reinforced by modern just-in-time supply chain practices.

Large roasting plants slot incoming containers into the production line on the basis of the quality, i.e. to be used in blend or production run number X. The quality is known in the sense that the purchasing department has previously approved a sample of the coffee and it has been allocated a purchase or quality code. The plant has received the shipping sample and has verified its conformity with the purchase code.

It is extremely important to the roaster that the shipping sample is fully representative of the actual shipment because at the roasting plant the container is discharged directly into a receiving silo. This leaves little room for manoeuvre – reversing the operation is both awkward and time-consuming. Of course someone watches the actual discharge to ensure no excessive foreign matter or clumps of coffee are present. Clumps suggest water or condensation damage and a potential risk of mould.

After dumping the coffee passes through a transfer duct into the electronic weighing silo. During this passage a time switch opens a valve at regular intervals, permitting a small amount of beans to fall into a sample receptacle. In this way the entire load is automatically sampled, from beginning to end. The resulting sample is then thoroughly mixed and checked to ensure it indeed matches the purchase or quality code. This system is much more accurate than the old way of using a sampling iron on perhaps 10% of the bags. After approval and weighing the coffee is then transferred to the final storage silo pending supply to the roasting process. During this transfer any foreign matter, dust and chips are removed, again automatically.

## Weights and supervision

Weighing technology in importing countries has progressed from the random check weighing of a certain percentage of the bags to the accurate computerized weighing of each complete parcel, increasingly by using weighing silos.

The European Contract for Coffee (ECC) states that the sellers shall refund any loss in weight in excess of 0.5% of the shipping weight. Unless weighing at origin is extremely accurate some argue that this implies 'delivered weights' irrespective of what the contract states because many containers travel long distances to the coast from inland filling stations. But the underlying reasoning is that coffee in bulk does not dry out to any noticeable extent and so should not incur any noticeable loss in weight either.

Experience suggests that 90% to 95% of bulk containers discharge within the laid down weight tolerance of 0.5% and that any loss exceeding 0.2% is likely to be due to incorrect filling. There is therefore no particular reason for shippers to add a little extra weight to avoid weight claims (as is sometimes done for bagged coffee). Note though that large receivers seldom bother to claim for small weight differences, preferring to simply strike a recurrent offender off their list of approved suppliers.

Some receivers use the weighing mechanism in the container gantry crane to establish whether the gross weight of a container appears to be within acceptable limits. Should an individual box present cause for concern then it will be discharged and weighed under independent supervision. This is not feasible in arrival ports but is possible by special arrangement at inland container yards.

But, the container can only be discharged into the electronic weighing system of the roasting plant or silo park operation. This makes the term 'supervision' somewhat theoretical, since all that will be produced is a computer print-out and verification of the container and seal numbers. Of course the supervisor could certify that the weighing system had been correctly and formally calibrated in accordance with the laws of the country where it is situated. The operators of such weighing installations should be able to produce a valid calibration certificate on demand.

### Cost and convenience

Bulk shipments require less handling, cost less in terms of packaging, and incur lower port and freight charges than bagged cargo. At the receiving end they eliminate manual labour and reduce transport costs, with the product basically presented 'ready for use' at the roasting plant. With exact and reliable just-in-time scheduling, coffee increasingly travels directly from origin to the roasting plants.

European Union countries hold importers directly responsible for the disposal of waste materials such as jute and sisal bags, a task roasters can do without. The European Union is also increasingly pressuring road transport to travel outside peak traffic hours: coffee in bulk fits this development because at the terminals it can be handled mechanically, outside normal working hours.

## Outlook

It has been estimated that by the end of 2001 at least 50% of all international coffee shipments were in bulk, not just because of cost savings but also because of demand from receivers. Large receivers suggest that 70% or more of their intake is now directly shipped in bulk.

Most large modern roasting plants no longer accept bagged coffee and producing countries or exporters who persist in using bags will have to transit their cargo through silo parks at destination. Here the bagged coffee is de-bagged and transferred into silos for subsequent delivery in bulk, sometimes after blending. This is both costly and time consuming and will increasingly render uncompetitive those suppliers who cannot or will not 'do bulk'.

## Security

This and other chapters have referred to such security issues as quality, performance and finance. But there are also physical risks that may occur once the container leaves the loading station. It may be tampered with for reasons of theft or smuggling, both occurrences that are on the rise worldwide. Favourite locations for this type of crime are ports and container terminals, or during road or rail transport. The aftermath of the terrible events of 11 September 2001 brought much stricter inspection controls on containers and even coffee samples entering the United States and probably also other countries. There may be as many as 15 million containers in use worldwide, carrying much of the world's cargo, and relatively few of them are ever physically inspected since to do so would cause bottlenecks that would not sit well with just-in-time logistics. To deal with such concerns United States Customs has initiated C-TPAT (Customs–Trade Partnership against Terrorism), a government–business programme to strengthen overall supply chain and border security. For more on this go to *www.customs.treas.gov*.

### Seals

Apart from locks, the first defence against tampering are the numbered seals the shipping company provides to seal a container's doors. If a seal is broken then the container has been tampered with.

But instances have been recorded where traditional seals have been broken and replaced without any visible sign of this having occurred. Because of this some exporters add locks of their own to physically secure container doors. Seals must also be physically checked each time a container is moved to make sure they are intact and that neither the seal nor the container numbers have changed. The last check takes place just before the container will be opened.

Security of containers is not just to protect the coffee. In recent years, illegal drugs have also been found in coffee containers (as a result of port to port conspiracies, unconnected with the coffee trade). The international coffee trade and the shipping community are actively working with customs authorities worldwide to help stop the use of coffee shipments as a vehicle for illegal drugs. Obviously, container seals are the first line of defence in this battle.

Modern seals incorporate increasingly sophisticated technology that makes undetected tampering difficult if not impossible. But physical verification is still required. Seals by themselves cannot prevent containers being opened – they are not a deterrent but rather a means of verification. Even so, **seals are no better than the person who places them**. If that person cannot be trusted then one cannot be sure the seal was really placed at all, i.e. that it was not faked. It is not for this guide to explain different ways in which the placing of seals has previously been faked. Instead, one preferred solution is to use clear seals that show the mechanism, with the number printed on the inside under a clear elevation that works as a magnifying glass. Electronic seals are also being developed that will record all movements that might occur during a voyage. They will be read by scanning and may also become useful in cross-border trade, for example by reducing customs formalities in Europe.

In the end even intact seals prove only that the cargo seems not to have been interfered with after the seals were affixed. Bulk containers have been known to be attacked by forcing a pipe through the rubber door seals and into the liner, after which coffee is simply siphoned out. This is easily prevented by placing a plank upright on the floor inside and in front of the doors before shutting them.

*Even if a container's seals are sound on arrival, the exporter is still responsible for what is discharged at the receiving end, also if the stuffing took place under supervision. If the quality is incorrect or there is a weight shortfall then the receiver will still claim on the exporter if culpability can be traced to them.*

Shipping lines can be held responsible only for the apparent good order and condition, and number of the bags for goods shipped on LCL basis. When goods are shipped FCL, the responsibility lies with the person supplying them unless the bill of lading shows the container was accepted as sound but at destination it is delivered damaged. To repeat, the burden of proof always lies with the shipper.

### Container tracking

Most reputable shipping lines provide container tracking tools, track and trace, through their own websites. Containers are not yet tracked electronically (implanting micro-chip transmitters is still too expensive) but every move is notified and recorded in the tracking system, making up-to-date information available.

As individual carriers traditionally work with proprietary computer systems and programs for such services, receivers have to contact each carrier individually, which is cumbersome. However, shipping portals are being developed to standardize the way shippers, receivers and clearing agents interact with carriers, and to provide access through a single platform.

This is of considerable interest to large receivers, who supply or receive coffee just in time and who increasingly require total knowledge of traffic movements. Smaller operators will also be able to access such portals, simply by using an Internet-enabled PC. Not only shippers and receivers track containers. Banks and collateral managers are equally interested in monitoring cargo movements. Eventually, such portals will interact with both e-commerce and paperless trading systems. Other service tools will include sailing schedules, container bookings, bill of lading information and event notifications. For more on this go to *www.inttra.com.*

---

# Insurance

## Utmost good faith

All insurance contracts are subject to the principle of utmost good faith. The insured must truthfully inform the underwriter of every material fact that may influence the insurer in accepting, rating or declining a risk. This duty of disclosure continues throughout the life of the policy. Insurance is in effect a partnership between the owner of the commodity who wishes to avoid or minimize the risk of loss or damage, and the insurance company that will take on that risk against payment of a fee. The owner of the commodity must practise *risk avoidance,* just as the insurance company must make good legitimate losses.

Insurance is the most obvious and the oldest form of risk management, and has been practised since long before futures markets and other risk management instruments came into being. It is beyond the scope of this guide to go into the precise detail of what constitutes a good insurance policy – there are almost endless variations on a very basic theme: if the loss was unavoidable then the cover should stand.

But insurance cover is only as good as what is stated in the policy document. One view is that only what is expressly included is covered. Another and more attractive view is that anything that is not specifically excluded is covered.

## The risk trail to FOB

To judge the need for insurance cover one first needs to analyse the type of risk that exists, how prevalent it is and what potential loss it represents. Only then consider whether or not cover should be purchased. Always look at the monetary value of coffee when considering risk. As coffee prices fluctuate, so does the value of a truck or container load. It is not always recognized that a container load of coffee can be more valuable than a load of television sets or other electronic goods.

The following is intended to help the reader review the risk trail between purchase and delivery to FOB.

## Farm gate to processing

***Money in transit.*** An obvious risk – buying agents carry cash. An insurance company may offer a cash in transit cover as part of a general policy but the extent of such a cover is always limited so be sure to find out exactly what is covered and what is not. When coffee values change the amount of necessary cash will change as well.

***Ownership at inland buying stations.*** At this stage coffee is often packed in unmarked bags and is very difficult to identify. Keep stocks at such stations to a minimum and transfer them to a central location as soon as possible. Unless there is a good, formal record system at the buying station it may be difficult to insure risk at this stage. Be certain to advise the insurance company of all circumstances, including negative aspects, to prevent difficulties arising after a loss occurs.

***Inland transit.*** Often inland transit is by small trucks under variable conditions of transport quality. Arrivals must therefore be checked for quality, weight and moisture content. To make fraudulent manipulation more difficult samples should be taken by a member of the quality control department rather than by warehouse staff.

## Warehousing and processing

***Warehousing.*** The better organized this function is, the easier it is to obtain cover and negotiate the best terms and conditions. Like banks, insurance companies wish to know and understand how a business operates. Ensure coffee is stored in an easily identifiable manner, using a numbered bay system in the warehouse with the bay numbers and boundaries painted on the floor. Coffee must always be stored on dry, clean wooden baulks or pallets, off the floor, away from walls.

Keep back-up warehouse records in a secure and separate location. Otherwise the loss of both stocks *and* records can become very convenient for some while creating a nightmare for the owner. Make weekly stock checks, preferably using people who do not know what is expected and therefore can only report what they find. All stacks should bear a clearly visible stack card, showing the detail and history of the coffee stored. There should never be unidentified coffee in any warehouse. Unidentified can become unknown and may progress to non-existent – mystery disappearance or 'going over the wall'.

Make regular random weight checks to verify that bags are of the correct weight and that scales have not been tampered with. Occasionally tear down a stack, again at random, to verify there is no hole or empty drum in the middle.

Other obvious general risk factors include flooding, fire, lightning, explosion, aeroplane crash, theft, burglary and embezzlement. Others are deterioration due to excessive moisture content, prolonged storage or infestation (but not all these latter types of risk are insurable).

The buildings themselves can pose risk if roofs are not tight, drainage pipes are blocked, ventilation is inadequate or the walls and floor are of poor quality. The area in which the warehouse is located may pose risks if neighbouring buildings are used to store or produce hazardous or smelly goods.

***Processing.*** Usually the risk of faulty or improper processing cannot be insured. Processors must depend on the qualifications of their staff and good quality control at the purchasing end to achieve the expected results. Nevertheless, accurate storage and processing records with daily out-turn reports will go a long way to alerting one to any unexpected and unwelcome variations.

Processing is always a weak point in that out-turns cannot be forecast exactly. Ensure scales are correctly set, bags are weighed to the proper weight and, above all, do not allow any unmarked coffee to lie around. Unmarked bags or bags without tags could be the first stage of an unscheduled voyage out of the warehouse.

### *Transport to port*

There are no uniform patterns for inland transportation to the port. Each producing country has different arrangements, but all have some risk principles in common.

- The truck that collects the coffee at your facility must have been properly cleaned as you do not know what it carried before. Closely inspect all trucks for smells and other contamination. Look for holes in the roof or flooring through which water could penetrate or through which coffee might be stolen by the use of probes.

- The same applies when containers are used for inland transportation. In addition, take a very close look at the locking devices of the doors and at the door hinges.

- It is recommended also to check the moisture of any wooden flooring of any such truck or container with a moisture measuring instrument. Even a moisture content of well in excess of 20%, a situation in which coffee would definitely become damaged, cannot be verified by simply touching or feeling the floor.

- If the inland container is also to be used to ship the coffee then be sure that the container is properly lined, with the coffee fully enveloped by strong kraft paper or cardboard (depending on the season and your type of trade). (See Logistics, earlier in this chapter.)

- Depending on climatic conditions heat radiation may be a potential hazard. Even if that is not the case, coffee in a container should never be stored in the open for a prolonged period.

- Ensure that only known and trusted parties or persons handle the coffee. It is advisable to operate with as few truckers or trucking companies as possible in order to build a mutual relationship. It may also be wise to clearly define which trucks and which drivers may be used.

- Do not permit overnight trucking or prolonged stops at unknown places. If the distance to the port is too far to make it in a single day trip then make sure the driver reports with the truck at places that can be trusted, and stays overnight only in a safe and secured compound. Under certain circumstances convoy systems can also be of help.

- In some countries it is advisable to consider using security services. Before adopting such safety measures and so incurring cost, always ask yourself how quickly you will be notified of something being wrong, and who will do what within what period of time after such information is received. Have an established accident or crisis management procedure.

- Ensure the coffee is delivered to a safe and suitable location, and that the operator is familiar with the handling of coffee. On arrival the goods should be properly checked and a certificate of receipt issued. This is to ensure there is a credible paper trail that the insurer can verify.

- Remember, the climate in most shipping ports is far from ideal for coffee. In high temperatures and high humidity coffee absorbs moisture, possibly to a level where permissible limits for safe transportation are exceeded and where severe condensation and mould may become unavoidable.

*Exporters should bear in mind that at all times the coffee travels and is stored at their risk.* There is also the obligation to deliver a particular quality and quantity at a given time and place. Poor management of the risks to FOB may ruin any chance of claiming a mishap on *force majeure* (i.e. as unforeseeable events beyond anyone's control).

## Delivery to FOB – FCL (or CY) terms

Up to this point there is no difference between shipping FCL (full container load) (CY) or LCL (less than container load) (CFS), since it is always the shipper's responsibility and risk that the coffee arrives at the point and time contracted for, usually FOB a particular vessel.

(For a more detailed explanation of the terms LCL and FCL, see Logistics, pages 119-120.) The following are the additional responsibilities and risks an exporter assumes when shipping FCL.

- The shipper is responsible for selecting a suitable container. This is not limited to deciding whether a type of container is suitable in principle: each individual container must be suitable for the carriage of foodstuffs. As per the bill of lading only the shipper is responsible for selecting a suitable container, for controlling its condition, and for preparing it in every respect for the voyage.

- The shipper is responsible for proper lining of the container, or for enveloping the coffee in a suitable form.

- The shipper is responsible for loading the correct quantity. Only evidence that the container has been tampered with will absolve the exporter from having to make good any short weights. The shipper is responsible for what is loaded into the container, right until the doors are closed.

- It is solely the task of the shipper to prepare the container for the carriage of goods. Any damage that cannot be proved to have occurred from external causes is for account of the shipper. In this context changes in weather or temperature are not an external cause.

- The shipper is responsible for proper stowage and must request the carrier to 'stow away from heat, cool stow and sun/weather protected' or 'stow in protected places only/away from heat and radiation' (i.e. no outer or top position). The European Contract for Coffee also stipulates that shippers shall pass on all relevant shipping instructions received from buyers to the carrier.

Remember, the burden of proof is always on the shipper, who has to show that everything was in good order when the container left their premises or was loaded. If there is any doubt, the shipper will be held responsible, regardless of any supervision certificates issued by any party at origin.

Such certificates do not provide an ultimate safeguard because only the verifiable facts at destination count. This does not prevent shippers from employing trustworthy persons with good knowledge to control and verify what is being done – their simple presence may already be enough to avoid manipulations. But, unless expressly agreed, such inspectors or inspection companies seldom assume any financial liability arising from their work. (Some supervising agencies do provide loss cover. See Collateral management in chapter 10, Risk.)

## Delivery to FOB – FCL (or CY) in bulk

Bulk shipments are made almost exclusively on FCL (full container load) terms. In only very few ports do shipping companies offer the service of bulk loading coffee that is delivered to them in bags. For bulk shipments, be aware of all risks already mentioned above for FCL shipments, and also of the following additional factors.

- While the need to select a suitable container for bagged coffee is essential and obvious, this is even more so for coffee in bulk since separating out any damaged beans is far more difficult and expensive. In particular the container must be clean, free of taint, watertight, with locking and sealing devices intact. Only responsible, experienced and reliable persons should be entrusted with the checking of containers before stuffing.

- Using the appropriate liner is essential. These are made from woven polypropylene or similar material that allows the coffee to breathe. The liner must be fixed to the container in such a way that:

  - It does not slide out during tilting and emptying of the container;

  - The liner's roof does not lie on the coffee;

  - The bulge does not touch the doors but is well away from them (the bulging effect increases during transit).

- The liner must be filled properly with the correct quantity and quality of coffee. The surface of the coffee must be as level as possible to provide maximum distance to the container roof, and to prevent the liner from resting on top of the coffee.

- Sealing the container is a good option to secure evidence of what has been done. The carrier will probably also affix a seal – if so, check carefully that the seal is correctly applied, and the seal number is noted and mentioned in the shipping documents. (The European Contract for Coffee requires shippers to provide seal and container numbers in their shipping advices.)

### Delivery to FOB – LCL (or CFS)

LCL (less than container load) means the carrier is responsible for the suitability and condition of the container, and the stuffing thereof for which they charge an LCL service charge. The bill of lading will then state 'received in apparent good order and condition X number of bags said to weigh Y kg'. The carrier accepts responsibility for the number of bags but not the contents or the weight. The exporter's liability is reduced but not eliminated since, again, the carrier can only be blamed if the cause of any arrival discrepancies can be proved to be external.

### Termination of risk

Depending on the terms of the contract of sale contract, risk may terminate at different stages of the shipping process.

***FCA*** or ***FOT*** *(*can be either ***CY*** or ***CFS***)*. The buyer or their agent takes delivery at an inland place, probably at the seller's mill or warehouse, the receiving station or on the carrier's truck. No risk of physical damage or destruction attaches to the exporter after this point, but the exporter remains responsible for errors or omissions that occurred while the goods were under their care and responsibility.

In other words, if you deliver an FCL container that is unsuitable (e.g. tainted) then you remain responsible for all the consequences. The same goes for short weights beyond the permitted tolerance. But if the container is stolen after it leaves the premises, then the loss is not the responsibility of the exporter.

***FOB*** *(*and ***CFR***)*. As discussed in chapter 4, Contracts, there are differences between FOB according to Incoterms and FOB as per the ECC and GCA contracts for coffee. In insurance terms:

- Incoterms: FOB means that you must bring the goods safely and in sound condition under ship's tackle at your risk and expense.

- ECC: FOB means that the risk, or rather the obligation to keep the goods insured, passes to the buyer when the coffee leaves 'the ultimate warehouse or place of storage at the port of shipment'. This certainly does not mean that the entire inland haulage or storage is at the buyer's risk – all it means is the very short time span from the last place of storage immediately before shipment. (This stipulation removes any uncertainty regarding insurance cover being in place for FOB shipments. The seller's contractual responsibility ends 'when the goods cross the ship's rail' but for insurance purposes it is difficult to establish when exactly this happens.) In the case of container shipments it means the removal of the container from the stack in the port of shipment for direct placing under ship's tackle – not the removal of the coffee from the warehouse for stowing it into containers.

ECC then goes on to state that 'the sellers shall have the right to the benefit of the policy until the documents are paid for'. This ensures that the exporter has recourse to the buyers' insurance policy in case the goods or the container itself are damaged, destroyed or stolen between the time the container is placed in the export stack in the port and its receipt on board.

Under GCA contracts, however, title to the goods is transferred when they cross the ship's rail and the shipper is therefore obliged to insure up to this point. The structure of the American coffee trade is different from that in Europe: the vast majority of American roasters buy coffee 'ex dock' so it is the trade house or importer that deals with marine insurance matters whereas in Europe many roasters buy basis FOB.

***CIF.*** In addition to paying the ocean freight the shipper must also arrange and pay for an insurance that must be in conformity with the stipulation of the European Contract for Coffee: warehouse to warehouse, all risks including SRCC (strikes, riots, civil commotions commodity trade) risk and war risks at a value of CIF + 5%. (For more on this see chapter 4, Contracts. Very few CIF sales take place nowadays.)

## Insuring risk

The paragraphs above are intended to assist in assessing the risks and obligations, other than purely commercial ones, that accompany particular types of contracts. The need for insurance will be obvious to everyone – the scope of cover that is needed depends on the total exposure to risk and is best assessed by seeking professional guidance from an insurance broker, an underwriter or one's bankers. Obviously this guide cannot provide a comprehensive overview of all potential options and solutions.

Just as it is essential to fully appreciate and quantify one's exposure to certain risks, so one must understand the obligation to inform the underwriters fully of all the factors of the risk to be insured against. If this is not done it may be considered that the risk was misrepresented, rendering the insurance null and void. The relationship between client and underwriters is in many ways very similar to that between borrower and banker – full disclosure is the best approach.

Insurance is a business with firm rules and regulations. The costs of insurance coverage are not based on firm tariffs, however, but rather are the result of the underwriters' experience with the particular type of risk. Underwriters keep check of the amount of premium collected and the losses paid out. This loss experience will determine whether premiums are reduced, remain the same or are increased. Alternatively the scope of cover may be reduced or even cancelled entirely. It is therefore in the exporter's own interest to avoid losses and claims, that is, to practise loss avoidance.

## Types of cover

### Open cover

If you have regular needs for insurance, it is advisable to enter into a contract that is valid for a period of time – usually one year. Within the principal contract all necessary stipulations are discussed and agreed once, and they apply for the entire period. This means that within its period of validity the cover is always available when needed. Compared to insuring on a case-by-case basis this provides additional safety, better rates and a better relationship with underwriters.

### Maximum exposure or limit of liability

With an open cover the insurance contract will stipulate the limit of the underwriters' liability to compensate the insured for a single occurrence. The amount of liability may vary depending on each stage of transport or storage. On a case-by-case basis (insurance per certificate) the amount stated in the insurance certificate is the limit of liability.

### Extent of insurance – all risks

In reality the phrase **'all risks' certainly does not mean that all possible risks are covered**. Normal storage and transport insurance principally covers only losses due to physical damage to goods that occurs suddenly and originates from external sources or events. For example, underwriters will never cover the risk of goods becoming unfit for use as a consequence of excessive moisture content or improper preparation, and they will firmly reject all such claims.

'All risks' normally covers all the physical risks mentioned earlier. The contract may however also include a list of perils, particularly for storage insurance. Be very careful with such lists. Only the items (perils) they mention are covered by the insurance – nothing else. If the list states only fire, lightning and flooding, then risks such as contamination, infestation, wetting or theft are not covered.

## Claims

It is the duty of the insured and whoever is acting on their behalf to:

- Take all reasonable measures to avoid or minimize losses recoverable under the insurance.

- Ensure that all rights against third parties (warehousemen, transporters, port authorities, etc.) are properly preserved and exercised.

## Loss in weight

One matter clearly not covered under 'all risks' is loss in weight that does not result from obvious theft or torn bags. Exporters wishing to cover potential weight losses, for example when shipping coffee in bulk, must expressly apply for such cover. Carefully check first whether it would not be better instead to ensure that the correct quantity is always shipped, possibly even with a small excess or tolerance.

## Duration of cover

There will be a clear stipulation from which moment until which moment cover is granted. Read that part of the policy or certificate very carefully; if you experience a loss outside that given timeframe, you are not covered. Note too that 'warehouse to warehouse' does not mean any warehouse that may be suitable – it is always a warehouse at the stated place of destination. This may well be different from the final destination the goods may travel to.

## Exclusions

The policy or certificate may contain exclusion of particular risks, for example the nuclear energy exclusion clause. Another likely exclusion is for war on land, not to be confused with coverage against SRCC risks (strikes, riots, civil commotion). There will also be other exclusions, sometimes based on the location of a particular risk.

## Deductibles or franchises

It may well be that the underwriter does not cover all of the risk and only agrees to insure 80%. Alternatively the first so many thousands of dollars of any claim will not be paid. Indirectly, this is the same thing. The objective of such stipulations is to ensure that the client, the insured, makes every effort to avoid claims occurring, that is, they practise risk avoidance.

Agreeing to deductibles – also called franchises – will also save some premium, but avoid a situation where in case of a major disaster the total amount of such deductibles could put the company's financial health at risk.

## Premiums

The policy will stipulate the amount of premium to be paid, how the monthly declarations shall be made to the underwriters, and the way and time limit within which invoices need to be paid. Remember that unpaid premiums can result in cover lapsing. Underwriters usually view single risks as more speculative and more expensive to administer than declarations under an open cover or declaration policy. Rates under open covers are therefore generally much lower than those for single risks.

## Claims from receivers at destination

We know that the vast majority of shipments are contracted FOB, and that receivers therefore cover the marine insurance. In the context of this guide their relationship and arrangements with the providers of that cover are not of direct interest, but exporters need to understand why the receiver claims from them, rather than from the carrier or the carrier's insurance company.

The burden of proof rests on the shipper unless and until there is concrete evidence that the loss or damage was due to an external event that took place after the container was closed and sealed. At the same time it must be appreciated that serious partners of good standing are not interested in claiming loss or damage where it does not exist. Some receivers therefore take the trouble to immediately inform shippers when they believe there could be a claim on an arrival, perhaps adding a digital photograph showing the problem (e.g. wetness, mould or clotting of the beans).

Depending on the type of problem the shipper is then given a time limit within which to respond, for example by arranging for an appointed representative to witness the discharging. Since the shipper has only insured till FOB it is unlikely that their own insurance company will become involved, unless of course the evidence suggests that the damage or loss could have occurred before loading. As a precaution, shippers are therefore always advised to transmit such claims to their underwriters.

Even so, damage due to the improper selection of a container, improper lining or stowing etc. is never part of the insurance cover to FOB unless it has been expressly agreed (liability insurance for faulty workmanship). Unexplained differences in weight or number of bags will also not be covered unless the cover was against loss in weight 'irrespective of cause', something few underwriters will consider.

### *Appointment of surveyors*

'Appointment of surveyors' is an often-heard term. 'Lloyd's agents' is another. But the trade in coffee is increasingly specialized, and the burden of proof is increasingly placed on the exporter (in health-related issues too). It is unlikely that the average insurance surveyor will have the required expertise in condensation issues, for example. In some countries this kind of specialized expertise is more easily obtained than in others; if shippers consider they might be at risk they could be well advised to determine in advance whom they could call on to represent them in case of claims. Compiling information for different importing countries on qualified, professional surveyors and other available coffee experts (surveyors may not understand quality issues for example, and a coffee quality expert may not be expert in transport matters), would be a useful exercise in collaboration between coffee trade associations in producing and consuming countries.

In any case, when a notification of a potential claim is received, it is best to react with all due haste and in particular:

● Inform your own insurance company, and the carrier, as a matter of course.

● Obtain the fullest information about the extent of the loss or damage.

● If necessary request someone (your agent for example) to visit the site.

● If things sound serious, appoint a qualified surveyor to attend on your behalf, always keeping your own underwriters informed.

# CHAPTER 6

# E-commerce and supply chain management

## E-commerce and coffee

### Different views and uses

In a sense e-commerce development ran away with itself in the late 1990s as companies rushed to establish industry standards, offering Internet services that most of the coffee industry was not ready for. Internet trading sites were offered to people and organizations that were not comfortable working on the Internet and, indeed, many such sites have since closed down. Nevertheless, coffee companies worldwide are learning the advantages of using computers to save costs and give access to new markets – it is only a matter of time until all sectors of the coffee business will be looking for new and better services on the Internet, to improve their trading opportunities.

Growers and exporters are looking to Internet trading to gain better prices. They hope that by eliminating the 'coyotes', or middlemen, they will get better prices from the major roasters but it is doubtful whether this will happen for most of them. Following the marketing principle that you can eliminate the middleman but not his function, it is even possible that eliminating middlemen and the middle market for coffee might have the opposite effect on prices. Buying power in the import market is hugely concentrated. The mainstream coffee market accounts for close to 90% of all coffee business, and the specialty or gourmet market by itself is unable to drive prices. But origin will always try to gain ground and exporters may eventually find themselves on a more equal footing with the middlemen they are hoping e-commerce may eliminate. A stronger secondary (second hand) market for coffee, that also includes players from origin, might then be the result.

Importers see the opportunity differently although, like exporters, they too hope to save on back-office costs. Unlike exporters, who see coffee trading only once, that is from source to importer or roaster, importers hope the Internet will stimulate renewed interest in the second hand market. They imagine a cash market that operates with Internet efficiency and speed, where parcels of coffee might trade two, three, or more times between coffee merchants before finding a final buyer. Such secondary or second hand trades would be used by merchants to offset differential and market risk, and would link the speculative activity of the futures markets to the fundamental realities of the cash market.

If one growth of coffee traded out of the price range from comparable qualities, this second hand market would create opportunities for all participants to take advantage. Assuming a certain level of financial stability, exporters also could have access to such a secondary market. Internet trading sites may help this type of market development, but by no means can they guarantee its success.

Large companies, including roasters, are also looking to trim costs and back-office paper work. But, perhaps more importantly, they hope the Internet will bring coffee market transparency and better purchase audit trails.

*Transparency*. For large companies, the coffee market poses problems. Coffee buyers have always been technicians, and coffee marketing executives and financial controllers have always had to trust the judgement of these coffee technicians in the prices that they pay for coffee. Coffee buying departments have to be big as it takes a number of coffee specialists to keep track of the market. Market analysis and forecasting make these departments even larger. Back-office paper work aside, reducing the reliance on coffee buying specialists could reduce overheads substantially. Some large companies envisage an Internet coffee trading site where most of the coffee in the world would be on offer, and where it would be just a matter of looking at the site and logging the offers to know where prices were at any given moment. Exporters would be pre-screened by credit and quality specialists, so only offers from approved vendors would appear on the site. In essence, the coffee market would be constantly defined by the offers on the Internet site from such pre-approved vendors. But of course there should also be room for information from non-approved vendors, both to facilitate their entry to the market and to improve competition.

*Audit trail.* If the market is constantly defined online by offers of coffee, keeping track of this data, using snapshots of daily offers and activity, gives an organization a clear market history. This would be a very specific price history of specific growths and qualities of coffee, quite different from what futures markets or indicator prices provide. Matching purchasing information with this detailed market history would give a large organization an audit trail that could be used to measure fairly accurately how the buyers were performing.

## Efficient commerce first

However, no organization can seek the advantages of a paperless Internet business system without first having a relatively sophisticated internal control computer system. The Internet is a data transfer medium and users need a database of their own before beginning to think of sending and receiving data to and from third parties. Supply chain management is not e-commerce – instead of 'electronic marketplaces', what is required first of all is standardization of the way in which an industry or a group of companies operates. Before we can have successful e-commerce in coffee, we need *efficient commerce,* and this is where the Internet offers huge potential that is increasingly being exploited. Prime examples already operating in the coffee industry include the London LIFFE CONNECT™ futures trading system (see chapter 8, Futures markets), the GCA's XML contract (chapter 4, Contracts), the Bolero paperless documentation system (later in this chapter), and shipping portals and tracking systems (chapter 5, Logistics).

Until the coffee trade generally has adapted to the electronic environment, a hybrid form of e-commerce is likely to develop: neutral electronic platforms alongside independent brokerage services. Such combinations already operate in other industries and would answer the coffee trade's preference for contact and neutrality. They permit the immediate capture of all necessary data, which in turn enables automatic linkage into electronic execution of the contract, for example the Bolero system. The data capture also provides the necessary links to risk management options (physical and futures trading are inseparable for probably 90% or more of all coffee traded), and the credit lines provided by commodity trade banks (see chapter 10, Risk).

Whether and how soon a sufficient amount of the coffee trade will move to truly efficient commerce largely depends on the mainstream players. If a good part of the mainstream business moves then much of the rest will likely follow. Whether this would lead to large scale, real e-commerce is hard to say, however.

The technology already exists to make a sophisticated, Internet-based, e-commerce coffee trading system feasible. It will not work, however, until enough market participants are comfortable with using it to provide the critical mass necessary to make it viable. But it is likely that, in the not too distant future, enough people will meet daily at an Internet trading site to call that site a market for coffee. Until then, instead of this business to business (B2B) model, the most obvious e-commerce activity in the coffee world will likely remain that of business to consumers (B2C), in which roasters, importers and some specialized producers with the requisite logistical capability sell small amounts, often in retail packs, directly to individual consumers or wholesale to small retailers.

## Internet auctions

### *Traditional auctions*

There is growing interest in Internet auctions for selling specialty coffee. The concept and many of the legal, technical and practical aspects were developed under the auspices of the ICO/ITC/CFC Gourmet Coffee Project and involved the Brazilian Specialty Coffee Association (BSCA) working in association with the Specialty Coffee Association of America (SCAA). The first auction was successfully held in December 1999 for specialty coffees from Brazil and has subsequently been developed into the *Cup of Excellence* programme. Since then, further auctions have taken place in Brazil, Guatemala and Nicaragua.

Under the Cup of Excellence programme a number of coffee lots are submitted to a tasting panel of respected international judges and the top ten or so are auctioned via the Internet. Internet auctions have also been held in Costa Rica and Panama, outside the Cup of Excellence programme. As a result of this process the winning lots have achieved much higher prices than they otherwise would have, and indeed some have commanded premiums, which before were the exclusive preserve of coffees such as Jamaican Blue Mountain or Hawaiian Kona. However, the total quantity sold through Internet auctions has been very small and although extremely high prices have been paid for the top lots, the number of bags in each lot has been very limited (averaging between 20 and 100 bags only). The small size of these lots creates a major shipping problem as no one lot is sufficient to fill a container on its own. See chapter 5, Logistics, for more on this.

The logistics of hosting an Internet auction are quite complex and involve developing a suitable portal which can handle real time defined bids from different sources. The process of signing up international buyers and importers is also a difficult and time-consuming task, as is establishing a tasting panel of well-known cuppers. However, although the process is complex, a model now exists which other origins can adopt should they wish to do so. Origins interested in hosting a Cup of Excellence Internet Auction should contact the organizers via the Specialty Coffee Association of America – *www.scaa.org*. A further Internet auction capability for African coffees is being developed (2002) by the Eastern African Fine Coffees Association (EAFCA) in Kampala, Uganda – go to *www.eafca.org*.

Note though that such auctions focus on a small segment of the specialty market and as yet do not lend themselves well to broader based selling of coffee.

### *Reverse auctions*

Reverse auctions are used by large individual companies or groups of companies to procure bulk requirements from pre-approved suppliers who are invited to submit offers for a specific requirement. They differ from Internet auctions in that *reverse auctions are meant to achieve the lowest possible price* and so are *organized by the purchaser*. Traditional auctions on the other hand are meant to achieve the highest possible price and so they are nearly always organized by or on behalf of the seller. Like traditional auctions, reverse auctions must achieve critical mass – there must be sufficient active participants to ensure a competitive market. It is easier to achieve this critical mass in times of over-supply or weak trading conditions than when the economy is booming and supplies are tight or even short.

# Taking the paper out of the coffee trade: the Bolero system

## Why?

The overwhelming majority of the coffee trade still uses paper documentation in its dealings. While actual negotiations are conducted by phone, fax, email, and lately more and more over the Internet, final agreements such as contracts, delivery orders, bills of lading, letters of credit and other vital documents require an original signature and must be presented physically to the respective parties. Furthermore, the quality and type of shipping documentation that circulates is extremely variable and delays may be considerable when faulty documents have to be returned and resubmitted, or cargo release is delayed because the documents are not available, causing significant and unnecessary cost.

According to the World Trade Organization the cost of paper shipping documentation and related unnecessary costs is as high as 7% of all international trade (a cost therefore of US$ 420 billion in 1996). Clearly the concept of a facility which allows the issue of electronic original documents with electronic original signatures, 24 hours a day, 7 days a week, is highly appealing. Cost savings apart, this will also help to eliminate middle layers such as brokers, agents and branch-offices in coffee producing countries.

Banks and others in the trade chain are very interested both in *electronic security* and *the standardization of trade documentation*. Taken together, provided clear and enforceable standards apply, these would provide the certainty that the shipping documentation submitted is valid and negotiable, which is not always the case at present.

For many exporters the time lapse between actual shipment and receipt of payment, executed through physical transmission of paper documents, can take as much as 15 to 25 days. Using the Bolero system, the transfer of documents, transfer of title and financial settlement can be reduced to 4 days or even less, depending on the complexity of the business process. The following example is based on experience gained with Colombian coffee shipped to the United Kingdom (Japan and the United States are now also linked).

### *Typical traditional document flow*

| | |
|---|---|
| Day 1 | Coffee loads |
| Day 2 | Carrier prepares bill of lading |
| Day 3 | Shipper receives B/L (can be much later in some coffee producing countries) |
| Day 4 | Shipper processes B/L to bank |
| Day 5 | Bank receives B/L |
| Day 6 | Non working day |
| Day 7 | Non working day |
| Day 8 | Bank processes documents |
| Day 9 | Documents in transit to selected European bank |
| Day 10 | Documents in transit to selected European bank |
| Day 11 | The European bank receives documents |
| Day 12 | The European bank sends documents to buyer |
| Day 13 | Non working day |
| Day 14 | Non working day |
| Day 15 | Buyer receives and processes documents |
| Day 16 | Payment effected |
| Day 17 | Shipper receives payment |

### Typical Bolero enabled document flow

| | |
|---|---|
| Day 1 | Coffee loads, bill of lading raised by carrier |
| | B/L instantly transmitted to shipper |
| | Shipper uses B/L to generate other documents |
| | Shipper transmits to selected European bank |
| Day 2 | Documents received and processed by bank |
| | Bank transmits to buyer |
| Day 3 | Buyer processes documents and effects payment |
| Day 4 | Shipper is credited with the payment |

Clearly the benefits will vary from country to country but that they are potentially substantial is obvious, especially when credit is tight and expensive, and when exporters depend on fast turn-around of their capital.

---

*The Bolero Project, originally an EU sponsored project on Trade Facilitation, developed the notion of an electronic bill of lading from which evolved Bolero International. For more information go to www.bolero.net. Although a relative newcomer for coffee, the Bolero system is widely used in the international metals and minerals trade, and increasingly in retail generally. It is a stand-alone process covering trade documentation that can be used with or without association with an electronic marketplace. The SWIFT (Society for Worldwide Interbank Financial Telecommunication) inter-bank payments service is one of the founders of Bolero International and manages the system's technical operations.*

---

## How?

### Bird's-eye view

Imagine the electronic progress of a coffee shipment from sale to delivery as a highway along which there are a number of stops where different actions take place: the coffee is contracted, bagged, weighed, transported, stuffed into containers, cleared, shipped, invoiced, paid, discharged, cleared, trucked inland and delivered to the roaster. At each stop documents and advices are initiated and are slotted into the electronic master envelope that represents the physical shipment. When the envelope reaches the buyer it contains all the required documentation and the buyer pays for the goods.

This is no different from the traditional way of physically collecting all the bits of paper and signatures at every stage and couriering them to the buyer or their bank. Except the electronic method is entirely secure, it is neutral and it takes much less time. It also provides a precise and instantaneous record of each step or action that is taken along the way, and of who takes it. At all times each party will know what has been said to whom and by who, thus avoiding misunderstandings and mistakes.

### The electronic environment

Major international companies have seen that the electronic sharing of non-confidential data and information can shorten delivery, marketing and financing cycles while maintaining acceptable inventory levels, thereby reducing cost and liberating working capital throughout the trade chains. Optimizing the supply chain results in efficiency gains for all parties, and minimizes the complications and risks involved in international trade and shipping.

Electronic information flows also make it much easier to act proactively when a potential control issue looms: the situation at each stage of the execution of an international shipment is visible, instantly and constantly. Finally, increases in efficiency and security may also add to cash market liquidity.

Such major change does not happen overnight. We have seen the telex and fax gradually being replaced by email. But what to do with electronic data which is not standardized? How to make optimal use of Internet technology? How to bring the community of coffee exporters, traders, importers, roasters, carriers, warehousemen, government authorities, financial institutions and other service suppliers closer together in sharing data, thereby avoiding duplication and errors? How to create efficiencies for each member of the community in their function within the supply chain and for the coffee community as a whole? What about the security of the data transmission? Will such comprehensive data be used effectively and without compromising the competitive advantage individual companies may have developed over the years?

Various global shippers have focused their efforts on providing browser-based information services on contracts, delivery orders, shipments and quality. These initiatives have played a meaningful role in the process of automation and creation of supply chain visibility. But in the long run they are not a sustainable solution because they do not allow for efficient, industry-wide data integration. Two mainstream solutions have now evolved:

- E-marketplaces for commodity trading, and

- Secure messaging platforms to allow for data integration within the supply chain.

### From B2B-exchanges to e-marketplaces

When e-commerce over the Internet was introduced, the operations were rightfully considered as B2B exchanges. Bringing buyers and sellers together, price discovery, and matching supply and demand were the main criteria bringing coffee traders and roasters to the Internet. Through specialization these B2B exchanges then developed into private exchanges or evolved into e-marketplaces, enlarging their scope to cover several commodities.

These e-marketplaces facilitate the electronic execution of coffee contracts but this covers only the 'front-office' segment of trading coffee. The 'back-office' component (execution of contracts, shipments, payments) continues to be largely paper based. Logically, e-marketplaces need to be able to link the members of the coffee industry and service suppliers, so as to offer the best levels of service and data distribution to the back-offices and planning systems of exporters, traders, importers, roasters, warehouses and other service providers.

Providing back-office functions to industry participants is where the Internet can bring efficiencies. Electronic exchanges such as Comdaq and InterCommercial Markets already conduct business on a global basis and several companies and organizations representing origin countries have also established private exchanges. Other application service providers offer integrated logistics services (back-office functions) direct or via such e-marketplaces.

### Centrally available data versus straight through processing (STP)

While e-marketplaces provide electronic functions and may replace back-office functions within each of the individual trading partners, the data remain on the servers at the e-marketplace. For certain functions it is ideal if the various parties in the supply chain have access to these centralized data. However, certain types of data need to be held in the databases of the participants themselves, for reasons of corporate security or enterprise resource planning (ERP): production scheduling, accounting, contract and position management systems and so on, that are outside the scope of an e-marketplace. Such data need to be transferred between the different players.

In paperless trade this is done not through physical transfers of documents or rekeying the data, but rather through electronic messaging of the data, between participants or via the e-marketplace.

If the electronic data are in a standard format which can be recognized by participating systems, information can be transferred directly from computer to computer. This is also known as *straight through processing* (STP). This means the data do not have to be intercepted by users for verification and subsequent re-entry in the system (retyping or rekeying[19]), but can be integrated directly into the individual user's application or database.

When combined with the central functions provided by the e-marketplaces, STP allows for efficiencies and cost savings at all functional levels of the supply chain. Administrative tasks are reduced, and supply chain visibility and efficiency between trade chain partners is increased.

## *Legal framework required*

Managing and limiting risk is essential in the international coffee trade and shipping environment. Knowing and trusting one's counterparts is not always easy. Managing the risks inherent in negotiable documents requires security, non-repudiation and certainty of delivery.

Although some companies have been using e-commerce for some time despite the lack of specific international or national legislation, the lack of legal clarity has slowed acceptance. The electronic exchange of data does not in itself pose a problem. However, when the data represent contracts, negotiable instruments or payments, a clear legal and neutral framework is required. In the absence of uniform national legislation, this framework can take the form of a multilateral contract that binds all participants to rules of conduct that are necessary for these transactions to work.

## *Rulebook and title registry*

In the Bolero system, this contract is known as the Rulebook. It clearly defines which electronic messages replicate the provisions of the classic paper documents, such as contracts and bills of lading. It also provides data security and integrity, and establishes that these messages cannot be repudiated. These are all essential elements in electronic messaging.

It also sets up a central registry of titles (TR), so that legitimate transfer of title can be made. This TR is currently designed for bills of lading (called BBL in the system), but the same principle can be applied towards any type of negotiable documents, whether contracts, warehouse warrants or letters of credit. The legality of the system has been tested in a number of jurisdictions, between them covering many countries.

## *Compliance verification and settlement*

The Bolero system can handle and verify the compliance of all types of international trade documentation, from commercial documents to government-issued certificates and financial settlement tools. Through the Settlement Utility for managing Risk and Finance (SURF – also operated by SWIFT) the Bolero system incorporates aspects of existing settlement methods, such as document compliance checking and exchange of business documents against payment, and eliminates expensive and time-consuming manual activities. Also through the SURF facility, electronic documents of title can provide the basis for trade goods to be used as collateral for financing. The aim is to connect the entire trade community: exporters, importers, carriers, banks and other intermediaries, thereby making the movement of goods and financial settlement cycles entirely paperless.

---

**19** A McKinsey study (2000) found that the error rate in rekeying may be as high as 50% for some documents – that is half of all the documents circulating contain at least one error.

Other initiatives have also been formed. Some service providers offer web-based browser solutions that focus on particular functions, industries or geographic sectors, but they may not provide the same legal frameworks as the Bolero system. Other solutions such as TradeCard, SurePay and Identrus focus more on the financial settlement. Some service providers restrict themselves to specific markets, some overlap with others, and in some cases they are complementary.

In the United States cotton trade there is another type of service provider, which focuses on the issue and registry of warrants for the cotton industry, regulated through the United States Department of Agriculture. (USDA monitors ERW Inc., the cotton trade's service provider, but does not guarantee its performance.) The Uniform Commercial Code in each state of the United States spells out the power of an original warehouse receipt; if a state says that a paper warehouse receipt is the primary document, then all claims based on an electronic receipt would be subordinate. For agricultural commodities federal law therefore stipulates that electronic warehouse receipts are primary documents. Electronic warehouse receipts have been used in the United States cotton trade since the early 1990s.

### Secure transfer of data and documents

Neutrality is an important aspect when choosing a service provider. Exporters, traders and roasters will generally feel more comfortable with a visibly neutral platform. They also prefer a legal framework in which supply chain participants can communicate data and documents within a closed community, yet within an open technology environment providing more effective business processes throughout the supply chain.

Individual participants will continue needing to keep data on their own servers and will strive to establish 'straight through processes' to their particular customers. But over time communities served by different providers will require cross-provider links between those networks. Service suppliers to the trade who are active across multiple industries, such as carriers, warehouses and banks, require access and transferability.

Both the open technology used and the transparency of cross-provider transfer of data will eventually allow companies to interact across borders *and* industries. Already several systems such as Bolero, Identrus[20] and Transora[21] collaborate and promote collaboration between supply chain members, so they will seek similar connections between different networks.

But obviously such transactions must be handled through a provider or trustee who furnishes *depository services*. That is to say, all those wishing to use electronic transfer of original documents will have to be linked to a provider of depository services, at least until individual providers can themselves be linked to each other and carry out each other's deliveries, adhering to the strictest standards of integrity and verification of the documentation.

The international banking community has been using such protocols and systems for many years: SWIFT (Society for Worldwide Interbank Financial Telecommunication) and CHIPS standards (Clearing House Interbank Payments System). Today these systems handle approximately 95% of all international dollar payments. Bolero and Identrus are based on similar principles and are logical extensions of the original considerations that led to SWIFT's formation.

---

20  Identrus is a Certification Authority and Scheme that enables digital signatures to be deployed by applications. SWIFT provides network and interface services to Identrus. For more go to *www.identrus.com*.

21  Transora (*www.transora.com*) is a purchasing platform through which large players in the packaged goods industry, such as Unilever, Heinz and Coca-Cola, aggregate their demand and so use their joint purchasing power in reverse auctions. Another such platform is Covisint (*www.covisint.com*), which pools the buying power of a number of otherwise competing motor manufacturers.

SWIFT is one of the founders of Bolero and Identrus and manages the technical operations of the Bolero system under contract, thus linking Bolero directly into the international banking system. As at mid 2002, a total of 197 countries were on-line with SWIFT. Over 7,000 live users transmit well over a billion individual messages each year, at peak times more than 8 million messages in a single day. Details at *www.swift.com*.

## Specifics

### *Security, common ground, dispute resolution*

The trade in coffee would not be possible without security, some form of common ground and the effective, neutral resolution of disputes. The existing trade execution system has been developed and fine-tuned over many decades: electronic systems will have to satisfy the same concerns and meet if not surpass the same standards to address the new issues arising from the use of electronic documents.

In the paperless chain, security is provided primarily by the legal framework, supported by the participants in Bolero, exactly as is the case with SWIFT, CHIPS, Identrus and others.

Common ground is provided by the multilateral contract, with Bolero acting as trustee for the entire operation. Note that all the participants are direct or indirect service providers to the international trade. As in the traditional coffee trade, rules and regulations are clearly defined in the Rulebook, which is overseen by the system users themselves, coming together as the Bolero Association, rather as the coffee trade comes together in the GCA or ECF.

As the trade associations do for the trade in coffee, so the Bolero Association regulates the execution of paperless trade and lays down the rules that govern the electronic exchange of messages, ensuring always that such rules remain within the purview of the major trade associations as ECF and GCA. (For more on this see chapter 4, Contracts.)

### *Guaranteed originals and no mistakes*

The electronic chain has its own in-built security insofar as it guarantees that what is transmitted is the original. Changes, additions, deletions and any mismatches, including the identity of who submitted them and when, are noted, recorded and advised. This removes a major cause for loss and argument in the coffee trade: incorrect documentation and who is to blame for it. The electronic system guarantees that the documents are correct as received but of course cannot by itself say anything about the coffee these cover, so the importance of collateral management remains unchanged.

The Bolero system records exactly what was done, by whom and when, for each individual contract by means of a unique identifier which also tracks the progress of each individual document. An identifier is generated whenever a new transaction is initiated. This can be done by the buyer or the seller, depending on what was agreed between them.

In its simplest form all this means, for example, that a buyer who erred in the description of the goods in a letter of credit, or who instructed the wrong shipping marks, cannot later claim it was the shipper's fault and withhold payment.

### *What are the benefits?*

- Banks and their collateral managers can exercise better control over the execution of the transactions they fund, an important factor when financing trade in commodities. Depending on industry demand, electronic warehouse receipts could also be linked into the system, for example to start the funding chain of the coffee that is to be procured, processed for export and shipped. Or coffee could be tendered to commodity exchanges such as New York and London.

- All concerned, including the bankers, can *see* the progress of the goods and, therefore, the progress of the transaction.

- Shipping documents are prepared, issued and transmitted more quickly, resulting in earlier payment.

- Turnover is faster, meaning more business within the same amount of working capital, or a reduction of the working capital required. In Colombia, for instance, the time lag between loading and receipt of payment has been cut from two weeks or longer to just four days and sometimes less.

- Costs are lower: less interest, no errors, no lost or late documents, no arguments, no waiting for shipping documents.

- Sellers have better control. So do importers and roasters, who can trace both coffee and documents.

- In some consuming countries special arrangements permit coffee to be cleared through customs ahead of arrival, resulting in direct dispatch from ship to final destination. This could bring many exporters closer to participation in the just-in-time supply systems of larger roasters.

## Electronic trade execution in practice

*Contract.* Once a deal is established the contract details are automatically transmitted to the principal parties to the trade, using the secure messaging platform and the contract XML standard. (XML means extensible mark-up language.)

*Back-office link.* This is automatic, since both parties have received the contract confirmation and the information has been integrated into their back-office systems through their user interface. The contract data are now ready for further execution.

*Price fixing.* The price is fixed either by using an e-marketplace or directly between the parties by trading futures via their futures broker, using the network to confirm the transactions.

*Letter of credit.* If called for, the network is used to establish the letter of credit through a SURF XML message from the opening bank to the exporter's bank.

*Shipping instructions.* For an FOB contract the importer will provide shipping and document instructions to the exporter and the opening bank via the network. The opening bank in turn sends a SURF undertaking to the exporter's bank, detailing the commercial documents to be presented under the letter of credit.

*Pre-shipment finance.* On the basis of the letter of credit (or other undertaking) the exporter can apply for pre-shipment finance, using the protocols provided by the SURF functions (and their relationship to the banking system). Upon approval the bank's collateral manager will be automatically linked into the transaction.

*Freight.* The importer can negotiate freight through a carrier's electronic service provider (e.g. INTTRA or GTNexus), confirmed through the network's electronic messaging system.

*Shipment.* The exporter advises the coffee's availability and makes a container booking using electronic messaging. (This incidentally also facilitates the establishment of the ship's stowage plan.) The importer books for voyage and space with the carrier as per this advice. These messages are simultaneously copied to other involved parties, for example the handlers of the cargo to the export terminal, the warehouse and the agency supervising weighing and stuffing. Of course the foregoing presupposes that all of those involved, including customs, have updated their electronic back-office systems using data obtained from a web interface or using their own document management software.

***Bill of lading.*** Using details from the booking and document instructions received earlier, the carrier issues an electronic bill of lading and registers it under the network title registry for release to the exporter. The exporter is notified through the system, and will endorse the B/L to the appropriate party, usually the bank that financed the goods, who is then registered as pledgee on the B/L. Alternatively, the B/L can also be issued directly in a bank's favour.

***Shipment advice.*** This is sent via the network, using the XML standard for electronic shipping advices.

***Dispatch.*** The exporter combines the commercial invoice with the other export documents received from the different service providers and authorities, and packages these into a network message which the network forwards to either the buyer or the bank.

***Verification.*** The documents are verified electronically with the instructions registered under the SURF L/C undertaking. If there is any discrepancy SURF notifies all parties and asks for refusal or acceptance of the documents.

***Presentation of documents.*** If the documents are correct they are transmitted for inspection and/or approval (as per the L/C protocol) to the importer's bank or, in the case of CAD (payment cash against documents on first presentation) directly in trust to the importer. When the importer's bank makes payment, the electronic documents are released automatically to the importer. Alternatively, the L/C opening bank, which was acting as pledgee on the B/L, will endorse the B/L to the importer once the electronic funds transfer (EFT) has been confirmed through the SWIFT clearing system.

***At the receiving end.*** Before or upon arrival of the vessel, the carrier notifies all concerned (importer, clearing agent, customs, inland roasting plant, etc.) of the vessel's ETA, followed by a notice of arrival, using XML. The importer settles the freight, releases the B/L to the carrier or shipping agency at the port of destination, and copies the B/L together with the commercial invoice to the clearing agent, all through the electronic network system and all at the same time. Again, each party knows instantaneously who said what to whom.

***Final delivery.*** If the coffee is going to an inland roasting plant, notifications of cargo arrival, sample orders and delivery orders will pass electronically between the importer and the roaster. If the roaster operates on a VMI basis (vendor managed inventory) then the importer will place the coffee either at the roasting plant, or at an intermediate container station, or in a warehouse or silo park pending final delivery. All this is done through network instructions to the clearing agents, trucking company and warehousemen. Again, everyone knows what is happening, and the roaster can see where the coffee is.

Finally the importer issues an XML invoice and delivery order to the roaster, copied to the clearing agents, truckers and warehousemen. Upon payment this delivery order acts as transfer of title as per the conditions determined in the ECF or GCA standard form contract.

## End result

The above is a realistic scenario of the execution of a coffee contract from origin to delivery at the destination market to a roaster. It is in fact already happening, for instance between Colombia and the United Kingdom. The example makes optimal use of electronic means of transferring data without the need for rekeying.

All electronically issued data are reused through back-office integration, or through making the data available through online service providers or e-marketplaces, facilitating the trade or the services performed by different service suppliers.

It appears to be a complicated process, but thanks to electronic messaging, use of XML standards and secure electronic transfer of title and financial settlement, the administrative handling is far less cumbersome than in the paper environment. The efficiencies realized will translate into direct cost reductions and savings across the supply chain. Equally important are the reduction in finance cycles and the possible reduction in inventory cycles, easier management, and improved cash flow.

As mentioned at the beginning of this chapter, for many exporters the business process described above can take 15 to 25 days from shipment to receipt of payment when executed through physical transmission of paper documents. Using the Bolero system, the transfer of documents, transfer of title and financial settlement can be reduced to four days or less, depending on the complexity of the business process and the state of preparedness in the exporting country.

# Technical questions

## Who can use the Bolero system?

A local IT infrastructure and legal framework must be in place before using the Bolero system for coffee and other commodity exports. If they are, anyone with web access, or whose bank, coffee authority or IT provider is linked into the system, can access it, either as a full member or by buying the service on a retail basis.

In practice only those countries whose customs and possibly coffee industry authorities have accepted the system and have installed the necessary capability will benefit. It seems likely that larger producing countries will join up quite rapidly because for them the economies of scale are tremendous. The roasting sector will also participate more and more because of the control and information the network provides, which will permit some to move from just-in-time systems to vendor managed inventory systems.

Even if a roaster is not linked into the system, the importer can surrender the electronic documents and have them replicated as paper originals by the original issuing authority, for instance the carrier or warehouse.

For the buyer it is essential however that the exporter is linked into the system. Given the cost savings and reduced working capital requirements the system provides, this linkage can become an important issue when considering the viability of any particular transaction or business relationship with an origin country or an individual exporter.

## Standards

Easy communication of data and documents within the coffee supply chain requires certain standards for contracts and contract amendments, pricing, optional conditions, declarations and so on. Standards are also needed for the electronic documents for contract execution, such as sample and delivery orders, bills of lading, warehouse receipts and warrants.

Electronic standards have been developed for the United States coffee industry in collaboration with the membership of the Green Coffee Association (GCA), the National Coffee Association (NCA) and the New York Board of Trade (NYBOT). These use XML (extensible mark-up language) format so both humans and computers can read them, and to allow electronic transfer and integration into back-office systems (straight through processing). The GCA electronic contract was formally launched on 23 July 2001, and includes additional options: price fix letter, price fix rolling letter, and a destination declaration letter.

The technology provides both *simplification* and an optimal number of *choices* when creating a contract, transmitting a delivery order or shipment advice, or presenting a commercial set of documents.

## Access

The Bolero system is not an actual IT application or browser, but rather provides an 'electronic highway' between the different parties in the electronic community. In short, it is open platform technology. Like CHIPS or SWIFT, Bolero keeps track of all documents transmitted on its system (platform). It provides proof of who said what to whom and when, and it confirms that messages, contracts, shipping instructions, sampling orders, documents, delivery orders and so on were received in a timely manner and in good order.

To access this electronic highway participants use Bolero accredited application providers and possibly middleware companies. These have developed Bolero-enabled software that can be implemented as stand-alone document packages, or integrated with back-office systems or enterprise resource planning systems.

Different parties have different needs, so different applications are available for banks, carriers, traders, processors and others in the trade chain. Different solutions also apply to different sizes of companies. Bigger operations need packages to be integrated with their existing software, while smaller companies may not have the need, the knowledge or the means to acquire sophisticated software.

Accredited, stand-alone document management software can be used but smaller coffee exporters and others can also obtain access through a web interface. Bolero and other managed service providers (MSP) provide such access through a web browser. The same technology is also used by e-marketplaces and application service providers (ASP). This enables seamless messaging from their platform over the Bolero network to the members of the supply chain without any obvious Bolero activity – the screens are adapted to look like those of the e-marketplace concerned.

The Bolero web interface engine can also be used by a coffee company, a trader, importer or roaster, to engage suppliers and customers in a closed electronic community hosted by it. In this case the coffee company could act as host for the Bolero interface engine on which all parties provide the information through the web interface provided by Bolero or by another MSP. The databases are then hosted by the coffee company or the MSP, allowing all data to be integrated with the back-office systems of the coffee company driving the process. If the other parties have full Bolero membership, they in turn will be able to integrate the data into their back-office systems through the Bolero network.

In future even the smallest exporter will be able to link into the electronic highway, either through an e-commerce site or by simply buying into the service through a bank or other service provider. This will certainly be the case in countries with well developed and easy Internet access, provided customs and other government authorities are in agreement and the necessary legal steps have been completed. Banks in coffee producing countries are likely candidates to join the network; they will then retail the service to individual clients on a user fee basis.

## Document definitions status

Those intending to use the system should verify for themselves to what extent their own government authorities, customs and business service providers cater for and accept electronic documentation (for updates and more information go to *www.bolero.net/boleroxml/docdef/alphabetical.php3*).

The following documents could be handled by the Bolero system by mid 2002:

Advance shipment notice

Air waybill

Arrival notice

Beneficiary's certificate

Beneficiary's documentary credit amendment
  acceptance or refusal

Bill of lading

Booking confirmation

Cargo report export

Cargo report import

Certificate of analysis

Certificate of origin

Certificate of origin application

Certificate of quality

Certificate of weight

Collecting bank's collection instruction

Collection advice of non payment or
  non acceptance

Collection amendment advice

Collection amendment request

Collection status advice

Collection status request

Commercial invoice

Cover letter

Credit advice

Debit advice

Dispatch advice

Documentary credit

Documentary credit acknowledgement

Documentary credit advice

Documentary credit advice of discrepancy

Documentary credit advice of discrepancy
  discharge

Documentary credit advice of discrepancy refusal

Documentary credit amendment

Documentary credit amendment request

Documentary credit copy

Documentary credit application

Documentary credit notification

Documentary credit reimbursement
  authorization

Documentary credit reimbursement claim

Export declaration

Exporter's collection instruction

Exporter's documentary credit presentation
  instruction

Firm booking request

Forwarder's cargo receipt

Forwarding instructions

Freight invoice

House air waybill

House bill of lading

Import declaration

Insurance certificate

Insurance policy

Issuing bank's documentary credit
  presentation instruction

Packing list

Paying bank's documentary credit presentation
  instruction

Payment instruction

Presenting bank's collection instruction

Pro forma invoice

Provisional booking request

Purchase order

Purchase order acceptance

Purchase order cancellation

Remitting bank's collection instruction

Sea waybill

Shipping instructions

Standby documentary credit

Trade confirmation

# CHAPTER 7

# Dispute resolution – arbitration

## Introduction

Keep in mind that a contract becomes final and binding when buyer and seller agree on a transaction, verbally or otherwise. This implies that all standard terms and conditions have been agreed to previously, including provisions for the resolution of possible disputes.

Remember, too, that although some clauses of the GCA and ECF contracts provide a certain amount of latitude, buyers are fully entitled to lodge a claim if they suspect deliberate manipulation. For example, ECC's provision for a tolerance of 3% in shipment weight, more or less than the contracted quantity, is meant to provide some flexibility if circumstances beyond one's control make it impossible to ship exactly the number of bags or tonnage that was contracted – it does not make sense to frustrate a shipment because of a minor difference. But the clause does not confer an automatic right to vary shipment weights for purely opportunistic reasons.

A further point to bear in mind is that not all buyers, especially larger firms, bother to pursue claims to the very end. Some may not even bother to lodge them. Instead an offending exporter is simply struck off their list of approved suppliers, which can be very damaging to an exporter who may not even be aware of the fact.

### The principle of arbitration

The international trade in coffee is complex by nature. Dispute resolution can therefore be quite complicated, requiring experience and insights not easily found outside the coffee trade itself. Disputes also need to be resolved quickly and fairly, preferably amicably, with buyer and seller agreeing to a mutually acceptable solution. But if this proves impossible, arbitration provides the means to resolve the matter in an impartial manner without involving a court of law where proceedings could be subject to delays and could be very costly. The standard forms of contract of both the Green Coffee Association of America (the GCA Contract) and the European Coffee Federation (the European Contract for Coffee, or ECC) therefore bind all parties to a contract to the resolution of disputes through arbitration and only arbitration. All parties to a dispute are legally bound to cooperate with any arbitration proceedings that may be lodged against them.

There are two types of disputes:

● Quality disputes – resolved through quality arbitration, and

● Technical disputes (which are any other type of dispute) – resolved through technical arbitration.

The standard contracts stipulate how and when claims must be lodged, but there is a major difference between the United States and Europe regarding where arbitrations shall be held.

Under GCA, arbitration automatically takes place in New York. Under ECC, arbitration can take place in various European countries, depending on what the parties agreed at the time the contract was concluded. All commercial contracts based on the ECC must therefore state *where* arbitration shall take place. If no place of arbitration is stated and the parties cannot agree on one, then the venue of the arbitration is decided by the ECF Contracts Committee. Failure to stipulate the arbitration venue in the contract can cause delays, and may result in having to deal with arbitration proceedings in an unfamiliar location.

Arbitration proceedings are subject to the law of the country where they take place and so, as different European countries have different laws, there are minor variations in procedures and aspects of law. But in all instances arbitrations are conducted by experienced members of the coffee industry and, usually, the awards in similar disputes are comparable. Nevertheless, anyone wishing to ensure that a particular arbitration procedure will apply *must* stipulate the place or venue of arbitration in the sales contract. Countries that provide facilities for arbitration services have their own *arbitration rules.* Exporters should obtain these from the various national associations.

In this context the most important European arbitration venues are the United Kingdom (London), Germany (Hamburg but also Bremen) and France (Le Havre), followed by Italy (Trieste), Belgium (Antwerp) and the Netherlands (Amsterdam). The national associations in these countries have established arbitration boards or panels, and have laid down rules and procedures that are applied by qualified, impartial arbitrators drawn from the ranks of the coffee trade in the country concerned. This is important because only qualified trade arbitrators can fully understand and appreciate the diversity of problems encountered in the coffee trade, and the **awards of arbitral bodies are enforceable in a court of law**.

## Failure to comply with an award

Under ECF rules, if one of the parties fails to comply with an arbitration award which has become final, the other party may request the coffee association under whose rules the arbitration was held to post (publicize) the name of the defaulting party and/or bring it to the notice of the members and, through the ECF, to any person or organization with or having an interest in coffee. Each of the recipients of such notification may in turn bring it to the notice of its own members or otherwise publicize it. In addition, in order to enforce an arbitration award, a party may also have direct recourse to the courts of the place where the defaulting party is established. GCA rules allow 30 days for an award to be satisfied, after which a comparable procedure kicks in if the party in whose favour the award was given so requests.

## Variations to standard forms of contract

Of course contracts can be, and very many are, concluded with conditions differing from those of the standard forms of contract (GCA and ECC), as long as these are well understood and are clearly set out in unambiguous language, leaving no room for differing interpretations. For example, one might agree to change the weight tolerance in Article 2 of the ECC from 3% to 5%, in which case the contract should include a paragraph to the effect that 'Article 2 of ECC is amended for this contract by mutual agreement to read a tolerance of 5%'.

If a modification to an existing contract is agreed then this should be confirmed in writing, preferably countersigned by both parties. Adding the words 'without prejudice to the original terms and conditions of the contract' ensures that the modification does not result in unintended or unforeseen change to the original contract. A modification that is not confirmed in writing could subsequently be repudiated or disputed by one of the parties, for example during arbitration proceedings. Human memory is fallible and there is nothing offensive in ensuring that all matters of record are on record.

# Arbitration rules and procedures in selected European markets

## United Kingdom

### *Introduction*

The Coffee Trade Federation Ltd (CTF) provides a two-tier arbitration service: arbitration at first stage and, if required, an appeal procedure. Alternatively, to minimize time and expense, the parties may opt for hearings before a board of arbitrators against whose decision there is no possibility of appeal. If this option was not already provided for in the contract, the parties to a dispute may, if they so wish and in mutual agreement, opt for board arbitration.

CTF arbitrations are governed by the provisions of the Arbitration Act 1996, except where such provisions are expressly modified by or are inconsistent with the CTF arbitration rules. The juridical seat of any arbitration or appeal under CTF rules is England, as designated under the rules pursuant to section 3 of the Arbitration Act 1996.

Parties to an arbitration have no right to appeal to the courts on questions of law arising out of an award. But they do have the right to apply to the courts to determine questions as to the substantive jurisdiction of the arbitral tribunal, or to challenge an award on the ground of serious irregularity affecting the relevant arbitral tribunal.

Notices to be given under CTF rules shall be sent within the relevant time limits by prepaid first class mail or airmail, or by any other recognized international carrier, or by fax, telex or email, in which case evidence of receipt should be obtained. Under CTF rules all written statements must be in English. Supporting evidence in a language other than English must be accompanied by an independent translation.

### *Time limits for introducing arbitration claims*

It is essential that claimants adhere to the rules of the standard form of contract on which the sale was based. ECF rules require quality claims to be submitted not later than 21 calendar days from the final date of discharge at the port of destination. All other claims must be submitted not later than 45 calendar days from:

- The final date of discharge at the port of destination, provided all documents are available to the buyers; or

- The last day of the contractual shipping period if the coffee has not been shipped.

If amicable settlement (always the preferred solution) proves impossible then the formal decision to initiate arbitration proceedings must be notified within the following time limits:

- Quality disputes: not later than 28 calendar days from the date the claim was formulated; and

- Other disputes: not later than 90 calendar days from the date one party formally notifies the other that the dispute apparently cannot be resolved amicably and arbitration proceedings will be initiated.

These time limits must be respected, or the outcome of an arbitration can be jeopardized. If unavoidable delays do arise then, in the interests of justice or avoiding undue hardship, ECF rules authorize the arbitral body at the place of arbitration to extend the time as it may think appropriate.

## Appointment of arbitrators

*Arbitration at first stage.* The parties (claimant and defendant) appoint one arbitrator each who jointly appoint an umpire. If the two arbitrators cannot agree on an award the umpire will decide the outcome instead.

*Appeals and hearings before a board of arbitration.* In both these cases the CTF appoints the arbitrators: three for quality disputes, and five for all other (i.e. technical) disputes.

The parties to the dispute may object, in writing, to the appointment of any arbitrator or arbitration board member. No arbitrator or arbitration board member may be, or become, directly or indirectly involved in a case they are officiating in.

## Fees

Under CTF rules the arbitrators and umpire, or the board of arbitration, set the level of fees and costs and apportion them between the parties if necessary. In addition there are fees and deposits payable to the CTF as follows:

- Appointment of arbitrators: members £40; non-members £100.
- Arbitration fee: members £40; non-members £100.
- Deposit: appeals £1,000; board of arbitration £500.

## Procedures

*Initiating arbitration at first instance.* Having initiated the arbitration procedure, the claimant selects a member of the CTF panel of arbitrators – the list of names is available from the CTF. Even though an arbitrator signifies his or her willingness to act in the dispute, this does not mean he or she now becomes an advocate for the party who nominated him or her: all arbitrators act totally impartially. The selection of arbitrators should therefore be based on the specialist knowledge that they may have. A party may also ask the CTF to appoint an arbitrator on their behalf.

The arbitration is deemed to have been initiated when the notice of appointment of the arbitrator is served on the defendant. The defendant then has 14 days to appoint a second arbitrator. If they fail to do so the claimant may ask the CTF to do so on their behalf instead, with copy to the respondent. All requests to CTF for appointment of arbitrators must include:

- Brief details of the dispute;
- The current CTF fee;
- Evidence that the other party has been advised of the action to be taken;
- A statement that London is the stipulated place of arbitration;
- The name of the arbitrator already appointed (where applicable).

*Directions.* Once the panel of arbitrators and umpire has been appointed and the arbitration registered with the CTF, the arbitrators will instruct the parties how the case is to be conducted.

*The claimant* will be instructed to submit, usually within 21 days or slightly longer, a clear statement of the problem, how it arose and the remedy sought. (It is not sufficient simply to state 'I claim an allowance' – if an allowance is sought then it must be quantified, e.g. 'US$ 4 per 50 kg is claimed on quality grounds'). The statement must be in writing and must be supported by copies of all relevant documentation, including copies of exchanges between the parties. All should be catalogued, numbered and presented in chronological order and sent to the nominated arbitrators of both parties and to the other party to the dispute. If the dispute concerns quality the arbitrators will give directions on the production of the necessary samples.

*The respondent* is required to respond, in writing, if the claimant so wishes. They too must provide all relevant documentation, properly catalogued, to all concerned and should specifically address the points raised by the claimant. Usually, 14 days are allowed for this – failure on the part of the respondent to respond leaves the arbitrators no option but to advise the parties that the case will be judged on the basis of the claimant's submission.

It is a fundamental principle that claimants are allowed the final word and, usually, they are therefore given between 7 and 14 days to make any further observations on the submissions by the respondent.

### Hearing and award

Both parties are notified of the date and place of the hearing. Parties wishing to attend in person, or who wish to be represented by a member of the trade, must give written notice to the arbitrator appointed by them or for them within seven days of such appointment. Legal counsel is not permitted to attend and indeed no one else may attend without prior agreement of the arbitrators or umpire. The arbitrators or umpire board themselves may however employ legal advisers, assessors or other experts to advise them and such persons may attend the hearing. The arbitrators or umpire shall have the power to conduct the arbitration in such a manner in all respects as they consider necessary while giving each party a reasonable opportunity of putting their case and dealing with that of their opponent. The arbitrators or umpire may adopt procedures suitable for the particular case and for avoiding unnecessary delay and expense. They may also make such interim orders as they think fit for the interim protection, warehousing, sale or disposal of the subject matter of the arbitration.

Within a reasonable time from the date of hearing, the arbitrators or umpire shall make in writing and sign a reasoned award on the official award form of the CTF. Subject to any valid appeal under CTF rules the award shall be final and binding. If so claimed the award may direct that any amounts awarded in it shall carry interest, simple or compound, at the rate specified in the award. It shall also state the costs and expenses of the arbitration, the fees payable, and which of the parties shall be responsible for paying them. The arbitration fees are set at the discretion of the arbitrators and umpire. If the award is not taken up within 30 days the CTF can direct one of the parties to take up the award and pay the fees, costs and expenses. If it is not then taken up within 10 days the CTF may by action recover all outstanding amounts from any or all of the parties, or deduct these from any amounts that may have been deposited in advance.

### Appeals

*Notice and appointment of board of appeal.* Either party may appeal against the award by giving written notice to the other party and to the CTF, to be received by each within 30 days of the date of publication of the award. The CTF notice must include copies of the award, the contract, the notice of appeal sent to the other party and the usual deposit towards fees, costs and expenses.

The CTF Arbitration and Contracts Committee then appoints the board of appeal, three members for quality disputes and five members for all other disputes. The board decides by majority vote, with the chairperson having a casting vote in the event of any equality of votes. The board may require the appellant to deposit such security as it deems fit; failure to make the deposit within the laid-down time limit will render the original award final and binding. Objections to a member or members of a board of appeal may be lodged, in writing, not later than 14 days before the commencement of the hearing.

*Submission of written statements.* An appeal constitutes a new hearing, and fresh evidence (if any) will be admitted. The board may confirm, vary, amend or set aside the original award as it thinks fit.

A statement giving the appellant's case must be sent, together with supporting evidence and in eight copies, to the CTF secretary not later than 21 days after giving notice of appeal.

Failure to do so will render the original award final and binding. The CTF will copy the statement and supporting evidence to the defendant who must, not later than 14 days from receipt, submit a statement of their defence together with any other supporting evidence, again in eight copies. The appellant then, again, has the final word of reply within 14 days of receipt. All these limits may be extended if the board so permits.

*Hearing and award*. The board of appeal shall have the power to conduct the arbitration in such a manner in all respects as it considers necessary while giving each party a reasonable opportunity of putting their case and dealing with that of their opponent. The board may adopt procedures suitable for the particular case and for avoiding unnecessary delay and expense. It may also make such interim orders as the members may think fit for the interim protection, warehousing, sale or disposal of the subject matter of the arbitration. The board may employ legal advisers, assessors or other experts to advise it and such persons may attend the hearing. But the parties to the dispute may appear or be represented at the hearing by legal counsel only if they so requested in their statements of claim or defence, and then only with the prior approval of the board of appeal. This it may grant or withhold at its discretion. In any case the original arbitrators or umpire may not represent any of the parties.

Within a reasonable time from the date of the hearing, the board of appeal shall make in writing and shall sign a reasoned award which, subject to any valid appeal to the High Court (if available under the CTF rules), shall be final and binding. Such an appeal may only be made on a point of law, not just because one disagrees with the award. Should the court agree that grounds do exist on a point of law then the most likely outcome is that the award is remitted back to the board of appeal with directions to reconsider a specific aspect. The award also states the costs and expenses of the appeal, the fees payable, and which of the parties is responsible for paying them, and the board may direct that any amounts awarded shall carry interest, simple or compound, at a rate set in the award.

The arbitration fees shall be set at the discretion of the board of appeal. If the award is not taken up within 30 days the CTF can direct one of the parties to take up the award and pay the fees, costs and expenses. If not then taken up within 10 days the CTF may by action recover all outstanding amounts from any or all of the parties, or deduct these from any monies that may have been deposited in advance.

## Board of arbitration

The board of arbitration procedure is designed for those wishing to minimize the cost and time associated with arbitration at first instance and possible subsequent appeal. It is only available if it was stipulated in the original contract, or subsequently agreed between the parties to the dispute. There is no appeal against the award of a board of arbitration, so in effect the parties are ensuring that they only need go through the arbitration proceedings once to settle the dispute.

The appointment of the board and the entire procedure are exactly the same as in the appeal procedure described above. The procedure is initiated when the claimant sends the CTF secretary an outline of the dispute, a copy of the contract, the request for appointment of a board of arbitration, the requisite deposit and, if it is not already stated in the contract, details of the agreement between the parties to have a board of arbitration hear the dispute.

## Germany

The Deutscher Kaffee-Verband e.V. (DKV) in Hamburg is the umbrella organization for the German coffee industry. It also conducts arbitrations but only on technical disputes. Quality disputes are dealt with by the Hamburg Coffee Association (Verein der am Caffeehandel betheiligten Firmen in Hamburg), the Association of Hamburg Coffee Import Agents, and the Bremen Coffee Association. The latter also deals with technical disputes, but very seldom. Since Germany offers three possibilities for quality arbitrations (one Bremen and two Hamburg associations) and two for technical arbitrations (DKV and the Bremen association), contracts specifying arbitration in Germany must therefore also state the city and the arbitral body that shall conduct the arbitration.

## Technical arbitrations by the DKV

*Arbitration panel.* The panel usually consists of three members. Each party to the dispute appoints an arbitrator from the official list, who together appoint an umpire. If they cannot agree on the umpire then the DKV chair will appoint one if both parties are DKV members. If they are not then DKV asks the Hamburg Chamber of Commerce to do so. The panel of arbitrators may be increased to five before or even during the hearings at the request of any of the parties or the sitting arbitrators themselves. In this case the sitting arbitrators must agree on the additional members; if they cannot then again the DKV chair will nominate them instead. Remember that arbitrators in a dispute are not partial to one or the other side – they are neutral members of the official arbitration board.

*Requests for arbitration* must be made in writing to the DKV secretariat and must include:

- A full explanation of the dispute and of the remedy sought; and

- The name and address of the claimant's arbitrator and proof of willingness to serve.

DKV informs the other party of the request, requesting a written response that must include the name of the arbitrator who will act for the respondent and proof of willingness to serve. Unlike some other markets, there is no fixed time limit within which the defendant must respond. Instead it is left to the discretion of DKV to set the limit for the first response but once the arbitration panel is constituted it sets all subsequent time limits. If a respondent fails to nominate an arbitrator then the DKV chair or the Hamburg Chamber of Commerce will appoint one as above. All submissions must be in writing: five copies for a three-member panel and seven copies for a five-member panel.

*Hearing and award.* The date and the organization of the hearing are arranged by the umpire and DKV notifies the parties in writing. Arbitrators examine the written submissions and may invite further voluntary evidence from outside witnesses and experts. Both parties to the dispute are also summoned for oral pleading of their case. A legal adviser, nominated by the panel, attends all meetings and participates in the deliberations but has no vote. Decisions are reached by simple majority vote and the award, setting out the grounds for the verdict, is delivered in writing through the DKV secretariat.

*Appeal.* There is no appeal as such against a DKV award. An award can be submitted to a Hamburg Superior Court of Law for a ruling on its enforceability, but only if the claimant considers that Article 1041 of the German civil process law applies. If the court disaffirms the award on formal legal grounds then the arbitration must be repeated, with the same arbitrators and umpire officiating unless the court specifically ruled otherwise.

Costs and fees are linked to the value of the dispute: up to 2,500 euro the fee is 1,000 euro. Then an additional 7% for the next 3,000 euro, 6% for a further 6,000 euro, 5% for a further 6,000 euro, 4% for a further 40,000 euro, 3% for a further 160,000 euro and for amounts thereafter 1%.

## Quality arbitrations in Hamburg and Bremen

The contract must clearly state where arbitration will be held and under which rules. Hamburg arbitration is more frequently used.

### Arbitration panel

*Hamburg Private Arbitration in the Coffee Import Trade.* Each party appoints their own arbitrator; together the arbitrators appoint the umpire. If a contract was concluded through an agent that agent is assumed to be the seller's arbitrator unless the agent appoints someone else to act for them. If the arbitrators fail to appoint an umpire then the chairperson of the Association of Hamburg Coffee Import Agents and Brokers will do so.

*Bremen Coffee Association.* The association chair appoints four people from the roster of approved arbitrators: two must be importers and two must be agents, brokers or representatives of the membership category known as inland firms. A trustee, usually a legal adviser, is also nominated to organize the arbitration. This is to ensure the anonymity of the parties – the trustee is sworn to secrecy.

## Requests for arbitration

*Hamburg.* Requests must be made in writing to the association. If asked to do so the Association will also appoint arbitrators or umpires. No time limits are laid down for these appointments but they must be made without undue delay.

*Bremen.* Requests must be made on form A/B and submitted together with the original contract. Part A of the form provides details of the quality description; part B identifies marks and type names required for the conduct of the arbitration. The parties must present details of any quality guarantees given and submit sealed arbitration samples, drawn and sealed by a qualified body (i.e. independent, sworn samplers). If they wish to make additional statements they must do so on forms I (original) and II (copy). Both parties countersign the reverse of form I (although this does not signify acceptance of the other party's statement) but only form II is submitted to the arbitrators.

## Hearing and award

*Hamburg.* The hearing is based on the original contract submitted by the claimant. Unless otherwise agreed, for bagged coffee arbitration samples must be drawn from 10% of the lot and must be sealed, either by both parties jointly or by an independent sworn sampler. For coffee shipped in bulk a 2-kg sealed sample is required, usually of each individual container. If the arbitrators fail to reach agreement then the decision of the umpire will be final. In the interest of neutrality the parties' identities are withheld from the umpire until after a verdict has been reached. Should the umpire inadvertently become aware of the buyer's identity then the umpire must withdraw, thereby necessitating a new hearing. Awards are issued on the official Association certificate and signed by both arbitrators and the umpire.

*Bremen.* All arbitrations are anonymous. The arbitrators do not know the identity of the parties and the parties do not know that of the arbitrators. However, if the proceedings so require the trustee may inform the arbitrators of contractual details such as prices and shipping period. Sealed arbitration samples must represent at least 10% of a lot in the case of bagged coffee (at the rate of not less than 100 grams per bag, although the degree of sampling may be reduced if both parties agree). For coffee in bulk a 2-kg sealed sample is required, usually from each individual container. Samples must be drawn and sealed by a qualified body (sworn samplers), and other relevant samples such as type or stock-lot samples must be sealed by both parties.

The panel arrives at its decision by simple majority vote although the aim is to achieve unanimity. If unanimity is impossible then the average of the allowances, if any, proposed by the individual arbitrators will be taken to be the award. The award is entered in form B and signed by all concerned. The trustee then enters the award in form C, signs it and submits it to the parties.

*Unsound coffee or radical quality differences, including excessive moisture content.* ECC Article 7 states that where arbitrators establish that the coffee is unsound or of radically different quality, and award invoicing back, then they shall also establish the price having in mind all the circumstances. As an example, the quality difference might be so enormous that it is obvious the shipper made no serious attempt to supply what they had sold. Hamburg and Bremen arbitrations deal with this somewhat differently but both sets of rules make special provision for such cases, and describe them as 'fraud and negligence'.

*Hamburg.* The question of fraud or negligence can be pursued only if the claimant requests this. In this type of case the arbitrators and three umpires are limited to pronouncing a 'suspicion of fraud and gross negligence' and to fixing an adequate allowance. The claimant may contest this and demand a technical arbitration to order annulment of the contract rather than payment of an allowance. The panel's reasoning must therefore be provided in writing to the Association by the umpires for possible use in such an arbitration.

*Bremen.* If a verdict is required on 'fraud and negligence' then the vote must be secret with at least three votes in favour for the request to succeed. The award may provide for an adequate allowance. As in Hamburg the panel provides its reasoning in writing for possible use in a later technical arbitration. The buyer then has two weeks in which to demand a technical arbitration panel to order annulment of the contract instead of payment of a penalty.

### Appeals

Neither the Hamburg nor the Bremen rules allow for appeals against awards in quality arbitrations. The awards are final and the arbitrators and umpire need not provide the grounds for their verdict, although in Bremen the trustee may provide additional information to the parties if the arbitrators consider this appropriate.

### Costs and fees

*Hamburg:* 1–1,000 bags: 100 euro per arbitrator. For each additional 1,000 bags or portion thereof: an additional 100 euro per arbitrator (two arbitrators and an umpire).

*Bremen:* Up to 250 bags: 50 euro per arbitrator; up to 500 bags 70 euro; and up to 1,000 bags 100 euro per arbitrator. For each additional 1,000 bags or portion thereof: an additional 50 euro per arbitrator (four arbitrators).

## France

The Chambre arbitrale des cafés et poivres du Havre (CACPH) is the main arbitral body for coffee. CACPH conducts both quality (*arbitrage de qualité et expertise*) and technical arbitrations (*arbitrage de principe*). Linked quality and technical issues within the same dispute can be dealt with simultaneously in a 'joint arbitration' (*arbitrage mixte*). Requests for arbitration must be made in French on the official form provided.

The parties to the dispute are bound to translate any document or information in another language into French. If legal counsel is to be involved this must be indicated on the request form. The rules provide for a two-tier system of adjudication: arbitration at the first instance and an appeals procedure. All time limits are calendar days and run from the date material is forwarded, including 72 hours deemed necessary for transmission. Late delivery automatically extends the time limit according to the delay involved.

### Documents to be submitted and time limits

#### Quality disputes

- Contract or sales confirmation;

- Invoice;

- Out-turn sample, sealed under independent supervision or by the parties jointly;

- Where relevant, a jointly sealed original sample of the coffee that was sold.

The request to CACPH must be submitted no later than 30 days from the formal notification by one of the parties that they are to proceed to arbitration. The defendant has 15 days from the date CACPH dispatches the notification to countersign and return it. Failure to respond will result in the arbitration proceeding without any input from the defendant.

### Technical disputes

- Statement of the matters in disputes and claims made;

- All relevant documents (contracts, invoices, bills of lading, certificates, etc.).

The request for arbitration must be lodged within 30 days as above, to be followed by the complete dispute file in five copies, including statements of facts and claims, within a further 10 days. The other party must lodge their defence within 30 days from the date CACPH transmits the dispute file to them.

The plaintiff then has 15 days to respond after which the defendant has a further 15 days to make a final response. Failure to respond will result in the arbitration proceeding without any input from the defendant.

## Arbitration panels

All arbitrators are designated by CACPH and their names are made known to the parties. Arbitrators may not have any connection with the matter in dispute – if they find that they do then they must withdraw unless the parties agree that they can continue.

*For quality arbitrations and appeals:* three arbitrators, appointed by the board of directors.

*For technical arbitrations:* in the first instance three arbitrators and on appeal five, again appointed by the CACPH board.

Parties to a dispute may challenge arbitrators only on grounds which arose, or became apparent, after they were appointed and must do so within three days of the event, failing which the panel shall stand as nominated. All arbitration hearings are private but in technical arbitrations the parties may be present or may be represented by legal counsel. They can also be represented by a member of the coffee trade but only with the prior approval of the panel.

## Awards and appeals

*Quality.* The award is issued within eight weeks from registration of the original request. Any appeal must be lodged within 15 days from the date the award was dispatched, copied to the other party. Appeal procedures and time limits are the same as for arbitration in the first instance.

*Technical.* Awards are made within three months from the date of hearing although this can be extended with the agreement of the CACPH board. Any appeal must be lodged within 20 days from the date the award was dispatched, copied to the other party, with the complete dispute file in seven copies being lodged with CACPH not more than 10 days later. Procedures and time limits are the same as for arbitration in the first instance.

*Costs and fees* are set by the arbitrators, who also stipulate who shall be liable for them. No arbitration procedure will be initiated unless the required deposit for costs and fees (determined by CACPH for each individual case) has first been made.

## United States

### Introduction

The rules of the Green Coffee Association Inc. (GCA) set out comprehensive arbitration and appeal procedures. Over 95% of the coffee imported into the United States and Canada is sold under GCA contracts so these rules apply to a large part of world imports and are therefore of some considerable importance.

The rules differ in some important aspects from those in Europe. For example, for technical disputes GCA sets no time limit for lodging the claim and instead sets a limit of one year from the date the issue first arose for the filing of the demand for technical arbitration hearings. ECF on the other hand sets a time limit for lodging the claim of 45 days from the date of discharge at port of destination (provided all documents were available to the buyers), or from the last day of the shipping period in the case of non-shipment. This is followed by a further 90 days for the filing of the demand for arbitration, counted from the date one party formally notifies the other that arbitration will be initiated.

GCA permits the use of legal counsel whereas ECF requires prior approval for this. And while the GCA freely permits the use of witnesses and legal counsel it does not allow new evidence to be presented at an appeal, whereas the London Coffee Trade Federation's rules allow new evidence at any time. In the United Kingdom and Germany two arbitrators are selected by the claimant and defendant and they together select a third, the umpire. GCA arbitrations are also heard by three arbitrators but all three are selected by the GCA administration, by lot, from the GCA arbitration panel.

GCA members annually submit names of coffee professionals who they feel are qualified to settle quality and/or technical disputes. The Arbitration Committee reviews the experience of each individual, and determines for which list he or she is qualified. These lists form the pool of names from which the GCA administrator then chooses arbitrators by lot. The administrator must also be vigilant not to select arbitrators who may have a conflict of interest because of relationships with either party to a dispute.

Once the arbitrators are selected, the arbitration is entirely under their control as stated in the GCA Rules of Arbitration:

> The Association does administer and interpret the arbitration procedure and these Rules and it designates the arbitrators. It is, however, the arbitrators who conduct the hearings, determine and decide the issue, and they alone have the power and authority to make an award. Arbitrators shall be in complete charge of the arbitration. They shall conduct the same with the purpose of establishing equity and fair dealings in matters of trade and commerce.

All GCA arbitrations are monitored by the legal staff of the New York Board of Trade (NYBOT) to ensure they are run efficiently and that the results are both impartial and in full compliance with the laws of the land. Since 1999 the administration of the GCA has fallen under the auspices of NYBOT.

### Quality arbitrations

The GCA contract stipulates that:

> Coffee shall be considered accepted as to quality unless within 15 calendar days after discharge of the coffee, or within 15 calendar days after all Government clearances have been received, whichever is later, either:
>
> a.    Claims are settled by the parties to the contract, or
>
> b.    Arbitration procedures have been filed by one of the parties in accordance with the provisions of the contract.

If neither a. nor b. has been done within the stated period, or if any portion of the coffee has been removed from the point of discharge before representative sealed samples have been drawn by the GCA, in accordance with its rules, seller's responsibility for quality claims ceases for that portion so removed.

To initiate a quality arbitration, the claimant must submit a signed and notarized demand for arbitration in triplicate explicitly setting forth the precise complaint(s) in detail on GCA form A-2. This must be accompanied by the original contract, a sampling order to the order of the GCA, and the requisite arbitration fee. When GCA receives the defendant's answer it copies it to the claimant, who may either file a reply with GCA or allow the arbitration to proceed in accordance with the original submission. All arbitration forms are available from *www.green-coffee-assoc.org*.

On receipt of the arbitration demand, the defendant responds by filing their signed and notarized answer in triplicate on GCA form B-2, together with the requisite fee. This answer must be filed with GCA within five business days from receipt of the arbitration demand if the defendant's office is located in New York City. If the defendant's office is not in New York City, the GCA administrator can, at their discretion, extend any time requirement beyond that prescribed to give the defendant an equivalent period to that allowed to a resident.

If the claimant files an answer to the defendant's reply, the defendant can file an additional response or they can allow the arbitration to proceed on the basis of their original answer.

### Procedure

After GCA has received the final replies from both parties, the administrator authorizes a sealed sample to be drawn by an approved sampler.

The administrator determines the classification of the arbitrators to be selected, based on the nature of the controversy. Any arbitrators known to be connected with either party must be removed from the list. The administrator then selects, by lot, three names from the remaining arbitrators on the list. The identity of the arbitrators is never disclosed to either party to the dispute.

GCA notifies the arbitrators of their selection. The arbitration should then take place within three days of this notification. The arbitrators must take an oath before the arbitration proceedings.

GCA prepares an extract of the arbitration papers that have been filed, deleting all names and references to the parties, including all marks on the samples to be tested.

The arbitrators independently grade and cup the samples, according to the claimant's demand, and make their own conclusions. The arbitrators review their findings and issue either a unanimous decision, or a majority and a minority decision. GCA notifies the parties to the dispute as quickly as possible, but not later than five days after the decision on the award is reached.

The arbitrators are also required to assess the costs of the arbitration against the unsuccessful party; they can however also instruct the parties to share the costs.

### Award and appeal

An award must be made and the parties notified by GCA within five business days after a quality arbitration is held. If the award is to be contested, an appeal must be filed with GCA within two business days after receipt of the award, on GCA form E in triplicate, duly signed, notarized and accompanied by the requisite fee. No new claims or counter-claims may be submitted on appeal.

In the event of an appeal, a panel of five new arbitrators (i.e. excluding the original three) is selected. They grade and cup the original sample in the same way as the first panel to reach a decision. Their decision to uphold or change the original award is final. The appeal award must be made within five business days of the sitting.

The unsuccessful party must settle the award within seven calendar days of the date of receipt of the notice of the award.

## Gross negligence and fraud

Under GCA rules all quality issues under FCA, FOB, CFR, CIF and DAF contracts are settled by allowance.

GCA considers that it is a technical issue whether or not quality is inferior to such an extent that the normal remedy of an allowance is insufficient. Therefore the claimant must file a demand for a technical arbitration. The technical arbitration panel might in its turn convene a quality panel to verify whether negligence or fraud took place but this would not be made known to the claimant who would only receive the decision of the technical panel.

## Technical arbitrations

*Actions the claimant and the defendant must take.* These are the same as for quality arbitrations, but the demand and response must be submitted on GCA forms A–1 and B–1. All relevant papers (shipping documents, correspondence, certificates, statements, etc.) must accompany these forms, which are available from *www.green-coffee-assoc.org*.

Each party has the right to request an oral hearing. If they exercise this right, they may appear with an attorney and witnesses provided the arbitrators and the other party have been given prior notice of this and the arbitrators have not objected. The other party may then also appear with an attorney. The arbitrators always have the option of asking GCA legal counsel to be present.

All oral testimony must be made under oath; the entire procedure is recorded stenographically. All communications must be addressed to the chairperson of the arbitration panel; no one is permitted to communicate directly with the arbitrators or witnesses, except with the chairperson's approval.

### Procedure

After the final replies have been received from all parties, the GCA administrator selects a panel of three arbitrators from the association's register of technical arbitrators and ensures that they have no connection with any of the disputants. A mutually satisfactory time and a date are set. The arbitrators may approve a delay of five days if acceptable reasons are submitted in writing.

The arbitrators receive copies of all the documents that have been filed and review them independently before the date of the arbitration. They elect their own chairperson to conduct the arbitration and hearings. The arbitrators may request the GCA counsel to attend and act as a legal adviser, but GCA counsel has no voice or vote in any decisions.

The arbitrators assess costs on either or both of the parties.

### Award and appeal

The award must be made within five business days of the arbitrators receiving copies of the transcript of the proceedings.

If the award is to be contested, an appeal must be filed within two business days of receipt of the award on form E in triplicate, duly signed, notarized and accompanied by the requisite fee. Five new arbitrators are selected to hear the appeal. They can review only the original documents and transcripts; no new evidence may be submitted. Their decision is final. The appeal award must be made within five business days of the arbitrators receiving the transcript of the hearings.

Settlement of the award must be within seven calendar days of the date of receipt of the notice of the award by the unsuccessful party.

## *Practical considerations*

Although the GCA arbitration system is designed so that exporters can use the system directly from source countries, it is advisable to have local representation at the arbitration. The GCA administration will provide all reasonable assistance to assure a fair hearing regardless of how far away a respondent may be, but there are certain facts and procedures of which the system assumes all participants have a good understanding. To protect oneself from oversight, it is a simple matter for an exporter to nominate a local importer to appear on their behalf in an arbitration. Most importers will perform this service free of charge and the practice is quite common.

Local representation helps in a number of ways. First of all, documents and sampling usually move along more efficiently. When a piece of paper or a sampling order is misplaced, local people can trace the problem more quickly. Second, local representatives usually have more experience with the arbitration system and can guide the exporter through some of the details.

For example, it is clearly stated that blanket contentions are not admissible in quality arbitrations. That is to say, one cannot simply ask for a quality allowance because 'the coffee is bad'. On the other hand, an experienced person would point out that a quality complaint should not only be detailed, but also be all encompassing. There have been quality arbitrations where a claimant has complained only about the grade of the coffee. When reviewing the samples the arbitrators also found cup deficiencies but felt unable to include the cupping problem in their award because the claimant did not claim on the cup. An experienced claimant would make a claim for certain grade defects (e.g. black beans, sour beans or husks) 'that sometimes reflect in the cup quality'.

The need for local representation in technical arbitrations is more obvious. The details of why and how contractual obligations are determined can be complex. An exporter's experience is usually mostly sales oriented, whereas importers (and most technical arbitrators for that matter), have the broader experience of being both buyer and seller in the international coffee market.

The final advantage to having local representation is gaining a better understanding of the award. Most awards are very simple statements like: 'Based upon the evidence submitted, we award X to the seller [or buyer], and the cost of the arbitration to the buyer [or seller]'. It is rare that an award includes any explanation as to why the arbitrators decided the way they did.

Because most arbitrators are experienced coffee people, with equal experience as international buyers and sellers of coffee, they understand both sides of the transaction. Those who see the coffee trade from only one side, such as exporters, do not always appreciate why and how certain actions or lack of actions can cause their counterpart to suffer loss or damage, and it is not uncommon for some to feel they have been treated unfairly in the arbitration proceedings. Someone who has not experienced the business from both sides cannot always see how the other party was legitimately hurt by their actions and may sometimes think that the other party won the award because of a bias in the arbitration system.

In quality arbitrations the arbitrators do not know who the parties are. They see only the complaint and the defendant's reply, without names. After this the coffee does the talking. Therefore, bias in quality arbitrations is virtually impossible. In technical arbitrations, the arbitrators do see the names of the parties but they are both buyers and sellers of coffee and so understand both sides of the business; before being appointed they are pre-screened about any personal contacts they may have with the parties to the dispute, and GCA legal counsel monitors the proceedings.

A local representative might not know exactly how the arbitration award was decided, but they should have a clear view of the proceedings and be able to explain more or less how an outcome was determined. This is very helpful for an exporter in deciding whether or not to appeal.

## Fees and other charges

The arbitration fee for members of the association is as follows:

● US$ 375 minimum up to 250 bags on any question solely of grade or quality of coffee. For each additional bag over 250 bags up to 500 bags there is a fee of 35 cents per bag; for each additional bag over 500 bags the fee is 50 cents per bag.

● US$ 525 minimum up to 250 bags from appellants only on the appeal from the award rendered on any question solely of grade or quality of coffee. For each additional bag over 250 bags up to 500 bags there is a fee of 45 cents per bag; for each additional bag over 500 bags the fee is 70 cents per bag.

● US$ 605 minimum up to 250 bags on any question other than one solely involving grade or quality of coffee. For each additional bag over 250 up to 500 bags there is a fee of 35 cents per bag; for each additional bag over 500 bags the fee is 55 cents per bag.

● US$ 775 minimum up to 250 bags from appellants only on an appeal from the award rendered on any question other than one solely involving grade or quality of coffee. For each additional bag over 250 bags up to 500 bags there is a fee of 55 cents per bag; for each additional bag over 500 bags the fee is 90 cents per bag.

From the fees received the association pays a fee to the arbitrators as follows:

● Arbitrations on any question solely of grade or quality of coffee, US$25 per arbitrator.

● Arbitrations on any question other than solely grade or quality of coffee, US$35 per arbitrator.

If an arbitration is withdrawn or cancelled before an answer is filed, US$ 200 is retained by the association as a filing fee out of the arbitration fee deposited. If the answer has been filed but the hearing has not yet begun, US$ 200 is withheld from the respondent's deposit. The balance of the arbitration fee is returned to the depositor, except for any non-member fees paid (see below). When a hearing has been scheduled and held on a technical arbitration or appeal and the parties reach a settlement or mutually agree to withdraw the arbitration or appeal, such settlement or agreement shall provide for forfeiture of the arbitration fees to the association by one or both of the parties as the panel sees fit.

When the panel makes a decision, the arbitrators assess one or both arbitration fees as they see fit. All other expenses incurred are also fixed in the award. Other deposits received are refunded to the parties entitled to them, except for non-member fees or any cancellation fees.

All non-members party to an arbitration are charged an additional fee for each arbitration or appeal, over and above the scheduled fees charged to GCA members as provided above. The non-member fees when arbitrating against a GCA member are as follows:

● US$ 200 on any question solely of grade or quality of coffee; or

● US$ 300 on any other question.

The non-member fee when arbitrating against another non-member is:

- US$ 500 on any question solely of grade or quality of coffee; or

- US$ 2,000 on any other question.

This additional fee is retained by the association regardless of the result. It must be paid, together with the regular arbitration fee charged to members, to the association at the time the statement, joint submission to arbitration, and/or answer thereto are filed with the administrator of the association.

# CHAPTER 8

# Futures markets

## Introduction

The extreme volatility of the price of coffee brings drastic price changes over months, weeks or days, or even within the same trading day. Crop prospects vary widely due to unforeseen events, for example drought, frost or disease. High coffee prices encourage production growth while low prices result in falling output. The balance of supply and demand is subject to many uncertainties that affect price trends and therefore represent price risk. All levels of the coffee industry are exposed to risk from sudden price changes.

Futures markets (also known as terminal markets, from the French *marché à terme*) exist because of price risk in the cash market for the underlying industry. No price risk means no role for a futures market. This basic fact is crucial to any understanding of the purpose and function of futures markets. Coffee futures represent coffee that will become available at some point in the future, based on standard contracts to deliver or accept a pre-determined quantity and quality of coffee at one of a known range of delivery ports. The only points to be agreed when concluding a futures contract are the delivery period and the price. The delivery period is chosen from a pre-set range of calendar months, called the trading positions. Market forces determine the price at the time of dealing.

There are two main futures markets serving the global coffee industry:

- *The New York Board of Trade (NYBOT),* the parent company of the Coffee, Sugar and Cocoa Exchange (CSCE) and the New York Cotton Exchange (NYCE), for arabica (market symbol KC). Delivery periods (trading positions): March (symbol H), May (K), July (N), September (U) and December (Z). *www.nybot.com.*

- *The London International Financial Futures and Options Exchange (LIFFE),* since early 2002 part of the Euronext group, for robusta (market symbol LKD). Delivery periods (trading positions): January (symbol F), March (H), May (K), July (N), September (U) and November (X). *www.liffe.com.*

Smaller futures markets trading in coffee are found in Brazil, France, India and Japan – for more information see later in this chapter.

### Internet access

The growth of the Internet has made access to the main markets easier than ever. The exchanges have their own websites, and all the major commodity news services (Reuters, CRB, etc.) supply price quotes for the major coffee futures markets. There are also Internet sites relating specifically to the coffee business that provide market quotes. Most sites are easy to navigate and usually include a page with the latest futures price quotations.

To locate market information on the Internet, it is helpful to understand the market coding systems. Using the symbols mentioned above, LKDX03 would refer to a quote on the London LIFFE robusta market for the November 2003 delivery period. In the same way,

KCZ04 would symbolize a quote on the NYBOT arabica 'C' contract for the December 2004 delivery period. Some Internet sites are easier to navigate and read using these official market symbols; other sites spell everything out in plain English.

Free access price quotations are subject to a 20- to 30-minute delay. Anyone requiring up-to-the-minute quotations must register with a subscription service, which means paying monthly fees for real-time quotes. There are numerous such subscription services with fees ranging anywhere from US$ 200 to US$ 1,000 per month, depending on what other news and trading services the subscription package includes.

# The function of futures markets

The coffee futures exchanges were originally created to bring order to the process of pricing and trading coffee and to diminish the risk associated with chaotic cash market conditions. The futures prices that serve as benchmarks for the coffee industry are openly negotiated in the markets of the coffee futures exchanges (primarily NYBOT/CSCE and LIFFE).

To support a futures market, a cash market must have certain characteristics: sufficient price volatility and continuous price risk exposure to affect all levels of the marketing chain; enough market participants with competing price goals; and a quantifiable underlying basic commodity with grade or common characteristics that can be standardized.

The futures exchange is an organized marketplace that:

- Provides and operates the facilities for trading;

- Establishes, monitors and enforces the rules for trading; and

- Keeps and disseminates trading data.

***The exchange does not set the price!*** It does not even participate in coffee price determination. The exchange market supports five basic pricing functions:

- Price discovery;

- Price risk transfer;

- Price dissemination;

- Price quality;

- Arbitration.

The exchange establishes a visible, free market setting for the trading of futures and options which helps the underlying industry find a market price (*price discovery*) for the product and allows the *transfer of risk* associated with cash price volatility. As price discovery takes place, the exchange provides *price dissemination* worldwide. Continuous availability of pricing information contributes to wider market participation and to the *quality of price*. (More buyers and sellers in the marketplace means better pricing opportunities.) Greater participation means that price discovery reflects the conditions of the commodity market as a whole. To ensure the accuracy and efficiency of the trading process, the exchange also resolves trading disputes through *arbitration*.

## The two markets

To clearly understand the coffee futures market, a distinction must be drawn between physical (cash) coffee and coffee futures.

In the *coffee cash market,* participants buy and sell physical, green coffee of different qualities that will be delivered either immediately or promptly. The cash transaction therefore involves the transfer of the ownership of a specific lot of a particular quality of physical coffee. The cash price for the physical coffee is the current local price for the specific product to be transferred. (Note that sales of physical, green coffee for later (forward) delivery, called forward contracts, are not to be confused with futures contracts.)

In the *coffee futures market,* participants buy and sell *a price* for a standard quality of coffee. The futures transaction centres around trading a futures contract *based* on physical coffee (or its cash equivalent) at a price determined in an open auction – the futures market. The futures price is the price one expects to pay, or receive, for coffee at some future date.

- Cash price = price now for coffee (by trading the physical product for immediate or prompt delivery)

- Futures price = expected price for coffee (by trading the different positions of the futures contract)

*The futures contract* is a standardized legal commitment to deliver or receive a specific quantity and grade of a commodity or its cash equivalent on a specified date and at a specified delivery point. Its standardization allows the market participants to focus on the price and the choice of contract month.

Traders in the futures markets are primarily interested in risk management (hedging) or speculation, rather than the physical exchange of actual coffee. Although delivery of physical coffee can take place under the terms of the futures contract, few contracts actually lead to delivery. Instead purchases are usually matched by offsetting sales and vice versa, and no physical delivery takes place.

In addition to its pricing functions, the coffee futures market also serves to establish standards of quality and grade that can be applied throughout the industry.

## Price risk

Since the futures contract is standardized in terms of the quantity and quality of the commodity, the futures price represents an average range of qualities and is therefore an average price. The price for each individual origin and even quality of physical coffee is not necessarily the same: it may be higher or it may be lower. Historically the futures price and the cash price tend to move closer together as the futures delivery date draws near. While such convergence does occur in an efficient market, prices for physical coffee often fluctuate quite independently from the futures market. The physical premium or discount, the *differential*, represents the value (plus or minus) the market attaches to such a coffee compared to the futures market. This price differential can reflect local physical market conditions, as well as coffee quality and grade.

Price risk therefore has two components:

- *The underlying price risk*: prices for arabica or robusta futures as a whole rise or fall;

- *The differential risk* or *basis risk*: the difference in price between physical and futures for a particular physical coffee (the basis) increases or decreases compared to prices on the futures market.

Futures markets can be used to moderate exposure to the price risk because they represent the state of supply and demand for an average grade of widely available deliverable coffee. They cannot be used to moderate the differential or basis risk, which attaches entirely to a particular origin, type or quality of coffee. Price risk is almost always greater than differential risk, so the risk reduction capability of the futures market is an important management tool.

Differential or basis risk can, admittedly, be very high at times and should never be ignored. It is helpful to examine historical differential pricing to identify periods of increased differential risk. There might be seasonal patterns, for example.

## Liquidity and turnover

Liquidity is a crucial factor in determining the success of a futures market. A futures market must have enough participants with competing price goals (buyers and sellers) to ensure a turnover high enough to permit the buying and selling of contracts at a moment's notice without direct price distortion. Large transaction volumes provide flexibility (liquidity) and enable traders to pick the most appropriate contract month, corresponding to their physical delivery commitments, to hedge the price risks inherent in those physical transactions. More bids to buy and offers to sell in the market at any given time create greater pricing efficiency for the participants seeking a price for the commodity. Currently only the New York and London markets provide this flexibility on an international scale.

Speculators and hedgers competing for price generally means that futures and cash prices move in the same direction over time and as a futures contract approaches delivery the futures price and the cash price will often converge. Futures prices do not always reflect cash market reality though, especially over the very short term when large volumes may be traded for purely speculative reasons. The volume of futures trading and the underlying quantity of physical coffee it represents easily exceed total production of green coffee, or indeed the volume of the physical trade as a whole.

The large volumes on the futures markets not only influence futures prices but inevitably have an influence on the price of physical coffee as well. It is important for those involved in the physical coffee business to be aware of the activity of speculators and derivative traders. For that reason, the futures industry regularly examines and publishes the ratio of speculative and hedging activity in the market.

Speculators are absolutely necessary to the efficient function of a futures market. Speculative activity directly improves liquidity and therefore serves the hedgers' long-term interests. During the last ten years or so, the activity of hedge funds and the development of options on futures markets have both led to an increase in short-term speculative activity.

| Table 20 | Annual turnover in futures compared with gross world imports, 1980–2001 (millions of tons) | | | |
|---|---|---|---|---|
| Year | NYBOT | LIFFE | Total | World imports* |
| 1980 | 15.2 | 5.5 | 20.7 | 4.1 |
| 1985 | 11.1 | 5.1 | 16.2 | 4.5 |
| 1985–1989 | 17.7 | 5.4 | 23.1 | 4.7 |
| 1990–1994 | 37.3 | 5.5 | 42.8 | 5.3 |
| 1995 | 34.0 | 5.2 | 39.2 | 5.0 |
| 1996 | 34.6 | 5.9 | 40.5 | 5.4 |
| 1997 | 39.0 | 7.7 | 46.7 | 5.6 |
| 1998 | 35.6 | 6.4 | 42.0 | 5.8 |
| 1999 | 44.9 | 7.8 | 52.7 | 6.0 |
| 2000 | 33.7 | 7.4 | 41.1 | 6.1 |
| 2001 | 37.4 | 7.7 | 45.1 | 6.1 (est.) |

* Re-exports ignored.

| Table 21 | Annual turnover in options and futures, 1990–2001 (millions of tons) | | | |
|---|---|---|---|---|
| Year | NYBOT options | LIFFE options | Total options | Options + futures |
| 1990 | 4.8 | 0.2 | 5.0 | 41.0 |
| 1990–1994 | 12.9 | 0.7 | 13.6 | 56.3 |
| 1995–1998 | 16.9 | 0.8 | 17.7 | 42.1 |
| 1999 | 23.3 | 0.9 | 24.2 | 76.9 |
| 2000 | 15.5 | 0.6 | 16.1 | 57.2 |
| 2001 | 13.6 | 0.4 | 14.0 | 59.1 |

While options on futures provide another speculative opportunity in the futures market, options also represent an important risk management tool that has become very useful in recent years. Options are discussed further in chapter 9, Hedging and other operations.

Not all options result in actual futures contracts. However, they do represent potential quantities to be traded on the strike dates should the holders decide to exercise their options rather than simply letting them expire. In any event, the large turnover in actual futures demonstrates the impact of the futures markets on the daily trade in physical coffee. In recent years physical prices have largely been determined by applying a differential to prices in the futures market; that is, the combination of the differential (plus or minus) and the price of the selected futures position gives the price for the physical coffee.

## Volatility

The extreme volatility of coffee prices can be seen historically in both the size and suddenness of price moves. In April 1994, for example, NYBOT 'C' contracts were around 85 cts/lb – after frost damage in Brazil they reached 248 cts/lb: a rise of close to 300% in less than three months. Eventually values fell back to around 90 cts/lb, but by May 1997 prices had reached over 300 cts/lb. And by mid 2001 the nearest position on the NYBOT 'C' contracts had fallen to below 50 cts/lb: a 30-year low just four years after the 1997 highs. Figure 17 on page 212 shows monthly price movements from 1993 to 2002.

Modern communications can move markets quickly, ensuring that all events affecting price become known to all market players more or less simultaneously. And when as a result everyone wants to buy or sell but there are no sellers or buyers, then without any trading the price may jump or fall by as much as 10 cts/lb or more, depending on the starting price level. In times of extreme volatility this gap means a trader can be left with a position they cannot liquidate when they wish to because there is no trade.

It is also critical to understand that the hours of trading futures are arbitrary and restricted, while activity in the cash market continues around the clock. Events that occur after trading hours can translate into a big gap in price from the previous day's closing to the next day's opening.

## Leverage

Leverage is a significant characteristic of the futures market. In light of coffee price volatility, it is important to be aware that futures contracts are *leveraged instruments*, meaning that a trader does not pay the full market price for each contract.

Instead, futures traders pay a small portion of the contract's total value (usually less than 10%) in the form of margin, a good faith deposit to ensure contract performance. A NYBOT

Coffee 'C' contract trading at 100 cts/lb would be worth $37,500 (each contract is for 37,500 lb of coffee). If the margin requirement is about US$ 3,000 dollars per contract, buying 10 contracts at 100 cts/lb means posting a margin of US$ 30,000, representing a long (unsold) position worth US$ 375,000. Leverage offers advantages, but it carries an equal amount of risk. If the market moves down 10 cents before a selling trade can be achieved then the loss of US$ 37,500 in this case represents 125% of the original investment of US$ 30,000 and will require payment of a variation margin (see later in this chapter). Of course the hedger would be realizing a comparable gain in the cash market of the value of the planned physical transaction.

Large *margin calls* (additional payments necessary to maintain the original margin level) sometimes further increase volatility when inability or unwillingness to raise the additional deposits causes traders or speculators to liquidate their positions, thus fuelling the price movement up or down still further.

# Organization of a futures market

## Clearing house

The clearing house conducts all futures business, including the tendering (delivery) of physicals under the terms of the futures contract. Usually set up as a corporation, separate and independent from the exchange, the clearing house guarantees and settles all exchange trades. Through its system of financial safeguards and transaction guarantees, the clearing house protects the interests of the trading public, members of the exchanges and the clearing members of the clearing corporation. The New York Clearing Corporation (NYCC) is the designated clearing house for all the NYBOT exchange markets. Although a subsidiary of the NYBOT exchanges, NYCC has its own separate membership and board of directors. In London the clearing house is owned by leading banks.

## Trading

Trading of futures contracts is permitted only between exchange members. Members must own or lease a membership (a seat) on the exchange, but may sell their membership to other firms. In late 2001, for example, the cost of a class A NYBOT membership[22] was between US$ 62,000 and US$ 80,000. These member firms transact considerable volumes between themselves, as well as trading contracts on behalf of non-member firms representing both the coffee trade and speculators.

Purchases and sales positions for the same contract month offset each other and are built up on a daily basis. Rather than carry such trades until maturity, the members turn to the clearing house to match offsetting positions and clear them from the records of the brokers who handled them. The clearing house takes the place of the buying or selling member: it performs the role of seller to all buyers, and that of buyer to all sellers. In this way a maximum number of direct settlements is automatically possible at the close of each trading day.

In New York, the transactions take place in 'rings' or 'pits' on a trading floor where exchange members gather during market hours to trade contracts. In London transactions take place in an electronic setting where trades are entered and completed in a screen-based environment. The futures markets in Europe have generally moved toward computer-based trading, while the United States exchanges have maintained the traditional 'open outcry' form.

---

22   A class A full membership was formerly called a CSCE seat, while the Cotton seats are now referred to as class B NYBOT membership.

## Financial security

Financial security for the market is assured by the clearing house, which establishes and enforces rules and guidelines on the financial aspects of all exchange transactions. The clearing house checks, settles and reports each day's business and guarantees the fulfilment of each contract. This is assured through the payment of margins and the collection of all outstanding obligations from members within 24 hours. In addition members pay into a permanent guarantee fund, enabling the clearing house to assume financial responsibility if a member defaults.

The clearing house also assigns tenders and re-tenders of deliverable coffee after ensuring each lot meets certain set standards of quality, storage, packing and so on.

# The principal futures markets for coffee

## The New York Board of Trade – NYBOT

### *The New York Board of Trade Coffee Futures Contract ('C' contract or 'C' for short)*

The original Coffee Exchange of the City of New York was founded in 1882 to deal in futures contracts for Brazilian arabica. The New York Board of Trade was established in 1998 as the parent company of the Coffee, Sugar and Cocoa Exchange (CSCE) and the New York Cotton Exchange (NYCE). Today's 'C' contract or NYKC, listed on the CSCE, covers mild arabica coffee and currently allows delivery of coffee from 19 producing countries. Some of these coffees are traded at basis price while others are traded at differentials above or below the basis price (see text table overleaf).

***Deliveries*** can be made at the ports of New York, New Orleans and Miami; deliveries to the latter two ports incur a discount or penalty of 125 points, or US$ 468.75 per 37,500 lb contract (100 points = US$ 0.01, i.e. 1 point = 1/100 cent). Commencing with the December 2002 trading position (KCZ02), the exchange will also accept delivery of coffee at the European ports of Antwerp, Bremen and Hamburg, subject again to a 125 point discount from the New York delivery price.

***Trading hours*** traditionally are 9.15 a.m. to 1.35 p.m., New York time, Monday to Friday all year, except for specified holidays. The closing call always commences at 1.30 p.m.[23]

***Quotations*** for all bids and offers are in United States cents and decimal fractions of a cent. No transactions, except against actuals (AA) transactions, are permitted at a price which is not a multiple of five one hundredths of one cent per pound, or five points per pound. (See later in this chapter for an explanation of AA transactions.)

***Limits.*** There are no general limits for daily price fluctuations on the 'C' contract. The Board of Managers, however, may prescribe, modify, or suspend maximum permissible price fluctuations, without prior notice. In times of maximum volatility it is common to have limits imposed; historically, these limits have been between 4 and 8 cents per pound maximum daily fluctuation.

Based on the New York 'C' contract size of 37,500 lb, a 4-cent variation is equivalent to US$ 1,500 per contract. Jobbers and floor brokers calculate this by taking US$ 3.75 for every point of movement, so each 1 cent move equals 100 points times 3.75, or US$ 375.

---

**23**   Following the World Trade Center attacks and the destruction of the original NYBOT trading floor, the coffee market hours have been modified to run from 9.00 a.m. to 11.45 a.m. These interim hours will remain in effect until the NYBOT moves to the NYMEX building in mid 2003.

The delivery months are March, May, July, September and December. Seven trading positions are always quoted, for example: December 2002 (Z02), March 2003 (H03), May 2003 (K03), July 2003 (N03), September 2003 (U03), December 2003 (Z03) and March 2004 (H04). The number of trading positions will increase to 10 during 2002 to provide a two-year period. The first or nearest month is known as the current or spot month. When months repeat, like December and March in this example, the further out positions are sometimes referred to as red December or red March.

| Tenderable growths and differentials | |
|---|---|
| **Tenderable growths** | **Deliverable at** |
| Costa Rica, El Salvador, Guatemala, Kenya, Mexico, Nicaragua, Panama, Papua New Guinea, Uganda, United Republic of Tanzania | Basis or contract price |
| Colombia | Plus 200 points per pound |
| Honduras, Peru, Venezuela | Minus 100 points per pound |
| Burundi, India, Rwanda | Minus 300 points per pound |
| Dominican Republic, Ecuador | Minus 400 points per pound |

***Certification.*** No coffee can be submitted for tendering without having first obtained a certificate of grade and quality from the exchange. All coffee submitted for certification is examined by a panel of three licensed graders. The examination is blind, or neutral, as the graders know the country of origin but not who submitted the sample. The quality is determined on the basis of six evaluations and measurements:

1. Green coffee odour (no foreign odours)
2. Screen size (50% over screen 15, no more than 5% below 14)
3. Colour (greenish)
4. Grade (defect count)
5. Roast uniformity
6. Cup (six cups per sample)

If a lot is passed the exchange will issue the certificate, which includes a complete rating on any grade imperfections. One appeal against rejection is possible on each lot with the whole process repeated by five graders instead of the original three. The appellant has the option to submit a new sample or to run the appeal on the original sample. It is quite normal for coffee that grades well but has failed on cup to be appealed automatically in the hope that the unsound cup in the first test was an anomaly.

| New York 'C' contract: maximum permissible imperfections | | |
|---|---|---|
| | **Colombian coffee** | **Other growths** |
| Basis | 13 | 8 |
| Maximum over basis | 10 | 15 |
| Total imperfections permitted | 23 | 23 |

The certificate establishes the basis, or standard, deliverable for these growths. Each growth is allowed a maximum of 23 imperfections (out of 350 grams), with a deduction of 10 points for each full imperfection by which it exceeds the number permitted in the basis. Sample size is 5 lb for parcels up to 300 bags, 8 lb for 301–500 bags and 10 lb for more than 500 bags.

Exchanges continuously monitor cash market conditions and adjust contracts or create new ones to reflect those changes. This reflects the fundamental relationship between cash and futures. If the futures market does not accurately represent the cash market, then it cannot perform its primary pricing functions. As an example, over a two-year period, the 'C' contract added Panamanian coffee to its tenderable growths, reduced the discount for Peruvian coffee and added European delivery points. In addition, new grading procedures as well as changes in bagging standards have been implemented by the New York Board of Trade.

NYBOT's direct involvement with the grading, certification and warehousing of physical coffee is an indication of how interconnected the futures and cash markets have become. The New York Exchange is also directly involved in the establishment of electronic transfer of ownership of lots of coffee through standardized electronic contracts and other paperwork that must accompany the movement of coffee through the marketing chain. Work commenced in April 2002 to extend its existing Commodity Operations Processing System (COPS) into a fully fledged electronic platform (eCOPS) for the full automation of coffee and cocoa deliveries for the exchange. Initially the system will handle electronic versions of warehouse receipts, delivery orders, sampling orders, weight notes, invoices and insurance declarations. Other areas such as bills of lading and customs entry documentation will be added as the system grows.

## Supervision

The United States Commodity Futures Trading Commission (CFTC) is charged with the supervision of trading in commodity futures. The CFTC reports directly to the United States Congress and its aim is to protect the trading public from abuses by the futures industry, such as manipulation of the market and other deceptive practices that might prevent the market from correctly reflecting supply and demand factors. It also seeks to ensure that the members of the exchange are financially viable. Incidentally, the NYBOT exchange bylaws, rules and regulations are statutory and therefore have the force of law. The provisions of the CFTC Act require every intermediary who deals with members of the public investing in futures to be registered with the National Futures Association, a self-regulatory body created by the Act. The NYBOT exchanges, through the use of electronic surveillance and professional personnel, actively monitor trading activity and enforce trading rules and regulations.

## Commitment of traders report

The CFTC actively promotes market transparency and to this end publishes the Commitment of Traders (COT) reports which clearly show the position of large commercial and non-commercial traders. Positions of 50 contracts or more must be reported to the CFTC. This is of great value to small players in that it allows them to see information that otherwise would be available only to very large operators. In the coffee market it is not uncommon for large speculative hedge funds to hold 20%–25% of the open (uncovered) interest, long or short, (see Mechanics of trading in futures, page 185) and it is important for producers and exporters to know in which delivery months these funds hold their positions. Because of the speculative nature of such fund positions it is equally important to know their size because if the tonnage of either their long or short position moves to extremes, very fast action could become imminent (liquidation of the longs or buying against the shorts as the case might be). The CFTC produces a weekly COT on futures, and a fortnightly COT on futures and options combined (available at *www.cftc.gov*).

## Mini 'C' contract

The regular 'C' contract quantity of 37,500 lb is not always practical for smaller producers, especially for roasters and retailers of specialty coffee who generally tend to deal in much smaller quantities. The price risk on such transactions can usually be hedged against the regular 'C' contract only by combining a number of small lots, and then lifting the hedge again if the quantity at risk has been halved. In addition, because of the highly leveraged nature of futures trading and the natural volatility of the free coffee market, the daily price movement can be significant when calculated in terms of the regular 'C' contract. In 1999, for example, the average daily price movement was US$ 1,392 per contract.

Recognizing this, on 15 March 2002 the New York Board of Trade introduced the Mini 'C', representing just 12,500 pounds of coffee, to enable small producers and small operators on the importation and consumer side to initiate and maintain hedging programmes within a smaller capital and credit availability. For speculative traders, the smaller margin for the Mini 'C' can reduce capital exposure during periods of great volatility while still providing opportunities for gain. Larger traders can fine-tune their market positions by taking advantage of combination strategies that create greater flexibility.

An interesting aspect of the new Mini 'C' is that it provides for cash settlement only, thereby removing the potential delivery concerns that arise when a delivery month nears expiry.

**Features**

- Each Mini 'C' futures contract is for 12,500 lb of exchange-certified arabica coffee, making it one-third the size of the regular 'C' contract (37,500 lb). As an example, at 60 cts/lb, the Mini 'C' contract would have a total value $7,500, as opposed to $22,500 for the regular 'C' contract.

- The Mini 'C' contract is priced in cents per pound to two decimals. The minimum unit of price fluctuation (tick value) is 0.05 cts/lb ($6.25 per contract compared to $18.75 for the regular 'C' contract).

- The contract trades five delivery months: February (Feb), April (Apr), June (Jun), August (Aug), and November (Nov). Each Mini 'C' contract month is associated with or corresponds to a regular 'C' contract month for final settlement purposes as follows: Mini February/'C' March; Mini April/'C' May; Mini June/'C' July; Mini August/'C' September; Mini November/'C' December.

- While the regular 'C' contract has physical delivery provisions, the Mini 'C' is *cash settled* against the *weighted average* of all ring-traded contracts in the corresponding 'C' contract month during the last five bracket periods of trading on the last trading day of the Mini contract (excluding spread trades, which are the simultaneous buying of one delivery month and selling of another – see Straddle operations in chapter 9, Hedging and other operations).

Because the Mini 'C' is cash settled, it will not be fungible (offsettable) with the regular 'C' contract. That is, Mini 'C' contracts cannot be used to offset regular 'C' contracts when determining the overall market position or a trader's commitment to the exchange. Traders can execute against actuals (AAs) however, in which a futures contract can be exchanged for the cash commodity (also called exchange for physicals – EFP).

There will be no options traded against the Mini 'C' contract. All New York coffee options will continue to trade against the regular 'C' contract.

## The London International Financial Futures and Options Exchange – LIFFE

### *Pure electronic trading environment*

Following the removal in 1982 of exchange controls in the United Kingdom, LIFFE was set up to offer market participants better means to manage exposure to both foreign exchange and interest rate volatility. In 1992 it merged with the London Traded Options Market, and in 1996 it merged with the London Commodity Exchange (LCE). This is when soft and agricultural commodity contracts were added to the financial portfolio. Contracts currently traded are cocoa, robusta coffee, white sugar, wheat, barley and potatoes. There is also a weather contract. Following the purchase of LIFFE by Euronext in 2001 the exchange was renamed Euronext.liffe although it is still referred to as LIFFE.

Commodity futures have been traded in London for many years. The current robusta coffee contract (exchange contract no. 406) has been trading since 1958; its most recent version dates from February 2001 when some minor amendments were made. Originally trade was in pounds sterling, but since April 1992 robusta futures have been quoted in United States currency instead.

In November 2000 LIFFE abolished traditional open outcry trading in favour of an electronic trading environment, based on LIFFE CONNECT™, an electronic trading platform. The entire trading floor system was replaced by computers, signalling among others changes the disappearance of floor brokers. Whereas previously the floor brokers making offers or bids would be known, trading is now anonymous and purely order-driven. Traders do not know who their trading counterpart is, either before or after the trade.

Dramatic as this move seemed at the time, the end-result has been increased liquidity and considerably easier access through linkages with global communications networks that provide electronic access on an equal footing, virtually regardless of location.

Trading takes place by submitting an order, via a trading application (front-end software) into the LIFFE CONNECT™ central order book. Having received the orders the system's Trading Host stores all orders in the central order book and performs *order matching* with corresponding orders (this is an electronic representation of the marketplace) where the criteria for determining trade priority depend on the contract being traded. Traders can submit orders; revise price, volume or a 'Good till cancelled' (GTC) order's date; pull orders, and make wholesale trades. After a trade has been executed, trade details are sent into the Trade Registration System in real-time throughout the day for post-trade processing.

---

### Trade priority/matching

*LIFFE CONNECT™ matches orders in the central order book. The trading host configuration allows the trade matching algorithm to be set by contract. One of the following algorithms will be used:*

#### Price and time priority

**Price.** *Highest bid/lowest offer has priority over orders in the same contract month/strategy/option strike. (See Options in chapter 9, Hedging and other operations.)*

**Time.** *The first order at a price has priority over all other orders at the same price which will, in turn, trade according to the time they were accepted by the trading host.*

#### Pro-rata with minimum/maximum caps

**Price.** *Highest bid/lowest offer has priority over the others in the same contract month/strategy.*

**Time.** *All orders at a price have the same priority; orders are filled in proportion to the volume.*

---

Participants may change or withdraw unfulfilled orders at any time and are able to 'see' all available offer and bid prices, including the number of lots on offer or bid for at those prices, and many other market details at any one time. Price information is also available free of charge at *www.liffe-nonfinancials.com*, but with a 15 minute time delay. To find out how to link into the LIFFE CONNECT™ trading system go to *www.liffe.com*, or ask for their brochure 'How the market works'. LIFFE has broken new ground in that rather than obliging market participants to use LIFFE access software, a series of independent software vendors were contracted to design 'tailor-made' front-end solutions. At the end of 2001 there were 493 active direct and indirect Internet access sites in 43 countries in all three major time zones.

### The robusta contract (exchange symbol LKD)

**Contract details.** Trading hours are from 9.40 a.m. to 4.55 p.m. United Kingdom time. The exchange is open Monday through Friday except for listed public holidays. The contract unit is 5 tons with a minimum price fluctuation of US$ 1 per ton. Delivery months are January (F), March (H), May (K), July (N), September (U), and November (X). As in New York, seven trading positions are always quoted. The last trading day is the last business day of the delivery month (till 12.30 p.m.); tenders may be made any day during the delivery month.

| Tenderable growths | Deliverable at |
|---|---|
| Angola, Brazil (Conillons), Cameroon, Central African Republic, Côte d'Ivoire, Democratic Republic of the Congo, Ecuador, Ghana, Guinea, India, Indonesia, Liberia, Malagasy Republic, Nigeria, Philippines, Sierra Leone, Thailand, Togo, Trinidad, Uganda, United Republic of Tanzania and Viet Nam. | All growths can be tendered at the base price, in 5-ton lots, provided the coffee meets the required quality standard. |

Grading samples are examined by three members of the exchange grading panel, who award a grading certificate based on the defect count only as the coffee is not liquored (tasted). Price variations are applied according to the grading results as follows:

- Type 1: Up to 150 defects per 500 g = full base price

- Type 2: 151–250 defects = discount of US$ 15/ton

- Type 3: 251–350 defects = discount of US$ 30/ton

- Type 4: 351–450 defects = discount of US$ 45/ton

**Screen size.** Coffee passing more than 25% through screen 14 and less than 10% through screen 12 (both round holes) are tenderable at a discount of US$ 60/ton.

Coffee is not tenderable if:

- It has more than 450 defects per 500 grams;

- It is unsound, i.e. for any reason other than those already listed, as determined by the graders;

- It contains more than 10% passing through screen 12 round;

- It contains more than 5 fully mouldy or 10 partially mouldy beans or any combination such that the total exceeds the equivalent of 5 mouldy beans per 500 grams.

**Delivery points.** Exchange-nominated warehouses in London and the United Kingdom home counties, or in Amsterdam, Antwerp, Barcelona, Bremen, Felixstowe, Genoa-Savona, Hamburg, Le Havre, Marseilles-Fos, New Orleans, New York, Rotterdam and Trieste.

### Supervision

The London Clearing House (LCH) acts as the central counter party for all trades executed on the LIFFE exchange, and is contractually obliged to ensure the performance of all trades registered by its members. Only LIFFE shareholders can apply to become LIFFE clearing members, subject to their also applying to become LCH members.

Apart from LIFFE's internal regulations on members' financial resources, staff competency and systems suitability, a considerable body of United Kingdom legislation governs the general trade on futures markets. The Financial Services Act 1986 requires, among other things, every person dealing with the futures-trading public to register with the Securities and Futures Association. This is a self-regulatory body created by the Act that seeks to assure the financial viability of all exchange members. The Financial Services and Markets Act 2000, which came into force on 1 November 2001, sets still more requirements

On a day-to-day basis, the LIFFE trading platform not only provides perfect price transparency but, like the Bolero electronic documentation system, it records each and every trading move made by members accessing the system: the time, what was done, and by whom.

### Outlook

LIFFE is the largest electronic exchange in the world in terms of value, and has the potential to cope with substantially higher trading volumes. Depending on market demand it could also be expanded to incorporate acceptance of electronic warehouse warrants for tendering purposes. Clearing of physical coffee against futures (against actuals) is already available.

Through electronic documentation systems as Bolero it is theoretically also possible to link coffee purchases in origin countries and the subsequent export shipments with the relevant hedging positions on the exchange. Such additions are of interest especially to the banking system that finances such operations but would require considerable further development. (See chapter 10, Risk.)

# Other futures markets

## The Tokyo Grain Exchange – coffee futures

Futures trading in rice started as early as 1730 in Japan. In 1893 Japan enacted the Exchange Law giving birth to the Tokyo Rice Exchange, which traded rice, cotton, sugar and raw silk futures. The present-day Tokyo Grain Exchange (TGE) was formed in 1952 and merged with the Tokyo Sugar Exchange in 1993. It has a membership in 2002 of over 80 firms, known as Futures Commission Merchants or FCMs. Trading in arabica and robusta futures started in June 1998. As yet options are not traded. (See *www.tge.or.jp.*)

The exchange is open to foreign participation through non-resident FCMs provided these are members of their own national futures exchange or are registered with a government regulatory authority such as the United States Commodity Futures Trading Commission. Non-resident FCMs must operate through an exchange FCM with whom they have opened an account.

The contract units clearly demonstrate that this is a futures market designed for an importing country with many types of buyers, ranging from large to very small. The contract unit for arabica is just 50 bags of 69 kg, or 3,450 kg. The delivery unit though is 250 bags, or 17,250 kg. For robusta the contract unit is 5,000 kg and the delivery unit is 15,000 kg. The minimum price fluctuation is equivalent to 500 yen per lot (arabica and robusta).

### Clearing house

TGE has no clearing house as such and, unlike the New York and London exchanges, is also not the counterpart to each member and each transaction. Instead individual members clear their own transactions at the end of each trading day and any open positions are marked to the market by the exchange. TGE then collects the difference from members showing a loss and pays this to those showing a profit. FCMs hold margins and other client funds in segregated trust accounts.

## Computerized trading

Trading is exclusively by dedicated computer screens linking the members (FCMs) into the TGE system. Coffee futures are traded only in sessions, not continuously as in New York and London. Five daily trading sessions are held at 9.30 a.m., 10.30 a.m., 13.30 p.m., 14.30 p.m. and 15.30 p.m., with an average duration of 7–8 minutes for arabica trading and slightly less for robusta trading. Each session takes the form of a *competitive auction* for each delivery position in which the total number of buy and sell orders per delivery position is matched through the raising or lowering of the price according to the imbalance of orders. If there are more sell than buy orders, the provisional price is lowered to draw out additional buying orders. More buy than sell orders: the price is raised to draw out more sellers. The provisional price becomes fixed once the totals match and then applies to all contracts for that position in that session.

The timing of orders during a session is therefore irrelevant, again unlike New York and London. Until the provisional price becomes fixed members can add orders. They can cancel orders by entering counter-orders of the same volume. If it proves impossible during any one session to match selling and buying orders for a given trading month then there will be no trade in that position unless the provisional price is at the daily price limit. In this case matching orders will be allocated by lot.

| Tenderable growths | Deliverable at |
|---|---|
| **Arabica** | |
| Mexico (Prime Washed, High Grown, Strictly High Grown), Guatemala (Extra Prime Washed, Semi Hard Bean, Hard Bean, Fancy Hard Bean, Strictly Hard Bean), El Salvador (Central Standard, High Grown, Strictly High Grown), Costa Rica (Hard Bean, Good Hard Bean, Strictly Hard Bean), Honduras (High Grown, Strictly High Grown) and Nicaragua (Strictly High Grown) | All deliverable at contract price |
| Colombia (Excelso and Supremo) | Plus 10 yen/kg |
| Brazil (type NY 2 and 2/3) | Minus 20 yen/kg |
| **Robusta** | |
| Indonesia EK-1 (G4a basis and G3, G2, G1), Thailand (FAQ) and Viet Nam (G2 basis and G1) | All deliverable at contract price |
| Indonesia AP-1 (G4a, G3, G2, G1) and India Cherry AB | Plus 12.5 yen/kg |
| Indonesia AP-1(G4b) | Plus 8.50 yen/kg |

Authorized delivery warehouses are situated in the ports of Yokohama, Nagoya and Kobe.

## Turnover

Considering TGE started operations only in 1998, its turnover is quite impressive: 4,465,044 arabica contracts and 420,419 robusta contracts during the calendar year 2001.

To date the main interest has been from coffee importers, foreign exporters and speculative trading. Roasters have shown less interest, possibly because they see the futures market as mostly speculative in nature, not as a potential source of physicals in that they cannot know what origin or grade of coffee they might receive. This appears to be borne out by the small number of actual tenders (845 tons arabica, and 405 tons robusta). Certain tax complications currently also limit roaster participation in the TGE market for hedging purposes.

## Bolsa de Mercadorias & Futuros (Brazilian Mercantile & Futures Exchange)

The first commodity exchange in Brazil was founded in São Paulo in 1917. The present Bolsa de Mercadorias & Futuros (BM&F) was established in 1985; in 1991 it and the original exchange merged and in 1997 a further merger with the Brazilian Futures Exchange of Rio de Janeiro consolidated BM&F's position as the leading derivatives trading centre in the Mercosur free trade area. The exchange conducts business in many fields of which coffee is just one (see *www.bmf.com.br*). Through the GLOBEX system BM&F is linked to exchanges in the United States and elsewhere and its coffee contracts are accessible to non-residents of Brazil. This enables foreign traders and roasters to hedge purchases of Brazilian physicals against Brazilian futures, thus avoiding the differential risk that comes with hedging on other exchanges.

### Separate contracts for spot and futures

The contract size (100 bags of 60 kg each, meaning it is accessible also to smaller growers), clearly demonstrates that this exchange operates in a producing country.

*The **spot contract** trades physical coffee:* type 6 or better, hard cup or better, graded by BM&F and stored in licensed warehouses in the city of São Paulo. Prices are quoted in Brazilian reals per 60 kg bag and all contracts must be closed out at the end of each trading day. This contract is aimed at operators in the local market: Brazil is not just the world's largest producer – it is also the world's second largest consumer of coffee.

*The **futures contract** trades seven positions:* March, May, July, September and December plus the next two positions of the following year. Basis: type 6 or better, good cup or better, classified by BM&F, with prices quoted in US$ per 60 kg bag. Delivery may be made in BM&F licensed warehouses in 24 locations in the states of São Paulo, Paraná and Minais Gerais (deliveries outside the city of São Paulo incur a deduction for freight costs). Using United States dollars facilitates linkage with the export market.

***Put and call option contracts*** are also traded, based on the BM&F arabica futures contract expiring in the month after the delivery month of the option, also priced in United States dollars. There are seven trading positions: February, April, June, August and November, plus the next two positions in the following year. Buyers may decide to exercise options from the first business day following the day a position has been initiated up to the last trading day before expiry as follows:

- *Put option:* the buyer (holder) of the option may decide to sell, and the seller (issuer) of the option must buy the corresponding position on the arabica futures contract.

- *Call option:* the buyer (holder) of the option may decide to buy, and the seller (issuer) must sell the corresponding position on the arabica futures contract.

All transactions are at the strike price for which the option was taken and settlement is effected according to all the usual exchange regulations. Of course, options are exercised only if they show a profit – otherwise they are simply allowed to expire.

### Clearing services

Clearing services are provided by the exchange's clearing members, who are liable for the settlement of all transactions. Clearing members must maintain the minimum net working capital set by the exchange's clearing division and must post collateral to finance the clearing fund. They are also subject to limits in respect of the trading positions for which they accept liability.

Commodity brokers and local traders are in turn bonded to the clearing members for all transactions they execute, from registration to final settlement. Thus, as in Japan, there is no clearing house to take the role of counterpart in all transactions as is the case in New York and London.

*Turnover and liquidity*

In 2001 the total futures turnover was 490,000 contracts or 49 million bags – the open interest at the end of December 2001 stood at 17,300 contracts (1.73 million bags). Turnover in options is relatively small but is growing. Trade in the spot contract is negligible, however.

## The Coffee Futures Exchange India Limited

The Coffee Futures Exchange India Limited (COFEI) was established following the deregulation of India's coffee marketing system in 1996 and commenced trading in June 1998. Its objectives are to provide hedging opportunities against price risk, ensuring a platform for guaranteed delivery of coffee, and to provide a price discovery mechanism for future delivery. COFEI has been structured to permit even the smallest growers to take advantage of modern risk management tools in an effort to lessen the effects of price volatility.

At the end of 2001 COFEI had 405 members, spread over four classes of membership:

- Institutional clearing members (ICM): clear on behalf of others – do not trade.

- Trade and clearing members (TCM): trade on behalf of self and of others – also clear.

- Trading members (TM): trade on own account and for others – do not clear.

- Ordinary members (OM): must trade through TM or TCM.

COFEI closely reflects the make-up of the Indian coffee industry, which counts more than 130,000 small growers (200,000 ha) alongside larger growers and plantations (100,000 ha). Both arabica and robusta are produced, with trade taking place in both hulled and unhulled coffee. There are therefore four contracts: *Arabica Parchment* and *Robusta Cherry*, contract unit 1,000 kg, and *Plantation A* and *Robusta AB*, contract unit 600 kg.

In theory these small contract units make risk management possible for even the smallest growers, again indicative of the make-up of the industry.

***Clearing house.*** The clearing function is undertaken by COFEI itself in that the exchange takes the role of counterpart in all transactions and guarantees performance.

Trading is by open outcry supported by fully computerized post trade systems. Trading hours are from 2.00 p.m. to 5.00 p.m. Bangalore time, designed to link in more closely with trading hours at the London and New York exchanges. In October 2000 COFEI introduced experimental online trading but shifted back to the open outcry system again in October 2001. The introduction of Internet-based trading is being explored.

So far COFEI has met with limited success in that liquidity remains small – not altogether surprising perhaps as markets have been falling almost since trading commenced. Prevailing low prices and the general recession faced by the world coffee industry as a whole are said to be the cause of the slump in the 2001 turnover.

| Year | Contracts traded | Tonnage |
|------|------------------|---------|
| 1998 | 11,366 | 6,820 (June–December) |
| 1999 | 41,393 | 24,836 |
| 2000 | 77,036 | 49,470 |
| 2001 | 32,720 | 24,250 |

# The mechanics of trading in futures[24]

## Trading the contract

### Floor procedure

In traditional open outcry or floor-based trading, the initiation of a contract transaction takes place on the floor of the exchange. Exact floor procedures vary from market to market. Some exchanges, such as LIFFE and its robusta market, have moved trading to a screen-based environment and automated the entire process. In both floor and screen-based trading, there is usually some form of open auction during which buyers and sellers make their trades in public. Unlike the physical market, no privately arranged deals are allowed. The transaction is negotiated across the floor, providing all participants an opportunity to respond to the current bids and offers. The negotiation is concluded the moment a buyer and a seller agree with each other and the seller registers the contract as a sale to the clearing house. Thereafter, the two traders are responsible only to the clearing house. In this way, the clearing house is a party to every transaction made by both buyers and sellers.

Automated or electronic trading is different but maintains the transparency of open outcry trading in that all bids and offers can be viewed by all participants. The computer system matches equivalent bids and offers without human intervention. Once the orders are matched, the clearing procedure is exactly the same as the old open outcry system.

Futures contracts are standardized in that all terms are given, except the exact date of delivery, the names of the seller and buyer, and the price. The market rules are legally enforceable contract terms and therefore cannot be substantially altered during the period of the contract. Every futures contract specifies the quantity, quality, and condition of the commodity upon delivery, the steps to be taken in the event of default in delivery, and the terms of final payment.

### Delivery

***Most futures transactions do not result in physical delivery of the commodity.*** Depending on their strategy, futures traders usually make conscious decisions either to avoid delivery or to accomplish it. That is, they either make an offsetting transaction ahead of the delivery, thereby avoiding physical coffee being tendered to them; or they consciously force the exchange to deliver (tender) physical coffee by allowing the contract to fall due. Delivery must be completed between the first and the last trading days of the delivery month, although the exact terms vary from one market to the other.

While the futures contract can be used for delivery, its terms are not convenient for all parties. For example, the terms of delivery of futures contract provide the seller with the exclusive right to select the point of delivery. This situation can obviously create difficulties for the buyer. In addition, the actual coffee delivered, while acceptable under the futures contract, may not match the buyer's specific quality needs.

### Offsetting transactions

*A trader who **buys** a futures contract and has no other position on the exchange is **long**. If this purchase is not eventually offset by an equivalent sale of futures then the buyer will have to take delivery of the actual commodity. Alternatively, a trader who **sells** a futures contract without an offsetting purchase of futures is said to be **short**.*

---

24   Based on customs and procedures applicable to the New York and London exchanges.

Traders who have taken either position in the market have two ways of liquidating it. The first involves the actual delivery or receipt of goods. Most traders choose the second option, which is to cancel an obligation to buy or sell by carrying out a reverse operation, called an **offsetting transaction**. By buying a matching contract a futures trader in a short position will be released from the obligation to deliver. Similarly, a trader who is long can offset outstanding purchases by selling.

*Against actuals (AA).* It is possible to liquidate futures positions in the spot market privately under a pre-arranged trade. This type of transaction, called an against actuals trade, avoids the complexities of making a physical delivery under a futures contract. However, such AA transactions must take place under the rules of the exchange that supervises the futures contract.

*Open interest.* The total of the clearing house's long or short positions (which are always equal) outstanding at a given moment is called the open interest. At the end of each trading day, the clearing house assumes one side of all open contracts: if a trader has taken a long position, the clearing house takes the short position, and vice versa.

The clearing house guarantees the performance of both sides of all open contracts to its members and each trader deals only with the clearing house after initiating a position. In effect, therefore, all obligations to receive or deliver commodities are undertaken with the clearing house and not with other traders.

## Futures prices

*Futures prices and spot prices.* Futures markets provide a public forum to enable producers, consumers, dealers and speculators to exchange offers and bids until a price is reached which balances the day's supply and demand. (Remember that only a negligible proportion of the physical coffee trade actually moves through exchange markets.)

The futures price is intended to reflect current and prospective supply and demand conditions whereas the spot price in the physical market refers to the price of a coffee for immediate delivery. In the futures market the spot price normally reflects the nearest futures trading position.

*Carries and inversions.* When the quotation for the forward positions stands at a premium to the spot price, the market is said to display a *carry* (also called *forwardation* or *contango*). The price of each successive forward position rises the further away it is from the spot position. In order to provide adequate incentives for traders to carry stocks, the premiums for forward positions must cover at least part of the carrying costs of those who accept ownership. Therefore, when stocks become excessive, the futures market enables operators to enter the market to buy the commodity on a cash basis and to sell futures, thereby carrying it. The carry will eventually rise to a level where the premium covers the full cost of financing, warehousing and insuring unused coffee stocks. This level of the forward premium is known as the full carry. The holders of surplus coffee are now covered for the full costs of holding these stocks.

The size of the forward premium or discount between the various forward trading months quoted at any time reflects the fundamentals of the coffee market. When coffee is in short supply, the market nearly always displays an *inversion* (*backwardation*), with the forward quotation standing at a discount to the cash price.

This inversion encourages the holder of surplus stocks to supply them to the spot market and to *earn the inversion* by simultaneously purchasing comparable tonnages of forward futures at a discount to the spot price.

### Differences between forward and futures market prices

Forward markets are used to contract for the physical delivery of a commodity. By contrast, futures markets are 'paper' markets used for hedging price risks or for speculation rather than for negotiating the actual delivery of goods. On the whole, prices in the physical and the futures markets move parallel to each other. However, whereas the futures price represents world supply and demand conditions, the physical price for any particular coffee in the forward market reflects the supply and demand for that specific type and grade of coffee, and the nearest comparable growths.

Prices in both physical and futures markets tend to move together because traders in futures contracts are entitled to demand or make delivery of physical coffee against their futures contracts. The important point is not that delivery actually takes place but that delivery is possible, whether this course of action is chosen or not. Any marked discrepancy between the prices for physicals and futures would attract simultaneous offsetting transactions in the two markets thus bringing prices together again.

However, buying futures in the hope of using the coffee against physical delivery obligations is extremely risky because the buyer of futures contracts does not know the exact storage location or the origin or quality of the coffee until delivery is made. The coffee that is finally delivered may be unsuitable for the buyer's physical contractual obligations, leaving them with more rather than less risk exposure. On the other hand, physical coffee on a forward shipment or delivery contract that is of an acceptable quality can usually be delivered against a short position on the futures market as the buyer can choose the origin and where to make the physical delivery (or tender). This feature makes futures contracts particularly suitable as a hedge against physicals.

## Types of orders

*Fixed price order for the same day* means that an exchange member is asked to buy or sell a given number of lots (contracts) for a particular month at a set price, for instance, two lots of coffee for December at US$ 0.62/lb. The contract must be completed during the day on which the order is given. If possible, the broker will buy (sell) at a lower (higher) price but never at a higher (lower) price. This ensures that the client will get the desired price if a contract is made, but they run the risk of not having a contract made at all if the floor trader cannot execute the order on that day.

*Fixed price, open order* is a similar order, except that the instructions stand for an indefinite period of time until the order is satisfied or cancelled by the client. This type of order is popularly known as 'good till cancelled' (GTC).

*Market order* is an order that gives the broker more flexibility, and allows him to make a contract for the best possible price available at the time.

Different orders are often made, subject to certain conditions. For example, a broker may be instructed to make a contract if the price reaches a certain level. Orders that are conditional on specific terms set by the client can also be made. Examples of such orders are: those to be carried out only at the opening or closing of the market; or those to be carried out within a certain period of time. (Orders have to queue at the opening and closing of the market and are therefore not all filled at the same price, particularly when trading volume is high in an active market. If one stipulates a price then an order may not be executed if that price is not touched, or is exceeded.)

Market orders and fixed price orders for the same day are the most common but orders are also made to suit the requirements of clients. Clients who follow exchange movements closely frequently revise their orders in response to changing market conditions. Those less involved in hourly market movements usually place open orders, or orders subject to certain conditions. For example, a stop-loss order – which is triggered into action as soon as a predetermined price level is reached – limits the client's losses relative to the level at which the order is executed. Placing more general conditions on the order gives the broker greater flexibility to react to changes in the market and leaves the final decision to them.

## Positions

*Open position* is the number of contracts registered by the clearing house which are not offset by other contracts or tenders when the contracts become spot (the nearby contract month). For example, a coffee trader may have a position with the clearing house of 30 purchase contracts and 40 sales contracts. Some of the purchases and sales may be for the same delivery month but the trader may have labelled them as 'wait for instructions' if those contracts represent separate hedging transactions for that trader. This means the trader will enter into additional futures deals to offset them once they unwind the physicals against which the original hedge was taken. In other words, the open position of that particular operator remains 70 lots until some of the contracts are offset or 'washed out'.

The clearing house reports only the total of all operator positions, rather than that of any one member, which is left to the broker to report. The CFTC's commitment of traders (COT) report breaks down the total open interest on the New York 'C' contract by category of traders. Large traders are called reportable, while small traders are non-reportable. The COT report then further breaks down the open interest by commercial and non-commercial reportable traders. It is a very handy tool for exporters to get an idea of the long or short positions of the large speculative hedge funds.

## Margins

*Trading deposits (margins)* are required upon initiation of a futures trade. Further deposits may be required daily to reflect the changes in the price of the contracts, when the market moves against a trader's position. If additional funds are required to restore the original margin (ranging from 5%–10% of the contract's nominal value) then *variation margins* must be paid in unless adequate security, for example treasury bills, had already been deposited when the account was established. Conversely, if the futures price move is favourable to the trader, the gains transferred into the account above the margin requirement level become immediately available to the trader.

Clearing house members must maintain specific margins depending upon their net open position with the clearing house. Margins are also needed for members of the trading public who lodge their contracts with members of the exchange. *Original margins* are normally set at approximately 10% of the market value of a contract and *variation margins* must be paid in full upon demand. Margin money collected by the exchange member from the public must be deposited in *segregated customers' accounts*. Note that the original margin requirements in this category are minimum figures and that exchange members may require additional security from their clients if they feel the minimum margin is not enough.

Original and variation margins are adjusted from time to time for the following reasons: to reflect increased or decreased market levels; to add security to volatile positions, particularly in months carrying no limit; and to discourage excessive concentration of trading positions in any one month. Investors should note that margin requirements can be changed without prior notice.

## Financing margins

Financing margin calls on open contracts can make the use of futures markets very expensive for producers and exporters, partly because variation margins are always paid in cash. This does not apply to trading deposits, which can be covered by securities such as bank guarantees and treasury bills.

Any user of futures markets should be aware that unanticipated calls for variation margins can be costly in terms of demands on their cash flow and the interest forgone on cash deposited with the clearing house. Therefore, a user should carefully consider how margin calls will be financed before entering into any commitments. (See also chapter 10, Risk.)

An (extreme) example: on 24 June 1994 the 'C' contract closed at 125.50 cts/lb. Just two weeks later the market closed at 245.25 cts/lb owing to frost damage in Brazil. This translated into a variation margin of US$ 45,000 per lot so an exporter with a short of 10 lots against physical stocks would have had to pay US$ 450,000 to meet the margin call – and within 24 hours at that! As a result of margin financing problems the open interest at that time was halved within weeks. Of course exporters would benefit from the increased value of their physical stocks in a situation like this, but might not always find it easy to convince any but the most experienced commodity finance banks of the validity of this argument.

Merchants and brokers are often willing to help producers and exporters to overcome the problems that margin calls can create. In some cases, the broker will finance all the margin costs but in return the broker will expect a higher rate of commission or a discount on physical contracts. Brokers can be particularly useful in solving the additional problems connected with distant futures transactions. Often a high premium can be picked up for forward physicals but there is no liquidity for such far dates in the futures markets. However, most if not all of today's forward business in physicals is conducted on a price to be fixed basis, which has reduced the need to enter into far forward futures deals. (Price to be fixed, or PTBF, is discussed in chapter 9, Hedging and other operations.)

Someone who pays their own margins is entitled to receive cash payments of all credit variation margins. Additionally, if they pay the trading deposit in cash, they are entitled to receive interest on that money. A producer or exporter can reduce liability for margin calls by becoming a clearing member of the market (assuming that regulations in their country permit this). This means that all trades are held in their account with the clearing house and not by various brokers in the market. Once they become a clearing member, their liability is reduced because they are liable only for margin calls on their uncovered position with the exchange. A clearing member can offset their position on one contract against their position on other contracts. By contrast, a non-member's liability for margin calls is calculated separately for each contract. There are other advantages in becoming a clearing member: there is no longer the worry about the risk of a broker defaulting, and in some markets business can be transacted through *locals* who may give better service than the larger brokers. *Locals* are exchange members who trade on their own account but do not deal with clients outside the exchange.

Trade houses play an important role in aiding producers, exporters and industry to overcome margin requirements. When a trade house enters into a transaction for physical coffee, either on a price to be fixed basis or on an outright price basis, it is usually also the trade house that takes up the obligation and risk of margin financing. This is of significant benefit to the coffee trade and plays an integral part in establishing long-term delivery contracts. Of course, the trade house itself must have strict financial and third party (counter-party) risk controls in place in order to avoid any excess margin calls in times of increased market volatility.

# CHAPTER 9

# Hedging and other operations

## The principle of hedging

Hedging is a trading operation that allows a person to transform a less acceptable risk into a more acceptable one. This is done by engaging in an offsetting operation in the same commodity under roughly the same terms as the original transaction that created the risk. Futures purchases or sales that are equal and opposite to a physical sale or physical transaction are made with the expectation that any loss on the physical transaction will be largely or fully compensated by a gain on the offsetting futures operation. In other words, the primary purpose of futures markets is to provide an efficient and effective mechanism for managing price risk. Individuals and businesses seek to protect themselves against adverse price changes, which they do by buying or selling futures contracts. This practice is called hedging.

Hedging serves all levels of the marketing chain: those who are exposed to the risk of falling prices (sellers), rising prices (buyers), or both (buyers/sellers).

The principle of hedging is quite basic, but one critical premise applies: hedging is based on the idea that prices of the physical commodity and the futures contracts generally move closely together. But it should be understood from the outset that some risk (the differential risk) cannot be hedged in the futures market.

As buyers and sellers, coffee exporters or traders face two potential loss risks: one before purchasing physical coffee and the other following a purchase of physical coffee.

### The risks

*Before physical (green) coffee purchase – risk of rising price.* If the exporter or trader has a commitment to supply physical coffee at some future date and has no coffee stocks, i.e. they are 'short' physical coffee, then they will be sensitive to the development of the buying price.

*After purchase of physical coffee – risk of falling price.* The exporter or trader, who now is 'long' unsold physical coffee, will be sensitive to the development of the selling price.

### The protection

*Long coffee* → *short futures.* Someone who is 'long' physical coffee will enter into an offsetting transaction by selling futures contracts (going 'short' futures) in proportion to the physical contracts at risk.

*Short coffee* → *long futures.* Conversely, that someone will seek to minimize their risk when they are 'short' physical coffee by buying futures contracts (going 'long' futures) to keep their book or position in balance.

The offsetting transactions are liquidated at the same time that the physical deals are completed, i.e. when the trader *sells* the physical coffee they have previously bought, they will at the same time *buy* the futures contracts needed to *wash out* (offset) their original sale of futures. On the other hand, when the trader *buys* the physical coffee they have originally sold short, they will simultaneously *sell* and wash out the futures contracts they had purchased to offset that short position in physicals.

Participants at other levels of the coffee industry, such as producers, are primarily concerned with one side of the market. Obviously producers are very vulnerable to falling cash prices and therefore will be concerned with protecting a selling price.

# Basic function of hedging

The most important role of the early futures markets was to hedge unsold stocks. During the peak marketing season of a commodity, traders often bought enough supplies to meet both their current orders and future demand until new supplies became available. Those with heavy stocks of an unsold crop could face serious losses in the event of a fall in prices. Similarly, those who chose to save on storage costs by relying on purchasing stocks at a later date, and made forward sales based on current cash prices, would incur losses if prices rose sharply. Hedging therefore focuses on transferring the risk of drastic price changes to other parties in the market.

Hedging is sometimes also described as a form of insurance but this is not entirely correct. Buying or selling futures contracts involves buying or selling at a specific price, thereby committing to a specific price. In contrast, the strike price in an option is used to establish a price floor or ceiling to provide some level of price protection or insurance. As with insurance, the premium paid for the option determines the level of protection purchased. See later in this chapter for more on options.

The traditional view of hedging as risk transferral has evolved into the more dynamic concept of risk management. Under this concept, hedging is viewed as a tool for decisions on buying and selling. The basic principle of hedging consists of buying or selling a futures contract that is equal and opposite to the physical trading commitment entered into outside the exchange. Any loss on the physical or cash market resulting from a disadvantageous movement of prices would be offset by a profit on the exchange transactions.

**Cash market losses = futures markets gains**

**Cash market gains = futures markets losses**

In order to effectively use futures markets for hedging it is important to understand what they can and cannot do.

- Futures markets by themselves do not create volatility or price risk for industry users. The *basis* for volatility and risk originates in the cash market.

- Futures markets *cannot* remove volatility or price risk. They are not a magic device to solve all management problems.

- Futures and options markets *can* help risk managers transfer cash price risk by locking-in prices.

- Futures and options are *tools* for managing risk.

The main motivations for hedging stem from the need to reduce or eliminate the price risk that results from being long in actuals (carrying unsold stocks of physical coffee) or short in actuals (selling forward in the physical market without already owning the physical coffee). Although dealers may be short or long in the physical commodity, they may be square overall if they also have some compensating transaction so that, whether the whole market goes up or down, the advantage or disadvantage is neutralized. The compensating, or hedge, transaction may be another physical deal or a futures deal. In other words, whatever physical transaction one may be planning or committed to carrying out can be countered by an equal and opposite move in the futures market. The hedge can also come from a fixed price, forward contract arrangement in the physical market, or a combined physical and futures hedging plan. The idea is to protect a profit margin or, at the very least (in the case of a producer) to cover all or part of the cost of production.

A long holder (that is, one likely to hold stocks of a commodity, such as a coffee producer or processor) enters the futures market in order to transfer risk in the physical market to another party. In this sense they have 'bought a price' by locking into a futures contract to protect against declining cash prices. Conversely, they have forfeited the chance of making a profit if cash prices rise. Traders who do not hedge can enjoy extra profit if prices rise, but are unprotected if prices drop. Many traders finance their operations with substantial short-term credit facilities. It is not at all unusual for bankers to insist that traders offset their trading risks through hedging, thereby limiting the consequences of unexpected disturbances in the market.

*The producer's position differs from that of other players* in the coffee market in that their buying price is in fact their production cost. This cost may not necessarily bear any relation to the current prices in the physical or futures markets. Thus, producers can hedge the risk that sales prices will be lower in future months but cannot offset their cost price if current market prices do not cover production costs. Operators who are not constrained by production costs will always have an opportunity to offset their purchase price in physicals with a selling hedge and vice versa, regardless of market levels. A trader in physical coffee engages in hedging to protect a *profit margin*, rather than an absolute price. The trader needs only to achieve a positive difference between their buying and selling price.

However, when there is a lack of correlation between the movements of the futures price and the cash price, that is they move in opposite directions or one rises/falls more than the other, then hedging serves only to reduce risk rather than eliminate it altogether, and traders and exporters may therefore be exposed to **differential risk**. If prices in the physical and futures markets have not moved in parallel, the trader makes either a residual capital gain or a loss, depending on the way the prices have spread or the basis has changed. For example, prime washed Guatemalan coffee beans for April shipment might be quoted at 3 cents (the differential) over the New York May future, in which case the basis would be expressed as 'three over'.

Even if there is no change in the market as a whole, the trader who bought at three over may find they can only obtain one over when they sell the physicals, for example because of greater selling pressure from the origin in question. Their basis has changed and they lose 2 cents per pound: this is the *differential risk* that cannot be offset. The price risk is that the market falls as a whole: this can be offset or hedged. Of course hedging is not entirely risk free but it does reduce the potential losses that can result from sharp market fluctuations.

The differential can also move in the other direction, of course, meaning that three over could become four over, thus adding another cent of profit. Either way, the differential or basis risk must always be considered separately from the primary risk management concern, the price risk.

## The selling hedge

A party holding unsold stocks of a commodity – a producer, exporter, processor or importer/dealer – is interested in safeguarding against the risk that the price may fall. This risk is offset by a forward sale of a corresponding tonnage on the futures market: the *short* or *selling* hedge. If prices decline, long holders would lose on the physical coffee they own. However, they would be compensated by profits made at the exchange because the futures contract would have been bought back at a lower price as well. This relies on the assumption, usually accurate, that futures prices also decline when physical prices fall.

A straightforward example (see box below) would be that of an exporter in Guatemala who on 15 September buys 1,000 bags of prime washed arabica coffee ready for shipment in October. As there may be no buyers on that day willing to pay their asking price (FOB), the exporter sells four lots of the New York 'C' December position instead. They do this because the price obtainable is equivalent to their asking price for the physical coffee. If the market for the physical coffee goes down, they will protect themselves from the lower price they may eventually have to sell at, by simultaneously buying in their short sale of New York 'C' December. Should the market go up, they will make up their loss on the December futures by the higher price they will receive when they sell the 1,000 bags of physical coffee – assuming that the prices for futures and the physical coffee move in tandem.

---

### EXAMPLE

**The market goes down**

*Physical transaction:*

| 15 September | Exporter buys 1,000 bags of 152 lb each from grower | @ US$ 0.82/lb |
| 30 October | Exporter sells 1,000 bags | @ US$ 0.81/lb |
| | Loss of $0.01/lb on 152,000 lb | = (US$ 1,520) |

*Futures transaction:*

| 15 September | Exporter sells 4 lots December 'C' (150,000 lb) | @ US$ 0.92/lb |
| 30 October | Exporter buys 4 lots December 'C' (150,000 lb) | @ US$ 0.90/lb |
| | Profit of 200 points x 4 lots or $0.02/lb | = US$ 3,000 |
| | Gross profit before commissions | = US$ 1,480 |

**The market goes up**

*Physical transaction:*

| September 15 | Exporter buys 1,000 bags of 152 lb each from grower | @ US$ 0.82/lb |
| 30 October | Exporter sells 1,000 bags | @ US$ 0.85/lb |
| | Profit of $0.03/lb on 152,000 lb | = US$ 4,560 |

*Futures transaction:*

| 15 September | Exporter sells 4 lots December 'C' (150,000 lb) | @ US$ 0.92/lb |
| 30 October | Exporter buys 4 lots December 'C' (150,000 lb) | @ US$ 0.94/lb |
| | Loss of 200 points x 4 lots or $0.02/lb | = (US$ 3,000) |
| | Gross profit before commissions | = US$ 1,560 |

---

NB: Most countries in Latin America use bags of 69 kg although bags of 46 kg and 75 kg are also seen. Brazil and most Asian and African countries use 60 kg bags. All ICO statistics are expressed in 60 kg bags equivalent though.

**Differentials** usually tend to be lower when futures prices are high, and higher when futures are low. A differential of 'plus 10' on arabica when the 'C' contract is at 60 cts/lb may change to 'even money' in the producing country when the 'C' for example goes to 120 cts/lb. This is favourable for exporters who need to buy physicals against a PTBF sale because when they fix the purchase the physicals will only cost 'even money'. A differential of 'minus 50' on robusta when LIFFE is at 700 US$/ton may perhaps change to 'even money' in the producing country when London goes to 500 US$/ton. This is unfavourable for exporters who need to buy physicals against a PTBF sale because when they fix the purchase the physicals will cost 'even money' against an open sale of 'minus 50'. (For more on PTBF, see later in this chapter.)

But differentials in producing countries may also buck the general market trend, for example because of drought or other production problems.

## The buying hedge

Roasters may have customers who want to purchase a certain percentage of their requirements at a fixed price for monthly deliveries up to a year ahead. But it would be both economically and physically impractical to purchase spot green coffee and finance and warehouse it for that period of time, so the roaster's alternative is to buy futures positions for as far forward as necessary to cover the sale of the roasted coffee.

Thus, in covering their needs for green coffee in a general way by purchasing the various forward months on the exchange, the roaster is in a position to buy a specific growth and quantity of physical coffee as and when needed for roasting, to fulfil their spread sale of roasted coffee. Upon purchasing the actual coffee they require, they then either sell out their position on the exchange or tender it as an 'AA' (against actuals) through the exchange with the agreement of the dealer from whom they are purchasing the physicals.

The dealer or importer who has sold forward a spread of up to 12 monthly deliveries to a roaster can purchase the various trading months of the futures contract to protect their sale until they are able to buy the physical coffee to be delivered against the forward sale. Once physical coffee is purchased, they sell back that part of their long position in futures on the exchange. As in the selling hedge, both parties have protected their price risk, regardless of market fluctuations up or down. The following example demonstrates how the buying hedge should work.

On 2 January, a roaster sells roasted coffee equivalent to 500 bags arabica coffee per month, February through to January at the (fixed) price of US$ 0.93/lb (GBE – green bean equivalent). They now protect their price by simultaneously buying the monthly positions of the 'C' contract as follows:

| | |
|---|---|
| 5 lots (1,250 bags) of March | @ US$ 0.88/lb |
| 5 lots (1,250 bags) of May | @ US$ 0.90/lb |
| 5 lots (1,250 bags) of July | @ US$ 0.92/lb |
| 5 lots (1,250 bags) of September | @ US$ 0.94/lb |
| 4 lots (1,000 bags) of December | @ US$ 0.96/lb |

i.e. 24 lots (6,000 bags) at an average of 91.83 cts/lb or 1.17 cts/lb below the selling price.

With this activity the roaster has immediately hedged most of the price risk involved. They can now deal with the purchase of the physical coffee at their convenience by periodically buying physicals to roast and ship to their customer, while simultaneously selling the corresponding amount of futures. For example, on 1 February, they buy 1,250 bags of spot milds at US$ 0.90/lb, and simultaneously sell the five lots of March 'C' at US$ 0.90/lb. They apply their profit of 2 cents from the sale of the 'C' to lower the cost of their physical purchase to US$ 0.88/lb. On 1 April, they buy 1,250 bags of spot milds at US$ 0.89/lb and sell the five lots of May 'C' at US$ 0.89/lb. They apply the 1 cent loss from the 'C' sale to the cost of their physical purchase, resulting in a price of US$ 0.90/lb. And so on.

The roaster continues to buy in the approved physicals of their choice as needed, whether 250 bags at a time or 1,250 bags at once, and sells out the equivalent futures. Their hedging objective is to maintain their average differential of 1.17 cts/lb or better on the purchase of their physical coffee compared to their position on the futures market.

# Trading physicals at a price to be fixed: PTBF

The discussion and examples above assumed that buyers and sellers worked with fixed or outright prices. They also focused on the primary market or price risk, not on the basis or differential risk that cannot be offset by hedging. In recent years more and more physicals have been traded at prices that are to be fixed against the futures markets: *the PTBF contract*.

## The principle

When the market outlook is very uncertain, many traders and roasters are reluctant to purchase physical coffee outright on a forward basis. The international trade has therefore developed a system of selling coffee without specifying a price for it, i.e. at a price to be fixed (PTBF). A relevant delivery month of the futures market is chosen: its price at a given moment will determine or fix the price of the physicals contract. If the quality of the physicals is worth more or less than the quality on which the futures contract is based, the price stipulation will read (for example) 'New York "C" December plus (or minus) 3 cts/lb', or 'London robustas November plus (or minus) US$ 30/ton': *the plus 3 or plus 30 is the differential*.

The contract constitutes a firm agreement to deliver and accept a quantity of physical coffee of a known quality and under established conditions. These conditions are based on the quotation for the specified delivery month of the futures market at the time of fixing, plus or minus the agreed differential. The advantage to the buyer and seller is that each has secured a contract for physical coffee, but the price remains open.

In other words the buyer has now separated the operational decision to secure physical coffee (thereby avoiding problems of shortages), from the financial decision to fix the cost of that coffee, which they prefer to postpone. This arrangement provides flexibility for both buyer and seller. The obligation to deliver and accept physicals now exists but as the price remains open, both parties can continue to play the market. The system of PTBF has been honed to such an extent that prices are sometimes fixed only when coffee is delivered to the roaster's premises.

## Producers, exporters and PTBF

Exporters who enter into PTBF contracts must have a similar view of the contract as the end-user. The exporter of arabica is making a commitment to deliver a type of coffee at a differential from the 'C' contract, or robusta at a differential against the London LIFFE price. There is commitment to a delivery and a differential but, until the contract is fixed, there is no firm price commitment. In theory this means that at this stage neither party is overly concerned about the 'price of coffee' as such: their risk now lies in the development of the differentials. But it is very different for producers to whom the actual price of coffee is of overriding importance.

The volume of trade on the futures markets is huge, far exceeding the trade in physical coffee. The average daily turnover in New York futures is between 1.5 million and 2 million bags and it is estimated that on some days close to three-quarters of the total volume may consist of speculative trading by brokers, trade houses, commodity funds and outright speculators. (Note though that speculators are generally responding to hedgers and will take positions partly based on perceived trends in hedging activity. They move the price to adjust their positions during the day, but overall that can benefit the hedger who has placed an order and is seeking a particular price range. The price movement during the day can increase the chances of getting a 'good fill' on the floor during a trading session.)

Price movements can represent factors far removed from the actual physical market at origin, especially for small producing countries. It would be unwise for producers to feel comfortable with their crops committed only on a PTBF basis because in fact they have committed themselves to deliver their coffee at no matter what price.

*Producers selling PTBF without any form of price protection must accept that they are losing all control over the final sales price.* When prices are very low in any case, as in 2001/02, this is probably not an issue, but when prices have ample room to fall, as in the late 1990s, then entirely open PTBF sales expose the producer to huge risk.

The apparent advantage of PTBF to the producer is that, for example, by selling part of their expected crop in July for shipment in October to be fixed against the New York December position, they have gained the time to fix the price at their option until the first notice day (the day when notice of intended delivery against the futures spot position can first be given) in late November. They will sell PTBF if at the time of selling they believe that the current price is too low and they expect to benefit from the higher prices later in the year. PTBF 'seller's call' (see below) does not require the producer to operate on the futures market as such and there are therefore neither margin payments nor commissions involved.

The producer should realize they have only secured the market differential and that they remain exposed on the actual sales price until an instruction is given to fix. But they have secured a home for their physical coffee, enabling them to plan ahead and to make arrangements for quality control, delivery and shipment. Producers and exporters generally should have a well-balanced mix of PTBF and outright priced contracts in order to spread their price exposure while ensuring they market their crops to coincide with harvest or arrival schedules.

## Main methods of selling PTBF

### *PTBF – Seller's call contracts*

- Generally are written to allow the price to be fixed by the seller prior to the first notice day for the specified futures contract.

- Allow the seller to ask the buyer to fix the contract price based on the futures price ruling at the time (therefore does not require the seller to have a futures trading account).

### *PTBF – Buyer's call contracts*

- Sometimes allow the buyer to fix the price any time before the delivery of the physicals, but usually before the first notice day of the specified futures contract.

- Allow the buyer to ask the seller to fix the contract price based on the futures price ruling at the time (therefore, does not require the buyer to have a futures trading account).

This means that the hedging operation is built into the transaction for the physical coffee but the hedge remains to be executed – the transaction price has not yet been fixed. Knowing how prices are fixed makes it easier to fully understand this principle.

## Ways to fix PTBF contracts

*Pricing order.* The exporter has covered (bought in) the physicals they sold, or they simply decide they like the current price on the exchange. They ask the buyer to execute the futures (the hedge) at the current price. Usually, the buyer then sells the futures and so fixes the price for the physicals without the exporter needing to be involved on the exchange at all. *But the buyer is not obliged to trade the futures:* they can also fix the price for the physicals by simply accepting the futures price that ruled at the time the seller asked for fixation.

*Against actuals – AA.* Many roasters fix prices on buyer's call contracts by trading the futures against actuals through a pre-arranged deal on the exchange, usually but not necessarily at a price within the day's range. This avoids the complexities of physical delivery against futures contracts and is easily done when the roaster's counterpart is an importer or a trade house. Exporters can accommodate this only if they have access to a futures trading account.

*Give up.* This is another way to fix prices on buyer's call contracts with roasters, and is also often used to fix PTBF contracts between dealers. It differs from AA in that, after executing the futures order, the buyer (or seller) instructs their broker to give the deal up to the other party. The futures are therefore actually transferred between accounts when the physicals are fixed.

## Selling PTBF seller's call

This is the easiest way to sell PTBF. With seller's call, an exporter does not need to have a futures trading account as they do not have to trade the futures. They can simply call the buyer and fix all or part of their contract as they cover the physical coffee for shipment. However, roasters almost always insist on purchasing basis buyer's call, so exporters who do not have access to the exchanges therefore often end up selling to trade houses or importers who can handle the hedging operations relatively easily. A number of large trade banks also provide risk solutions that enable producers and exporters to access price protection tools without necessarily having to deal directly with the futures exchanges.

**Example**

- On 20 August 2002 the exporter sells short 2,000 bags of Prime Mexican October 2002, shipment PTBF against NYKC December 2002 less 6 cts/lb, FOB Laredo.

- On 20 September 2002 the exporter is able to buy the physicals at 50 cts/lb FOB equivalent and decides to buy or lock in at this price. NYKC December is trading at 59 cts/lb. The exporter calls their buyer and asks to fix the contract.

- The buyer puts in the order to sell 8 lots December at 59 cts/lb with their futures commission merchant (FCM). There is a market uptick and the FCM is able to sell at 59.50. Thus the contract for the physicals is fixed at 59.50 less 6 = 53.50 cts/lb FOB Laredo. (In real life exporters should watch prices on the futures market, but should only expect to obtain the price they indicated for their fixing order.)

A seller might want to delay price fixing beyond the time delivery is made or the documents are to be presented. Provided this has been stipulated in the contract, after shipment the coffee could be invoiced *pro forma* at a price ranging from perhaps 70% to 90% of the day's NYKC or LIFFE value plus or minus the differential. This would include a proviso that if the futures value fell, say 5 cents, the seller would have to put up margin or be closed out.

## Need for discipline

A PTBF sale does not mean the seller has made their price decision – that will only be the case once they fix! But many a seller has been unable to bring themselves to fix at an unattractive level, and in falling markets a good number even roll open fixations from one futures position to the next, preferring to pay the cost, usually the difference in price between the two positions plus the buyer's costs. In other words, a PTBF sale is like being a passenger in an elevator without knowing whether it is going up or down, with 'fixing' being the floor buttons. If you do not push the button you may end up somewhere unexpected.

To avoid falling into the 'fixation trap' (an inability to decide), set internal stops to ensure that fixing takes place automatically when a certain time has elapsed or a price, up or down, is reached. Fixing orders can be given basis GTC (good till cancelled). But, as explained previously, in a very volatile and fast moving market situation the 'gap trading' phenomenon may make the timely execution of such GTC orders difficult if not impossible.

The producer or exporter who has both the coffee *and* a PTBF sale (i.e. they have the differential but no base price), must appreciate that although they have eliminated the differential risk, a decision not to fix leaves them totally exposed to the market or price risk. This is not very different from straightforward speculation.

When fixed price sales are not feasible, one simple alternative is to sell PTBF and to fix immediately, thereby fixing both the futures price and the differential that, together, make up the final sales price. Concerns such as 'are we fixing too early?' or 'what if the market goes up?' can be dealt with by also buying a call option, accepting that the cost of this comes out of the sales price for the physicals.

## Selling PTBF buyer's call

An exporter with access to futures trading who sells PTBF buyer's call can lock in their final price ahead of the buyer's fixation in one of two ways.

### Example one

- On 20 August 2002 the exporter sells short 2,000 bags of Prime Mexican October 2002, shipment PTBF against NYKC December 2002 less 6 cts/lb, FOB Laredo.

- On 20 September 2002 they could buy or lock in the physicals at 50 cts/lb.

- The exporter cannot fix as the sale was **buyer's call** but sees New York is trading at 59.50 cts/lb. They call their FCM and sell 8 lots December for *their* account at 59.50, giving them an FOB value for the physicals of 53.50 cts = a profit of 3.50 cts/lb.

- On 1 October 2002 the buyer fixes the contract by buying 8 lots December at 52 cts/lb. The contract is now fixed at 46 cts/lb FOB. This leaves the exporter a loss of 4 cts/lb on the physicals that had been bought at 50 cts/lb FOB.

- On the futures side the exporter shows 8 lots sold at 59.50 cts/lb against the buyer's purchase of 8 lots at 52 cts/lb. The buyer *gives up* their futures to the exporter, resulting in a gain for them of 7.5 cts/lb on the futures against a 4 cts/lb loss on the physicals, leaving the original profit of 3.5 cts/ lb.

### Example two

- On 20 August 2002 the exporter sells short 2,000 bags of Prime Mexican October 2002, shipment PTBF against NYKC December 2002 less 6 cts/lb, FOB Laredo.

- On 1 October 2002 the buyer fixes the contract by buying and transferring 8 lots December NYKC at 52 cts/lb to the exporter. The physicals are now fixed at 46 cts/lb FOB.

- As the exporter has not yet bought the physicals they remain long on the futures instead.

- On 15 October 2002 the exporter buys in the physicals to be able to ship on time. The market has risen and they must pay 50 cts/lb, thus losing 4 cts/lb.

- They sell the December futures at 59.50 cts/lb, or a profit of 7.5 cts/lb, leaving the same profit as in example one, even though in this case the physicals were bought after the fixation.

Both examples yield the same result because the assumption is that the differential (price difference between futures and physicals) remained the same. In neither case does the direction or extent of the general market movement matter, but had there been an unexpected shortage of Mexican Prime then of course the differential would have moved against the exporter and they could have lost money because of this. This basis or differential risk exists regardless of whether one sells PTBF buyer's call or seller's call – it cannot be hedged in the futures market (although, given the huge number of PTBF trades it is not inconceivable that this could change in the future).

*It is much more complex for exporters to sell buyer's call as they will need access to a futures account, either directly or indirectly.*

An exporter without access to futures trading is entirely exposed, not only to the buyer's whims but also to the risk that the market may collapse without them being able to cover themselves. (As discussed in chapter 10, some trade banks provide all-in credit packages that include hedging and provision for margin calls.) In the United States most buyers fix their purchases by AA (against actuals) transfers, or on a 'give up' basis, so a seller needs the financial ability to handle the margin requirements when accepting the buyer's longs on the exchange when the buyer gives them up.

An AA transfer is an open outcry transaction allowed by the exchange that can be executed at any price, without others able to participate. AA transfers were developed only for trading against cash market coffee. If the market is volatile, payment of variation margins might become a factor. While most AA transfers are priced within the daily trading range, some buyers may want to give up futures lots at prices that are well out of the day's trading range. A seller who has previously agreed to this will have to come up with the variation margin on such high-priced longs. They will recoup this when the coffee is delivered but the cost of financing that variation margin will be lost.

In each strategy – straight futures hedging, PTBF or AA – the common goal is to lock in a price and thereby manage risk exposure.

# Options

Another approach has also demonstrated a growing usefulness: the purchase of options on futures as price insurance. This strategy has the appeal of limiting the losses in the futures market while protecting upside price potential. It is particularly attractive to small producers who may wish to establish a price floor (above the cost of production) without committing capital to a margin account.

Options alone or in combination with futures offer greater flexibility for risk managers in the design of their hedging strategies. There are two options around which all option strategies are based: the call and the put.

A *call option* confers the right, but not the obligation, to buy a futures contract at an agreed price between the date of concluding the contract and the time the option contract expires. If the buyer decides to exercise the option then the seller of the option is obliged to deliver the futures.

A *put option* confers the right, but not the obligation, to sell a futures contract at an agreed price: the seller of the option is obliged to accept the futures if the option is exercised.

Of course the option holder will only exercise the option if it makes financial sense, that is, if the option shows a profit.

The main thing to remember about options is that when you purchase an option, you pay a premium and your potential for loss is limited to the amount of that premium. The option can be exercised at any time, no matter how far the market moves, so there is potential for unlimited return less the amount of the premium. Also, you are not required to deposit any margin when purchasing options. Options work rather like insurance: *the payment of a premium provides a level of protection against loss.*

When you sell (or write) options, the reverse is true. The option writer is paid a premium (limited return) and must perform no matter how far the market moves (unlimited risk). Option writers must maintain margin accounts. Because of the potentially unlimited risk, only experienced hedgers and traders should consider selling or writing options.

The price for an option is based on three factors, the intrinsic value, the time to expiration (or time value), and the implied volatility. The cost of an option is related to how close the strike price is to the market price ruling at the time the option contract is concluded. As with futures there is an active trade in option contracts.

The **strike price** is the price quoted in an option; the price at which the option can be exercised.

The **intrinsic value** of an option is the strike price as a differential to where the market is trading. If this intrinsic value is negative then it is considered to be zero.

The **time value** of the option is also a factor in determining the premium. A longer time until expiration of the option increases the likelihood that the option will be exercised.

### Example

If December futures are trading at 54 cts/lb then a *December call* with a 50 cts/lb strike price might be quoted at a 6.50 cts/lb premium. The intrinsic value then is 4 cts/lb because the option is *in the money*. But a December call with a strike price of 60 cts/lb might trade at a 3 cts/lb premium, meaning the intrinsic value is nil because the option is *out of the money*. Of course the buyer of an option has the choice of paying a higher premium to establish a greater level of price protection.

'Out of the money' options will not usually be exercised.

*Implied volatility*, which is based on a mathematical formula, evaluates the premium on the expected price volatility of the underlying futures contract. It is important to realize that the price of an option can change because of time and volatility factors even when the underlying futures price does not move.

Option strategies are extremely diverse, and almost any strategy can be developed using options (obviously at a cost and a risk). A variety of names have been attributed to various strategies – strangles, condor, calendar spread, butterfly, and many others. The scope of option trading is vast and an explanation of all the strategies would take a book in itself. Call options are of little direct interest to producers and exporters. Selling or writing options is only for experienced hedgers and involves potentially unlimited risk. Both therefore fall outside the scope of this guide. (More information can be obtained from both NYBOT and LIFFE.) But for the purposes of this guide here is an example of how a producer or exporter could use a put option.

## Using put options

Instead of selling futures, producers and exporters can establish a minimum price, or price floor, by buying a put option. With a put option in a falling market one can still have a short hedge at a reasonable level. For calculating value, the price floor will be the strike price less the premium paid for the option. The advantage of the option is that if the market goes up the option can simply be allowed to expire, while the physicals can be sold at the higher level (from which the premium paid for the option should of course be deducted to arrive at the net sales realization).

### Example

If December futures are trading at 54 cts/lb an exporter or producer might perhaps be able to buy a December 50 cts/lb put for a premium of 2.5 cts/lb. A put is an option to be short, so there is no intrinsic value in being short at 50 cts/lb in a 54 cts/lb market. Furthermore, the right to be short at 50 cts/lb costs 2.5 cts/lb, so the value of the option is really 47.50 cts/lb. In this scenario, the option holder is guaranteed a price floor at 47.50 cts/lb if the market goes down, but they will still be able to take advantage of any upswing in prices if the market rises.

## Summary

Hedging offers definite advantages to commodity producers and costs comparatively little. Hedging with futures allows a producer to lock in a price that reflects the producer's business goals (a profit). The producer should therefore determine the actual price available in the futures market that will support the cost of production plus a profit. If prices fall, the producer still achieves something near the originally intended pricing goals. If prices rise, the producer foregoes a larger profit margin.

The loss of this potential (speculative) extra profit is balanced by the protection afforded against dramatic and damaging declines in the market. There are also other advantages in addition to this price-insurance aspect of hedging.

First, hedging offers a flexible pricing mechanism. Anyone who feels they have made the wrong decision on the exchange can have an alternative order executed easily and immediately. Second, hedging operations involve only small initial outlays of money. If the price of futures goes up, the producer who has sold futures may be asked to pay additional margins; but the price of their physicals will also have risen. Third, because a futures contract provides considerable price protection, banks and other financial institutions are more likely to finance producers, exporters and traders who hedge their crops and positions than those who do not.

Finally, commodity trade banks and risk solution providers put together different *risk mitigation instruments* that are *tailored* to a client's requirements. For example, a put option can be graduated to extend over the usual marketing season by spreading equal portions over two or three futures trading positions, at different strike prices if so wished. Each individual portion can then be exercised individually. Alternatively a solution provider may simply guarantee a minimum price. For payment of a premium, they undertake to make good any shortfall between the insured price (the minimum price the producer wishes to secure) and the price ruling for the stated futures trading positions (New York or London), either at a given date or based on the average price over a number of trading days. In doing this the producer buys a 'floor': a guaranteed price minus the cost of the premium.

## How trade houses use futures

### Introduction

After the Second World War, most companies who bought coffee from source referred to themselves as importers. Communications were rather slow, but otherwise the business was relatively simple. Coffee was bought from reliable shippers or exporters in origin countries and sold on, with a margin or a commission, to a major roaster.

Some origin governments were involved in marketing their own coffee and offered special time or volume agreements. The importers brokered these arrangements as well as the coffee transactions themselves.

In the mid 1970s, importers began to refer to themselves as traders. This was a new aspect to the business. Young traders who knew how to use the futures markets began to offer coffee at prices equal to, or sometimes even better than, what was being offered from source. The old established firms had a great deal of trouble understanding how to compete and slowly new importing and trading companies were born.

To sell coffee cheaper than producers themselves are offering it involves taking risk. Using various types of operations, applicable to different types of market, traders can make money. These operations fit into three main categories: hedging, arbitrage and speculation.

## Trade hedging

Traders use the same basic hedging techniques described earlier in this chapter. They sell coffee short and buy futures against the short. They also buy coffee long and sell futures against it. Traders also use PTBF contracts to assure hedging differentials both on physical purchases and sales.

There are different aspects to trade hedging. A good trader will know how to play the seasonality of the coffee they are transacting. Obviously, the buying differentials are usually better when the coffee being bought is in the middle of the crop and availability is plentiful. Selling differentials on the other hand are usually best when the type of coffee being sold is between crops and therefore not in plentiful supply just then.

A good trader will also be aware when a type of coffee is being oversold or undersold. Sometimes producers hold back on their sales. This is usually a sign that over time the differential for that type of coffee will become a more attractive buy. On the other hand, sometimes traders are too quick to sell a certain type of coffee short. Later, short covering can then push the differential for that coffee to a premium over the normally expected physical/future spread. Trade houses are usually prepared to offer physical coffee up to one year in advance provided they are comfortable with the differential.

In order to secure a large forward sale trade houses would usually be prepared to offer a discount from the prevailing price for prompt shipment offered by exporters provided they expect a normal supply of coffee over the period. Trade houses have an advantage over exporters in that they can offer a range of different origin coffees for the industry to use in their blends. This enables them to transfer to an alternative origin if there are supply problems. However, the trade house also has to manage the risk of margin payments, which can be significant during the life of a long-term supply contract. Trading in and out against forward sales together with effective use of hedging can sometimes enable trade houses to be more competitive than origin on long-term contracts.

The specialty business in the United States has made new hedging demands because many transactions represent less than one lot of futures. To effectively hedge a position in specialty coffee it is therefore necessary to *basket trade*: the trader has to group the purchases and sales together, into a *basket* if you will, and adjust those hedges from the position as a whole, for example by lifting a hedge when the equivalent of two-thirds of a box of physicals has been sold. The introduction by the New York Board of Trade in March 2002 of a Mini New York 'C' contract of just 12,500 lb (the Mini 'C'), was in part meant to address such issues and to facilitate access to hedging operations for smaller growers and exporters, and smaller operators on the import and consumption side. (See Mini 'C' contract in chapter 8, Futures markets.)

The examples of the selling hedge and the buying hedge have been discussed earlier. How effectively one puts these hedges on and takes them off again is a lifelong training exercise. It is not just the trader's feel for numbers – they must also have a feel for the coffee they are transacting.

## Arbitrage

The most common form of arbitrage for coffee is the robusta/arabica quality spread because the two major futures markets clearly show the arbitrage value, New York being arabica based and London robusta. If the price difference between two comparable arabica and robusta delivery positions is considered overstated or understated then the arbitrageur will buy the one and sell the other according to their convictions, speculating that the difference will move in their favour.

Trade houses for the most part go far beyond simple robusta/arabica arbitraging. Remember, there are over 60 countries that produce hundreds of different qualities and types of coffee. A good trader will look to all the quality options. Perhaps they will buy Brazil coffee trading at 8 cts/lb under New York 'C', while selling short Colombians at plus 12 cts/lb New York 'C', arguing that, comparatively speaking, Brazil is cheap and Colombians expensive. This sounds good, but in recent years it has been entirely possible to lose on both sides of such an arbitrage.

There are other forms of arbitrage. One that is very common in an oversupplied market is the 'cash and carry'. When the spot position is at a discount, high enough to cover the costs of carrying inventory to the next delivery period, this is called a 'cash and carry'. A 'cash and carry' in itself is not an arbitrage, but when the costs to carry are different for different markets, one can arbitrage the variation in carry costs.

**Example**

The carry cost for the NYKC September 2002 to December 2002 is based upon the following costs:

- Financing (cost of money);
- Insurance;
- Storage;
- Weight discounts (0.5% after the first two months of storage, 0.125% for each month stored after that);
- Age discounts (0.5 cents or 50 points for the first 150 days, after that 25 points per month for the first year, 50 points per month for the second year, 75 points per month for the third year, and 100 points per month for coffee over three years).

The costs for a simple August shipment of cash market coffee on 'cash and carry' basis, September through December, are all of the above, except for any quality discounts. Depending upon the type of coffee and its actual arrival date, there might be no weight discount. One can take delivery of fresh coffee in September and deliver it on in December without a discount. It is thus possible to arbitrage the cash market 'cash and carry', which is approximately 2.5 cts/lb, with the futures market 'cash and carry' of approximately 4 cts/lb based upon the average age of the certificates. In this example, a trader can pick up 1.5 cents for every pound of coffee carried from September to December.

- In August buy fresh coffee at September less 1 ct/lb.
- Simultaneously sell the same coffee at December less 1 ct/lb.
- September/December is trading at 4 cents: the cash and carry for the futures market.
- Effectively the trader bought fresh coffee September delivery at a 4 cent discount to the price they sold December.
- It costs 2.5 cts/lb to carry the coffee from September to December in the cash market (storage, interest, and insurance only) leaving the remaining 1.5 cts/ lb as profit.

## Trader speculation

When a trader says they are *fully hedged*, it is usually a sign that they have a bad position. In order to cover costs as an importer or trader, one simply must speculate. This speculation is not always outright long or short, but most of the time it is. Traders do however play quality and time differentials, and these are a different type of speculation.

A good trader is disciplined. Operations are always accounted for as what they are. A good trader will never use a hedge lot to offset a bad speculative trade. Nor will a good trader mix quality arbitrage with spread trading.

Keeping 'the book' well defined sounds easy but it is the downfall of many traders that they try to dress up their positions, that is, make them look better than they really are. Another sign of a good trader is the ability to take a loss. Traders cannot be right all the time. They only need to be right 60% of the time to be profitable. As one master trader once taught many years ago, a good trader must be able to cut off a finger before losing a hand, and cut off a hand before losing an arm. The ability to take losses and move on is an essential element in trading, applicable to exporters as well.

# Commodity speculation

Commodity speculation is the purchase and sale of a commodity in the expectation that the reversal of the purchase or sale will yield a profit as a result of a change in the market value of the commodity. There is a certain amount of pure speculation in commodity futures, although its magnitude is difficult to gauge.

Throughout the 1970s high levels of inflation and exchange rate uncertainty were associated with a greater degree of nominal price volatility for primary commodities. This in turn gave a tremendous boost to futures speculation, sometimes referred to as the other side of the exchange. The participation of speculators in the futures market contributes to that market's liquidity, essential for avoiding undue price distortions that can be caused by laying on or lifting hedges.

However, excessive speculation can lead to wider price fluctuations – markets become 'overdone on the upside and on the downside' (prices move to greater extremes than expected) – until the excess of either the long or short positions is finally unwound. By virtue of an individual or firm's expectations and willingness to take risks, speculators aim to make an uncertain profit from their operations in the market. Speculators may form their price expectations on the basis of the futures prices, the spot price, both spot and futures prices, or perhaps on the basis of the price spread alone, and take positions reflecting their expectations in the markets.

Certain features of futures exchanges attract speculation. These include the standardization of the futures contract, the relatively low costs of transactions, and the comparatively low initial funding required (leverage).

## Differences between hedging and speculation

Hedging is often confused with speculation. In both cases operators are concerned with unforeseen price changes. They make buying and selling decisions based on their expectations of how the market will move in the future. However, where hedging is essentially a means to avoid or reduce price risk, speculation relies on the risk element. For instance, it would be irrational to carry out a selling hedge if the market were absolutely certain to rise. In the absence of absolute certainty about future market movements, *hedging offers an element of protection against price risk*, whereas *speculation involves deliberately taking a risk on price movements, up or down, in the hope of obtaining a profit*. One of the principles of speculation involves the opportunity for gain that the investor achieves by agreeing to accept some of the risk passed off by the hedger. In other words, *the hedger gives up some opportunity in exchange for reduced risk. The speculator on the other hand acquires opportunity in exchange for taking on risk.*

Buyers and sellers of coffee who aim to minimize their price risks in the physical market assume opposite positions, or risks, in the futures market. At any moment there will be a number of buying and a number of selling hedge operations. However, it is unlikely that demand for hedges against buying risks will exactly balance demand for hedges against selling risks. The resulting surplus of buying and selling risks that has not been covered by the usual hedgers is taken up by speculators. To absorb the vast amounts of futures entering the coffee exchanges, numerous speculators willing to buy one or two lots are required. Likewise, considerable purchasing pressure occurs when traders or roasters hedge to cover their future needs. Prices would increase unless speculators were willing to step in as sellers.

If producers who wish to hedge could always find counterparts who also wished to do so, there would be no need for speculators. However, this situation is unlikely to occur regularly, partly because the periods in which producers carry out hedging operations normally do not coincide with the periods in which consumers try to hedge. The speculator provides the link between these two different periods and interests.

## Types of speculator

In any futures market the extent of speculative involvement can be high. The coffee markets are no exception. The New York market attracts the most attention, and longer-term speculative involvement can reach as much as 30% of the open interest. Day traders can account for an extremely large percentage of the daily volume.

*Day traders* are so-called because they always square their position at the end of each trading day – they never carry any long or short position overnight. The *day traders in coffee are referred to as 'locals'* as many operate for themselves. They take short-term positions (for minutes or hours) based on the order flow they see in the market and are well positioned to take advantage of price aberrations caused by other market participants. They will be prepared, for example, to deal at a few points under the market level if they judge that the distortion will be short-lived and that prices will return to their previous levels. Thus, locals can liquidate their contracts at a profit, although the profit may be quite small. Since the locals receive a beneficial commission rate they can repeat this operation several times a day.

*Commodity funds* provide the greatest source of speculative activity and their financial power can greatly influence price movements. Funds operate on a variety of mathematical trigger mechanisms such as moving averages, trends and momentum indicators. Over the years they have become more sophisticated in the complexity of systems they use and some now incorporate an element of in-depth market research within their strategies. The fund managers generally have a large portfolio of markets to trade and will therefore view coffee as only one facet in their total risk management. A hedge fund could lose in coffee and make profit in other non-related markets (such as bonds or currencies) to return an overall profit. Professional coffee traders do not have the luxury of this diversification or the financial backing that the funds control and thus must be aware of the fund positions in the market in order to manage their own coffee books accordingly. Hedge funds normally take longer-term market positions.

Both *coffee trade houses* and *large non-coffee related speculators* take strategic positions in the futures market. Such positions could be to anticipate a directional move or to take advantage of price differences between different market positions, for instance a discounted switch structure in the same market or an arbitrage between the New York arabica and London robusta markets.

*Non-professional speculators* operate in commodity markets that are likely to experience sudden changes in price and hence offer a greater profit potential. They tend to be guided by information and comments from second-hand sources such as bulletins published by brokers, daily newspapers and, more recently, information on the Internet. This category of speculators normally involves small investors, many of whom rely on the advice of commission houses.

## Speculative strategies

### The market trend

Speculators normally follow the market trend. In a **bearish market – marked by declining prices** – speculators are usually reluctant to enter long. Such a measure would be justified only if the speculator was attempting to buy at a minimum price before a new upward trend occurred. Speculators will sell in a **bullish market – marked by rising prices** – only if prices are believed to have peaked and a new downward trend is imminent.

The practice of attempting to buy when prices have sunk to their lowest point and sell when prices are at their highest is risky and difficult. Often luck, rather than skill, is responsible for success in such endeavours. As a rule, speculators try to forecast the market trend and take a position when they reach a conclusion about market prospects. If a market shows a distinct bullish trend, the price rise has already started and it is too late to buy at the lowest price level. Speculators will liquidate their position only when the market has reached its highest level and has begun to fall.

### Stop-loss order

Just as margin calls protect the clearing house from overexposure to the risk of financial losses, stop-loss orders offer protection to the speculator. Although they are willing to bear some losses from an adverse movement of prices, speculators cannot risk seeing a large proportion of the value of their assets wiped out. Speculators give a stop-loss order in order to moderate their losses. This order is triggered once the price of the *stop* is reached, at which time the broker seeks to trade at the price given in the order or as close as possible if the market permits the order to be executed. Since the object of the stop-loss order is to get out of a position, such orders have to be carried out ruthlessly. Stop-loss instructions are given the moment a trading position is taken, or sometimes even before, so the taking of any position automatically puts them in place. It is also quite customary to employ a *trailing stop*. For example, if the initial position taken is good and the market trend continues as expected, the stop can be moved accordingly and so *trail* the trend, thereby locking in increasing amounts of profit.

There are several aspects worth considering: first, the position to be adopted (long or short) as suggested by the market analysis, and the size of the transaction; second, the financial resources available for the operation; third, the target profit expressed in points; fourth, the loss, also expressed in points, that the speculator is prepared to absorb if the market moves in an unexpected direction; and finally, the changes in the level of the stop-loss orders that will ensure a paper profit.

It is important for speculators to decide the maximum loss they are willing to bear before taking a position. Once a position begins to lose points, there is a strong temptation to justify the losses and continue to invest, rather than to accept that the original decision was a mistake.

Likewise, speculators should define the expected profit (in points) and only liquidate their position when the target has been reached. It is just as common to attempt to take the profits before the positions have reached the maximum level as it is to continue to sustain losses even after prices have sunk below reasonable levels.

### Pyramiding

When speculators use the profits from their existing futures position as margin deposits to increase the size of their position, they are said to be pyramiding. This type of operation is extremely speculative and plays no role in the normal daily business of coffee producers and exporters. It is not, therefore, discussed here.

## *Straddle operations*

Straddling, another method of trading on the commodity markets, involves *simultaneously purchasing one delivery period and selling another delivery period*. This can be undertaken in a variety of ways.

- The transactions can be carried out with two futures positions on the same exchange. This is sometimes referred to as a spread or switch.

- The two futures positions can be taken on two different exchanges.

- Positions can be taken on two separate exchanges of related merchandises, for example, arabica in New York and robusta at the London exchange. This is also generally called *arbitrage*.

Straddle operations have the advantage of offering lower risks to operators although, not surprisingly, at lower profits. In a sense, a straddle is a form of hedge. Markets usually encourage straddling by requiring less deposit than for a single purchase or sale. When operators undertake straddles they are long and short of futures contracts for different months or maturities, usually in the same commodity market. Operators buy one month's contract in a product and sell another month's contract in the same product or, in some cases, a related product.

The purpose of taking two futures positions is to take advantage of a change in price relationships. The intention is to earn a profit from expected fluctuations in the differential between the prices of the two months. If during the interval prices rise, the profit made from the long position will be compensated by the loss on the short position, and vice versa if prices decline. What really matters in a straddle operation, therefore, is the price spread between periods. It is of no consequence in which direction the market moves. If, for example, the price spread between the July 2002 and December 2002 position seems greater than usual, with the forward position at a premium, it makes sense to buy the near position and sell the forward position. This assumes that the differential will be reduced at a later date, in which case the speculator will gain. The spread will narrow if one of the following situations arises:

- The near position rises while the forward position remains unchanged;

- The near position rises higher than the forward position;

- The near position remains unchanged while the forward position falls;

- The near position falls less than the forward position.

### Example

A speculator sells New York 'C' December (KCZ02) and buys March (KCH03) at 360 points premium March. In abbreviated fashion, they are buying March/December at 360. As December gets closer to the first notice day and the level of certified stocks is rather high, the market will move out to a full 'carry' estimated by the trade to be 425 points. Our speculator now buys December/March (buys KCZ02 and sells KCH03) at 425, locking in a 65 point profit per lot. At $3.75 per point, the profit is $243.75 per lot. (See chapter 8, Futures markets, for more on 'carries and inversions'.)

# Technical analysis of futures markets

Technical analysis is the study of the market itself rather than an evaluation of the factors affecting the supply of, and demand for, a commodity. The important components of technical analysis are prices, market volume and open interest. As this technical approach only considers the market, it must take into account fluctuations that reflect traders' actions and that are not necessarily associated with supply-and-demand cycles. The basic assumption of all technical analyses is that the market in the future can be forecast merely by analyzing the past behaviour of the market (although many in the coffee trade find this hard to accept).

Detailed technical analysis is not possible for all or even most traders. The most important elements for accurate decision-making are close contacts with the markets and with knowledgeable individuals in the trade. However, if charting specialists supply the analysis within a usable period of time, technical analysis can provide useful additional information, particularly for medium-term forecasts.

***The main tools of analysis are past price patterns that are shown in various forms of charts or graphs.*** The changes in the volume of open positions (i.e. the number of futures or option contracts outstanding on a given commodity) and the total volume of operations in the market are also examined. Charts often use a moving average to record and interpret price trends. In most charts, an average moves with time as the newest price information is incorporated into the average and the oldest price is discarded. For example, a simple three-day moving average of the daily closing price of a commodity changes as follows: on Wednesday, the sum of closing prices on Monday, Tuesday and Wednesday is divided by three; on Thursday, the sum of closing prices for Tuesday, Wednesday and Thursday is divided by three; and so on. Analysts can average prices over a period of hours, days, months or even years, depending on their needs.

The value of the moving average always lags behind the current market price. When prices are rising in bull markets, the moving average will fall below the current price. However, the moving average in a bear market will be higher than the current price. When the trend in prices is reversed, the moving average and the current price cross each other.

While advocates of charting accept that fundamental factors are the prime determinants of commodity prices, they point out that these factors cannot predict prices. They argue that the graphs incorporate all the fundamental factors that shape prices and also reflect the subjective market reaction to these factors. The alternative argument holds that although the price curve and other elements of the graph are real and objective, the interpretation is necessarily subjective. Thus the same graph can give contradictory signals to different readers.

In reality there is likely to be substantial overlap between the fundamental approach and the charting approach. It is common for operators to determine the market trend by studying fundamental factors and to then select the right time to enter the market by referring to the charts. Similarly, chart advocates also study other factors beyond the limit of technical analysis. They may consider the number of marketing days left before a position expires, the amounts notified for delivery on the exchange, the situation of the longs, and the possibility of accepting deliveries on the exchange without adverse results.

Many companies specialize in producing charts for various commodities and most have their own websites where it is possible to access charting information such as price history, volumes, open interest and technical studies. In addition all of the Internet coffee information sites, such as *www.nybot.com*, *www.liffe.com*, *www.intercommercial.com*, *www.coffeenetwork.com* and *www.tradingcharts.com* have charting ability and analysis. Most carry not only price, but also volume and open interest, all of which are discussed below.

## Open interest

*The total of a clearing house's outstanding long or short positions is called the open interest.* If a broker who is long in a futures contract sells their position to another trader who wants to be long on futures, the open interest does not change. However, if they sell their position to a trader who is short and is therefore closing out their position, the open interest is reduced. The total size of the open interest indicates the degree of current liquidity on a given market.

When considering the open interest, it is important to distinguish between the types of operators entering the exchange. The term '*strong hands*' describes those who are able to make margin payments over an extended period of time whereas '*weak hands*' are operators who cannot easily meet the substantial variation margins demanded whenever prices move significantly.

In general, strong hands are comparatively resilient to price changes. One type of strong hand is an operator who uses the exchange for hedging purposes. They may want to liquidate a position, not as a result of price movements but because of an opportunity to carry out an operation in physicals. Once the hedging operation has begun they will not be affected by price changes. Another type of strong hand is the speculator who holds large amounts of capital. Such operators can withstand a setback on the market without being forced to sell their positions because they have the financial resources to cover the margins. Small non-professional speculators who generally operate through a broker are considered weak hands because they are more vulnerable to changes in price.

Looking at prices in isolation can give some indication of whether buyers or sellers are dominating the market, but it will not distinguish new purchases from hedging operations. If new purchases are the predominant activity, it is possible to forecast the continuance of the market's upward trend as these purchases signify that new operators are entering the market in the hope that the market will rise. However, if these purchases are largely for hedging purposes to cover short positions, the market is considered weak because once these short positions are covered the buying pressure will subside.

## Volume of operations

The volume of operations, or turnover, is equivalent to the number of trades in all futures contracts for a particular commodity on a given day. Technical analysts regard volume and open interest as indicators of the number of people or weight of interest in the market and thus of the likelihood of a price rise. A gradual increase in volume during a price upturn could suggest a continuation of the trend.

The rise in volume could also result from an anticipation of higher prices in the future, but, in fact, it may indicate that long or short positions are leaving the market because of a fall in prices. In general, the volume of trade is a good guide to the breadth of the outside support given to a price movement on the market.

## Relationship between open interest, volume, and price

The elements of charting must be interpreted together as they are meaningless on their own. When changes in open interest and volume are analysed in conjunction with the price charts, they may indicate several trends, described in the paragraphs that follow.

When both volume and open interest are expanding against a background of rising prices, a **bullish trend** on the market is indicated. A rise in open positions is a consequence of the ongoing entry of new long positions and new short positions into the market. However, with every subsequent upward movement in prices, the shorts that previously entered the market will incur worsening losses that will be increasingly difficult to sustain. Eventually, traders with short positions will be forced to buy, which will add more buying pressure to the market.

A persistent rise in both volume and open interest with prices rising is a good indicator of a bull market. In this scenario more new participants are willing to enter the market on the long side, looking for higher levels. When the volume and open interest start to decline this could be a signal of a trend reversal. As mentioned earlier, for the New York market, the commitment of traders (COT) report, published by the CFTC (*www.cftc.gov*) yields a great analysis of the opened interest, not only by trader category, but also by weekly change.

If daily volume and open interest are falling and prices are declining, a ***bearish trend*** is confirmed. When there are more sellers than buyers in the market, long positions suffer increasing losses until they are forced into a selling position. Declining volumes together with declining prices in turn mean that it will be some time before the lowest price of this bearish trend is reached.

An explosion of volume can also signal a turning point in the market if a day's trading at very high price levels is recorded against a very large volume and if subsequent price movements, either up or down, are accompanied by lower levels of volume. This is a good sign that a reversal is imminent. Similarly, a collapse in prices after a severe downtrend, recorded against a high volume, can signal an end to the bearish trend.

## Charting

The two most commonly used charts in technical analysis are the bar chart, and the point and figure chart. There are many technical studies which can be added to these charts such as trend lines, moving averages and stochastics (probabilities).

***Bar charts*** use a vertical bar to record the high and low range of a price for each market day. The length of the bar indicates the range between the highest and lowest quotations. The vertical line is crossed by a small horizontal line at the closing price level. Therefore, in just one line per day it is possible to show the closing price as well as the minimum and maximum quotations registered for that day. A record is made daily, forming a pattern that may cover several weeks, months or even years. Some chartists insist that a new bar chart should be started as soon as a new futures position is opened. However, it is common to continue the original chart with the new position following the position that has just expired. As the new position may have discounts or premiums in relation to the old position, the chart should be clearly marked to indicate where the new position starts and where the old position ends.

***Continuous plotting*** can be done in various ways. One way is to show the first position until it expires and then to continue with the new first position. Another way is to show only one position until it expires and then to continue with the same month of the following year. The drawback of the second method is that once a position expires, e.g. in December 2002, and the next position taken is December 2003, prices may have changed significantly and the chart may therefore show either a large increase or decrease.

***Trend lines*** on charts reveal significant trend changes but obscure subtle changes in supply and demand factors. The trend line is best suited for recording long-term changes in indices or other financial and economic data. The market registers three types of trends: a bullish trend when prices are rising, a bearish trend when prices are falling, and a steady or lateral trend when prices are neither rising nor falling. A steady trend sustained for a comparatively long period is known as a *congestion area*. The larger this area, the greater the possibility that the market will begin a definite trend, either bullish or bearish.

The simplest patterns to recognize are those formed by the three types of trend lines. These are: the support line, which is drawn to connect the bottom points of a price move; the resistance line, which is drawn across the peaks of a trend; and the channel, which is the area between the support and resistance lines that contains a sustained price move.

The **point and figure chart** differs from the bar chart in two important respects. First, it ignores the passage of time. Unlike a bar chart, where lines are equidistant to mark distinct time periods, each column of the point and figure chart can represent any length of time. Second, the volume of trade is unimportant as it is thought merely to reflect price action and to contain no predictive importance. The measurement of change in price direction alone determines the pattern of the chart. The assumptions underlying the point and figure chart primarily concern the price of a commodity. It is assumed that the price, at any given time, is the commodity's correct valuation up to the instant the contract is closed. This price is the consensus of all buyers and sellers in the world and is the result of all the forces governing the laws of supply and demand.

Moreover, no other information needs to be included in this chart because the price is assumed to reflect all the essential information on the commodity.

Real time and delayed charts can be obtained from various sources, e.g. *www.nybot.com*, *www.tradingcharts.com* and *www.coffeenetwork.com* – just to mention a few.

**Figure 16**    **Example of a daily coffee futures price chart (September 2002); Coffee – CSCE/NYBOT 2 August 2002**

*Source:* TFC commodity charts – *www.futures.tradingcharts.com*.

MACD:    Moving average convergence/divergence

RSI:    Relative strength index

**Figure 17        Example of a monthly coffee futures price chart; Coffee – CSCE/NYBOT, 31 July 2002**

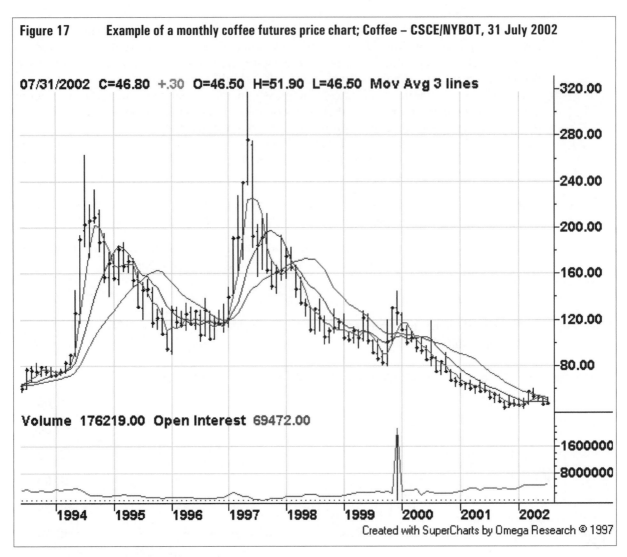

07/31/2002  C=46.80  +.30  O=46.50  H=51.90  L=46.50  Mov Avg 3 lines

Volume  176219.00  Open Interest  69472.00

Created with SuperCharts by Omega Research © 1997

***Source:*** TFC commodity charts – *www.futures.tradingcharts.com*.

# CHAPTER 10

# Risk and the relation to trade credit

Many producers and exporters have difficulty in accessing competitively priced finance. Often this is because finance is not available, but sometimes they do not approach the issue correctly and, as a result, their applications are turned down. This chapter offers some views on the hows and whys of accessing trade finance and the role of 'risk' therein under two headings: commercial risk and risk related to credit.

## Commercial risk

In terms of the coffee and general commodity trade, risk can be divided into four main categories:

*Physical and security risk*: physical loss or damage as well as theft and fraud, to be covered by insurance against payment of a premium. (See chapter 5, Logistics.)

*Quality or value risk*: the goods are not what they are supposed to be – at worst they are unsaleable.

*Price or market risk*: the price of goods may rise or fall to the detriment of the owner, depending on the type of transaction they have engaged in. The value of unsold stocks falls when prices decline – conversely the cost of covering (buying in against) a short or forward sale increases when prices rise.

*Performance risk*: one of the parties to a transaction does not fulfil its obligations, for example because of short supply or unexpected price movements, resulting in loss for the other party. A seller does not deliver, delivers late, or delivers the wrong quality. A buyer does not take up the documents, becomes insolvent or simply refuses to pay. In some countries this particular type of non-performance risk is also known as *delcredere risk*.

Some trade aspects and terminology require a brief explanation.

### Long and short positions

'Long' means unsold stocks, or bought positions against which there is no matching sale. The total unmatched quantity is the 'long position'. Short is the opposite, that is, sales exceed stocks and one has outstanding sales without matching purchases – the 'short position'. When large holders sell off their 'longs' the market speaks of 'liquidating'. Conversely, when traders buy in against 'shorts' then the reports speak of 'short covering'.

### Physical and paper trade

There are two very different types of coffee trade. Exporters, importers and roasters handle green coffee: they trade 'physicals'. Others trade purely on the futures markets and are known as 'paper' or technical traders because they do not habitually deliver or receive physical coffee. Paper traders include brokers acting on behalf of physical traders wishing to offset risk (hedging), market makers, individual speculators (day traders) and institutional speculators (funds).

Physical traders perform a supply function. Trading physicals requires in-depth product knowledge and regular access to producing countries. Futures traders, on the other hand, trade the risks players in the physical market wish to safeguard against. Most futures contracts are offset by matching counter transactions through the clearing houses that manage the contract settlements of the futures markets and debit or credit traders with losses or profits. Very rarely therefore do futures traders handle physical coffee: instead they specialize in market analysis and trend spotting. Coupled with considerable financial strength this enables them to take on the risks the physical trade wishes to offset by providing market liquidity.

Exporters on the other hand combine analytical ability with product knowledge. Like their clients they can put a value on physical coffee (quality!), and they know which quality suits what buyer. Most paper or technical traders are not very conversant with 'quality', and do not need to be.

When *physical* traders wish to guard against future price falls on unsold stocks they sell futures, and the *paper* trade buys those futures contracts. When the delivery time draws near, the physical trade will want to buy those contracts back and the paper trade will then sell them. Because the clearing house is always between buyer and seller (and deals only with approved parties) the identity of either is irrelevant. The system works because a futures contract represents a standard quantity of standard quality coffee, deliverable during a specified month (the trading position) and so matching trading positions long and short automatically cancel each other out, leaving just the price settlement.

## First and second hand

Coffee sold directly from origin (from producing countries) is *first hand* – there were no intermediate holders. If the foreign buyer then re-offers that same coffee for sale, the market will know it as *second hand*. But international traders also offer certain coffees for sale independently from origin: in so doing they are going 'short' in the expectation of buying in later at a profit. To achieve such sales they may actually compete with origin by quoting lower prices. Market reports then refer to *second hand offers* or simply *the second hand*. Traders can buy and sell matching contracts many times, causing a single shipment to pass through a number of hands before reaching the end-user: a roaster. Such interlinked contracts are known as *string contracts*.

## Volume of physicals versus futures and second hand

The volume of physicals is limited by how much coffee is available, but there is no such constraint on the trade in futures or second hand coffee. The huge volume of trade on the futures markets contributes strongly to the volatility of physicals. Futures can cause prices for physicals to move abruptly, sometimes for no immediately obvious reasons. In addition, the volume of trade in some individual coffees regularly exceeds actual production because many second hand or string contracts are either offset (washed out), or are executed through the repeated receiving and passing on of a single set of shipping documents. Producing countries are therefore but a single factor in the daily trade and price movements.

## The differential

The differential is the difference, plus or minus, between the price for a given trading position on the futures markets of New York (NYBOT, trading arabicas) or London (LIFFE, trading robustas), and a particular physical (green) coffee.

Briefly, the differential takes into account (i) differences between that coffee and the standard quality on which the futures market is based, (ii) the physical availability of that coffee (plentiful or tight), and (iii) the terms and conditions on which it is offered for sale. By combining the ex dock New York or London futures price and the differential, one usually obtains the FOB (free on board) price for the green coffee in question. This enables the market to simply quote, for example, 'Quality X from Origin Y for October shipment at New York December plus 5' (United States cts/lb). Traders and importers know the cost of shipping coffee from each origin to Europe, the United States, Japan or wherever, and so can easily recalculate 'plus 5' into a price landed final destination.

## Price to be fixed – PTBF

Parties may agree to sell physical coffee at a differential (plus or minus) to the price, at an as yet undetermined point in the future, of a specific delivery month on the futures market, for example, 'New York December plus 5' (cts/lb) or 'LIFFE July minus 25' (dollars/ton). The contract will state when and by whom the final price will be 'fixed': if by the seller then it is 'seller's call', if by the buyer then it is 'buyer's call'. (See chapter 9, Hedging and other operations.)

# In-house discipline

## Avoid over-trading

People often associate risk management with price protection but there are many different types of risk and risk management. At a cost, exporters and traders can *buy* protection against many forms of risk. But there are other risks inherent to the trade in coffee that only they can 'manage'.

The serious exporter's long-term strategic objective is to trade steadily and profitably, and to seek regularity of business; not to chase potential windfall situations involving speculative moves with the potential to put the day-to-day business at risk. Solid seller–client relationships are founded on confidence and regularity of trade. Regular purchases maintain producer links; regular offers and sales help to convince clients to place at least part of their business 'with us'.

Purely speculative trading has no place in such a strategy but many an exporter has unwittingly fallen foul of speculative markets. When prices are low, the potential risk of a sudden rise is often high. Conversely, when prices are very high then the potential risk of a sudden fall increases accordingly. This conventional wisdom is reinforced by an old but accurate saying in the coffee trade: 'When prices are down coffee is never cheap enough, yet when prices are on the up then coffee is never too expensive.' In other words, when high prices fall the herd does not buy, yet when low prices rise people buy all the way up and beyond. This often causes either movement to be exaggerated.

A speculative long position in physicals in expectation of a price rise needs to be financed. If one allows such speculation to take up most available working capital and the market turns – it falls – the competition will be able to buy and offer at the lower levels. The choice is then: sell at a loss, or lose business and perhaps lose buyers as well by letting the competition in. The only consolation, perhaps, is that in theory the loss potential of long position holders is limited to their investment. Those with short positions potentially face an open-ended price risk.

Selling physicals short in anticipation of price falls usually does not require any direct investment (as opposed to selling on the futures markets where margin payments have to be put up), but the risk is entirely open-ended. Should an unusual event occur, the market may rise beyond all reasonable expectation. In extreme cases it may become impossible to cover the shorts at any price. Because the uncovered sales are showing a serious loss one becomes reluctant to make further sales, even though buyers are now prepared to pay more. This again opens the door to the competition to grab both business and clients. Worse, with higher sales prices more can be bid in the local market thus squeezing the short seller from both sides.

Quick turn-around? A trader who decides early enough that the market is definitely turning against them can quickly cover their shorts and go long. Or, in the reverse instance, sell stocks and in addition go short. *But only if they can finance all these transactions.* If they cannot, *if they have overextended themselves by over-trading*, then the party is over, at least for this season.

Price protection, hedging, options and other risk management tools may be available in theory. But such instruments will not necessarily save those who *overextend* themselves and do not manage their physical or position risk.

## Long and short at the same time

Strictly speaking, *long* or *short* represents the *net* difference between purchases and sales. But this assumes trading is in one type or quality of coffee only. What happens if stocks consist of one quality and sales are of another? For example, an exporter might believe that having at least some coffee in stock will act as a hedge against the shorts and limit exposure to price risk, even if stocks and shorts are of different qualities.

Or the expectation might be that the 'spread' (price difference) between the two types of coffee will change in the exporter's favour. In both cases the simple statement 'we are X tons long or short' hides the fact that there are not one but two positions. The qualities are not substitutional: the trader is *long* in quality A and *short* in quality B. If the market for B rises then the shorts must be covered: if funds must be liberated to do this then the longs must be sold.

But if others are short of B as well then covering in may produce substantial losses and at the same time A may have to be sold at a loss simply to release the funds necessary to pay for B. Incidentally, this does not change if the short sales were made basis PTBF. Shortage or surplus in a particular type of physical coffee immediately forces the differential for that coffee up or down, often independently of the market as a whole.

> **Spread trading** *is the forecasting or anticipating of changes in price differences between two qualities or markets, for example New York arabicas and London robustas.* **Arbitrage**, *on the other hand, is making use of (small) differences or distortions between different markets or positions for the same commodity. Unlike spread trading, arbitrage is therefore virtually risk free.*

## Volume limit

Exporters deal with physical coffee. Unless they have easy access to a suitable futures market, they will always be directly exposed to physical or position risk. And that risk has to be managed by limiting or mitigating it. Any operation, large or small, should establish its exact position at least at the close of business every day.

The **daily position report** will show total stocks, forward purchases, and sales awaiting execution, concluding with an overall long or short *position*. At first glance it seems safe to assume that by imposing a *volume limit*, a maximum permitted volume or tonnage long or short, one avoids traders going 'overboard' and possibly putting the firm at risk.

In reality this is not the case. As mentioned above, long or short is the net difference between stocks and sales, *but only if both are of the same quality*. Therefore, a number of different position reports are required for the full picture to be seen:

- Tonnage and cost of stocks (including forward purchases) that cannot be offset against existing sales.

- Tonnage and estimated cost/value of uncovered (open) sales, i.e. sales for which coffee still has to be purchased.

- Tonnage and cost of stocks (including forward purchases) awaiting allocation against existing contracts, cost of shipments under execution, and total outstanding invoices (receivables).

## Financial limit

A volume limit is meant to avoid excessive risk. However, at a price of US$ 2,000/ton a 500-ton limit long or short represents US$ 1 million, but at US$ 4,000/ton the same 500 tons represents US$ 2 million. So, at US$ 2,000/ton, US$ 1 million is needed to cover a short position of 500 tons; double that amount if the price goes to US$ 4,000/ton. Conversely, at US$ 2,000/ton a long position of 500 tons costs US$ 1 million to finance but US$ 2 million at US$ 4,000/ton. Clearly, because exporters deal in physical coffee that must be financed, the volume limit by itself is not enough.

A *financial limit* is needed as well to ensure the operation, the book, can be financed. However, the volume limit is equally important. A price change of US$ 200/ton against the exporter means a loss of US$ 100,000 for 500 tons; double that if lower prices had caused their financial limit to permit a position of 1,000 tons. To take a real-life example, in December 1999 the ICO 'other milds' indicator stood at 124 cts/lb ex dock: by the end of December 2001 the same indicator had fallen below 60 cts/lb.

*Both* types of limit are needed therefore to protect against drastic price changes. The financial limit kicks in when prices rise, and the tonnage limit kicks in when prices fall. The objective is to avoid exceeding one's financing capacity or incurring unsustainable trading losses.

By adding the third position category (pending shipments and outstanding invoices) the daily position report will show both the funds applied by category, and the firm's total trading exposure. Unfulfilled contracts, shipments in progress and outstanding invoices should be subdivided to show the total exposure *per individual client*.

The combination of financial and volume limits is also important for those trading on the futures markets where financial leverage or gearing may enable traders to turn, for example, a margin investment of US$ 100,000 into a US$ 500,000 coffee position (if they are permitted to trade at the ratio of 5 to 1). In this situation a 1% position profit means a 5% profit on the actual investment; conversely, a 1% position loss means dropping 5% on the investment. (In futures the volume limit would be expressed as a number of contracts.)

## Margin calls – a potential hedge liquidity trap

Producers, traders and exporters are increasingly seeking ways and means to hedge price risks. When such hedging is done on a futures exchange, directly or through brokers, then deposits and margin calls are part of the deal. Usually producers and exporters sell futures short to hedge unsold crops and stocks. If futures prices then rise, additional and often substantial margin calls can pose real liquidity problems: there may be insufficient liquid funds available to cover the margin calls, even though the underlying trading position is sound and profitable. If there are heavily geared or leveraged speculative positions in the market, then margin calls by themselves can move the price of futures.

Hedge positions, and their associated potential margin demands, should therefore also be included in the daily position report, as should any gearing or leverage involved in the futures transaction. The difficulty is of course that margin calls can be neither predicted nor quantified in advance, and in extreme cases a company's liquidity may not be adequate to finance them. Commodity banks understand this and their credit packages will make provision for margin calls to avoid otherwise sound operations being derailed.

Smaller banks in producing countries cannot always offer similar facilities, unless they act as agents for such commodity banks or other providers of risk management solutions.

## Currency risk

The vast bulk of the world trade in coffee is expressed in United States dollars and coffee is known as a 'dollar commodity'. But in many producing countries the local currency is not linked to the United States dollar. Exporters therefore face the risk that the dollar exchange rate will move adversely in relation to their own local currency, affecting both export revenues and internal coffee prices.

Usually, the currency risk can be limited by borrowing in the currency of sale, provided local regulations permit such foreign currency advances to be offset against the export proceeds. If advances are immediately converted into local currency that in turn is immediately used to pay for spot goods whose shipment will be invoiced in United States dollars, then the cost of goods is expressed in dollars and not local currency. If the cost of goods represents say 80% of the sales value then one can say that exposure to currency risk is limited. But in many countries local banks are unable to make *substantial* advances in United States dollars.

Historical evidence suggests that in most coffee producing countries the local currency is more likely to depreciate (exporters ought to profit on stocks bought in local currency) than appreciate (exporters are likely to lose because they will receive less local currency on export). But there have also been numerous examples where local currency movements have gone against exporters, for example due to intervention by local monetary authorities. Individual companies and bankers approach currency risk in different ways, but the guiding principle should always be that commodity export and currency speculation do not go together.

Exposure to potential currency risk therefore needs to be reported and monitored in exactly the same way as purely coffee trade related risk. (In many coffee producing countries currency risk can be hedged, but the complexity of currency markets and trading places this subject beyond the scope of this guide.)

# Risk in relation to credit

## Introduction

Risk is often assumed to concern only sellers and buyers but there are other parties to a transaction. Usually finance for the deal is directly or indirectly provided by banks or other financial institutions whose risk is that after they have advanced funds to enable a transaction things somehow fall apart and part or all of the funds cannot be recovered. So there are three principals to almost all transactions: sellers, buyers and financiers, each of whom have different but interlinked risk concerns.[25] Therefore *credit and risk mitigation are irrevocably linked.*

Few producers, traders, processors, exporters, importers, trade houses or roasters are able to finance turnover from 'own funds'. If they were able to do so then the financiers' preoccupations with risk would not concern them, except to say that in a well run business

---

25    Insurers or underwriters are also party to risk but as service providers, not as principals.

many of those concerns are taken into account as a matter of course. But if one aspires to borrow working capital then all the lender's preoccupations have to be addressed satisfactorily: otherwise there is little chance of obtaining any finance.

Simply put, there are two perspectives to risk and risk management:

* The **commercial perspective** or **trade perspective** is mainly preoccupied with managing physical and price risks, although performance risk also plays a role.

* The **financial perspective** or **lending perspective** on the other hand is mainly concerned with performance risk.

All the other risks associated with commerce also feature, but a lender can insist on many types of risk 'insurance' against these, ranging from insurance against loss or theft to the hedging of unsold stocks or open positions. But what of the risk that a borrower does not perform – that is, someone becomes unable to refund a loan, misrepresents the company's financial or trading position, misstates the quality of goods financed, or engages in pure speculation without the knowledge of their financial backers? What if the suppliers or buyers a borrower depends on default against that borrower? For example, unfavourable price movements cause a supplier to renege on sales contracts, thereby rendering the borrower unable to fulfil their own obligations, through no fault of their own.

Each type of trade has its peculiarities and coffee is no exception. An added factor is that a coffee's value depends not only on supply and demand but also on **quality**. No-one without at least some ability to assess and value quality would be expected to make a success of the physical or green coffee business as a trader, processor, exporter, importer or roaster. But assessing that quality, and therefore a coffee's commercial value, is not an exact science. Market analysis is not exact either, with many price movements difficult to anticipate or explain. These uncertainties complicate the business of raising loan finance because banks dislike uncertainty in any shape or form.

The risks that attach to monies lent for investment in visible physical assets (i.e. land and buildings) are very different from the risks on monies lent to finance trade in coffee. Commodity trade finance is a highly specialized activity, usually undertaken not by the average retail bank but rather by corporate lending or commodity trade finance banks.

The term **'trade finance'** is self-explanatory: these banks finance *trade*, not speculation. Prospective borrowers should understand this from the very beginning. Therefore, before any credit limit or *credit line* can be agreed, the *types* of transactions that are to be financed have to be agreed, to avoid each and every deal having to be individually approved. Usually, but not always, the borrower can then trade freely within the limits that have been agreed and needs to apply for additional approval only if, for example, they wish to increase their credit line.

Different risks attach to financing the trade in coffee. Some of these could be termed *trend risks*, in that changing trends in the coffee world can have negative effects on those who borrow trade finance. Other, more *transaction specific risks* attach to the type of coffee trade engaged in. (This discussion is limited to the financing of coffee that has been harvested, i.e. 'off the tree'. 'On tree' financing criteria would be based on many of the considerations described below but also on many others that go beyond the scope of this guide.)

## Trend risks

*Market risk.* World demand for coffee is stable with limited growth potential only. High production keeps prices generally low and there is little scope for expansion of trade profitability other than through competition, consolidation, or expansion or diversification of activities. Diversification usually means getting involved with a larger number of commercial counterparts, which can increase performance risk.

*Margin (profitability) risk.* The concentration of roaster buying power and the large roaster's need for increased transparency in green coffee pricing both put pressure on margins, again potentially affecting trade profitability, while costs rise because of changed buying patterns and a greater need for risk management (hedging). Having fewer and larger partners also means having larger performance risks. Margins are also likely to be affected as e-commerce sites gain recognition and price transparency increases, certainly for the more standardized qualities of coffee.

*Volatility risk.* For many it is becoming more and more difficult to trade back-to-back (make matching purchases and sales simultaneously), and more and more position taking is required. While the *base price risk* can be hedged (the market as a whole rises or falls), it is impossible to hedge the *differential risk* or *basis risk* (the value of the coffee bought or sold rises or falls compared to the underlying futures market). Modern communications provide instant price news worldwide, bringing increased price volatility.

*Country risk.* This is a risk rating applied to all international lending, based on the lender's assessment of the political, social and economic climate in the individual country where the funds are to be employed. Country risk often weighs quite heavily in the total risk assessment attaching to the financing of trade with coffee producing countries. The more unstable a country or its economy, the poorer the country risk rating will be. Such ratings will also include an assessment of the probability that a country may suddenly introduce or reintroduce exchange controls. Poor ratings increase the cost of borrowing and may result in the bank demanding loan guarantees from sources independent of the country concerned. If banks feel the country risk is unacceptably high then they will buy country or credit insurance.

What is not always appreciated is that country risk also applies to the *buyer's country of residence*. If an exporter trades with bank-supplied finance then the bank will usually reserve the right to pre-approve the exporter's buyers and sometimes even the individual transactions. If a sale is to be made to an unusual destination, country risk will play a role in that approval process. It is easier for an international bank than for an individual exporter to make such judgement calls.

## The market is not static – and neither is risk

General change or evolution has an effect on the positioning and exposure of exporters and traders or trade houses. Examples are the ever-increasing concentration of buying power in the hands of a small number of very large roasters, also now in the specialty trade, and the ongoing switch to the just-in-time supply chain. Large roasters concentrate more and more on their core business: the roasting and marketing of coffee. Procurement at origin, delivery and financing the supply chain is therefore increasingly entrusted to specialized trade houses and in-house trading firms, usually in the form of long-term supply contracts for a range of coffees. Such contracts may even stipulate delivery dates at roasting plants.

Another example of change or evolution in the marketplace is growing transparency in the coffee pricing chain. This limits trading margins, certainly for the more standardized qualities that very large end-users require. At the same time, near instantaneous global access to information means 'the market' as a whole learns more or less at the same time of important developments, which undoubtedly serves to increase price volatility. E-commerce again plays a role through the running of tenders and, sometimes, reverse auctions that price standard qualities accurately and quickly.

All this evolutionary change impacts on the way the coffee trade does business and, by implication, changes the risks it incurs as well. Having fewer but very large business partners, for example, also means having fewer but larger performance risks, and the trader or trade house may be more or less forced to dance to their partner's tune.

The concentration of buying power is not limited to roasters. The same development is evident in the coffee trade, where today a small number of really large trade houses dominate.

The just-in-time system can be said to increase trade risks. But it also enables trade houses, especially larger ones, to add value because their turnover and their total range of activities both increase, often when they establish operations in producing countries in competition with local operators. The large trade houses' relatively easy access to cheaper international credit than is available to local operators has obviously facilitated their entry as direct players into origin markets.

Smaller exporters, traders and importers are having to become more professional and specialized if they are to maintain or add to their traditional functions. If they cannot satisfy the demands of the larger roasters then they must concentrate on niche markets and smaller counterparts therefore, for example in the specialty or gourmet market.

Their functions and margins may also be under threat from e-commerce or Internet trading. This may not necessarily compete with them, but may limit their ability to maintain adequate margins. If trading margins are inadequate then turnover has to rise or other activities have to be added – again factors that can have an impact on risk.

If this involves them in more position taking, then their hedging requirements will increase accordingly, accompanied by exposure to unwelcome margin calls. Smaller operators mostly lack the margin cushion that large houses with direct or indirect exchange membership enjoy: large operators with direct access to the exchanges usually pay margins calls only over their net open position (long minus short). Margin calls can present particularly unwelcome and difficult swings in liquidity. Perhaps this is one more reason why so much trading has been on a PTBF (price to be fixed) basis in recent years. Until such contracts have to be 'fixed', hedging is not necessarily required because the price remains open. (See chapter 9 for more on trading PTBF.)

Unless a transaction is back-to-back, banks usually require outright purchases at fixed prices to be hedged immediately. Open hedging sales or purchases on the futures exchanges expose one to margin calls that need to be financed.

Importers dealing with the strongly growing specialty or gourmet market need to 'carry' their customers: they must hold green coffee in stock for them, they must stock a range of different green coffees, and more often than not they must provide their clients with credit terms ranging from 30 to perhaps as much as 120 days *after* the actual delivery takes place. Risk attaches to all of these activities.

Exporters wishing to sell to the specialty market must guarantee a certain minimum availability over a certain period of time. This automatically translates into price risk on the unsold stock holdings that need to be maintained as a result. If exporters want to secure a permanent foothold in the specialty market they may have to make crop finance advances to certain producers in order to safeguard supplies from future crops – risk again. Long-established and well known exporters may be able to offset such transactions against forward sales to importers or roasters who also want to secure longer term supplies of a particular coffee. The introduction in March 2002 of the New York Board of Trade's mini arabica futures contract for lots of just 12,500 lb each (the Mini 'C') demonstrates the growing need for hedging tools adapted to the specialty coffee market.

Clearly, long-term trends require careful monitoring. Most change has an effect one way or another on a risk situation somewhere, sometime.

## Transaction specific risks

To the points above we must add the risks attaching to the actual type of trade to be financed. These are *the operational risks* associated with the operations that are to be conducted, and *the transaction risks* that attach to each and every individual transaction.

## Operational risks

Different categories of traders have different strengths and weaknesses. Weaknesses can of course be equated with potential risks.

| Category | Advantages | Weaknesses |
|---|---|---|
| International multi-country traders or trade houses | Long-term supply contracts provide buying power and opportunities to add value by offering services.<br><br>Global sourcing means being able to hedge some or much risk in-house while country risk is mitigated.<br><br>Usually strong management, and financial strength/backing | Global trade requires complex organization.<br><br>Multi-location risk centres.<br><br>Just-in-time commitments may translate into need to carry high stocks.<br><br>Dependency on large roasters.<br><br>Must be 'in the market' at all times. |
| Exporters | Local expertise. Can invest 'upstream' in processing and even production. Can add value by tailoring quality for niche markets. | Country risk if stability becomes problematic.<br><br>Supply risk if crops are poor or fail.<br><br>Often higher financing costs and competition from international trade houses.<br><br>New exporter faces all these and also lacks track record and client base. |
| Importers | Local expertise.<br><br>Can add value by adding services and servicing niche markets.<br><br>Specialized products can mean higher margins. | Can face reducing client base because of concentrations of buying power.<br><br>Services often include holding stocks and providing credit.<br><br>Supply, quality and price risks on specialized products higher. |

There are also the in-house buying or trading companies of the very large roasters and some retail chains (who have coffee roasted for them by third parties), whose strength lies in buying power and strong financial resources that permit them to negotiate favourable terms of trade, either with trade houses or directly with origin. The fact that such in-house buying companies have guaranteed outlets for their purchases obviously appeals to banking system. In partnership with collateral management providers (discussed later in this chapter), this combination of interested bank and strong buyer is therefore able to get closer to origin through all-encompassing credit packages that extend backwards from the roaster-buyer to the exporter and indirectly enable the exporter to purchase the necessary coffee at the farm gate.

Last but not least, there are speculative operations, technical or paper traders, and investment or commodity funds. The latter in particular have access to huge capital resources. They can therefore invest in top-flight personnel and can afford to buy the best (and certainly the most expensive) analytical services available. But as they have no real trading function, they tend not to have much 'feel' for the physical market. Their risk exposure is therefore substantial.

## Transaction risks

It is not always appreciated that the lender and borrower have the same interest: that the transactions for which the funds are used come to a fruitful and profitable conclusion. Many of the average lender's preconditions are no more onerous than those any sensible owner or manager of an operation would apply in-house in any case.

| *Category* | *Description* | *Potential remedies* |
|---|---|---|
| *Speculative risk and volatility* | *The deal is not fully hedged or not hedged at all.*<br><br>*Prices for physicals affected by speculation on futures markets.*<br><br>*Differentials move 'against us'.*<br><br>*Increasing visibility of prices brings more volatility.* | *Strict hedging rules and controls over 'open' positions.*<br><br>*Strong management.*<br><br>*Knowledgeable staff/brokers/agents.*<br><br>*Pre-approved credit line for margin calls.* |
| *Performance risk (technical)* | *Supplier or buyer reneges on contract, for example because prices have moved sharply up or down.*<br><br>*Inferior quality or weight is supplied. Coffee is rejected.*<br><br>*Non-adherence to contract terms.* | *Deal only with well-established reputable parties on approved list.*<br><br>*Possibly provide pre-finance.*<br><br>*Establish independent quality and weight controls.*<br><br>*Strong monitoring and administrative skills.* |
| *Performance risk (documentary)* | *Exporter presents inaccurate or invalid shipping documents.*<br><br>*Documents are delayed or lost.* | *Standardize documentation and documentary processes.*<br><br>*Facilitate access to electronic documentation systems.* |
| *Performance risk (financial)* | *One of the parties is declared insolvent.* | *Limit total exposure to any one client or supplier.*<br><br>*Monitor changes in behaviour which may point to difficulties ahead, for example gradual slowing down of payments.* |
| *Currency risk* | *Currency of purchase and sale are different.*<br><br>*Currency rates move 'against us'.* | *Match currency of purchase, borrowing and sale.*<br><br>*Strictly control 'open' positions.*<br><br>*Use pre-finance expressed in United States dollars.*<br><br>*Use forward cover.* |

## General conditionalities

When banks and other institutions finance trade in coffee they indirectly but automatically share in all these risks. Clearly their assessment of the degree of risk presented by each borrower or type of operation plays a role in determining the *credit line* (the amount of finance to be provided), and what conditions and costs will apply.

As well as setting a limit on the amount of finance to be provided, banks will also stipulate under what circumstances and for which purposes funds may be drawn. For example, funds meant for trading coffee may not be used to finance other operations.

As a rule, international banks will only finance the trade in coffee in foreign currency (in most cases in United States dollars), and under an agreed set of pre-conditions including limits on a borrower's total exposure to open and other risks, and a predetermined programme of actual transactions. The exact credit structure will depend to a large extent on an individual borrower's solvency, balance sheet and general standing. As a general rule though smaller operators are likely to be subject to more stringent controls than substantial and well-known companies. Banks will also clearly distinguish between, and assess separately, the price (value) risks and the physical (goods) risks inherent in each lending operation.

Trade or commodity banks provide *short-term credit* to finance transactions from the purchase of stocks through to the collection of export proceeds. Usually this means the credit is self-liquidating – funds lent for the purchase of a particular tonnage of coffee *must* be reimbursed when the export proceeds are collected.

Credit buys stocks that turn into *receivables* (invoices on buyers, usually accompanied by documents of title such as shipping documents) that generate incoming funds which automatically offset the original credit.

## Security structure

To safeguard its funds and the underlying transaction flow the lender will establish a *security structure*. The elements can be summarized as follows:

***Exporter.*** Assignment of accounts, mortgages on fixed assets, pledges of goods. Assignment of contracts, receivables, insurances. Business experience, track record. Fixed price contracts, risk management or hedging. Monitoring of trading 'book', independent audit of accounts.

***Price risk during and after transaction.*** Agreed transaction structure, hedging tools, in-built margin call financing.

***Contract reliability.*** Pre-approved buyers only; agreed structure; fixed price or agreed hedging arrangement. (Who decides when and how price fixing takes place? For example, is it the trader or someone else? Are there specific time limits? For example, fix no later than so many days after date of contract, or so many days ahead of shipment.)

***Physical stocks.*** Stored in eligible (approved) warehouses. Properly marked, stored separately and identifiably. Commingling with other goods not permitted.

***Stocks as security.*** Pledge agreement with title to the goods = warrants. (Note that depending on local law, warehouse receipts are not always title documents in the legal sense and may need a court order to enforce rights.) Take ownership of the goods. (Note though that this does not protect the lender where export licenses are required, or where local law may require collateral to be auctioned locally – sometimes within just 14 days after the default is confirmed. How to ensure no other lender, creditor or authority may have prior assignment over the goods? For example, if the national revenue authority's claims take precedence the goods may remain blocked for long periods.)

***Stock values.*** Daily verification of market value versus credit outstanding, based on futures exchange values where goods are quoted, or basis to be agreed. Top-up clause in lending agreement in case collateral value becomes inadequate. Monitoring of processing cycles and turnover speed.

***Collateral management agreement (CMA).*** External legal opinion on the CMA itself, the fiduciary transfer of goods and the power of attorney to sell the goods. Due diligence on transport, shipping, warehousing, inspection and collateral management companies. (Due diligence is the thorough analysis of operations, standing, strengths and weaknesses, profitability and credit worthiness.) Performance insurance including cover against negligence and fraud by collateral manager. What pre-emptive rights, if any, do warehousemen and collateral managers have over goods under their control? Do their storage and management charges take precedence?

*Export.* Goods must comply with industry, government and contract specifications. In case of default, does a bank require any special licence to trade or export the goods? What will be the cost of export taxes, shipment, insurance? When does risk move from performance to payment risk? (At what stage does the lender get possession of actual negotiable shipping documents?) Are funds freely transferable in and out of the country? It is no good collecting local currency against an outstanding invoice in foreign currency if that local currency is not convertible or transferable.

*Buyer.* Exposure to price risk and volatility (affects both exporter and importer). Due diligence; pre-approved buyers only. Limit total exposure to any one buyer. Buyer must accept that lender may execute contract in case of exporter default.

## Specific conditionalities

All or some of the following preconditions, *the conditions precedent*, must be met before any lending agreement will be considered.

- The borrower has obtained all necessary authorizations to export.

- All levies, fees and taxes are paid up to date.

- Legal opinion confirms the rights of the lender and the right to execute these without needing a court order.

- The borrower's entitlement to enter into the lending agreement is evidenced by, for example, a directors' or shareholders' resolution.

- Statements are available showing there are no outstanding or pending claims from tax or other authorities or institutions which could impinge upon the free and unconditional execution by the lender of its rights or the free and unencumbered movement of the goods.

- Grading, bagging, inspection and quality certificates are available.

- The goods are and will be stored separately under the full control and responsibility of an approved collateral manager.

- Suitable commercial all risks insurance cover is in place, covering storage, in-country transit and loading onboard ship.

- Suitable political risk insurance cover is in place, covering seizure, confiscation, appropriation, exporter default due to export restrictions, riots, looting, war, contract frustration and so on.

- Cash deposit or collateral deposit of X%.

Usually, the lending agreement will take effect only if:

- The goods are covered by fixed sales contract(s), pledged to the lender.

- All rights under the sales contract(s) are assigned to the lender with the acknowledgement of the buyer, authorizing the lender to execute the contract in case of default by the borrower.

- The export proceeds (receivables) under the contract(s) are pledged to the lender.

- The borrower's export account (escrow account) and other assets with the bank are also pledged to the lender. (An escrow account is an account under a third party's custody or control.)

- All insurance policies are assigned to the lender with acknowledgement that the lender is the loss payee or beneficiary.

- A collateral management agreement with an eligible and approved collateral manager is in place.

- The coffee (stock in trade) is pledged to the lender. Weekly stock statements are issued by eligible (approved) warehousing companies under collateral management agreements, or countersigned by an independent collateral manager confirming that the quantity and quality are equivalent to or higher than required for tender against the pledged sales contract(s).

- All relevant forwarding and shipping documents, issued by eligible (approved) transport, warehousing and shipping companies, are assigned to the lender.

- The transaction structure and control over the goods is such that there are no obvious 'gaps' in the transfer of title documents.

## Other aspects

### *The borrower's balance sheet*

The borrower's balance sheet is of course important – if it is not sound then not much else is likely to be sound either. But in any case international trade finance for coffee producers and exporters is nearly always, if not exclusively, based on *realizable collateral security*. Only very large 'blue chip' companies can obtain substantial credit lines on the strength of their balance sheets. At the other end of the borrowing scale are those who can obtain only *fully collateralized* credit (sometimes only against offsetting sales) because there is less balance sheet security.

Less substantial and smaller firms will usually be subject to detailed day-to-day scrutiny by both banks and collateral managers – more substantial or *highly secured* borrowers will fall somewhere in-between.

### *Availability of credit*

The availability of credit depends on a bank's overall exposure to a given country (each bank applies a 'country limit') or commodity, and the net collateral value (assets, stocks) an individual borrower may be able to provide (pledge). The ratio to pledgeable assets at which banks provide overdraft facilities varies but will never be 100%.

Non-pledgeable assets are not considered, and banks always cap (set a limit to) their exposure to each individual borrower. Borrowers must appreciate that while gaining market share and making margins is important to banks, these are not the primary considerations when evaluating credit applications.

### *Cost of credit*

The cost of credit to a borrower is built up from the regular lending rate to include all the considerations discussed under trend and trade specific risks. Each consideration adds to the base lending rate until one arrives at an interest rate at which both the risk factors and the bank's profitability are adequately covered. This is why lending rates differ from country to country, and from borrower to borrower.

*Monitoring*

Monitoring of a borrower's entire operation is vital to avoid the chance that certain transactions are kept hidden – an 'audit trail' needs to be established. Even so, it can still be difficult for a bank to determine whether a client is entirely truthful with them, for example when it comes to forward transactions. Other than the exchange of contracts, a forward PTBF sale or purchase for completion six months ahead need not immediately generate visible action or disclosure, and could therefore be kept secret. But differential volatility has proved to be a risk factor in itself. Unless a deal is back-to-back (the differential on both the purchase and the sale has been fixed), the company's position contains an unknown price risk. This is another reason also why banks dislike financing unsold stocks.

Similarly it is not always easy for banks to determine whether someone is speculating. The 1990s saw spectacular collapses of loss-making speculative operations in a number of commodities, usually because at least some of 'the book' was hidden from both top management and the banks. Loss-making deals were kept secret and were rolled over until the loss became too high to manage. But there have also been instances where rogue traders declared insolvency while keeping profitable transactions hidden. Most banks will therefore regularly audit the borrower's procedures and administration, including retrospectively checking adherence to position limits and contract disclosure. This may be done as often as once a month.

Banks also watch for gradual changes in client behaviour. They will, of course, also control as much as possible the use of loan finance, for example by making payment direct to authorized suppliers and by using collateral managers. (Collateral management is discussed later in this chapter.)

In some producing countries local commercial banks have had bad experiences with lending to agriculture and commodity trading in the past. Admittedly this has sometimes been due to government interference. Nevertheless it has caused many local banks to cease such lending altogether, and others are now extra careful 'because soft commodity financing is dangerous and requires intimate knowledge of the trade'.

The degree to which a bank follows the borrower's operation will vary from case to case. It is not unusual for a bank to price or 'quantify' its risk on a particular borrower on a daily basis. *It is important to understand that unsold stocks will be valued at the purchase price or at market value, whichever is the lower. Stocks held against forward contracts that are to be shipped at some later stage, may also be valued on the same basis because they do not constitute receivables.* This is because if shipment is subsequently frustrated then it is likely that neither the exporter nor the bank will be able to realize the sales value of the original contract and the goods may have to be disposed of at the then ruling market price.

Cumbersome as all this may seem, the bank is a direct partner in the risk the business entails and as such is entitled to all relevant information. As with buyers, so too with banks: the early and frank disclosure of unexpected events usually leads to solutions being found. Good relationships and optimal support in banking are based on openness. If a bank rules out a particular buyer perhaps the exporter should be grateful rather than annoyed, as the real message being conveyed is 'watch out!'

## Risk management as a credit component

Banks increasingly insist on risk management as a credit component. As every trader or exporter knows, depending on just the futures markets for this can be quite restrictive (specifications, timing, financial requirements). Using futures does not always fit the bill for traders or their banks, or simply might not be possible. As a result more and more 'off market' risk solutions are being created by the banks themselves, tailored to the individual client's requirements. Such individual packages can include facilities for the automatic financing of margin calls, for example, when an exporter sells PTBF 'buyer's call' to an importer or roaster on the bank's 'approved list' and wants to hedge (sell futures) to protect their base price.

For larger deals and more important clients the main commodity banks often create such risk solution packages in-house. They do not necessarily offset these against the futures markets but rather do so independently 'over the counter', sometimes even in-house. This may also be done at the request of the importer or roaster rather than the exporter. This can be important for exporters who otherwise may be unable to trade directly with large roasters who insist on buying PTBF 'buyer's call'. The golden rule here is that the more the bank is involved in a transaction, for example if it is financing both the exporter and the receiver, the easier it will be to have access to such tailored credit or risk management packages. But banks will never provide such facilities for transactions with unapproved buyers: should there be a default the bank's loss could be double.

Obviously all this comes at a cost but at the same time it enables exporters at origin to compete on a more equal footing with the international trade. Once they can hedge their price risk, they will also be able to sell directly to roasters who habitually purchase 'buyer's call'.

The audit trail must always be clear and dependable, though. Much depends therefore on the quality of the control systems that are in place, their ability to prevent fraud, and whether or not the fraud risk is insurable.

## Like risk, the availability of credit is not static either

The last decade of the twentieth century saw substantial economic crisis in Eastern Europe, Latin America and Asia. Major losses were suffered by the international banking system. These have resulted in much more stringent risk assessments for lending, and new rules on the ratio 'own capital to lending' banks must maintain: the higher the risk factor, the higher the ratio of own capital to such lending will have to be. Such rules 'block' capital, reduce the amount of available credit and increase costs. Despite globalization and talk of the world as a single marketplace, banks have in general therefore become much more selective as to how much, for what purpose and to whom they will lend in which countries.

Faced with such limitations, some in the banking world are looking to hedge their own exposure by *securitizing* some of the risk. For example, if funds are lent against warehouse receipts in a coffee producing country and these warehouse receipts are of good quality (from a substantial issuer) and they are freely negotiable, then in theory such receipts can be 'securitized'. That is, like any other financial instrument they can be passed to other financial institutions, thereby reducing the exposure or risk factor of the original lender. Such warehouse receipts must have the same negotiable status as warehouse *warrants* but many other preconditions must also be satisfied.

Liberalization and deregulation in the 1980s and 1990s brought huge change in the export marketing of coffee worldwide: new rules, open markets and different players. But not all of the new players were creditworthy from an international banking perspective, and price volatility became huge. As a result the financing of coffee trading has become less 'bankable', more risky and less attractive.

Add to this some fairly spectacular defaults caused by sudden price changes, over-trading, over-pricing, and quality problems, and it is no surprise that many banks consider such business to be long on risks and short on margins. As a result the number of banks willing to lend to commodity producers and traders is decreasing rather than increasing. But those that remain are more commodity focused, see new opportunities, and have the expertise to gather the necessary information. Therefore they have better insight into the actual business. Often such banks finance the entire chain, from roaster or importer back to the exporter, *especially where the buyer actively supports the borrower's application.*

Other initiatives aim to make risk management tools available to individual growers and smallholder groups as an integral part of producer credit. (Electronic) warehouse receipts will likely play a significant role in all this eventually. In general, though, modern coffee trade financing solutions are increasingly coming from specialized foreign banks rather than from banks in coffee producing countries themselves.

## Risk remains risk remains risk

Such banks place trade credits where risk is manageable, that is, where collateral can be realized and genuine debts can relatively easily be recovered through a reasonably modern and properly functioning judicial system, and the funds so obtained can be remitted out of the country.

International trade houses co-exist well enough with all this but local exporters are often faced with weak internal banking systems that are unable or unwilling to become substantially involved. They have to pay higher rates of interest, and they cannot easily or cannot at all directly access international finance. But the large commodity banks cannot easily or cannot at all work 'in the field' in producing countries, so in-country financing requires local solutions. Sometimes this is achieved by a foreign bank taking a shareholding in a local bank. Even then, local banks remain first and foremost commercial institutions with specific limits and regulations. They cannot always accommodate modern risk management solutions, no matter which shareholder or international development agency backs them or provides the funding for specific packages.

It has to be recognized that risk remains risk for the seller *and* their bank until such time as the bank obtains receivables (invoices, with shipping documents) on a pre-approved foreign buyer. Even if the foreign bank is only involved 'at distance', perhaps by providing credit through a local bank, not directly to the borrower, it will nevertheless evaluate both the credit risk and the value in the entire transaction, even if the deal is 'fully collateralized', for example by warehouse receipts or warrants.

## Warehouse receipts as trade finance collateral

In most countries a warrant automatically provides *title* to the goods but with warehouse receipts this is not necessarily the case. National legislation may be unclear or silent on the *enforceability (execution) of rights* over the underlying goods. Although warehouse receipts have been in existence for centuries, not all country legislation recognizes them as negotiable documents of title. Even if the common law framework and trade legislation provide sufficient basis for using warehouse receipts as negotiable documents of title, banks and other creditors may still encounter unexpected obstacles when trying to execute a warehouse receipt and take title to the goods. In some countries there will be 'reasons' why a creditor may have title but cannot *enforce* the rights this supposedly confers.

Where rights under a title are obtained, the execution still needs to be supported by legislation that will permit the creditor to trade or export the underlying goods. Does the creditor need a trade license? An export license? Can the sales proceeds be transferred out of the country? Can the execution process be interfered with or delayed? In some countries the execution of debt presents banks with huge problems. No credit risk assessment can avoid examining the legal and sometimes physical difficulties surrounding the execution of the lender's rights.

The usefulness of warehouse receipts in general is well established, for example as a source of credit for producers of seasonal crops who may thus avoid having to sell during seasonal periods of oversupply and therefore low prices. But for the coffee export industry, warehouse receipts may represent only part of the answer to the banks' concerns about debt security and debt or collateral execution.

Incidentally, freely negotiable warehouse receipts present a different potential for fraud, in that the documents themselves may be stolen or falsely endorsed. Some international collateral managers therefore prefer to issue their own, non-negotiable receipts as part of 'guaranteed total performance' packages, which they back with liability and indemnity insurance. It could be argued that the *real* value of such insurance will emerge only when a real claim, a really *huge* claim arises, because insurance cover is only as good as what is stated in the policy document. One view is that only what is included is covered; the more attractive alternative view is that anything that is not specifically excluded is therefore covered by implication.

To recapitulate, in the context of coffee export trade finance, warehouse receipts may generally be considered as valid collateral if:

- The receipt is issued by an approved entity (public warehouseman, collateral manager).

- The goods are identifiable, records are maintained and no commingling is permitted.

- No superior rights (liens) are held over the goods by the issuer (the warehouseman).

- The receipt can be transferred by endorsement or assignment (it is negotiable), or it is issued in favour of the lender.

- The receipt can be used to pledge or sell the underlying goods.

- Insurance cover against loss or unauthorized release of the underlying goods is adequate.

- No third party can have superior rights over the underlying goods.

- Local legislation enables the beneficial holder to *enforce* their rights over the underlying goods, that is, *the debt the goods represent can be executed* ahead of any claims that others (for example revenue authorities or warehousemen) may have. (See end of this chapter for an example of the development of such legislation in Uganda and the United Republic of Tanzania.)

# Trade credit in producing countries

## Introduction

Earlier chapters have discussed many aspects of the coffee trade. The box below recaps briefly some of the terminology and definitions. For full explanations consult the earlier chapters.

*Physical coffee* – *green coffee.*

*First hand* – *coffee sold from/by origin.*

*Second hand* – *coffee subsequently sold on by overseas traders.*

*Long* – *coffee bought in expectation of later sale.*

*Short* – *coffee sold against expected future purchases or arrivals.*

*Spot* – *immediately available coffee.*

*Forward sales* – *coffee sold for later shipment, sometimes months ahead.*

*Futures market* – *trades standard qualities and quantities of coffee for future delivery at pre-determined ports during specific months or trading positions.*

*Paper trade or paper coffee* – *trade in futures and other contracts that are offset against each other, i.e. do not result in physical delivery of coffee.*

*Differential* – *premium or discount of 'our coffee' with respect to futures market.*

*Outright sale or fixed price sale* – *the full selling price is set at the time of sale.*

*PTBF* – *price to be fixed: selling now at a known differential against the futures market with the futures price being determined later.*

*Fixing* – *the action to determine the futures price that, combined with the differential, will become the contract price for the physical coffee.*

*PTBF seller's call* – *futures price to be called or fixed by the seller.*

*PTBF buyer's call* – *futures price to be called or fixed by the buyer.*

*Price risk* – *the risk that the coffee price generally moves against us.*

*Basis risk or differential risk* – *the risk that the differential moves against us.*

*Collateral* – *underlying security for advances, for example stocks.*

## Types of coffee trade finance

The most common types of coffee trade finance are the pre-financing of coffee to be purchased, advances against actual stock holdings, and the financing of the goods during processing for export and shipment.

### Pre-financing

Processors and exporters engage in pre-financing to secure future supplies of particular coffees. Bank support for such deals depends very much on the track record of the parties concerned, and whether the buyer has a guaranteed sale for that coffee. It is difficult enough to obtain finance for unsold stocks, let alone for 'promised' stocks.

This is one of the strengths of the trade houses that engage in long-term supply contracts with large roasters. They usually have a guaranteed outlet for their coffee with little performance risk *and* they are able to raise funds internationally, often at lower rates than those available in the producing country itself.

As a result of liberalization measures in the 1990s, international houses have gained considerable ground in a number of producing countries, mostly at the expense of local operators. But the individual exporter who deals with importers and smaller roasters will usually find that this type of buyer is not interested in providing any kind of finance; they may even be looking for credit themselves.

### Collection credits and stock advances

The main issues with collection credits and stock advances are what proportion of the value can be borrowed, what type and quality of coffee will be bought, at what prices, and how the coffee will be physically handled. It is often assumed that borrowing against stocks, or against coffees for which there is already a sales contract, is relatively risk free. But although the lender will have a formal lien over the goods, what if the weight or the quality is misstated? What if warehouse receipts are issued for non-existent goods? Of course all exporters should ask themselves and their own staff these same questions.

### Pre-shipment finance

Pre-shipment finance is usually obtained when the ready goods are lodged for shipment (as pre-shipment finance) or when shipment has been made and the documents become available (as negotiation of documents). The term 'negotiation of documents' is often misunderstood – the bank merely makes an advance of all or part of the invoice value against receipt of the shipping documents, which it then presents to the buyer for payment. If the buyer does not pay, the bank has *automatic recourse* to the exporter because although it 'negotiated' the documents, it did not take over the non-performance risk, that is, the risk that the buyer would not pay. Letters of credit, which are discussed later in this chapter, are an option here, but not all buyers are willing to establish them.

## Associated risks

Of course, all the risks mentioned in previous chapters are present. How do you know that the goods are what they are said to be? When a bill of lading simply reads 'received one container said to contain (STC) 20 tons of green coffee, shipper's stow and count', where does that leave everyone?

All forms of credit expose the lender to physical risk, price and value risk, and performance risk.

- *Physical risk:* the goods are simply not there, or are somehow lost.

- *Price risk:* the market value falls and the loss cannot be recovered, or the quality is not up to standard and so the value is less than expected.

- *Performance risk:* the foreign buyer does not buy the goods, reneges on the contract or is declared insolvent.

### Physical risk

When funds are advanced against stock in trade, the goods so financed are usually pledged to the lender as guarantee of repayment: they become the security or *collateral*. Banks do this by taking out a general *lien* over stocks and collectables (outstanding invoices) through which beneficial ownership rests with the bank until all outstanding advances have been refunded in full.

In long-established relationships banks may be satisfied with this. They may leave the management and physical control of the goods to the borrower, especially if general international guarantees are in place, for example from a trade house's parent company.

But for smaller operators, and certainly those in new or relatively recent relationships, the banks will want to be satisfied that checks and balances are in place. These checks could include having the goods stored by public warehousing companies that issue warrants or warehouse receipts in the bank's name or hand warrants to the bank 'endorsed in blank' which permits the bank to freely transfer or assume title. The bank's lien will extend to the proceeds of any insurance claim that may arise, since all the goods must be insured with an agreed insurer, on conditions acceptable to the bank. Even so, banks may still demand additional security guarantees.

## Price risk

In this context, price risk is the risk that the market as a whole (the price risk), or the differential (the differential or basis risk), will change to the borrower's disadvantage. Remember that banks do not normally encourage or finance speculation: whether a bank will permit a client to hold stocks without hedging them depends on the relationship and the guarantees that the borrower may have provided.

Unless the goods have been bought to fulfil a fixed price contract, it is likely that the bank will insist on the regular hedging of the price risk on all stocks. In a general sense, smaller exporters especially should understand that banks are risk averse and do not like to finance speculative transactions. That is, they do not really approve of 'open' positions. *But only the price risk can be hedged. The differential risk cannot be hedged.*

## Differential risk or basis risk

Banks are well aware that the differential risk can be substantial, especially for those trading single origin coffee, but also that for them insight into the way differentials move is difficult and that as yet there is no immediately obvious solution for this. They mostly depend on the borrower's track record and judgement, especially when coffee is bought against offsetting fixed price sales.

But where purchases are made against an open price sales contract, a PTBF contract that specifies only a *selling differential*, then the *buying differential* will only be determined when the physical coffee is bought and 'fixed'. If the market differential for that type of coffee has substantially changed since the sale was made, then the difference between the hedge price and the buying price of the physicals may be substantially different as well, which could cause the transaction to be unprofitable.[26]

## Currency risk

When advances in United States dollars are immediately turned into coffee stocks that will later be sold in United States dollars, the currency risk is limited and mostly of local concern. Nevertheless, if the local currency subsequently loses value then other traders or exporters may lower their United States dollar offer prices, thus reducing the United States dollar value of unsold stocks, a market reaction that may put recovery of the original United States dollar advance at risk.

## Performance risk

The first line of defence against performance risk is a correctly structured transaction. Further safeguards can then be put in place through the use of collateral management, beginning at the point of purchase and ending with the handing over of shipping documents. On the selling side this is more difficult, as it is impossible to know the financial status and health of all potential importers or roasters.

This is why banks will insist that trade is only with 'authorized buyers' – companies that are known and in which they have confidence. In addition the bank may require that a sales contract is in place before *any* monies are advanced to buy stocks. In that case selling PTBF facilitates matters. The contractual obligation to supply and accept the goods can be

---

26 Differentials tend to be lower when futures prices are high, and higher when futures are low. A differential of 'plus 10' on arabica when the 'C' contract is at 60 cts/lb may change to 'even money' in the producing country when the 'C' for example goes to 120 cts/lb. This is favourable for exporters who need to buy physicals against a PTBF sale because when they fix the purchase the physicals will only cost 'even money'. A differential of 'minus 50' on robusta when LIFFE is at 700 US$/ton may perhaps change to 'even money' in the producing country when London goes to 500 US$/ton. This is unfavourable for exporters who need to buy physicals against a PTBF sale because when they fix the purchase the physicals will cost 'even money' against an open sale of 'minus 50'. Differentials in producing countries may also buck the general market trend, for example because of drought or other production problems.

established without the buyer being committed to an actual price long in advance of the actual shipment: only the differential has to be agreed. (Many, if not most, roasters insist on buying PTBF 'buyer's call'.)

This resolves the performance issue but still leaves open the questions of price and differential risk. Because of this, but also as a general rule, most banks dislike advancing the entire cost of a purchase, often preferring to stick to a percentage of the value, say 80%. This provides reasonable cover against a worst case scenario. This percentage will vary according to the risk rating of the country where the borrower conducts their business, and the bank's assessment of the borrower.

## What any borrower must show

| Advances at each stage | Borrower must show | Ratio and cost of advance | Conditions | Financing of margin calls |
|---|---|---|---|---|
| 1. Document negotiation | Real function, i.e. adds value.<br><br>Track record. (Defaults are most likely to occur in the first 3 to 5 years of new operations.)<br><br>Quality management.<br><br>Understanding of the coffee business.<br><br>Deals are correctly structured. | Ratio or percentage of advance: highest.<br><br>Interest rate: lowest. | Sold to approved buyer.<br><br>Documents and/or payment via bank. | Exposure has been hedged, or PTBF sale has been 'fixed'. |
| 2. Pre-shipment | Appropriate business plan and reporting systems.<br><br>In-house financial and volume limits.<br><br>Clear document flows, proper stock rotation. | Ratio: lower.<br><br>Cost: higher. | Pre-sold to approved buyer or hedged.<br><br>Collateral manager. | Depending on package and borrower's 'book'. |
| 3. Export processing | Own capital.<br><br>Visible, permanent and pledgeable assets. | Ratio: lower again.<br><br>Cost: higher again. | Pre-sold to approved buyer or hedged.<br><br>Collateral manager. | Depending on package and borrower's 'book'. |
| 4. Interior buying | Adequate warehousing and insurance.<br><br>Access to collateral management. | Ratio: lowest or even nil.<br><br>Cost: highest. | Pre-sold to approved buyer or hedged.<br><br>Collateral manager. | Depending on package and borrower's 'book'. |

---

### *Some common errors and misconceptions*

- *Borrowers are not frank enough. If the bank feels it is not receiving all information, it will wonder why. In any case, banks do not want uncertainty – they want control. Shared knowledge is also beneficial to both parties and enables the bank to be proactive.*

- *Applications are not based on adequate 'homework', resulting in a poor first impression or outright rejection.*

- *Borrowers do not realize how important it is to have quality independently audited financial statements ('financials'), delivered by reputable auditors.*

- *Internal control and reporting systems are inadequate.*

- *Transactions work when everyone wishes it – sudden change (weather, prices, buyer turns 'nasty', politics) can alter this and result in 'blameless' default.*

- *It does not really help a bank to become the owner of the borrower's stocks. If these have to be sold off at a loss (10%–20% is not unusual) it may take years of new lending to recoup the money lost.*

- *The local legal system may make the realization of collateral or debt recovery a nightmare. If so, local collateral in whatever form, including warehouse receipts, may be (almost) without value.*

---

## Letters of credit

### *Documentary credit*

Letters of credit can serve a dual purpose:

- A guarantee of payment once shipment has been made, to reduce the exporter's credit risk.

- A means of advancing credit to an exporter, enabling goods to be bought and shipped.

In the first instance the exporter is paid against submission of the complete and correct set of shipping documents as stipulated in the letter of credit (L/C): *the documentary credit.* This is a guarantee of payment once shipment has been made. It is not a specifically designed instrument to enable one to raise credit although occasionally banks may accept documentary credits as a form of collateral.

Documentary credits include:

- *Sight letter of credit*: payable on first sight (presentation) of the documents to the bank.

- *Usance* or *time letter of credit:* payable after a certain period has elapsed.

- In addition there is the *performance* or *bid letter of credit*, whose value is forfeited if the party concerned fails to perform (i.e. does not deliver, or does not establish the requisite documentary letter of credit). These are sometimes used for large, long-term supply contracts or in conjunction with tenders (a form of bid bond). For more on using documentary letters of credit see also chapter 4, Contracts.

### *Advance credit*

Here the letter of credit becomes a means of raising credit. The buyer or (more likely) a bank agrees to release funds whenever an agreed set of circumstances arises and certain pre-conditions are met. In this category there are three main types of letters of credit.

***Red clause letter of credit.*** This is a combination of documentary and open credit in that it provides unsecured credit to an exporter against an agreed transaction. Under this type of

L/C the issuing bank agrees to advance part of the estimated sales proceeds of the coffee to be shipped, without tender of the shipping documents. The balance is then paid once the shipping documents are presented. If a 'green clause' is included as well then the exporter can obtain additional advances upon submission of warehouse receipts as collateral. Obviously the issuing bank will issue strict directions to the correspondent bank in the exporter's country as to how, when, by whom and under what circumstances funds may be drawn. (The correspondent bank is a bank with which the issuing bank has an established relationship.)

A red clause letter of credit allows an exporter to obtain pre-shipment finance, although the amount of available credit is usually only part of the estimated value or even the sales value. This is one way for a buyer to expand their sources of supply. Most buyers are reluctant to become involved in financing goods that have not yet been shipped, but exporter and buyer may be linked together through a normal contract with the trade bank establishing the red clause L/C against a registered contract with an approved buyer.

***Advance letter of credit.*** This is similar to the red clause L/C but it limits the amount that can be drawn without presentation of documents to a percentage of the invoice value and requires the exporter to present an original set of bills of lading before a specific date. Again, inclusion of a 'green clause' can extend the availability of credit through presentation of warehouse receipts as collateral.

Both red clause and advance letters of credit are used when local financing is not available or is available only at excessively high rates of interest. From the point of view of the trade bank or the buyer, the credit provided is unsecured.

***Green clause letter of credit.*** This is a normal documentary letter of credit, which provides a secured form of credit in that exporters can draw an agreed percentage of the value of the goods to be shipped against presentation of warehouse receipts as collateral. Such receipts will be issued by an authorized party (public warehousing company, bonded warehouse, collateral manager), and issued or endorsed in favour of the bank in question. Proof of adequate insurance cover, with the bank as beneficiary, may also have to be submitted.

This type of credit can provide an exporter with working capital during the buying season and while processing takes place. The credit will be revolving, in the sense that it must be self-liquidating with export proceeds offsetting the relevant outstanding advances in the order these were incurred. At the end of the season or other agreed period all outstanding advances are liquidated when the last shipment takes place. The advantage is that the lender (bank or buyer) has some control over the goods. Depending on their assessment of the exporter's reliability, the lender may decide to appoint someone to supervise the stocks on their behalf – such supervision is usually called collateral management. This is discussed in detail under 'Warehouse receipts as collateral' earlier in this chapter, and below.

## All-in collateral management: another option

### *Functions of the collateral manager*

The collateral manager (CM) is an independent operator who 'manages' the collateral (the stocks) for a fee on the bank's behalf. The action that triggers the release of bank funds usually determines the stage at which the collateral manager enters the process. Depending on circumstances this may entail CM personnel supervising or managing the borrower's premises, or the storage of goods at public warehouses owned and managed by the CM. Usually the CM is engaged by the borrower and the bank jointly, with the fees paid by the borrower.

To have true value for the banks the CM's obligations have to be guaranteed as well. This is usually done through appropriate liability and indemnity insurance, acceptable to the bank.

Today's collateral managers offer a host of traditional and new services, for example:

### Verification of funding

- The funds are applied to the agreed purpose.

- The timing and level of advances applied for is as agreed or is realistic.

- The purchase price is as agreed or is realistic.

### Verification of borrower's and warehouseman's insurance arrangements

- Quality and scope of cover are acceptable.

- Lending bank is named as loss payee (beneficiary).

- Premiums are paid up to date.

- Premises and goods are adequately described.

### Verification of premises

- The premises are secure, safe and fit for storage.

### Tally-in and weighing

- Bags received are counted.

- Bags are weighed and stacked.

### Verification of quality

- The goods are what they are supposed to be.

- Goods can be monitored from farm gate to ship's hold.

### Issue or certification of warehouse receipts

- Certifying receipt of the goods.

- Providing proof of existence, which is collateral for funding.

### Stock administration and control

- Goods are properly accounted for.

- Goods cannot be dispatched independently.

- Goods are stored separately, they can be readily identified and no commingling is permitted at any time.

### Export process

- Supervision of export processing; quality control; goods match the sales contract.

- Goods are handed over against approved waybills, receipts or bills of lading.

- Waybills, receipts and bills of lading stipulate the bank as beneficial owner and are handled and dispatched correctly.

The stage at which the CM leaves the process depends on the bank. The bank's back-office will have monitored the entire process and the CM's role often ends when the goods are handed over for shipment with the bank assuming title through the issue of bills of lading in the bank's name rather than the exporter's.

**Full out-turn guarantee**

- The CM guarantees that the weight shipped is what will arrive.

- They will make good any shortfall.

- In some cases they may offer a similar guarantee for the quality.

Guaranteeing that a coffee has the requisite clean cup is difficult, and guaranteeing that an expensive quality coffee has the requisite cup is almost impossible for a CM. But the quality of bulk standard grades or types of coffee is relatively easily verified through defect count, screen test, moisture test, an OTA (ochratoxin A) test for mould, and general examination. In some countries CMs take responsibility for 'quality' from the farm gate through to discharge at the end-user's premises. Verification services and full out-turn guarantees have been available for many years already – they now slot neatly into modern collateral management arrangements.

## Modern collateral management facilitates credit

Collateral management in coffee producing countries is a logical extension of the traditional 'supervision' business of independent verifiers and sworn weighers. Where previously such companies certified that goods loaded on ships were of the prescribed quality and weight, they now begin the verification process at the very first point in the collection marketing chain. Modern collateral management increasingly means that a single company coordinates all the logistics, guarantees the integrity of the physical circuit, and provides security over the export documentation process, thus eliminating all unsecured gaps. In other words, they are in the business of 'moving collateral'. As such they can play an essential role in the financing of coffee traders and processors or exporters, especially where the same bank is financing both the end-user and the exporter.

Some international CMs provide complete packages, linking customers with lending institutions on the strength of the CM's performance guarantee, based on standard packages and procedures which they apply worldwide. And as the coffee trade moves into the paperless trade with electronic documents of title and so on, so the role of the CM will take on more importance.

## Guarantees

Banks need the guarantee that warehouse receipts will become receivables: that is, commercial invoices backed by negotiable bills of lading or other relevant documents of title to the goods. All the gaps and risks in the process from the first purchase to this point need to be quantified and covered. For CMs the risk is enormous. Cases of quality fraud, physical theft and document falsification do occur!

Therefore, if their guarantees are to be truly solid then they need to be backed by fidelity (indemnity) and liability insurance of a quality and level that is acceptable to banks. To be readily enforceable, the insurance policy, and if possible the underlying collateral management contract, must be based on an acceptable jurisdiction, for example English law. (See also 'Alternative solutions' at the end of this chapter.)

If a CM's overseas parent company provides the guarantees, then it could be said that the collateral manager takes at least part of the country risk on board. This makes it easier for banks to approve certain lending operations, especially when the total credit and risk management package encompasses both the end-user and the producer or exporter.

Coupled with the 'total' credit and risk management packages offered by commodity banks, modern 'all in' collateral management has become an essential component of credit. The increased collateral and transaction security it offers facilitates access to credit, and can help to bring also smaller producers and exporters closer to buyers and end-users in consuming countries.

# Trade credit and risk management in the smallholder sector

## Credit channels

Commercial credit for smallholders is linked to risk in much the same way as it is for commercial growers and exporters. The risk principles are the same, although the detail may be different.

- Performance: will the crop be delivered as agreed?

- Price: will the value cover the outstanding credit?

- Value: will the quality be acceptable and saleable?

- Collateral: can any collateral be provided, and if it is, can it be realized?

Obviously it is difficult if not entirely impossible for the average commercial bank to evaluate performance risk, let alone potential quality and value, on an individual basis for thousands of smallholders.

Providing collateral can prove difficult for smallholders.

*Land is nearly always unsuitable as collateral.* Even though for most smallholders it may be their only form of visible asset, in many countries such land is often held through traditional ownership structures that make the realization (the sale in debt execution) of the collateral impossible. Even where rural agricultural land is held under title deed, communal and political pressure may make its sale impossible, so smallholder-owned land is often if not mostly unsuitable as collateral.

*Crops on the tree are also not meaningful as collateral* until they become goods entered into store against warehouse receipts. That is, credit will be advanced only once the harvest is stored. This is a most suitable arrangement for crops that might otherwise have to be sold quickly to raise cash during seasonal periods of oversupply and consequent low prices, but it is not necessarily right for coffee.

Coffee is usually best marketed when it is still fresh (new crop). Prolonged storage, (beyond the usual marketing season), or retention for speculative purposes cannot really be recommended.

*The most likely credit channels* for smallholders are therefore well run cooperatives or other forms of grower organizations that have the required critical mass and that are in a position to guarantee and discipline their members. Credit to such organizations will then largely be based on the same principles discussed earlier in this chapter.

## Risk management

Of all coffee producing countries only Brazil has been able to establish a successful internal futures market for coffee, the Brazilian Mercantile and Futures Exchange. Growers in *all* other producing countries must look abroad, directly or indirectly, if they wish to make use of futures markets. (See chapter 8, Futures markets.) In many countries small growers and smallholders are mostly locked out of risk management markets anyway, for reasons that include a lack of knowledge, high costs, and inappropriate contract sizes. (Note though that the LIFFE futures exchange robusta contract size is just 5 tons, and the new NYBOT mini arabica contract is 12,500 lb, or 5.7 tons.)

Just as for gaining access to credit, potential solutions include the aggregation of production and financial capacity through the establishment of cooperatives or other forms of producer groupings. Such groups can then decide how they approach price risk management: simply as an insurance that they purchase, or as part of the marketing process. (It should not be ignored here that in a number of countries the performance record of cooperatives has been less than impressive.)

### Price risk management as pure insurance

Price risk management as pure insurance means there is no direct link between the insurance of the price risk and the marketing of the coffee.

*Straight hedging by selling futures* exposes the seller to margin calls, bringing with it the risk of potential hedge liquidity traps. Whether any lending institution or risk solution provider will finance such an operation without firm guarantees and collateral is doubtful. Indeed the notion will be a non-starter for most, small growers and solution providers alike.

*Buying put options,* the right to sell futures at a stated price at some point in the future, is much simpler than hedging. The cost that needs to be financed is known up front, and no margin calls need to be faced. The premium will depend on circumstances, but can at times be very substantial. Even so, it may be easier to raise finance for this than for straight hedging. As always, the provider will still need to be reassured about how the cost of the option will eventually be recouped.

*Tailored solutions.* Risk solution providers *tailor* risk instruments to clients' requirements. For example, options can be *graduated* to extend over the usual marketing season by spreading equal portions over two or three futures trading positions, if so wished, at different strike prices. Each individual portion can then be exercised individually.

Alternatively the solution provider may simply guarantee *a minimum price*. Against payment of a premium, they undertake to make good any shortfall between the insured price (the minimum price the growers wish to secure) and the price ruling for the stated trading positions in New York or London, either at a given date or based on the average price over a number of trading days. The producer has bought a 'floor': the guaranteed price less the cost of the premium. (Consumers would buy a 'cap' to protect themselves against future price rises.)

*Swap agreements.* Producers can also 'swap' price risk by giving up the benefits from future price rises in exchange for a guaranteed minimum price. Swap agreements could also cover more than one crop year, with tonnages and settlement dates set for each quarter. The concept is nothing new, and has been extensively used to limit exposure to currency and interest rate fluctuations. Innumerable variables are possible, making it impossible to provide a standard model.

**Note:** Solution providers and commodity trade banks can put together different risk mitigation instruments but only for parties with the required critical mass, who are organized and who can find and afford the finance necessary to buy the price insurance they require.

### Price risk management as part of marketing

*Forward sales of physical coffee at a fixed price* are the most straightforward form of price risk management as part of marketing. The size of the expected crop is reasonably well known, prices are satisfactory, and buyers have enough confidence in the seller to commit to them on a forward basis. This is perhaps the ideal situation, but it is seldom encountered nowadays. And when prices are very low, fixed price forward contracts look attractive only to the buyer.

***Selling physicals forward PTBF buyer's call*** means growers lose all control over the fixation level, and therefore the price, unless they simultaneously also sell a corresponding amount of futures. But this would expose them to margin calls and potential liquidity problems, assuming they could even find the funds to finance the initial deposits. (For more on this see Options in chapter 9.)

***Selling physicals forward PTBF seller's call*** might appear to be the answer but this is not necessarily so either. Unless the seller *fixes immediately*, all such deals establish is a contractual obligation to deliver and accept physical coffee.

The PTBF sale sets the differential the buyer will pay in relation to the underlying futures position(s), *but the general price risk and the decision when to fix remain entirely open.* In other words, the PTBF sale does not mean the seller has made a price decision – that will only be the case once they fix. Many sellers are unable to bring themselves to fix at unattractive levels, and in falling markets a good number even roll fixations from one futures position to the next, preferring to pay the cost (usually the difference in price between the two positions) to gain more time in the hope that prices will eventually rise. This does not happen only when prices are generally low. In a falling market it is sometimes very difficult for sellers to accept that today they must fix at less than they could have done yesterday or the day before. To avoid such fixation traps one should set internal 'stops' so that fixing takes place automatically when a certain price (up or down) is reached. Such orders to fix can be given to whoever is responsible for the actual execution, basis GTC or 'good till cancelled'.

**Note:** When fixed price sales are not feasible the simple alternative is to sell PTBF and to fix immediately, thereby fixing both the base price and the differential which, together, make up the final sales price. If there are concerns about 'fixing too early' or 'what if the market goes up', then one also buys a call option accepting that the cost of this of course comes out of the sales price for the physicals.

## Alternative solutions

In many countries growers can and do sell basis PTBF to local exporters and so they do not necessarily need to have direct access to the overseas market for this type of operation. But, if to access price insurance they *must* sell locally then their bargaining position may be weakened. And in countries with indirect marketing systems, such as central auctions, the grower has no direct access to the exporter in any case so this option is not available.

Together with the international banking system, institutions such as the United Nations Conference on Trade and Development (UNCTAD), the International Coffee Organization, the World Bank and the Common Fund for Commodities (CFC) are actively and imaginatively seeking new credit and risk insurance solutions for small growers, through pilot projects in a number of countries. Ever-lower coffee prices have in recent years starkly demonstrated the need for such initiatives, but the unprecedented scope of those price falls has also made it more difficult to mobilize the resources and motivate the active grower participation necessary for these initiatives to be launched.

**Collateral management.** Using United States experience and systems as a basis, pilot projects in Uganda and the United Republic of Tanzania have been financed by CFC and implemented by the United Nations Office for Project Services (UNOPS). They are setting some of the stage through the drafting and introduction of *specific national legislation dealing with all aspects of collateral management for the coffee industry*, including addressing the vexed question of how lenders can legitimately and efficiently turn collateral into true collectables. This is a step in a lengthy process that must also include providing the necessary expertise to the jurisdictions that will have to deal with such issues. As of mid 2002, draft legislation was being prepared in both Uganda and the United Republic of Tanzania. A further CFC financed project, dealing specifically with price risk management for smaller growers, commenced work in March 2002 to compliment the collateral management initiative with which it will be linked in due course.

**Price risk management.** The International Task Force on Commodity Risk Management in Developing Countries (ITF) was first convened in January 1999. It comprises major international institutions, producers' and consumers' groups, major commodity exchanges, commodity trading firms, academia, and private sector entities. Its work is carried out by the Commodity Risk Management Group of the World Bank. The ITF aims to provide smallholder producers in developing countries with access to the same risk-management instruments available to producers in industrialized countries. This involves identifying rural institutions to serve as local transmission mechanisms for such insurance. The ITF provides technical assistance, training, and 'honest broker' services to local institutions (e.g. cooperatives, domestic banks, or traders) in the use of price risk management instruments and serves as an honest broker for the delivery of these instruments to smallholder producers.

The ITF has undertaken numerous feasibility studies to determine how price risk management instruments (price insurance) can be put in place for coffee producers. Feasibility studies have been completed for the coffee sector in El Salvador, Mexico, Nicaragua, Uganda and the United Republic of Tanzania. In each of these countries the ITF has identified local counterparts with sufficient outreach to small-scale coffee producers and the ability to deliver price insurance to these producers. Local counterparts include producer organizations, exporters, and rural financial institutions. By mid 2002, the project studies in Nicaragua, Uganda and the United Republic of Tanzania had moved into the operational phase, with price insurance transactions being designed for the upcoming crop season. In addition, focused technical assistance was being provided to train managers of producer groups and banks and individual producers in understanding the use of price risk management instruments.

Further details on ITF at *www.itf-commrisk.org*.

# CHAPTER 11

# Coffee quality

## Introduction

Coffee (Coffea) is the major genus of the *Rubiaceae* family, which includes well over 500 genera and over 6,000 species. The genus *Coffea* itself comprises numerous species. Only two of them are currently of real economic importance:

- *Coffea arabica*, referred to in the trade as arabica and accounting for 60%–70% of world production.

- *Coffea canephora* (or *Coffea robusta*) called robusta in the trade and making up 30%–40% of world production.

Two other species are traded to a very limited extent: *Coffea liberica* (liberica), and *Coffea excelsa* (excelsa).

The share of arabica fell from about 80% of world production in the 1960s to around 60% by the turn of the century, initially because of strong growth of robusta production in Brazil and parts of Africa but more recently because of the emergence of Asia as the world's leading robusta producing region.

The original arabica strains generally produce good liquors with acidity and flavour but they are susceptible to pests and diseases. This has led to the development of a number of different varieties that show better tolerance. Some quality purists consider that some of these varieties lack the quality characteristics that created coffee's popularity – others argue that the bottom line for many producers simply does not permit them to concentrate on just the traditional or original varieties.

***There are two main primary processing methods:*** the *unwashed* or *dry process*, which produces naturals, and the *washed* or *wet process*, which produces washed coffees. In the dry process the ripe cherries are dried in their entirety after which they are mechanically decorticated to produce the green bean. In the washed or wet process the ripe cherries are pulped and fermented to remove the sticky sugary coating called mucilage that adheres to the beans (this can also be done mechanically), and the beans are then washed and dried.

There is a third process in which the ripe cherry is pulped and dried 'as is' with the mucilage still adhering to the parchment skin. Originally called semi-washed in Africa, this process is gaining importance in Brazil where it occupies a place in-between the dry and wet processes and is simply called 'pulped natural'. In other countries, for example in the Great Lakes region of Central Africa, semi-washed coffee has been (laboriously) produced for many decades using small hand pulpers.

In all procedures the parchment skin is later removed mechanically after drying.

**Figure 18        Processing of coffee cherries and green coffee beans***

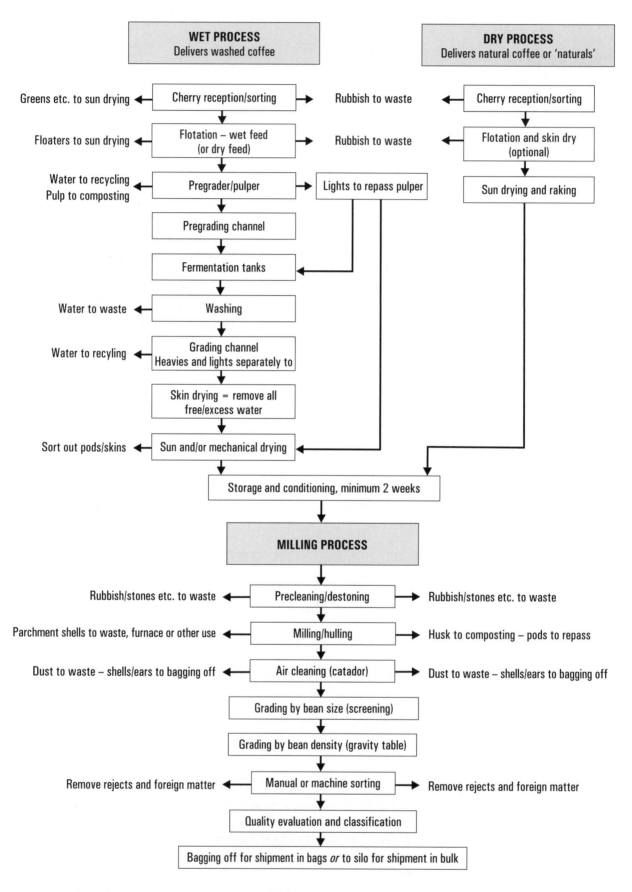

* The process may obviously differ from one country to another.

# The definition of the quality of green coffee

There are many differing views as to what constitutes 'quality', just as there are about beauty. But it can be said that the quality of a parcel of coffee comes from a combination of the botanical variety, topographical conditions, weather conditions, and the care taken during growing, harvesting, storage, export preparation and transport.

Botanical variety and topographical conditions are constants and therefore dominate the basic or inherent character of a coffee. Weather conditions are variable and cannot be influenced, resulting in fluctuating quality from one season to another.

Growing, harvesting, storage, export preparation and transport are variables that can be influenced. They involve intervention by human beings, whose motivation is a key factor in the determination of the end quality of a parcel of green coffee. Depending on their marketing priorities people's efforts will fluctuate between the highest possible level, regardless of the cost, and the bare minimum, in order to reduce costs and optimize revenues and margins. Efforts to promote quality are prejudiced by world market prices and the degree to which buyers are willing to reward attention to the safeguarding and improvement of quality with adequate premiums for better than average quality.

# Quality in relation to marketing

## The basics

The basics of quality in relation to marketing are simple. Coffee must:

- Be suitable for human consumption. European Union legislation now imposes full accountability and responsibility on all participants and stages in the food chain, who must therefore be clearly traceable and identifiable, from producer to consumer. See Quality control issues, later in this chapter.

- Be free from extraneous matter, live pests and moulds.

- Fully conform to the contract description or selling sample, and be of uniform quality throughout the entire shipment.

- Be clean in the cup, i.e. free from obnoxious flavours.

The first two points cover the general *acceptability* of a coffee, while the third and fourth deal directly with the *quality*. Without an agreed description of the quality, or a sample of the actual coffee, there could not be any trade in coffee because *quality* is a subjective term, open to many interpretations depending on who is making the judgement.

For the serious, committed producer and exporter the focus should always be on *quality*. Price should never play a role when preparing a shipment of an established type of coffee. It is only by strictly adhering to contractual obligations and always supplying exactly what was sold that solid reputations are created. Solid reputations attract equally solid buyers, which leads to repeat business that in turn raises the level of interaction between seller and buyer from just *price* to *quality and price.*

Probably the worst offence an exporter can commit is to *knowingly* ship a coffee that does not meet the contract specification. Roasters purchase coffee with specific purposes in mind and *if a shipment is not up to standard then it cannot be used*. Usually, even the offer of a subsequent reduction in price (an allowance) does not help. Respect for quality and impeccable contract execution are an essential, and may even be the most important part of an exporter's marketing arsenal. Both large and small roasters tend to reject coffees that on arrival do not match their requirements, something that can cause major problems. And roasters are increasingly purchasing *subject to approval of quality on arrival*. For the exporter, prevention is *always* better than the cure.

## Quality and availability determine the target market[27]

The trouble with the pursuit of *quality* is not just that the term itself is a somewhat nebulous concept. First of all, the vast bulk of world coffee exports consists of medium to average quality coffee: mainstream coffee. Secondly, the extra effort to produce top quality may not always be adequately rewarded and, thirdly, there is also a lively and substantial world trade in coffee of poor and inferior quality.

Quality discussions are further complicated when one separates coffee by species or by type of processing. There are arabicas and robustas, both wet and dry processed, and each with different quality aspects. Then there is also the question of whether the coffee will be sold as whole bean, as roast and ground, or as soluble. Appearances can also cause some confusion. It would be a mistake to think that *quality* means only exceptionally good looking (visually perfect), bold beans: small bean coffees can also show excellent *quality*. Conversely, visually perfect, bold beans could in fact hide very unpleasant cup characteristics. The pursuit of *quality* is therefore not restricted to top or exemplary coffee.

This is probably just as well, because not everyone is capable of producing exemplary quality. In reality there is a market for almost everything, from expensive top quality to qualities at the other end of the spectrum. There is room in the marketplace for just about anyone who honours their contractual obligations *and who adequately satisfies the market's quality expectations for the type of coffee they produce*. Different markets have different preferences. Producers and exporters should therefore know where their coffee is likely to receive the best response and, as far as possible, *tailor the quality* to the requirements of the buyer.

## Quality segmentation of origin coffees

Quality can be broadly ranked into four categories, from highest to lowest quality.

### *Exemplary quality*

Exemplary quality coffees have a high intrinsic value with a fine or unique cup, and are usually of quite limited availability. They are mostly retailed under straight estate or origin names. These are usually very well presented washed coffees, including some superior washed robustas, but also include some naturals (Ethiopian Harars, Yemeni mochas, some Indonesian arabicas) and top organic coffees. They are true niche coffees.

### *High quality*

High quality coffees are good cupping coffees, well presented, but not necessarily visually perfect. They are retailed both as straight origins and as blends. This category includes good quality, well prepared organic coffees, and washed as well as superior quality natural robustas. The market for this quality band is much broader and includes a good percentage of today's specialty coffee.

---

27　This chapter is targeted mainly at assisting smaller operators, growers and exporters alike, to make headway in the development of coffee quality (and marketability). It therefore deals mostly with arabica quality as it relates to the quality expectations in the exemplary and medium quality segments of the market. Mainstream type coffees and robustas are dealt with separately, although the discussion on 'quality' is relevant to all those producing and exporting coffee. Quality requirements for exemplary type robustas, and for those used in espresso, are largely comparable to those for arabica and just as stringent.

## *Mainstream quality*

Mainstream quality coffee is fair average quality, reasonably well presented but certainly not visually perfect. It will offer a decent, clean but not necessarily impressive cup. Many robustas are included in this category. It is estimated that mainstream qualities account for 85%–90% of world coffee consumption, while the share of exemplary and high quality coffee is less than 15% of the world market.

Mainstream qualities are often traded on description. Descriptions can be fairly loosely written in the contracts, but usually there is some degree of quality understanding. That means seller and buyer have jointly established the quality parameters which the seller is expected to respect, for shipment after shipment. It is to be hoped that buyers will take this into consideration when *talking price*. The advantage to the buyer is that they are virtually certain that the coffee will do for them what they expect from it, and the seller knows the buyer will come back time and again for more of the same, irrespective of whether the market is up or down. This is one of the main factors that work towards creating market security, although given how easily interchangeable they are, for most of the more mundane coffees price will always play the major role. Note that no roaster will accept a coffee without tasting it first, regardless of of how it was described, which means that no exporter should ship any coffee without having done the same.

Quality descriptions without an accompanying understanding between buyer and seller as to *quality* can lead to problems. For example, 'Fair average quality (FAQ)', or simply specifying the screen size and defect count together with 'guaranteed clean cup' or 'sound merchantable quality', all leave much to the imagination. Such descriptions say the absolute minimum about a coffee's quality and therefore the quality often fluctuates within a fairly wide range. Deliveries can be good, mediocre or really disappointing. Although the buyer has a quality *requirement*, they are likely to be modest in their *expectations* of coffees bought on a relatively vague description. Usually, this is reflected in the price that is offered.

## *Undergrades or lowgrades*

Finally, there are the undergrades or lowgrades, which are basically everything that does not fit into any of the above descriptions. There has traditionally been an active trade in undergrade coffees because there was a definite demand for them. Not everyone always knows 'the price' for such coffees, which can make trading them very opportunistic.

For the United States market, undergrade coffee is any type of coffee that grades below GCA type 6 (120 defects per 370 grams. In mid 2002, United States Customs regulations prohibited the importation of coffee below GCA type 8 (610 defects per 370 grams) with suggestions from some quarters that this should be raised to type 7 (240 defects per 370 grams). Other importing markets do not normally specify that particular grades of coffee should not be imported, relying instead on general food and hygiene regulations.

The ICO is moving to introduce worldwide minimum export standards in an attempt to remove the lowest coffees from the market altogether. The higher risk of mould and therefore OTA occurring in lowgrades is also likely to reduce the demand for such coffee. (See Quality control issues, later in this chapter.) As a result it is increasingly likely that over time lowgrades and rejects will lose their commercial value, thereby becoming part of the producer's or exporter's cost calculation rather than representing an exportable coffee.

## Quality in relation to production

Much but not all quality evaluation is subjective, and many people buy certain coffees because they get what they want from them. All exporters should know the market for the type of coffee they produce; it is pointless to offer the wrong coffee to the wrong market. Once the 'right' quality is established, it then needs to be produced in the most efficient and *consistent* manner.

Production and processing systems influence quality. Exporters can never be certain of all the components and inputs that make up consistent quality, but they should know the basic norms in climate, soil, and other agricultural factors in the growing areas. Once this is known exporters can adjust their processing techniques to get the best result for the given agricultural environment. Even annual variations in climate can often be at least partly offset by processing adjustments. Some of the major influences on quality are discussed below.

### Rain fed or irrigated

Stressed trees cannot produce decent, well formed cherries. Coffee is drought-resistant, but not drought-proof. It has remarkable recuperative power from dry spells, but like all living things it needs water to produce.

Only very few coffees from marginal rainfall areas have made it to the ranks of truly notable coffees. These notable coffees have specific, inherent quality aspects (linked to their variety) which command premiums high enough to compensate for very low yields. Non-irrigated coffee in marginal rainfall areas usually shows the greatest seasonal quality variation.

### Wet or dry processed

Washed arabica not only needs adequate rainfall or irrigation for growth, but also requires water for wet processing. In many areas it is not uncommon to see multiple washing stations (or wet beneficios) using common sources of water, either small rivers or streams. Below-average rainfall can then result in insufficient or poor quality water for washing, which has a direct effect on the quality produced. The preparation of natural or dry processed coffee does not use water, but of course the trees still require adequate water for growth. Harvesting and drying need dry conditions and the best natural coffees are obtained from areas that have little rain in the harvesting season. Examples are Yemeni mochas and some Ethiopian Harars, but the largest group of natural arabicas comes from Brazil, with the best originating from dry areas where the cherry matures and dries quickly.

### Variety, soils and altitude

A vast number of different coffees are traded in the market. Together these represent an almost immeasurable number of combinations of variety, soil and altitude. The better combinations can obviously aspire to better prices but growers, especially smallholders, cannot easily change their location, that is, change their soil type or altitude. Commercial growers however can relatively easily change the variety they grow: depending on their cropping cycle, modern commercial farms automatically replant 10%–15% of their tree park annually. But the choice of variety can be difficult. It is in the best interest of growers to stay informed of the types of coffee available for planting, and to match the best variety to the soils and the altitude conditions of their farms. For smallholders uprooting and replanting are especially costly undertakings, requiring careful consideration and realistic advice concerning *all* the potential consequences. This applies equally to genetically modified (GM) coffee that may appear in future. As yet there is no commercially available GM coffee but work in this area has been underway during the last decade. For more on this see, for example, *Coffee Futures* by CABI Commodities (*www.cabi-commodities.org*; ISBN 958-332356-X).

### Cost and yield versus quality

If a coffee lacks the inherent quality to make it a best-seller capable of commanding premium prices, then most growers, and specifically estates, cannot tolerate low yields unless their input costs are low as well. Estates, especially when using irrigation, can optimize yields much more easily than can most smallholders. This can be done by planting high yielding and/or disease-free varieties, by increasing planting densities, or by applying larger amounts of inputs, especially fertilizer (although excessive use of fertilizer can result in thin, almost bitter liquors).

There is an element of truth though in the often heard lament that such actions at times reduce *quality*, especially when taken to excess (for example very dense plant populations necessitating very high fertilizer applications). But the bottom line return from higher yields of medium to sometimes mediocre quality is, unfortunately, often better than that from lower yields of superior quality, even when higher prices are obtained. The market does not always like such comment but in recent years this has been particularly true, with many decent coffees in 2001/02 selling, in real terms, at close to historical lows.

Estate managers can usually take these considerations into account and so make relatively well-informed decisions. But when smallholders replant it is sometimes perhaps more a case of being recommended to do so, rather than a well-informed choice on their part. Yet for many smallholders it is not an easy matter to maintain the level of inputs required by higher yielding hybrids. In times of trouble, such as when prices fall, they run into difficulty and may finally end up with neither yield nor quality. Respect for the old adage that 'low inputs equal low yields but also low and therefore sustainable cost' has in the past kept many smallholders going but, as some would argue, perhaps it has also kept them poor.

### Estate or smallholder grown

It is not true that smallholders can never match the quality standards of estates. For years and years many smallholders in Kenya have consistently outperformed large and well managed estates while growing the same varieties. But much depends on the personal circumstances of each individual smallholder and it is fair to say that many smallholders in the world face daunting circumstances.

There are no accurate data on the proportions of estate and smallholder coffee in the total world production, partly because there is no definitive measure of what constitutes a smallholder. But it is believed that over half the world's coffee crop is grown on farms of less than 5 hectares.

In Africa only about 5%–6% of the annual output of about 1 million tons is grown on estates. The remaining 95% or so is grown by people whose holdings range from perhaps one or two to ten hectares, to just a few hundred trees in all, sometimes even less than that.

The world's main resource of original coffees, and their future, probably lies within the smallholder sector. Ironically though because of the heterogeneity of most of these coffees (a single shipment is made up from many small growers), they often fail to get into the exemplary segment of the specialty market because they lack visual perfection, or they are 'unknown' and it is easier to market well-known coffees. On the other hand, their availability is also not always adequate or regular enough to match expectation, which limits their scope in the marketplace. Even so, it seems reasonable to say that apart from relatively small amounts of specialty coffee, the market's general failure in recent years to provide broad support for quality smallholder coffees is contributing to the decline in their availability. Without decent prices there is little reason for the average smallholder to invest in quality.

### Harvesting method

The best quality is obtained from selective picking in which only red, ripe cherries are gathered, by hand, in successive picking rounds until most of the crop has been harvested. When coffee prices are low this time and labour consuming method is expensive. But it is impossible to produce exemplary quality coffee when the cherries are simply stripped, all at once, regardless of the degree of maturity.

# Preparing high quality arabica

## The basics

Before targeting a market one should understand one's own product, and know how it might fit into one or the other of the many niches that make up the world coffee market. Even where individual producers grow the same varieties, there are differences in tree age, tree care, fertilization, processing, general maintenance and sometimes irrigation that cause coffee quality to vary from farm to farm, within the same geographical area, on the same mountain slope, and so on. When these differences are not too obvious it is possible to mix or blend such coffees into a stable, reasonably even quality. When the differences are too great, any blend becomes as good (or as bad) as its lowest components. One cannot hide poor quality by mixing it with better coffee.

*The degree of quality variation* will depend on the size of the production area or region, the variables in that area (altitude, soil, water), the number of individual growers, whether the coffee faces north or south, and so on. Although not always appreciated as such, the same applies to individual estates, though to a lesser extent. Estates may also have excellent, good and mediocre blocks. By mixing all the coffee as it comes off the trees an estate may produce an acceptable product, and if the variability is not too great it can even be a good product. Mixing is often the only way to obtain commercially viable quantities and there is no problem with this as long as it is done on *an informed basis*. Perhaps the most important message here is that the *uninformed* mixing of different qualities or production batches is nearly always bad for business and for profits. Knowledgeable buyers will always recognize mixing, and in the end the grower or exporter may have to start all over again. In the meantime the reputation of the coffee or even an entire region may have been affected.

*The meaning of the word 'quality' is often misinterpreted.* Unfortunately many producers and exporters appear to believe that all one needs to do to make *quality coffee* is to clean up the appearance of their usual standard coffee by some regrading and additional sorting. Expertise is sometimes lacking, not only at the producing end but also at the consuming end. Large quantities of so-called quality coffee are traded which show no quality at all. This is regrettable because, in the end, indifferent quality causes consumers to lose interest, as happened for example in the United States after the Second World War, with devastating consequences for consumption there. Fortunately, the market share of the United States specialty or gourmet segment is growing, and this may help to arrest if not reverse that trend.

Accepting that not every grower, region or even country can produce absolute top quality, or visually perfect coffee, then the alternative must be to present the best possible coffee for those markets that show appreciation for that quality by rewarding the effort that goes into producing it. Without reward, growers cannot afford to invest the time and energy required to produce quality. The words 'present the best possible coffee' are used here because it is not the intention of this guide to praise or condemn any one cultivar or variety. Preferences in different markets vary, and so do the prospects of different varieties, types and qualities of coffee.

Other than the wild, extremely bitter tasting *Mascarocoffea* (found wild in the forest on Madagascar), *inherently* bad tasting coffee does not exist. Even the poor Mascaro has its good point – it is entirely free of caffeine – but apparently it is also sterile when crossed.

True, certain new cultivars may not deliver the quality characteristics of the original lines and this disappoints many coffee enthusiasts. But there is no *inherently bad* coffee, at least not when it is still on the tree. What happens to degrade the quality from then onwards is nearly always caused by human intervention.

When discussing quality from the production perspective it is well to remember that someone, somewhere, is expected to drink the coffee. When recommending planting or replanting with disease-resistant or high-yielding hybrid varieties, one should ensure that the growers are exposed to all relevant information. So also, what is the expected quality and marketability of the coffee? What are the experiences with that coffee in the potential growers' own environment? The decision to change the variety one plants has to be an informed decision, one that includes an assessment of the quality and marketing potential.

## Defining quality

*Who defines quality?* Behind every successful importer and roaster stands a satisfied body of consumers. But the final judge for growers is, simply put, the importer (or roaster) who pays a satisfactory price for a coffee and who does so on a sustained basis. Once you know what this person takes into account when judging your coffee, you can relate this to your entire production process and see where you need to take corrective or supportive action.

*The first impression can make or break a coffee's prospects.* The first impression a potential buyer gets of any coffee is when a sample of the green coffee is put in front of them. If *the green* immediately creates a negative impression then the least that will happen is that the coffee will be subject to bias from then onwards. The worst scenario is that the sample is not even tasted and is simply thrown away.

Many exporters complain of getting no response to samples they send out, but green coffee buyers are usually very busy people. Getting them to take time out to taste a new coffee is not always easy, especially if their first impression is not very positive. Hence the need to *target* one's markets. It is not just costly but almost pointless to send samples to all and sundry in the hope of achieving the odd hit.

## The green

### The aspect (or style) and the colour should be 'even'

The green beans should be of compatible shape or style, colour and size. They (and the roasted beans or the roast) must give an impression of being reasonably even. This is most important for coffee that is to be retailed as roasted whole beans. Buyers know the green bean aspects that affect the liquor negatively and they consider these when evaluating any sample, irrespective of how they might use the coffee. Buyers dislike uneven greens because they can pose problems during roasting. The resulting uneven roasts do not appeal to consumers and in any case tend to produce lower liquor quality than do even roasts. Usually, uneven colour indicates the mixed harvesting of immature and ripe cherry, which also reflects negatively in the cup.

The bean shape or style can vary with the cultivar. Usually coffee from the same cultivar will not show great variation in terms of shape and style, whereas uniformity of size is determined by the degree of size grading which takes place. But mixing different cultivars within a single consignment can produce uneven looking coffees, even if all the beans conform to the same screen size. This is especially so if coffee from cultivars producing solid and softish beans are mixed into the same batch. Softish beans usually have quite a different shape and style from solid beans; this will be especially evident in the roast.

If different cultivars have been interplanted, as could be the case on a smallholding where there might be no room to separate them, then there is little to be done at the harvest stage. An estate with blocks of different cultivars could harvest and process them on different days, and hold them separately for example by colour coding each batch. But before going to this effort and expense, verify first through sampling if the end result warrants it.

If coffee is collected commercially from different geographical production areas, care should be taken to verify its compatibility before mixing it, if necessary by making small trial blends by hand in proportion to the quantities to be mixed (bulked).

## Colour is very important

*The colour should be even and bright*, especially so for mild, washed arabicas, which should never be dull, or mottled, or faded (going whitish).

Buyers dislike greens of uneven, faded, blotchy or dull colour because this hints at poor processing, incorrect moisture content and/or premature ageing of the coffee. All of these translate into reduced liquor quality, progressively becoming dull (bland) and common (ordinary). Remember that the buyer knows the actual shipment will still take time to reach them, so if the advance sample sent by air already shows such signs, the coffee itself may look still worse on arrival.

*Drying affects the colour.* Like wet processing, *drying* is also of extreme importance. At this stage a coffee's quality can literally be destroyed. Correct harvesting, processing and drying require *maximum management input*: having spent an entire year tending to and investing in the crop, do not then entrust its harvest and handling to poorly trained, unsupervised labour. Many potential candidate coffees fail to make it to the specialty market, and certainly to the exemplary segment, because their green appearance shows shortcomings during drying and storage.

The green appearance of naturals (dried in the cherry) habitually shows a brownish tinge and beans with brown silver-skins (often called foxy beans). In naturals this is quite acceptable, but for wet-processed (washed) coffees these are negative aspects because they can translate into fruitiness, sourness and even an over-fermented taste. The knowledgeable liquorer will usually downgrade such a washed coffee even before it is liquored. But even if the liquor is satisfactory, the coffee may still be rejected because the green appearance suggests it could hide something – *the coffee looks unreliable*.

## Causes of poor colour

*Dullish and sometimes brownish greens* often result from (too rapid) mechanical drying which also tends to *flatten* the liquor quality. Uneven colour is usually a consequence of poor drying techniques.

*Uneven, mottled greens,* often with mottled, blotchy, whitish or *soapy* beans, suggest the coffee was spread too thickly when drying, that it was not turned often enough, or that it was dried too rapidly. Such beans subsequently show up as mottled beans (also called quakers by some) in the roast.

*Mechanical drying* is often used if the climate or the tonnage to be handled do not allow one to depend entirely on sun drying, that is, if the weather is too unreliable during the harvest season, or the quantities of cherry to be handled are simply too big. For washed robusta it is also a means of avoiding (secondary) fermentation.

Collectors (those who buy parchment or dried coffee in cherry from small farmers) often use mechanical drying to bring the moisture content down to acceptable levels. Subsequent storage or *conditioning* in bulk bins with airflow capability then *evens out* the moisture content throughout the entire parcel or stack.

*Brownish tinges in arabica greens* can result from the harvesting of overripe cherries, or from allowing too many skins to enter the fermentation tanks. The use of dirty water, under-fermentation, insufficient washing after natural fermentation, or the mechanical removal of mucilage are other contributing causes. In washed arabicas foxy beans (where the silver-skin has turned reddish-brown) are usually due to the harvesting of overripe cherry, or keeping cherry overnight before pulping.

*Fading is an indication of problems.* A generally bleached or fading colour suggests that the coffee is ageing, or that it was over-dried, especially so in arabica. When the fading is more pronounced around the edges of the beans (which turn whitish) then this suggests the coffee was taken off the drying racks or grounds too early, or it was stored in moist, humid conditions, without adequate air circulation. If some of the beans are also generally softish and whitish then the experienced buyer knows such a coffee will never make it to the specialty market, let alone the roasted whole bean segment. Such a sample may find its way directly to the waste bin because such coffee has already lost its fresh taste and will definitely show a dull (bland) and common (ordinary) liquor.

### How to improve or maintain colour

*When drying mechanically*, experiment with the temperature. Some older types of dryers expose coffee to very high temperatures. Be careful coffee is not dried too rapidly or over-dried. Some modern (and quite simple) dryers use ambient air circulation, which minimizes such problems. Their suitability also depends on the prevailing climatic conditions.

For arabica coffee, try combining mechanical and sun drying, with the initial drying done mechanically followed by a finishing-off period of exposure to sunlight. This improves the colour generally and appears to reduce the effect on colour of the mechanical drying. Some flat bed dryers incorporate a sliding roof which permits managed exposure to sunlight.

*When sun drying*, do not spread drying coffee, cherry and parchment, thicker than one hand's width. Use an even drying surface and spread the coffee evenly, with no hills and valleys. Stir or turn the coffee regularly to ensure *even* drying. Cover parchment coffee during the hottest time of the day to avoid it cracking open and creating mottled beans. Cover all coffee during rain and of course at night. For smallholders, drying trays are an excellent drying method: easily taken out and returned to store. If they are combined with plastic covers as shown below, then one simultaneously achieves good air circulation, heat retention and cover against rain.

A solar dryer in Papua New Guinea.                                    Photo: PNG Coffee Industry Corporation

Solar dryer in Colombia.                                                          Photos: Cenicafé-Federacafe, Colombia

*Good housekeeping helps.* To avoid brownish greens and foxy beans in washed coffee, observe proper harvesting practices: where possible pick ripe cherry only, and avoid overripes (like green unripe cherry, overripes should also be put separately for sun drying). Do not allow cherry to be collected in plastic bags as they allow no air circulation. Do not allow full bags to be exposed to direct sunlight, as this causes heating, sweating and possibly over-fermentation. Remember, coffee starts to ferment immediately after picking so *always* pulp within the same day as harvesting. Ensure proper separation of skins from parchment (if necessary float excess skins off the top of the fermentation tank or basin); do not use contaminated water; ensure fermentation is complete before washing; and make sure coffee is washed properly to remove all vestiges of mucilage. Skin dry immediately after final washing – spread parchment very thinly to ensure rapid loss of water.

## Moisture content and drying

*There is no exact standard for ideal moisture content.* Not all coffee is the same, and circumstances differ from country to country. In general, 11% is probably a good target for most coffee. In any case roasters are increasingly insisting on a maximum moisture content on arrival. Coffee above 12.5% moisture should *never* be shipped.

If past experience suggests buyers are generally satisfied then stick to good established practice and monitor the moisture content regularly. Remember that when coffee is dried on flat surfaces (such as tarpaulins or concrete) it will heat up and thus dry out more rapidly than when it is spread on raised tables or trays that allow air to circulate around it. When getting close to the moisture target, monitor *every hour*.

Always use properly calibrated moisture meters and test them regularly, before each season. If in doubt about the exact percentage, take the coffee off a little earlier rather than letting it become noticeably over-dried. This is especially recommended if decent storage sheds or, better still, ventilated bins or silos are available for conditioning.

*Apart from later loss of cup quality, under-drying may also cause mould.* In severe cases, under-dried coffees may develop fungi and moulds. These have always been undesirable but increasing consumer attention to mycotoxins in agricultural produce, specifically ochratoxin A (OTA), is a real cause for concern for some coffee producers.

Clean, proper and efficient drying and storage of coffee is probably the best defense against mould growth and its potential consequences. This and other food safety issues are reviewed in detail in Quality control issues, later in this chapter.

To repeat once more: many receivers stipulate a maximum acceptable moisture content on both shipment *and* arrival. Producers and exporters need to develop appropriate *moisture content management techniques* if they are to cope with this.

*Over-drying costs money.* This makes it as serious as under-drying: not only is weight, and therefore money, lost unnecessarily, but the accompanying loss of colour also translates directly into lower liquor quality. When moisture drops below 10%, aroma, acidity and freshness begin to fade away and at 8% or below they have completely disappeared. For this reason the ICO wants to see shipments of coffee below 8% moisture content prohibited.

Like *under-dried* coffee, *over-dried* coffee should not be mixed with correctly dried coffee. They are not *compatible*. Remember also that climatic conditions in many storage sheds are not ideal: they may be keeping the coffee dry but they are certainly not keeping it cool and the coffee may therefore continue drying out. Quality loss due to over-drying cannot be reversed, and is unacceptable. Over-dried coffee also breaks up more easily during milling. This increases the percentage of ears, shells and broken beans, which further reduces both the quality and the value.

Finally, do everything possible to avoid letting coffee sit around endlessly after it has been containerized for export. This can be especially problematic for landlocked countries from where coffee must travel long distances to the port of shipment. If containers are kept in the open, exposed to open sun in holding grounds, on railway flatcars or trucks, then this can lead to overheating and condensation. (See chapter 5, Logistics.)

*Over-drying also affects the way a coffee roasts.* Coffees with a moisture content as low as 8% may certainly take the average specialty roaster by surprise. This is because such coffees tend to roast to completion *much faster* than these roasters expect. Smaller specialty roasters do not always have moisture meters, and they can and do get into trouble with such coffees. Quite apart from the reduction in acidity and flavour that over-drying causes, the end-user may also be embarrassed – all good reasons never to buy that coffee again.

## Avoid obvious defects

### *Appearance*

Coffees containing black beans, obvious stinkers, water-damaged beans and foreign matter *stand no chance,* not only in the quality market but also not for the great majority of roasters. This should be obvious to anyone in the coffee business, so what follows is limited to the perhaps not so well recognized appearance (green) defects that put off quality buyers and cause them to reject one coffee in favour of another. This explains why seemingly good samples are rejected or why some buyers simply do not respond to them at all.

*Coated.* The silver-skin has adhered to more than half a bean's surface. The immediate consequence is that the green appearance suffers because the silver-skin obscures the bean's surface and true colour. Too much coatedness does not look good. The roaster also knows that the silver-skin tends to burn off during roasting and the resultant chaff can pose problems.

Coated beans are caused by drought and by trees over-bearing. Both of these tend to affect the cherry in similar ways, and the coffee's style and general aspect are usually not impressive. General coatedness can also result from under-fermentation. Beans that are entirely coated may originate from unripe cherry.

Coffees with pronounced coatedness often produce common, ordinary liquors. The experienced coffee buyer will tend to instinctively discriminate against such coffees, also because the roast will usually contain ragged, soft and sometimes pale beans.

If possible one should not mix coffee from drought affected trees with that of others. However, many coated beans will lose their silver-skin during hulling (or polishing, where this is installed). Very coated beans are usually also ragged and smaller or lighter than the norm and may be removed during grading and sorting.

Before rushing into polishing to remove the silver-skin, first establish whether the coatedness of your coffee *is* a problem and, if so, what the cause might be. Polishing as such adds *nothing to coffee quality* but does improve the colour and overall appearance (unless the polisher has excessively heated the beans, which has the opposite effect). Correct (i.e. cool) polishing may make a coffee more easily saleable. Some robustas are polished as a matter of course, but for arabica it is advisable to first verify whether polishing makes commercial sense.

*Ragged or uneven.* Ragged refers to drought-affected and misshapen beans that give the green an uneven aspect. Too many ragged beans in a coffee suggest less than optimal quality, *neither green nor roast are pleasing to the eye* and such coffee is not usually suitable for sale as whole roasted bean. Ragged coffees often produce mediocre liquors – but one cannot generalize because some sought-after *original* coffees show beans with naturally meandering centre cuts as a matter of course. Great care must be taken therefore to distinguish between the *visual or cosmetic aspects* of different coffees and the *quality*.

An uneven green can also be the result of mixing different coffees, for example a roundish bean (Bourbon) with a flattish bean (Typica), or a boat-shaped (Ethiopian) variety. Where possible it is probably best to leave decisions on the mixing of different cultivars and types to the buyer.

The fundamental causes of raggedness can be addressed only in the field. All processing can do is: separate light and heavy cherry before pulping (by grading or flotation: smallholders can even do this using a simple bucket or basin); systematic washing and grading after pulping; and intensive size and especially density separation during dry (export) processing. The most useful tool in this respect is without any doubt the gravity table (*table densimetrique* in French). Properly set and supervised, this machine will eliminate many if not most ragged beans.

*Pulper-nipped beans* are the result of incorrectly set pulpers. They are very difficult to remove during export grading and sorting. If those beans are also discoloured they can also cause fermented, foul or unclean cups as described in the next paragraph. Experienced buyers will notice pulper-nipped beans and the risk message they convey.

### Insect and pest damage

Controlling insects and other pests can be a problem, especially in countries where coffee is grown in small patches, sometimes of a few hundred trees only and often widely dispersed and scattered over substantial areas. Such conditions make effective treatment difficult. Insect damage in the beans suggests less than optimal care of the tree park. It detracts from the coffee's visual attraction, and buyers know that insect damaged beans cause common, ordinary and sometimes tainted liquors.

Most insect damage may be quite obvious to the eye but insects can also be the cause of invisible stinkers with dirty water penetrating an insect-stung or pulper-nipped bean during fermentation and causing an internal chemical reaction. Such beans may look sound on the outside but can throw unclean or even fermented cups that degrade an entire consignment.

Insect and pest damage can be controlled only in the field. Eliminating damaged beans after harvesting costs more and does not address the root cause of the problem. However, the flotation (grading by density) of cherry before pulping is of great importance, as is the subsequent separation of parchment into lights and heavies in the washing and grading channel. These are important principles of wet processing. Smallholders who use hand pulpers should try floating the lights off in a bucket or basin filled with water before pulping – usually this makes a major difference to the end product.

Failing this, the coffee miller's best friend, the gravity table, presents the best and cheapest option for eliminating damaged and light beans. But of course the table works well only if it is properly set and operated: the attendants must know *why* they are doing what they are doing. Catadors (pneumatic separation using blast air) do the same job but less efficiently, and work best if the coffee has first been size graded.

This is not the place to argue for or against the wet processing or washing of coffee. There is no doubt however that correctly operated washing stations are an important quality control tool, *at the very start of the processing chain.*

## Bean size

*Below-size and light beans* in a consignment are a direct consequence of inadequate size and density separation, partly during primary processing but mostly during dry or export processing. Not only do too many smalls and lights spoil the coffee's green appearance, but large and small, or heavy and light beans also do not roast well together. This is because smalls and lights will *over-roast* during the time it takes for the roasting of the larger, heavier beans to be completed. There are strict limits to the proportion of smalls and lights roasters may tolerate in whole bean coffee; if a coffee exceeds their in-house tolerance for smalls and lights, then out it goes.

*Not all size grading is accurate.* Opinions differ on the accuracy of different size grading techniques (vibratory or flatbed versus rotary or cylinder graders for example) and this is not the place to argue for or against any of them. But, often, when operated at full design capacity, graders do not necessarily produce *accurate* separation, so the throughput must be regulated. This can be especially troublesome if a grader is directly auto-fed by a preceding

---

### Screen sizes

*Coffee is graded by size using rotating or shaking screens, replaceable metal sheets that have round holes in them that retain beans over a certain size and allow smaller beans to pass. Screen sizes are expressed as numbers (e.g robusta grade one screen 16), or by letters (e.g. arabica grade AA –indicating a bold bean), or by descriptions (e.g. bold, medium or small bean). It all depends on the trade custom in any given country. Intermediate screen sizes (e.g. 16.5), are important in some producing countries but disregarded in others. However, nearly all coffee for export is graded to exclude the largest and smallest beans, as well as broken beans and other particles.*

#### Standard coffee round screen dimensions

| Screen number | ISO dimensions (in mm) |
|---|---|
| 10 | 4.00 |
| 12 | 4.75 |
| 13 | 5.00 |
| 14 | 5.60 |
| 15 | 6.00 |
| 16 | 6.30 |
| 17 | 6.70 |
| 18 | 7.10 |
| 19 | 7.50 |
| 20 | 8.00 |

*It is not always easy or possible to achieve a 100% accurate screen (e.g. nil passing through screen 16). Where a 100% accurate screen is required then marginally increasing the size of the holes to give a small tolerance in the screen may provide the required result.*

*Slotted screens with oblong slits (usually 4.00 or 4.50 mm wide) are used in some countries to remove peaberries (single oblong beans in a cherry, the result of a genetic aberration because normally there are two beans in a cherry), which are sought after in some consuming countries.*

processing unit, or if the product quality is quite variable. It is always advisable therefore to have a supplier commission  any new milling, grading and sorting equipment, using the actual product that is to be handled. Regulating the intake flow by placing a buffer silo or feed hopper ahead of the grader can improve grading accuracy quite considerably, but constant supervision will always be necessary. The grading accuracy should be verified regularly, using hand or sample screens that should be kept handy, near the grader.

When grading whole bean type coffee bear in mind that some *very* large beans may not be particularly attractive as they are often soft or misshapen. Such beans become especially noticeable in the roast appearance. They can be easily removed by the insertion of a large size screen (number 20 screen for example) ahead of the regular screens. This is also helpful when *elephant beans* are present (beans which have become inter-twined in the cherry and which nearly always break up, if not during milling then during roasting).

One easy way to quickly verify whether a shipment corresponds to the selling sample is to check the coffee's size and density composition. Pass 100 g or 200 g of the original sample and the shipment sample over the appropriate size screens and compare the percentages. Do the same with the lights by counting them. Many shipments appear visually to be a match but turn out not to be when this simple test is applied. Buyers know this, and so should the exporter.

## Bean density

*Lights, shells or ears, brokens* are all beans or parts of beans that are notably lighter in weight (i.e. less dense) than the *average* bean in a particular size grade. Note this distinction: although a small but solid bean will weigh less than a large one, it does not automatically follow that it is a *light* bean. Lights usually have natural causes such as drought, stress, or picking of immature cherry. All of these result in misshapen, shrivelled and soft beans. The breaking up of beans during hulling and other processing actions (including over-drying) results in shells, ears, brokens, chips and so on. Such beans and bits and pieces detract from the green appearance. They cause similar roasting problems to smalls in large bean grades, and they very definitely depress the cup quality.

Not only do light and broken beans reduce the flavour, acidity and body of a coffee, but they often also introduce a flattish, common or ordinary taste. They can turn a potentially fine cup into a mediocre one. Proper density separation is therefore of extreme importance, especially when the coffee beans to be dealt with are also somewhat heterogeneous (uneven) by nature.

*Lights and brokens* are removed pneumatically using strong airflows (catador), or by a fluidization process (gravity table). Both separate coffee by density but catadors are usually less accurate than gravity tables. Catadors are most useful for the initial clean-up of a coffee, directly after hulling (and polishing if installed). The strong air current removes most chips and small lights that would otherwise complicate or slow the subsequent processing. Gravity tables on the other hand are at their most efficient when the coffee has already been size graded. This is because the size grader will have removed most of the remaining smalls, and the product to be separated is therefore already of reasonably uniform density.

Catador and gravity table settings must be based on the type and quality of the coffee under process and on the desired result. Constant, well informed supervision is essential, especially if the product is not homogeneous, for example if there has been no prior size grading. Again, an intermediate buffer silo or feed hopper permitting variable feed can ensure that the intake flow is correctly set. This is essential if optimal results are to be achieved.

*This applies to all grades of coffee, not only whole bean grades,* because the value of the small bean coffees that are an inevitable by-product of the larger, whole bean, grades must also be maximized. Small lights, ears and chips in a grade of whole but small beans (C grade, pea-berry, screen 15 and even screen 14) cause exactly the same problems: they make the coffee awkward to roast and degrade the liquor quality. There are good markets for decent *grinders* (used for roast and ground only) if the coffee is homogeneous and properly graded.

## *Sorting*

*Bleached, mottled, whitish, blotchy, soapy and discoloured beans* generally cannot be removed by size or density grading but there is no place for them in quality coffee (although there is probably some tolerance for them in the lower priced segment of the general market). Nearly all such beans are caused by moisture and drying problems, but discolouring can also be due to oxidization, contact with soil, metal, dirty water and so on. The gravity table can help but in the end the only effective way to remove these beans is through manual or electronic sorting.

Not only do such beans effectively ruin the coffee's green appearance but they also show up in the roast as softs or quakers, pales, mottled beans and so on, and they definitely affect the cup quality. The buyer of *quality* coffees will not tolerate such beans.

*Modern sorting equipment* is capable of many and extremely varied tasks. The most recent developments use laser technology. *Such equipment can be quite costly though whereas in some countries sorting by hand is an important source of otherwise scarce employment.* Deciding whether to hand or machine sort depends on individual circumstances, the tonnages to be sorted, and the cost of labour. Smaller producers of specialty coffee usually give their coffee at least a quick going over by hand, especially if labour is relatively cheap. Some expend much time and care on sorting, depending on their target market.

Individual countries and operators have different ideas, systems and methods when it comes to sorting green coffee and there is no point in discussing these here because different circumstances pose their own particular requirements and problems. But there are two general principles which are important and which are always valid:

- *Know your sorting capabilities.* When preparing advance samples for dispatch abroad, ensure that your expectations of your sorting capacity do not exceed reality. It is only human to remove more rather than fewer defects from an advance sample 'as the coffee will be properly sorted in any case'. It is exceedingly annoying for the buyer to find later that the coffee is 'almost' but not quite as well sorted as the advance sample.

- *Without a good working environment and decent lighting people cannot sort coffee efficiently and correctly.* Many manual sorting processes still consist of people sitting on the floor in dark and dingy warehouses, each facing a heap of coffee. The sorters closest to the door can see the best – the remainder have to make do. This will never do for the preparation of quality coffee, whether arabica or robusta, because the sorting will be neither optimal nor even, and the entire operation is best kept hidden from visiting buyers altogether. If sorting belts are too expensive, then at least invest in sorting tables and benches. These are easily made up by any competent carpenter. Such tables speed up the sorting process, which then is also more easily supervised. (Sorting belts are moving conveyor belts, usually with auto-feed and auto-advance, providing room for 12 or 24 sorters to sit on either side. Sorting tables are tables with a fluorescent light over them, seating 6 or 8 people. The table top is divided into squares with raised edges. A small hole in each square allows sorted coffee to fall into a bag hanging underneath; rejects go into receptacles fixed to the table's edge.)

## The roast

*As with the green, first impressions are very important.* A roast that is dull, uneven, open and/or soft (with ears or shells) immediately raises suspicion. Conversely, a bright or brilliant, even and solid roast is not just pleasing to the eye but also suggests good cupping potential. For the average consumer of whole bean roasted coffee the most obvious eye-catching aspect is probably the evenness. An even roast is therefore a prerequisite for almost any coffee to make it to the end consumer in whole bean form. *There are some exceptions:* a few very well established naturals with less than optimal roast appearance are sold as whole bean, but these are coffees with an established reputation. The consumer is convinced they are good even if they do not 'look so good'. But 'new' coffees whose appearance does not match the general perception of what quality coffee should look like do not stand much chance in the whole bean market segment.

The potential causes and remedies for many individual roast defects have already been identified in 'The green', earlier in this chapter. The following therefore deals with more general roast defects that are under the producer's and exporter's control.

## Type or quality

*An even roast is all-important.* In an even roast almost all the beans have roasted to about the same colour and brightness, with a white or whitish centre-cut that is not too irregular. There should be few obvious defects, preferably none.

Wet-processed coffees usually produce the best roasts, especially when the parchment has been properly sun-dried. Brilliant roasts with white centre-cuts are a hallmark of well prepared and well dried coffee: under-drying, on the other hand, produces dull roasts. The centre-cuts in particular are indicative of the care taken during the processing and drying of washed and semi-washed coffee. Naturals (dried in the cherry) usually show dullish roasts with brownish centre-cuts and this makes it difficult to present most of them as whole bean. Unless well managed, mechanical drying using hot air may also *dull* the roast appearance.

*A brilliant or bright roast almost shines up at the viewer.* It has a well defined, white to brilliantly white centre-cut and the beans are usually fairly hard or solid. When considering mixing or blending, one should always consider the roast of each individual component: mixing bright, solid roasts with dull and usually softer roasts may well result in an unattractive overall view that renders the coffee less suitable for presentation as whole bean.

*Dull and dullish roasts lack lustre and brightness.* This is usually caused by under-drying, or sometimes by mechanical drying. Over-fermentation and the picking of overripe cherry can also cause dull roasts and will especially affect the colour of the centre-cut.

In washed coffee, brownish centre-cuts or no center-cuts are suggestive of overripes, over-fermentation, use of dirty water or the presence of too many skins in the fermentation tanks. But naturals usually tend towards duller roasts, and brownish or almost no centre-cuts as a matter of course.

## Uneven roasts

*There are many potential causes of uneven roasts.* They include: the picking of immature or droughted cherry; uneven fermentation, including the mixing of different batches of washed or semi-washed coffee which have not necessarily been fermented or washed to the same degree; too rapid or uneven drying; and insufficient separation of light coffee during primary and/or export processing. Incomplete fermentation causes dull roasts, and when mixed with brighter roasting coffee this gives an aspect of general unevenness. Immature cherry usually translates into pales or semi-pales in the roast (beans which are yellowish to yellow in colour). But bleached or colourless green beans, including yellow beans or ambers, also cause pales in the roast. Not only do (bright) pales ruin the roast appearance and cause clearly visible yellow particles in ground coffee, they also introduce commonness into the liquor.

## Mottled and blotchy beans

Mottled and blotchy beans are caused by uneven drying. The end consumer may not necessarily notice them as a defect, but their appearance in the roast suggests to examiners that the quality of the coffee is likely to deteriorate rather quickly. This may cause them to reject it altogether.

## *Softs, brokens and raggedness*

Softs often go together with pales but a roast can also present a general aspect of softness. In this case the beans are generally open, and the centre-cuts are not well defined and may be brownish in colour. Some cultivars have a tendency towards soft roasts, especially when grown at low altitudes, but in the main softs are caused by poor drying and immature (very coated) coffee.

Bleached, soapy, mottled, discoloured and blighted beans usually show up in the roast as softs or quakers, and also as pales. Careful sorting of the green beans helps to eliminate them but it is difficult to achieve 100% accuracy.

Broken beans in a roast reflect inadequate separation during processing (both wet and dry), over-drying, incorrectly set equipment, and the presence of misshapen and deformed beans that have broken up during the roasting: all problems related to processing therefore, although some cultivars do produce larger proportions of deformed beans (elephant beans). In some cases, drought or nutrition stress seems to result in larger numbers of *small* elephant beans (these are of considerable concern to the grower as they mostly break up during processing and roasting).

Ragged roasts also suggest the wrong coffees have been mixed together. For example, droughted coffee has been mixed with good coffee, or incompatible cultivars have been mixed such as larger flat-shaped beans with smaller, rounder or boat-shaped beans.

## *Measuring roast colour*

Measuring roast colour is important. The type of roast – light, medium or dark – has a definite bearing on quality.

- The darker a roast, the less pronounced the acidity and different flavour aspects (as well as defects) of the liquor, but the heavier the body.

- The lighter a roast, the more pronounced the acidity and flavour (and defects), but the lighter the body.

Different markets roast coffee differently. Exporters should understand the type of roast their buyers need. But 'light, medium and dark' mean different things to different people: they are subjective terms. (See also Traditional versus espresso, later in this chapter.)

The Specialty Coffee Association of America (SCAA) has developed a points system to classify the degree – *the colour* – of different roast types. The system consists of eight numbered colour disks against which one matches a sample of finely ground, roasted coffee, usually pressed into a laboratory petri dish. In this way one assigns the roast an approximate number on what is commonly called the **Agtron Gourmet Scale**, ranging from #95 (lightest roast) at intervals of 10 down to #25 (the darkest common roast). This helpful tool enables producers and roasters to speak the same language when discussing 'the roast' of a coffee. (It is available from the SCAA's resource centre in Long Beach, California – see *www.scaa.org*.)

# The taste or liquor

## *The importance of liquoring*

*As said earlier, first impressions are vitally important.* If the green does not make it to the roasting room then the coffee will never be tasted. It is pointless therefore to send samples which do not demonstrate at least a minimal effort at creating a presentable product – the amount of effort one puts in depends on the market segment that is to be targeted or, perhaps, the premium one is trying to attract.

*Remember that, in principle, there is no inherently bad coffee.* If a coffee presents really poor quality, the cause can usually be traced to poor harvesting and post harvest processing, drying, storage and handling. *It is absolutely essential to maintain stringent standards of cleanliness at all stages, especially in wet processing*. If this is done, almost any coffee has the potential to show a presentable green with at least a passable cup or liquor. How your potential buyer judges that liquor will depend on the type of coffee, and on how it matches their specific preferences and objectives. A buyer will not buy a coffee that does not fit their requirements, even though they may have appreciated it for what it was. Aspiring sellers therefore need to understand the requirements of the market segment they are thinking of targeting.

*Without the ability to liquor one cannot be a successful exporter.* All coffee is sold to be drunk, and someone, somewhere will taste a coffee before it is roasted. Sending out samples of obviously unsuitable or even unpleasant coffee is a recipe for disaster. It conveys the impression that the seller does not know their own product, or does not care. Such samples also suggest that the seller might ship unclean-tasting coffee and many buyers, especially smaller ones, will therefore avoid them. Inexperienced suppliers represent potential danger: if on arrival the liquor is no good, then the coffee cannot be used. This causes a shortfall in supply which has to be made up from elsewhere, and the buyer has to find a way to dispose of the offending coffee, which meanwhile may be taking up finance and storage space.

*Liquoring is also important for other reasons.* A seller who cannot properly *evaluate* the quality of their own coffee also cannot *value* it against the price at which the competition or other origins are selling. Without liquoring it is nearly impossible to judge whether one's asking price, for example, is too high or too low.

## The basics

*At the very minimum the liquor has to be clean.* There should be no off-flavours or taints in the cup. The liquor must be reliable and constant: the coffee should liquor the same every time it is tasted. When making up a shipment it is no good tasting a single cup and thinking that the coffee is fine, when many buyers as a matter of course will taste five or ten cups over two or more individual roasts.

*When roasting your own coffee, remember the type of roast your buyer prefers and match it in your own preparation.* But also remember that sometimes a lighter roast may accentuate defective liquor aspects that darker roasts tend to hide. Specialty roasters in particular usually roast small batches and taste every batch. This means a coffee will be tasted many times over. If it is unreliable (meaning different or even unclean cups simply 'appear' from time to time) this will be spotted. Bulk users of commercial grade coffee also sample very accurately and will easily spot an unreliable parcel. See Quality and sampling, in chapter 5.

*What constitutes 'quality' is a subjective judgement.* Quality is open to many interpretations, but experienced tasters will seldom disagree on whether a coffee is clean in the cup or not. What they may argue about is whether the type and degree of uncleanliness, or off-flavour, is such as to render the coffee unacceptable. Clearly one will be more tolerant of quality defects in a bargain-priced grinder to be used in the general mass market, than one would be of taste defects in a top-priced, supposedly exemplary coffee.

*Experienced buyers have a fair idea what to expect from certain origins and types of coffee.* They know what those coffees can be used for. And so a sun-dried natural may present flavours that buyers know, accept and even appreciate in that type of coffee, but that they will absolutely *not* accept in a washed coffee. For example, the full body and often somewhat heavy, fruity taste of many good naturals does not appeal to buyers who are looking for acidic coffees instead. The experienced liquorer will know what coffee suits which buyer or market – anyone wishing to get into the business of selling *quality* will have to find this out if they want to make their mark.

*Understand your buyer.* Once a quality has been accepted it is most important to understand exactly why the buyer likes and continues to buy that particular coffee in preference to others. There can be many reasons, but the most important to mention here are continuity and mutual trust. *Continuity* suggests not that this coffee is just an isolated happening, never to be seen again, but rather that the seller knows where the coffee came from, how it was brought to the quality the buyer approved, and that within reason the seller can repeat the exercise in future. Of course, like wine, no coffee is exactly the same from season to season. There are good years, and then there are less good to sometimes even bad years. Experienced buyers know this and will never hold such variations against a seller.

*Buyers hate exporters who knowingly ship coffee whose quality is not up to standard.* If unforeseen circumstances mean one has difficulty in fulfilling a contract then the best and, really, the only option is always to inform your buyer as soon as you become aware of the problem. The buyer may be able to assist you by granting an extension to the shipping period, or may agree to take a slightly different quality (perhaps against a reduction in price), or may agree to release you from the contract. But the buyer will rightly be furious if the exporter simply ships a slightly different coffee hoping to get away with it. This can cause *real and serious trouble,* as shipping the wrong coffee disrupts the buyer's supply pipeline. Roasters buy coffee for a specific objective. If on arrival it does not suit, it becomes virtually useless to them. It is no good then to offer a price allowance or discount to try and settle the matter. After all, if the roaster could have used a lower quality they would presumably have bought that in the first place.

*Continuity and mutual trust* mean both parties understand what is important in the coffee, that within reason they will continue to offer and buy that coffee, and that they can rely on each other to respect their obligations in every respect. Not all obligations are specified in the contract. For example, keeping buyers informed about the status of pending contracts is an unwritten obligation, whether the news to be passed on is good or not so good.

### Serious liquor problems

There is a whole range of flavours, good and bad, whose impact on quality varies in importance depending on the type of coffee and on the type of buyer. But some flavours are unacceptable in *any* coffee to virtually all buyers, certainly in the quality business.

*Fermented or foul* is a very objectionable taste, not unlike the odour of rotting coffee pulp. In its worst general form this is due to over-fermentation, cherry left to rot in heaps, the use of polluted water or stung beans with pollutants entering them. Foul-tasting cups can also be produced by single beans left behind in fermentation tanks or washing channels, or by beans that have been partly dried and then re-wetted again under unsanitary conditions.

If a few such stinker beans are irregularly spread throughout a shipment then this is a typical example of an *unreliable* coffee that *occasionally* produces an unclean or foul cup. Note that there is no such thing as *only a little ferment*, just as there is no such thing as being *almost honest.* (See also information about pulper-nipped beans and insect damage earlier in this chapter.)

Most buyers would also consider *sour and onion* liquors as totally unacceptable, arguing that both are just a step away from ferment. This is a persuasive argument because sour and oniony liquors are caused by late pulping of cherry, and poor processing or drying techniques. Coffee does not naturally come off the tree with such taints. Remember that fermentation starts as soon as the cherry is picked. But there are clever blenders who know how to use such coffees in combination with other specific taste characteristics, and in so doing arrive at an acceptable final result. The real issue may therefore be whether such a coffee is *over the top or not.* As far as the quality market is concerned, however, one is best advised to stay well clear of such coffees.

*Musty or mouldy* is a very unpleasant coarse harsh flavour caused by the storage of under-dried coffee, or the re-wetting of coffee after it has already been dried. This flavour also suggests potential mould problems. (See Mould and prevention, later in this chapter.) *Earthy* is a close relative. Contact with bare earth or dust are the main causes, which also imply poor drying arrangements, and the possibility of mustiness and mouldiness.

*Very strong taints* will also render a coffee virtually unusable: contact with petrol for example. *Unclean* can refer to any offensive off-flavour or taint. It can also be taken to indicate that an unspecified off-flavour is present.

Most of these taste defects tend to intensify with ageing. The common thread linking them all is that they are not to be tolerated in reasonably decent coffee.

### Less serious liquor problems

Less serious liquor problems are difficult territory: very subjective and personal. What constitutes an acceptable or unacceptable liquor depends on the individual buyer's judgment, so it is vital to understand your buyer. Appreciate why the buyer takes certain coffees and not others – visit them and taste different coffees together, including your own.

*Fruity or winey* are a good example of less serious liquor problems because, within reason, such flavours can add something interesting to a coffee. But the next step down is *fruity-sour* and then *sour*, which is undesirable. Winey can move through *oniony* to *onion*, which is a relative of *ferment*. Within reason these are not always necessarily reasons to reject a coffee. However, in coffee to be used for espresso *fruity* or *winey* are not wanted under any circumstances because the espresso process often transforms them into rather different, intense and sometimes outright unpleasant tastes. So these tastes can be viewed as positive or negative – it all depends on the intensity and on the buyer's judgement. (See Traditional versus espresso, later in this chapter.)

*Ordinary, common or coarse tastes* are strictly speaking not off-flavours. Just as there is a market for *vin ordinaire,* so there is one for *café ordinaire.* These flavour characteristics are usually caused by problems such as drought, serious stress or insect damage, or by processing or drying errors. Such liquors are therefore unlikely to find much favour in the quality market. But there are also disease resistant or high-yielding cultivars that present rather common liquors even though the coffee may be of attractive appearance and style. Sometimes such coffees may be upgraded through blending, perhaps by adding another coffee with an oniony, fruity or winey flavour. The result may not be a candidate for the exemplary market, but perhaps not a candidate for outright rejection either.

A *woody or aged taste* is not unsimilar and is the direct result of the ageing of a coffee, usually accompanied by loss of colour. It is not at all uncommon to find woody tasting coffee at the retail end of the specialty business because it sometimes takes months before coffees are roasted. Poorly dried coffees age more quickly than do well prepared ones, and lose colour more rapidly as well. The coffee 'fades' quickly. For 99 out of 100 offer samples from origin, a woody taste or fading appearance suggests a risk of premature ageing during shipment and the time spent awaiting final sale.

*Grassy is a greenish taste* that tends to obscure the liquor's finer aspects such as flavour or aroma. This taste is reminiscent of hay and is mostly found in early season coffee. Under-drying tends to accentuate grassiness. *Bricky* is a close relative in that it also reduces flavour and acidity. Usually this commonish taste is associated with (slight) under-fermentation.

## Sampling

*The golden rule of quality coffee is to do the best possible within one's capabilities.* This means demonstrating first of all through the green appearance that a certain amount of care has gone into the coffee's preparation. Such care will automatically come through in the roast and in the liquor. If potential buyers do not see such signs of care in a green coffee sample they may discard it without even tasting it. *The liquor will always show a coffee's real character,* however exciting or dull that may be, but at least the liquor should never show any of the obvious defects mentioned earlier. If it does, do not send the sample to someone who you know buys only quality. Apart from the rejection that will follow, you may inadvertently ruin any chance of future business with that buyer because you have demonstrated an obvious lack of expertise.

*Samples must be representative.* When you send a sample be sure that it is fully representative of the actual coffee or, if you do not have the coffee in stock, that you can match the quality. It is useful to note the following sampling definitions:

- *Stocklot samples* are samples of the actual coffee that will be shipped if a contract is concluded.

- *Approval samples* are sent for coffees sold 'subject approval of sample'. Such samples must be drawn from the actual parcel intend for shipment. Remember, a sale subject to approval is not really a sale until the buyer approves the sample.

- *Type samples* represents a quality agreed with the buyer, expected to be matched in all respects. If you cannot match the sample quality in some respect, tell your buyer sooner rather than later.

- *Indication samples* are an indication of what you expect to be able to ship, usually followed later by an approval sample which shows what you actually propose to ship.

- *Shipment or outturn samples* are fully representative samples of the coffee that has actually been shipped.

# Mainstream quality

Mainstream quality makes up the bulk of the global trade in coffee. Standard type coffees are used by large and medium-sized roasters alike. These roasters have a supply obligation to keep the shelves in supermarkets and other retail stores filled with their product: a product that is always available and that is always the same in terms of appearance and taste. The largest roasters use many millions of bags of such coffee each year. For reasons of blend composition, logistics and simple supply security they cannot depend on just a single origin. Their main requirement therefore is that the supply be reliable, which means such coffees must be relatively easily substitutable and so they must be available from a number of countries.

To satisfy their long-term delivery commitments for roasted coffee, roasters also enter into long-term purchase contracts, usually on the basis 'price to be fixed – buyer's call' (see chapter 9). Such long-term commitments almost inevitably mean the coffee trade sells such coffees short and expects to cover their sales later. Selling short is risky by itself but, as discussed in earlier chapters, most of the risk can be hedged. But selling a single origin short (in quantity and over an extended period) is exceedingly risky in case of later supply difficulties in that origin, so the trade instead sells a 'basket' of acceptable coffees from a number of different origins. For example, 'Guatemala, Prime Washed, and/or El Salvador, Central Standard, and/or Costa Rica, Hard Bean,' against the appropriate delivery months of the New York arabica contract, the 'C'. Or, 'Uganda, Standard Grade, and/or Côte d'Ivoire, Grade 2,' against the LIFFE robusta contract.

The 'baskets' represent coffees that are acceptable for the same purpose in many blends of roasted coffee. Suppliers can fulfil their delivery commitments by providing one of the specified types. Each individual shipment is still subject to the roaster's final approval of quality on arrival, of course.

By coupling the use of these 'baskets' with just-in-time delivery and the often imposed requirement that any coffee not approved on arrival be substituted immediately, one could say that the large roasters have taken most surprises out of the procurement process. All except price; but even here their main objective is *not* to pay more than their competitors, rather than to look for bargains or play the market. Exporters must understand that there is no place for emotion in these buying processes. All that counts is price and performance.

Interestingly, this standardization of quality not only means that below par coffees are not acceptable, but also that coffees of better quality or better bean size are not wanted, and no premiums will be paid. The primary requirements are that the coffee must do for the blend what the roaster expects, and that every shipment is the same. There can be no question of accepting differences in quality, nor of settling such differences through payment of allowances or through arbitration. If the coffee is not right then it will be rejected. Not only must the quality of each delivery be comparable to the previous one, it must also be uniform throughout the entire parcel, from bag to bag and from container to container. *Consistency* is the key.

All that has been said earlier concerning respect for quality applies equally to mainstream or standard grades as well. But, clearly, the quality of such coffees is not as exciting; it would be fair to say that as a rule standard type coffees are not particularly inspiring and offer easily matched cup quality. For standard quality, price is a much more important business factor than it is for exemplary or specialty coffee where quality holds the key. Prices for standard quality are generally also well known so the only way for an exporter to beat the competition is to be more efficient, more reliable, more consistent and more flexible.

There are those who accuse the large-scale roasting sector of gradually lowering the quality of retail coffee through technical innovation and product changes (high-speed, high-yield roasting, steaming of robustas, the introduction of liquid coffee, etc.). Germany is sometimes quoted as an example of shifting quality preferences: in 1990 Colombian mild arabicas and other mild arabicas accounted for 73% of imports, with Colombia as top supplier, but by 2001 Colombian mild arabicas and other mild arabicas were only 49%. The share of Brazilian naturals (27%) and robustas (24%) had risen to 51% and Viet Nam was providing more than the former top supplier, Colombia.

On the other hand, others would argue that there simply is not enough quality coffee in the world to permit today's mega-roasters to raise the quality of standard blends without creating serious price distortions, although other agroindustrial products such as wine appear to cope easily enough with a widely segmented price structure. Also, the demand pattern in some countries is shifting in any case, as in Germany where acidic coffees are said to be in less demand.

Wherever the truth may lie, smaller origins and exporters cannot easily compete for what has become pure bulk commodity business. They have no competitive advantages, and lack the economies of scale of larger players. It is impossible for them to add value because only large quantities of standard products are wanted. Mega-roasters have neither the time nor the inclination to deal with small quantities of exemplary coffees. Some do participate indirectly in the specialty business, but do it through separate business units. Despite the excitement of the specialty market, never overlook the fact that the mainstream business represents 85% or more of world coffee imports and therefore should not be ignored.

# Robusta

## Introduction

*Coffea canephora*, popularly known as robusta because of the hardy nature of the plant, was first discovered in the former Belgian Congo in the 1800s. It is also known to be indigenous to the tropical forests around the Lake Victoria crescent in Uganda. It was introduced into South-east Asia in 1900, after coffee rust disease wiped out all arabica cultivation in Ceylon in 1869 and destroyed most low altitude plantations in Java in 1876. Currently it represents between 30% and 40% of world production. It is grown in West and Central Africa, throughout South-east Asia, and in parts of South America including Brazil, where it is known as *Conillon*.

The robusta plant grows as a shrub or as a small tree up to 10 m in height. Generally, it is planted at lower densities than arabica because of the larger plant size. Robusta exists in many different forms and varieties in the wild. The cross-bred strains of this variety of coffee are often hard to identify, but two main types are generally recognized: *Erecta*, or upright forms, and *Nganda*, or spreading forms.

Robusta is a diploid species. It is a larger bush than the arabica plant, and with robust growth. The root system of robusta, though large, is rather shallow compared to arabica, with the mass of feeder roots being confined to the upper layers of the soil. The leaves are broad, large and pale green in colour. Flowers are white and fragrant, and are borne in larger clusters than in arabica. The flowers open on the seventh or eighth day after receiving rain. Unlike arabica, robusta is self-sterile, that is, its ovule cannot be fertilized with its own pollen and hence cross-pollination is necessary. The cherries are small, but larger in number per node than arabica, varying from 40 to 60 or more. They mature in about 10 to 11 months and are generally ready for harvest two months later than arabica.

Robusta beans are smaller than arabica beans. Depending on the plant strain, the bean shape is round, oval or elliptical with pointed tips. The colour of the beans depends on the method of processing – grey when washed and golden brown when prepared by the dry cherry or natural method of preparation. The caffeine content of robusta beans is nearly twice as high as that of arabica beans (2%–2.5% versus 1.1%–1.5%).

Robusta coffee possesses several useful characteristics such as high tolerance to leaf rust pathogen, white stem borer and nematode invasion, and the potential to give consistent yields. For these reasons, the cost of robusta cultivation is relatively low compared to the arabica variety. On the other hand, inability to endure long drought conditions, late cropping, late stabilization of yields and slightly inferior quality compared to arabica, are some of the negative attributes of robusta coffee.

In general, robusta is hardier than arabica and grows well at low altitudes, in open humid conditions, with the cost of production being lower than the arabica variety. In some countries (Uganda and India, for example) robusta is also cultivated at fairly high altitudes (above 1,200 m) and under shade. These features have helped in the production of dense beans, with better cupping characteristics than those normally expected in the robusta cup, which could aid in the preparation of specialty and possibly exemplary coffees.

The natural wet process helps to mute and mellow the striking notes of fruit and bitterness that are often at the core of the robusta cup. Wet processing helps in developing 'soft buttery notes' in the cup, unlike the thick 'robust' notes that are observed in the average robusta cup. In a number of import markets, quality washed robusta has replaced a percentage of washed arabica in coffee blends. Such robustas have not only provided the froth and bubbles for the much sought after espresso, but have also helped in reducing the price of such blends. Robusta beans with robust but clean notes of strength and fruitiness (but not fermented, i.e. with a neutral liquor) also find ready acceptance in the preparation of soluble coffee.

Note however that the wet processing of robusta is riskier and more difficult because the mucilage in robusta coffee is thicker and stickier than it is in arabica. In some cases fermentation may not be complete even after 72 hours and, considering the high temperatures at the low altitude at which most robusta is grown, the process requires extremely careful monitoring to avoid over-fermentation. Such lengthy fermentation periods also require much more tank space than the average processing facility can economically operate. This has led to the development of frictional stripping of the mucilage, using so-called aqua pulpers. This procedure is costly in terms of power and water consumption and is therefore of little use to small growers and smallholders.

However, the development of small, transportable motorized processing units that combine depulping and frictional mucilage removal with minimal water use is creating new opportunities for smallholders to benefit from the growing demand for wet processed robustas. (For information on one such type of machine go to *www.penagos.com*.)

## Quality evaluation

Defectives and off-tastes found in robusta, and their causes, do not differ markedly from those covered in the preceding section. All the concerns and limitations concerning quality and moisture content already stated are equally valid for robusta coffee, both dry and wet processed. Nevertheless it is appropriate to review some of them in the context of robusta production.

### Defects in robusta coffees

Improper processing techniques, including use of incorrect equipment and improper handling, contribute to defects in quality. In washed robusta the major off-tastes caused by improper processing techniques are raw/green, fruity, overripe, fermented, medicinal, chemical, stinkers, stale, earthy, baggy/oily, spicy and to an extent metallic.

Unwashed robusta coffee is less susceptible to quality deterioration. Off-tastes such as raw/green, fruity/fermented, overripe, medicinal, chemical and stale occur mainly because of negligence during processing.

*Impact of immatures/greens, brown beans, fruity/overripe, fermented and medicinal off-tastes.* Selective picking of cherries is essential for the production of high grade robusta. The quality of the bags or baskets used for collection during harvesting should also be carefully checked. Cherries collected in fertilizer bags or in bags previously used for chemicals could absorb an off-taste, especially when such bags are tightly tied and left unattended for a length of time or directly exposed to strong sunshine.

The *raw/green* off-taste in robusta coffee has been attributed to incorrect harvesting techniques. For economic reasons, selective picking may not be practised. This results in unripe cherries being pulped or dried along with ripe cherries. The *green* or *immature* beans present among the unripe cherries give a raw or green off-taste to the cup.

On the other hand, the presence of *brown beans* and an off-taste of overripe could occur when the cherries have been picked in an overripe or even already dried condition. Where feasible, growers are advised to sort the cherry after picking, to ensure that the coffee to be pulped (or dried in the cherry for natural preparation) does not contain unripe or overripe cherries that lower the cup quality.

'Fermented' and 'medicinal' off-tastes have been observed in natural (dry processed) robusta. The cause for these could be delays in spreading the cherries for drying or the deterioration of overripe cherry. (Late harvesting means general overripeness = poor cups.)

*Causes of pulper-nipped beans/cuts, stinkers, putrid/rotting off-taste.* Invariably, not all coffee cherries will be the same size. If they are not sorted on size, with the help of mechanical cherry sorters, hand sieves or flotation then it is very likely that the beans will be cut during pulping. This can also happen if the pulper has not been suitably adjusted or fitted with flexible chops. Micro-organisms can enter pulper-nipped beans through the injury and cause the formation of stinkers or black beans, adversely affecting quality.

*Causes of earthy, fruity and fermented off-tastes.* The water used for washing, as for all the stages of processing, should be clean to ensure the quality of the end product. Unclean water or water contaminated with fine silt, and recirculated water with a high solid content, could cause earthy, fruity or fermented and other off-tastes.

*Causes of mouldy and faded beans and impact of improper drying and storage:* During the preparation of natural robusta, spreading the cherries in thick layers with no or inadequate stirring and raking could result in *mould* formation. This can adversely affect the visual appearance and the cup quality of the cherry beans. Lack of protection from rain and night dew during drying can also cause mould growth. (For more on this see Quality control issues, later in this chapter.) *The fading (of the colour) of coffee* and the cup being described as stale could be the result of inadequate drying facilities, storage of beans with a high moisture content, or the storage of well dried coffee in improperly ventilated warehouses. Stale cups can also be caused by improper storage on the farm, at the curing factory or at warehouses awaiting sale. Storage of coffee on the drying yards, inadequate covering of coffee stacks, poorly ventilated warehouses, or stacking coffee in a haphazard manner up to the ceiling of the warehouse can all cause a stale off-taste to develop in the cup.

*Spicy and chemical off-tastes* could be due to packaging in poor quality bags or bags in which spices or fertilizers have been packed earlier. Storing coffee with spices, chemicals, fertilizers or fungicides could also cause these off-tastes. Remember that coffee beans readily absorb taints and odours that could lower their aromatic quality and, therefore, value.

### Inspection and classification

Each coffee producing country has its own export presentation system. Whatever form this may take, it is essential to ensure that the coffee offered for sale does not contain excessive amounts of defective beans or foreign matter, and that it is clean in the cup. Some origins and exporters only assess robusta quality visually and do not liquor the coffee. This is to be discouraged: coffee is meant for human consumption and its taste is of paramount importance. The roaster liquors it before using it, so the shipper should liquor it before dispatching it.

**Based on visual quality,** robusta beans could be categorized into three grades: above FAQ (fair average quality), FAQ (average) and below FAQ.

**Above average** coffees would have good colour (grey with a hint of blue when washed and golden brown when unwashed), possess uniformity in size and shape and conform to the prescribed grade specifications, emit a normal smell (cereal-like when washed and fruity when unwashed), and would contain hardly any defectives. The beans would be free of extraneous or foreign matter, mould or toxins, and have a moisture content definitely less than 12.5%.

**Average** coffees would be of a colour that is not faded, conform to the grade description, have no mould or fungal growth and contain a limited proportion of defects that do not adversely affect the cup quality.

**Below average** coffees could be of varying qualities, ranging from beans which have high moisture content and are defective such as broken beans, blacks, browns or extraneous matter, to very poor, bleached and mouldy beans. Remember that coffees with more than 12.5% moisture content should never be shipped, and that many receivers stipulate their own moisture content limits, both at the time of shipment and upon arrival.

**Based on liquor quality,** robusta beans could be classified as follows:

**Fine and special**, where the liquor quality is soft, smooth and buttery, with good body, hardly any bitterness, and clean. This quality can be seen in robusta coffees which are washed and processed with care, in robusta beans which are grown at high altitudes and under shade, and in plant strains which have the inherent characteristics of lower caffeine content, softness and mellow flavour notes.

**Good**, where the liquor quality could be described as good body, neutral, light bitterness, clean, with a hint of chocolate notes.

*Average*, with a cup quality of fair body, fair neutrality, average bitterness, and clean.

*Below average*, where the liquor, though of fair body, has harsh notes of the robusta fruit, is bitter though clean, and is flat with no flavour notes.

*Poor*, a cup which is unclean, having medicinal, phenolic or rioy off notes, or strong harsh robusta notes, with or without body, bitter and unpleasant to the taste.

What has been said above is not a universal methodology followed by all robusta producing origins. It is only a means to explain the quality attributes that could be encountered in a robusta cup and the manner in which these attributes could be classified. Individual buyers have their own classification and evaluation methods, but usually the attributes and ratings will be comparable to those above.

## Specific aspects affecting quality and price

*High moisture content reduces coffee's shelf life.* Beans that are at equilibrium and are inactive would have a moisture content of well below 12.5%. Beans with a high moisture content could be very actively respiring, giving up moisture and undergoing changes both physically and intrinsically. Physically, there would be a fading in colour and, depending on the moisture content, the temperature and the humidity of the surrounding area, the fading could intensify, resulting in bleaching and finally mould growth. Intrinsically, the cup quality could fade from a clean, strong and neutral cup to a 'woody', 'aged' and 'musty' cup.

*Colour.* Poor visual colour, such as a brownish or whitish appearance in washed robusta, or a green shrivelled appearance in unwashed robusta, could result in a low value. The brown appearance of the beans in washed robusta coffee is a direct indication of incorrect processing techniques. In the cup this could result in a fruity or fermented off-taste. The whitish appearance of a consignment would result in heavy discounts for the coffee, as again it reveals both incorrect processing techniques and improper storage conditions.

Greenish shrivelled beans in unwashed coffee reflect improper harvesting techniques; the farmer has stripped the coffee plant of berries that were at different stages of ripening. This visual defect detracts from the cleanliness and quality of a good cup of coffee.

*Bean size* could, to an extent, influence the price that is paid for a consignment of coffee. Large sized beans roast well and could have a better cup profile, provided the processing has been carried out carefully and correctly. Broken beans, on the other hand, could result not only in a high roasting loss, but also in charring of the beans and a poor cup quality. Many robusta producing origins sell their coffee based on the size of the coffee beans and a permissible tolerance to defects, with a classification of AA or grade/type I and so on, each grade denoting the size of the beans and a measured tolerance of certain imperfections.

*The defect count* is the measured presence or absence of defects such as blacks, browns, greens, faded and bleached beans, insect damaged beans, pulper cuts, stinkers, sour beans and extraneous matter such as twigs, sticks or stones. The presence of defects could lower the value of coffee; their absence could result in a premium.

*Cupping or cup quality* would be the final determining factor for purchase or rejection of a consignment and for determining the price. The presence of defects could result in an unclean cup and thus lower the cup quality and price.

## Robusta in espresso and other coffee beverages

Until very recently, the Western hemisphere and many South and Central American countries have been the producers and exporters of specialty coffees. While 75%–80% of specialty coffee exports originate in Central or South America, the Caribbean and Hawaii, and over half the remaining 20%–25% are produced in Africa, Asia's contribution barely exceeds 10%.

Historically, Colombia, Ethiopia, Jamaica and Kenya, which are considered as producers of gourmet coffees, produce only arabica. The North American consumer market, where the specialty phenomenon was born, has so far mostly bought robusta for use only as a filler or for soluble coffee preparation.

Robusta coffees are strong in body and can be neutral and buttery in the cup. There are robusta varieties in Africa, India and Indonesia whose cup quality, when washed, is supremely soft and buttery. This taste profile, with the added attributes of high altitude and fairly low caffeine content, could help in creating designer and premium robusta coffees. (Liquor requirements and the liquoring of coffees for use in espresso blends are different from those used for traditional preparation. See Traditional versus espresso, later in this chapter.)

Using only arabicas limits the diversity of coffees available for consumption. Robusta origins, and the special acceptable tastes inherent to robusta beans, could provide a solution. Price could be an additional reason for creating exemplary and specialty robustas. Robustas are traditionally cheaper than arabicas, so there is an opportunity to develop premium robustas that are less expensive than premium arabicas, thus catering to a new group of consumers.

A point worth mentioning is that on the consumer side there has been no rejection of quality robusta. Even before the birth of the gourmet and specialty coffee phenomenon, select food stores all over the world were offering roasted coffees by origin: monsooned robustas from India, washed robustas from Papua New Guinea, and from Indonesia the famous well washed robusta (originally called in Dutch 'West Indische bereiding' or WIB = West Indian preparation, or pulped), have been very popular. Some have earned the status of being described as exemplary coffees. Increasing consumer awareness of the attractions of top quality robustas will in itself also help to promote such coffees.

Quality robusta can be used in the preparation of today's coffee beverages. Clean and fresh, strong bodied, neutral, with hardly any acidity and with an undercurrent of chocolate and malt notes, *unwashed robustas* can be used in the making of espresso, canned or liquid coffee, and regular or filter coffees. *Well washed, soft robustas* provide the aromatic *crema* for strong espresso, provided they do not show fresh or fruity tastes that can be unpleasantly accentuated by the espresso extraction process. High quality washed robusta coffees are excellent for fortification of milk-based drinks such as cappuccino or *café au lait* (latte), and as a component of high caffeine blends.

However, there are different tasting requirements when using arabica or robusta in espresso. The concentrated espresso cup exaggerates certain sensory aspects, not always positively. Only well matured and absolutely clean cupping coffees can be considered, and their suitability can only definitively be established by submitting the sample to actual espresso extraction. (See Coffee tasting, later in this chapter.)

# Quality control issues[28]

## Introduction

In many producing countries the liberalization of the coffee industry in the 1980s and 1990s meant considerable change in the way coffee was collected, processed and marketed. In some countries the situation went from total control of all aspects of the collection and marketing chain, to virtually no controls at all, referred to by some as anarchy. This is not to say that all

---

28  The information on mycotoxins in this chapter has been drawn from industry experts, from the findings of the ICO/FAO project 'The enhancement of coffee quality by prevention of mould growth', and from the book *Coffee Futures* published by CABI Commodities (2001).

had been well in those tightly controlled coffee industries, but quality did initially suffer in some countries. In recent years the pendulum has swung back and the need for quality standards is once again being recognized.

Quality control at the primary (farm gate) level can assume different forms.

- Government or coffee authorities attempt to 'police' harvesting, on-farm processing and drying. This is costly in terms of qualified staff and does not have a good track record.

- Penalties are imposed for lower than average quality. This is *passive* quality control: it does nothing to encourage better than minimal or average quality.

- Premiums are offered for better than average quality. This is *active* quality control: it rewards and encourages the production of better quality. It can be combined with a refusal to purchase inferior quality but this leaves open the question of what will happen to such coffee.

Different producing countries have differing quality control systems and attach differing values to certain aspects of quality. General information on coffee quality standards can be found at *www.iso.org* (for instance, ISO 10470, a draft defect chart, but there are also many other ISO standards of interest to coffee exporters, including one detailing correct sampling procedures). Information is also available from coffee authorities in producing countries, some of whom are listed in the appendix at the end of this guide.

When setting quality limits one should recognize that without active quality control, such as paying premiums for better quality, the maximum permissible limit (on defects, for instance) quickly becomes the new standard. In setting export taxes care should be taken not to penalize producers of better quality who manage to obtain premium prices as a result of their effort.

## ICO minimum export standards

Internationally, the very low coffee prices that resulted from surplus production in the late 1990s and early 2000s have brought calls for the lowest qualities to be eliminated from the market altogether, and the ICO Council has passed a resolution to this effect. The objective is to halt the export of substandard beans and thereby tighten supply lines in the expectation this will help lift prices. The ICO's Coffee Quality-Improvement Programme calls on producing members to no longer permit, from 1 October 2002, the export of arabica coffee with more than 86 defects per 300 g sample or robusta coffee with more than 150 defects per 300 g. The Programme also asks members not to allow arabica or robusta of any grade to be exported whose moisture content is below 8% or above 12.5%, with the proviso that this should not affect established, good and accepted commercial practice. Thus, where moisture percentages below 12.5% are currently being achieved exporters should endeavour to maintain or decrease these. Exceptions shall be permitted for specialty coffees that traditionally have a high moisture content, such as Indian monsooned coffees, provided such coffees are clearly identified by a specific grade label. (For more see Resolution number 407 of 1 February 2002, on *www.ico.org*.)

The programme's impact is to be reviewed in September 2003. It should be noted though that importing members did not agree to forbid the importation of coffee not meeting the ICO's minimum standard because they considered this might create a two-tier market, rather as happened when ICO export quotas were in force in the 1980s and before. The responsibility for enforcement thus rests mainly on producing countries.

# ISO 9001

ISO 9001 is a process-based quality management system that organizations can use to demonstrate the *consistent quality* of their products to customers and concerned regulatory institutions. Customer satisfaction is then further enhanced through continual improvement of their system. As an example, in an ammunitions factory it would be hopeless to inspect all the bullets manufactured – instead one monitors the *process* used to make them. Similarly one can describe in documented procedures such as production manuals the *process* of converting the fruit of the coffee tree into exportable green bean.

When an organization's quality management system complies with ISO 9001 and when the coffee is processed in accordance with these procedures, then the quality management system (not the product) can be ISO 9001 certified. During cultivation too many variables (weather, diseases, pests) are beyond the control of the producer, and this is why in the case of green coffee the process in the ISO system starts when the cherry is picked, and ends when the container is delivered to the ship's side. This can work for estate coffee that is exported under its own name, but is less easy to apply to smallholder coffee because numerous small deliveries to collection points or washing stations automatically lose their identity. And blended coffee shipped in bulk gains an 'identity' only upon loading.

Nevertheless, good harvesting and processing standards are essential to maintain quality, and ISO 9001 provides those who process their own coffee for export with identification and traceability for all the coffee produced. The batch number can lead back to the day of picking, where on the farm, what the weather was then, how long it took to dry the coffee, how well it was dried, and a number of other variables – all useful information in determining the cause of any quality problems that may subsequently arise. Perhaps none of this provides any immediate or direct economic advantage, but estate growers using the system say they have become better processors and are better able to provide the sort of quality guarantees that the larger commercial roasters demand. (For details go to *www.iso.org*.)

However, by themselves the ICO and ISO objectives do not provide answers to the ever more stringent food legislation being introduced at the consumer end, and the potential impact of this on coffee exporters.

# Hazard Analysis Critical Control Points – HACCP

The scope of quality control in developed countries has expanded enormously in recent years. Today it encompasses not just the traditional commercial concerns with 'quality' but also all food health and hygiene concerns associated with modern consumerism. Coffee is part of the modern food chain and health concerns are increasingly shaping quality controls at the receiving end.

Gone are the days of settling claims on mould or contamination damage 'internally' through the payment of a simple allowance. Not only may customs and health authorities in consuming countries order the destruction of 'hazardous' parcels, but they will also trace responsibility back to the source: the country, the shipper and even the individual grower. Relatively light-hearted sounding phrases such as tracking and tracing food products from *farm to fork*, *stable to table* or *plough to plate* are, in fact, the political outcome of consumer pressure. People want to know their food is safe and if one particular sector of the food industry is found to pose a problem, then all other sectors are affected as well.

Food health and hygiene concerns are relatively easily addressed in developed countries. The difficulty for developing nations is that the resultant procedures and regulations are then applied equally to food crops imported into developed countries. The import trade is increasingly passing such consumer-imposed food chain management issues on to exporting countries that, in most instances, have to find the answers or lose the business. A particular food safety issue for coffee is concern over the presence in foods and beverages of ochratoxin A (OTA), a mycotoxin that is believed to cause kidney damage. OTA is a probable human renal carcinogen (cancer producing substance – IARC evaluation Class 2B). Although the toxicological status of OTA has not yet been settled, importing countries are increasingly paying attention to its occurrence in coffee and other products and are requiring the adoption of preventative measures.

HACCP is a management system in which food safety is addressed through the analysis and control of biological, chemical and physical hazards from raw food material production to manufacturing and consumption. It involves seven principles.

1. Analyse hazards, for instance microbiological (e.g. bacteria, viruses, moulds, toxins), chemical (e.g. pesticide residues), or physical (stones, wood, glass etc).

2. Identify critical control points. These are points in the food's production (from raw to processed to consumption) at which a potential hazard can be controlled or eliminated.

3. Establish preventative measures with critical limits (values) for each control point, such as a minimum drying time to ensure mould growth cannot progress.

4. Establish procedures to monitor the critical control points (e.g. how to ensure that adequate drying occurs).

5. Establish corrective actions to be taken when monitoring shows that a critical limit has not been met, such as disposing of potentially contaminated cherry.

6. Establish procedures to verify that the system is working properly. For example, test drying facilities for leaks or contamination.

7. Establish effective record keeping to document the HACCP system, such as records of hazards and control methods, the monitoring of safety requirements and actions taken to correct potential problems.

Most enterprises in the coffee chain, including coffee producers and exporters, will at some point need to apply controls to guarantee product safety. These are usually represented in a concise process flow diagram with underlined points where hazards may occur. This must be documented in a HACCP plan, and also any discrepancies found, and the counter-measures taken to correct them, must be registered. In 2002 European Union food business operators were already being obliged to implement HACCP systems on the basis of existing legislation (Council Directive 93/43/EEC on the hygiene of foodstuffs). Of course, many food processors and their suppliers have always had stringent quality controls that, in practice, were close to a HACCP system. The difference now is that a HACCP system requires a detailed description that can be subject to verification by food safety authorities. For example, supplying an inferior grade of green coffee that is otherwise sound is a quality issue, and does not necessarily represent a food hazard. But a mouldy coffee does.

Control points can be divided into two groups. The main group includes all those points where certain controls have to be applied and where loss of control may result in *a low probability* of a health risk. These are known as control points, or CP. The other group includes a very few points where loss of control may result in *a high probability* of illness. These are known as critical control points, or CCP. For example, quickly passing a critical stage in the coffee drying process seems like a vital critical point in the HACCP system.

Both HACCP and GAP (or Good Agricultural Practice – there is also GMP or Good Manufacturing Practice) are quality assurance systems but they have different approaches. HACCP concentrates on a few critical points whereas GAP tries to make all-round improvements. GAP is easier to set up but does not necessarily zero in on the most important steps that influence the occurrence or avoidance of toxins in coffee. See *www.cfsan.fda.gov* and search under HACCP for a good introduction to the subject.

The two processes are complimentary in that GAP will improve coffee quality, whereas HACCP will provide the type of disciplined monitoring and control that supermarket chains and food manufacturers increasingly demand. More importantly, it is only through the HACCP process that one can establish where OTA enters the system and where the fungi causing OTA first appear. This is essential if one is to meet European Union and presumably in due course also United States requirements for the reduction and prevention of OTA contamination.

*Imports of coffee into the United States* are all subject to inspection by the United States Food and Drug Administration (FDA) under the provisions of the Federal Food, Drug and Cosmetic Act. To pass for importation coffee must be free of unapproved pesticide residues, have had no or only limited exposure to insect infestation in the field, and be free of all chemical and other contamination including mould and live insects. Insect damage by itself, pinholes for example, exceeding 10% may also lead to rejection. The Green Coffee Association (GCA) contracts routinely contain the clause 'no pass – no sale' which puts the responsibility for passing the FDA inspection firmly on the exporter.

The tragic events of 11 September 2001 catapulted both domestic and imported food security into top priority in the United States, with consequent strengthening of FDA surveillance of imported foods. This is visibly demonstrated by much stricter FDA and Customs inspection of coffee containers and even coffee samples, and the distribution of an FDA Food Security Preventative Measures Guidance circular to food importing operations. These measures also include a large 'track and trace' element. For more information on all this and FDA coffee regulations go to *www.cfsan.fda.gov*. Also, ask for the information booklet 'Health and Safety in the Importation of Green Coffee into the United States' from the National Coffee Association of the United States.

# Potential hazards in the coffee trade

*Mycotoxins* are caused by contamination by some naturally occurring moulds. Not every type of mould produces mycotoxins. Mycotoxins are 'selective' in the sense that a given type of mycotoxin occurs in specific foodstuffs: aflatoxins in peanuts, grains and milk; patulin in apple juice; ochratoxin A (OTA) in grains, grapes and derived products, beans and pulses, cocoa, coffee and others. For coffee OTA is the most relevant mycotoxin, but in the framework of an HACCP system it is recommended to envisage measures for mycotoxins in general.

The initial contamination of coffee with OTA takes place through spores in the air and in the ground. These spores may produce a mould but only if the right circumstances (humidity and temperature) prevail. The importance of proper moisture management throughout the entire processing and supply chain cannot be overemphasized. Farmers, middlemen and exporters should also be aware that in a shipment of coffee OTA contamination (mould) may be very localized, making sampling extremely complex. Careful inspection of visual appearance and any mouldy or earthy smells can be a useful tool for checking.

*Pesticide residues* in coffee have only very rarely exceed the limit values so far, but this does not mean that their monitoring is not a vital aspect of an HACCP system. It is absolutely essential that coffee growers maintain *chemical registers* that detail, in chronological order, the type and quantities of all chemicals used and the timing of their application. Obviously only chemicals that have been approved for use on coffee may be used and then only within the withholding limits specified by the manufacturers. Exporters and shipping lines must ensure only clean containers are used, thus avoiding cross-contamination by previous cargoes.

(See the Draft Code of Hygienic Practice for the Transport of Foodstuffs in Bulk and Semi-packed Foodstuffs of the Codex Alimentarius Commission at *www.codexalimentarius.net.*)

**Hydrocarbon contamination** is usually caused by jute coffee bags because of the 'batching oil' used to soften the jute fibres before spinning. There have been instances of contaminated oil being used (old engine oil for example). The International Jute Organization has established specifications (IJO Standard 98/01) for the manufacture of jute bags to be used in the food industry:

- *Analytical criteria.* Ingredients used as batching oils must be non-toxic and approved for use in packaging materials that will come into contact with food. Batching oils must not contain compounds that could produce off-flavours or off-tastes in food packed in jute or sisal bags.

- *Chemical criteria.* The amount of unsaponifiable compounds (which cannot be converted into soap by boiling with alkali) shall be less than 1250 mg/kg. The method described in British Standard 3845:1990 is recommended for the determination of the added oil content of jute yarn, rove and fabric. Method 2.401 of the International Union of Pure and Applied Chemistry (IUPAC) is recommended for determining unsaponifiable matter.

- *Organoleptic criteria.* Jute bags shall be analysed for their olfactory qualities. No undesirable odours, or odour untypical of jute, shall be present. No unacceptable odours shall develop after artificial ageing of the sacks. The ageing procedure to be followed shall be the one described in European Standard EN 766 for use on sacks for the transport of food. To read the EU Packaging and Packaging Waste Directive (PPWD) go to *www.europa.eu.int/scadplus/scad_en.htm* (look under official publications: EUR-Lex).

Organizations and private companies in India and Bangladesh have developed a hydrocarbon-free lubricant, based on vegetable oil, to soften the jute fibre. It is a non-toxic, biodegradable oil, and bags made with it can be classified as food grade bags. However, the fact that vegetable oil is used for batching is in itself not sufficient: the oil used must be stable and may not turn rancid.


## Mould and prevention – OTA

Mould is undesirable in any product, and coffee is no exception. In recent years mould in coffee has increasingly become associated with concerns over the presence in food and beverages of ochratoxin A (OTA). The toxicological status of OTA has not yet been settled but importing countries are nevertheless paying increasing attention to its occurrence in coffee and other agricultural products, and are requiring preventative measures. It may be safely assumed that in a few years all major coffee consuming countries will apply such measures. For this reason in December 2000 the ICO sponsored a US$ 5.5 million project, funded by CFC and managed by FAO, to establish guidelines for mould prevention throughout the supply chain. The project will be completed in 2004, and by early 2002 a number of good practice guidelines had already been disseminated and training of extension workers had commenced.

Extensive sampling and testing are already ongoing in a number of consuming countries. The Nestlé Research Center in Lausanne, Switzerland, has developed a rapid TLC (thin-layer chromatographic) screening method for detecting OTA in green coffee that is rapid, simple, robust and very cheap, which makes it particularly well adapted for implementation in producing countries. For more information on this see the *Journal of Agricultural and Food Chemistry*, issue 50, pages 243-7 (2002). For a source of testing equipment go to *www.vicam.com.*

In the European Union a decision on whether to impose limits on coffee and coffee products is likely to be taken before the end of 2003, and the United States and Japan are unlikely to lag far behind. In the meantime Finland, Germany, Greece, Italy, the Netherlands and Spain impose their own, national, limits. (For the full EU Regulation on OTA go to *www.europa.eu.int/eur-lex/en/index.html*; look for Commission Regulation No 472/2002 of 12 March 2002 in the *Official Journal of the European Communities* L75 dated 16 March 2002, page 18.) The danger is that once a producing country is identified publicly as a potential source of OTA contamination, the reputation and marketability of its coffee are likely to suffer, with obvious consequences. Italy has already established a system to identify 'high risk' origins. Identification of a shipment with an excessive OTA level automatically results in the producing country being placed on a 'high risk' list, and it will be removed again only once a number of 'clean' shipments have been received.

A further issue is how green coffee would be sampled for OTA. As yet there is no universally agreed OTA related sampling and testing method for coffee and the danger is that individual countries will establish their own individual procedures. It is in everyone's interest that sampling and testing procedures are standardized worldwide, including producing countries, and that adequate preventative measures are taken in producing countries since it is there that the problem can be addressed at source.

*The importance of this cannot be stressed enough. It is not at all impossible that at some stage the well known United States contract condition 'no pass no sale' will also be introduced for coffees shipped to Europe and elsewhere, with 'no pass' possibly leading to destruction of the goods.*

OTA is produced by fungi of the *Aspergillus* genus (*A. ochraceus, A. carbonarius, A. niger*). In coffee it is mostly concentrated in the husk, which suggests that naturals (coffees dried in the cherry) are most at risk of contamination. Identified factors affecting mycotoxin levels in the coffee chain include:

- Environmental factors: temperature, moisture, mechanical injury (insect or bird damage, micro-organisms);

- Harvesting factors: crop maturity, temperature, moisture;

- Storage: temperature, moisture;

- Distribution and processing: condensation;

Studies[29] have shown that inadequate sun drying of cherries leads to OTA formation in the pods and parchment husks, and that defectives (including black beans), pods and husks (and dust) are the most important sources of OTA contamination in green coffee. The drying stage is the most favourable time for the development of OTA. Adequate drying to uniformly low moisture levels and avoiding local wet spots, caused for example by uneven drying, rewetting or condensation, is crucial in prevention. Simple and cheap devices for solar drying of coffee can be of great help in improving drying practices, including prevention of rewetting by rain or dew.

The preventative steps below apply as much to wet processed coffees as they do to dry processed (natural) arabica and robusta. Good housekeeping is essential. Prevention is currently the only available effective way at farm level to combat OTA.

### Prevention during harvest

- Cover the soil below the trees with clean plastic during picking to prevent cherries coming into contact with dirt or soil, or getting mixed with old, mouldy cherries left behind from previous picking rounds or the previous season.

---

29   Useful websites include *www.ncbi.nlm.gov, www.fao.org* and *www.europa.eu.int.*

- Do not use cherries that have been in contact with bare earth – they are susceptible to developing mould growth.

- Process fresh cherry as soon as possible: either pulp them or commence drying on the day they are picked. Do not store fresh cherry, especially if fully ripe or overripe, as such storage promotes mould growth; do not hold cherry in bags.

- Never dry on bare earth, because mould spores remain in the soil and can contaminate cherry. Use mats, trays or tarpaulins. Raised drying tables, allowing air circulation, remain one of the most effective drying systems though.

- During the first two to three days of drying ensure the layer is as thin as possible to speed the process. After this, the layer of drying cherry should not be more than 4 cm (1½ in) thick. Drying cherry should constantly be raked and turned, and should be covered at night and during rainfall.

- Never allow partly or wholly dried cherry to get wet again: protect it at all times against rain, morning dew and accidental wetting.

## Prevention during wet processing

- Dispose of pulp from wet processing away from drying or clean coffee. Compost it before using as mulch in the field.

- Pulp on day of picking. Separate floaters and control water quality.

- Remove pulp and skins from parchment. Sanitize equipment daily.

- Skin dry wet parchment to remove water quickly. If necessary remove excess water with forced drying. Then dry the parchment slowly to avoid cracking. Turn regularly; do not spread more than 4 cm (1½ inch) thick.

- Remove any pods and skins from the parchment by hand.

- Use drying mats or drying tables where possible. Never dry on bare earth, because mould spores remain in the soil and can cause contamination. Use mats, trays or tarpaulins. Again, raised drying tables, allowing air circulation, remain one of the most effective drying systems.

## Prevention during dry processing

- Site the dry processing or hulling plant in a dry area, away from swamps.

- Do not buy or process wet coffee. If you must, then keep it separate and dry it immediately and correctly.

- Keep equipment and buildings clean. Do not allow dust and husk to accumulate and so contaminate clean (green) coffee.

- Ensure clean coffee contains *no husk*: more than 90% of mould originates from the husk of sun-dried cherry. Remove also dust, mouldy beans, unhulled cherries (pods) and so forth.

- Avoid adding husk or pods on purpose (in order to reach a maximum permitted defect level in the specification).

- Use only clean, dry bags for storage. Always keep cleaned coffee in a separate area, well closed off from the hulling area and the waste husk disposal site.

- Ideally moisture content should be even throughout. Use correctly calibrated moisture meters and ensure all meters are recalibrated at the start of each season.[30] See also Preventing condensation, below.

- The risk of fungi growth is at its strongest when coffee is stored with a moisture content of over 12.5% (ISO 6673) and at high temperatures (over 25°C).

- Cover bags during transport to avoid any chance of rewetting. Load and offload only during dry weather or under cover. Store in well ventilated, leak-proof warehouses. Always store away from walls and on pallets to allow ventilation and avoid storm water damage.

Obvious indicators of potential OTA presence in green coffee include wet or mouldy bags or beans, the presence of husks and pods, an earthy or mouldy smell, and earthy notes in the cup itself.

> *The ICO agreed method of moisture content analysis is ISO standard 6673: heating at 105°C during 16 hours, or moisture measuring equipment calibrated to the same standard. The sampling method referred to in ISO 6673 is ISO 4072. For details go to www.iso.org.*

### Preventing condensation during shipment

Condensation occurs because moisture is always present in the air and hygroscopic (water-attracting) materials such as coffee normally contain a certain amount of moisture as well. Coffee with a moisture content in excess of 12.5% (ISO 6673) should *never* be shipped, whether in containers or bagged, as beyond this point the risk of condensation and therefore fungi growth occurring becomes unacceptably high. Under ICO minimum export standards, the only exceptions could be specialty coffees that traditionally have a high moisture content, such as Indian monsooned coffees.

This is not to suggest that a moisture content of 12.5% is commercially acceptable for all coffee – for certain coffees, certain origins and certain buyers it is definitely not. The figure of 12.5% simply represents a known technical point at which the risk of damage from condensation and growth of mould during storage and transport becomes unacceptably high. *Shippers who normally ship their coffee at moisture percentages below 12.5% should definitely continue to do so.*

An increasing number of buyers now include a maximum permissible arrival moisture content in purchasing contracts. Increasing preoccupations with food health and hygiene in consuming countries suggest strongly that exporters will be well advised therefore to acquaint themselves with their buyers' requirements in this regard.

#### Bagged coffee in containers

Condensation cannot always be avoided but it is possible to avoid or reduce damage by observing these basic precautions.

- Containers must be technically impeccable: watertight; free of holes and free of corrosion on the roof or sides; intact door locks, rubber and sealing devices. They must always be swept clean and must be dry and odourless.

---

30 Websites where information on moisture meters can be obtained include *www.sinar.co.uk*, *www.farmcomp.fi/index.html*, *www.enercorp.com*, *www.agric.gov.ab.ca/index.html*, *www.decagon.com/aqualab/* and *www.geobirksales.com*.

- When stuffing takes place at the shipper's premises the shipper must inspect the containers. An inspector should go inside the container and close the doors. If *any* daylight is visible the container must be rejected immediately. Also check that all rubber door seals are whole and tight.

- The actual stuffing of the container should take place under cover, just in case a rain shower occurs during that time. Bags should be sound: no leaking, slack or torn bags; no wet bags; no stained bags.

- The saddle stow (see chapter 5, Logistics) is the best way to stow bags in a container as it minimizes air circulation between the bags and so reduces transport of moisture to cold spots (on roof or walls). Containers should never be filled to absolute capacity – always leave sufficient room above the stow.

- Best practice is to line the container with cardboard (ideal) or two layers of kraft paper, preferably corrugated, with the corrugation facing the steel structure, so bags do not come in contact with unexposed metal from the container. When stuffing is complete, fit a double layer of kraft paper on top of the bags all the way to the floor in the doorway. This will ensure that the paper will, at least partly, absorb any condensation from the roof. Note that although *dry bags* are meant to absorb moisture during the voyage they should only be used with the express prior permission of the receiver. Many receivers do not permit their use under any circumstances.

- Experience shows that most of the condensation problems encountered during maritime transport are caused at origin (containers are stuffed too early ahead of actual shipment, or not properly lined), or immediately after offloading (particularly for containers arriving in winter). It is therefore of utmost importance to limit both transit times and the dwell or intermediate storage periods and land legs of the transit as much as possible.

- When making a booking with the carrier always give the instruction 'stow away from heat, cool stow and sun/weather protected'. The term 'stow under deck' is no longer appropriate for modern container vessels.

### Bulk coffee in containers

Recent years have seen a substantial increase in the movement of coffee in bulk, using normal dry containers fitted with a liner. One advantage is the savings for shippers on the cost of bags (and no need to dispose of them at the receiving end), of course minus the cost of the liner. But there are other, not always immediately apparent advantages.

Coffee shipped in bulk, using normal dry containers fitted with a liner, always arrives in a better condition than coffee in bags when shipped under similar conditions. Shipping in bulk avoids most of the problems associated with bagged cargo: no baggy smells, no weight losses due to handling, generally better preservation of quality.

Air caught inside the closed liner is called interstitial air. Interstitial air in a bulk load hardly moves since the individual beans are obstructing the free flow of air, and so the hot air cannot easily move to the edge. As a result there is less transport of moisture to the roof and walls and the risk of condensation is thereby reduced.

Provided correct liners and procedures are used, and the coffee is shipped at *the correct moisture content*, then the incidence of claims on bulk cargo is vastly reduced compared to bagged cargo, according to some by as much as two-thirds.

The general principles for choosing a container are the same as when shipping bagged coffee (see above).

# Coffee tasting (liquoring)

Coffee quality is assessed in terms of the green appearance, the roast appearance, and by taste (cup or liquor), as described earlier in this chapter. The latter two aspects are deserving of more detail.

## The roast

Coffee quality is greatly influenced by the roasting process. Dark roasts tend to obscure the finer aspects but enhance the body. Light roasts emphasize acidity but result in a weaker brew. (See the Agtron system of roast colour measurements earlier in this chapter.) The degree of roasting depends therefore on one's marketing objectives. From the professional taster's point of view, it is easier to detect quality and any off-flavours when coffee is roasted lighter rather than darker. A light roast also makes it easier to spot immature and green beans, which tend to show up as yellowish pale in colour rather than brown when roasted. All pales affect the cup quality but extreme cases of pales (bright yellow beans) spoil the cup by giving it a *quakery* or *peanut* taste.

The roast of naturals (sun-dried coffees) tends to lack the bright whitish centre cuts of wet-processed arabicas. In general, dull roasts also suggest imperfectly processed or aged coffees, whereas bright roasts indicate freshness and good processing. The following descriptions are commonly used:

● **Fine roast.** Bright, brilliant, uniform and even, no pales.

● **Good to fine.** Bright, uniform, even, no pales.

● **Good roast.** Bright to dullish, reasonably even, occasional pale, no other defects such as ears or brokens.

● **Good to fair.** Dullish, slightly uneven, mottled, a few pales and other defects, can be soft and open.

● **Fair to poor.** Dull and uneven, a number of pales and other defects, generally soft and open, often containing many brokens.

● **Poor.** Anything below fair to poor.

Uneven bean size produces uneven roasts because small, broken and light beans roast faster than whole and solid beans. Very small pieces or chips may even burn up altogether. Some roasters prefer to roast coffees from different origins separately and then to combine them afterwards. Strong growth in the specialty and whole bean segments of the consumer market has rekindled the emphasis on a coffee's roast appearance, and at the retail end the roast is perhaps the first thing the consumer really looks at.

## The cup or liquor

The cup remains the most important determinant of a coffee's usefulness and value. All exporters grade coffee visually, by size and defect count, but not all cup test. Only the cup can reveal a coffee's true value, however, and exporters who cannot taste cannot bargain as equals with importers and roasters who *always* taste.

Taste is a highly subjective matter and different tasters or liquorers will have different opinions on the quality, appeal and value of a particular cup or liquor. There are no international cupping standards and nor is the terminology standardized. This adds to the subjectivity. Coffee tasting and wine tasting are comparable: both are done to determine quality, usefulness and price.

See the glossary at the end of this chapter for a review of some of the descriptive terms generally used in the coffee industry. As a rule of thumb, cup characteristics can be loosely characterized in the following ways:

**Robustas.** Mostly supplied as unwashed, sun-dried or naturals. Taste varies from *neutral* to *coarse with strong robusta flavour*. Neutral coffees are preferred for blending whereas those with strong robusta flavour are particularly suitable for soluble coffee. Well-prepared pulped and washed robustas are appreciated for their good body and neutral taste and the absence of off-flavours.

**Washed arabicas.** The most appreciated are those with a well-balanced (rounded) cup where good acidity and body, together with some flavour or aroma, complement each other. Marks for acidity range from *pronounced* through *good, fair* and *slight* to *lacking*; for body from *heavy* through *good, medium* and *light* to *lacking*; and for flavour from *excellent* through *good, some* and *slight* to *lacking*.

**Unwashed arabicas or naturals.** This group (mainly Brazils, Ecuadors and sun-dried Ethiopians) tends to have less well balanced body and acidity. Ecuadors are often fruity and occasionally sourish. Brazils frequently have a harsh or Rio taste, especially coffees grown in certain zones of the states of Esperito Santo, São Paolo and Rio de Janeiro. Unwashed Brazils that are free from Rio or Rio taint are known as *soft* or *strictly soft* and command a premium over *hard* or *Rioish* and *Rio-type* coffees.

**Pulped Brazils.** This is a relatively new form of coffee from Brazil in which the cherry is pulped immediately after harvesting and is then sun-dried, so without fermentation or washing as in the normal wet process. Such coffees tend to combine good body with a sweeter cup than is found in traditional Brazils that are dried in the cherry. These coffees are making inroads into the traditional market for secondary mild arabicas.

## The coffee liquorer

Most people can acquire the liquoring technique, but it takes years of on-the-job training in the liquoring rooms of exporters, importers and roasters. Exporters must understand the preoccupations of the roasters, and a top liquorer will have experience of both sides of the 'divide'. Trading quality coffee is *impossible* without liquoring expertise. It is surprising that not all producing countries offer formal training courses and official recognition to coffee professionals.

The liquorer's first objective is to determine if a coffee is acceptable in terms of type and standard. The less sophisticated the standard the easier it is to approve a coffee. But when it comes to better coffees then it is not only *acceptability* but also *marketability* that count. The liquorer must be able to assess not only a coffee's marketability and potential usage, but also its price range.

- *Marketability.* Who can use this? Who wants this? Know your markets and know your buyers. Travel and cup test with them.

- *Price.* What will they pay for this? Know the quality your competitors supply. Know what other origins offer. Again, travel, attend tradeshows, visit roasters. It is only by cupping your coffee against that of others that you can assess which has the advantage.

## Traditional versus espresso

Following the introduction of soluble coffee in the 1950s, the next major change at the consumer level was the introduction of the home coffee maker, the drip machine. This tended to split the market into roast and ground for those preferring convenience, and whole bean roasted for those who prefer to grind their own coffee at home. The next major change has probably been the huge inroads made by espresso in importing countries during the 1990s. Most coffee bars and cafés in the United States, Europe and Asia today have extended their product menu to include different types of espresso coffee.

Traditionally, coffee tasting has been done on the premise that the coffee would be used as soluble, roast and ground or whole bean. This permitted more or less the same methodology and terminology to be used to evaluate the quality. But there are significant differences between the brewing processes of traditional coffee and espresso, so much so that traditional liquoring alone cannot provide a correct evaluation of a coffee's suitability for use as espresso.

The steps before tasting the liquid coffee are always the same (examining the green and the roast, smelling the ground coffee and so on). For traditional tasting, about 10 g of ground coffee is brewed in cups containing about 230 g of boiling water. This is not a scientific process: the water temperature may vary, the weight is not always exactly 10 g and the water measure may not always be exactly right either. The temperature of the water changes as the cups are poured and so on. But experienced cup testers know all this and so will taste more than a single cup per sample. They may also taste the sample various times. In the end it is the cup tester's personal assessment of all the different factors and sensations that determines what they will do with the sample in question. In real life consumers do not use a scientific process to prepare or evaluate their coffee either. They like it or they do not, and it is the cup tester's job to make sure they do.

But this method does not work for espresso. The espresso cup is a concentrated beverage, which can be said to exaggerate all the aromas, and fragrances found in the coffee bean.

Unlike the traditional coffee served in many bars and hotels, espresso must always be fresh. It can only be made on demand: the customer has to wait for the coffee, not the other way around. It was the desire to supply many cups of fresh coffee quickly and efficiently that led to a major innovation for traditional brewing systems: Italian inventors introduced the use of water pressure to speed up the extraction process.

Today making espresso is a mixture of art and science. Italy is home to a large and fast-growing manufacturing and export business not only of espresso machines and all the accompanying accessories, but also of espresso coffee roasted and packed in Italy. Names such as Illy and Lavazza are but two of many found all over the world; they are even found in producing countries. The introduction of the espresso pod (pre-packed dosages of coffee ready for use 'as is' in the espresso machine), the growth of specialty coffee chains such as Starbucks, and increasingly efficient mini espresso machines for home use have all contributed to Italy's spectacular growth as a coffee processing and exporting centre.

### *What are the differences the coffee liquorer has to watch?*

Espresso is a brew obtained by percolation of hot, not boiling, water under pressure through a cake of roasted ground coffee. The energy of the water pressure is spent within the cake.[31] The pressure accentuates taste aspects that are not immediately obvious in cups prepared in the traditional way. Sharp acidity turns into bitterness, freshness or slight fruitiness turns into sourness and fruity turns into fermented because all the flavour components are extracted. And this is not all: espresso is nearly always sugared, and the interaction of sugar and these intense flavours can again alter the final taste palette the taster encounters. Some flavours benefit, others are 'turned' and become negative.

For example, a pleasant tasting coffee that is slightly winey may be eminently suitable for sale as an exemplary quality in a niche market. But it will probably never make the grade for espresso, because once concentrated, the same winey flavour may turn into something quite unpleasant.

---

**31**   From *Espresso Coffee* by Andrea Illy and Rinantonio Viani, Academic Press, London, 1995.

The other aspect to bear in mind is the foam or *crema* that is always present in every well made cup of espresso. Briefly, the machine pressure is allowed to drop which permits the cup to be filled. The drop in pressure releases dissolved gases into the cup and this is what produces the foam. The foam must survive at least a few minutes before breaking up and starting to show the dark surface of the liquid itself. A perfect espresso looks as good as it tastes.

Some coffees produce excellent foam; others do not. Most espresso coffee is therefore a blend of different coffees that together produce the desired combination of both taste and cup appearance.

Green coffee exporters wanting to supply the important espresso market on a sustained basis must familiarize themselves with the differences between their traditional cupping and the basics of espresso liquoring. Better still, they should practise espresso liquoring alongside their traditional cupping by acquiring the necessary equipment.

## Annex

# Glossary of commonly used coffee classification terms

**Green or raw coffee**

| | |
|---|---|
| Ambers | Smooth yellowish beans caused by soil conditions. |
| Antestia-damaged | Beans damaged by the Antestia bug, resulting in black depressions on the bean which is often completely shrivelled. |
| Black beans | Caused by harvesting immature beans or gathering them after they have dropped to the ground. Blacks are often taken as the yardstick for rating a defect count. |
| Blackish beans | Pulper-nipped beans which have partly oxidized. |
| Bleached beans | Colourless beans, often caused by drying too rapidly or over-drying. Also known as soapy and faded beans, usually associated with mechanical drying. |
| Blotchy beans | The result of uneven drying. |
| Broca-damaged beans | Beans partially eaten away by an insect (*Stephanoderes hampei*) which bores galleries through the bean. |
| Brown beans | Brown in colour. May be caused by faulty fermentation, improper washing or over drying – *see also* 'foxy'. |
| Coated beans | Beans to which the silverskin adheres. Caused by drought, over-bearing or harvesting of unripe cherries (*see also* 'softs' under Roasted coffee, below, and 'common' and 'harsh', under Liquor, below). |
| Crushed beans | Pulper-damaged beans, which often split and fade. Also caused by manual pounding of dry cherry to separate beans from husk (*pilonnage* in French). |
| Discoloured beans | Often pulper-damaged. Other causes are contact with earth, metal and foul water as well as damage after drying and beans left over in fermenting tanks (*see also* 'stinkers'). |
| Drought-affected beans | Either coated or misshapen, pale and light in weight. |
| Dull, unnatural coloured beans | Due to faulty drying, often associated with metal contamination. |
| Ears | Part of a broken *elephant* bean. |
| Earthy beans | Smell of earth, caused by collecting beans fallen on bare ground. |
| Elephant beans | A generic aberration resulting in two beans being joined together – usually deformed and likely to break up during processing/roasting (*see also* 'ears', above). |
| Faded beans | Beans from old crop or dried too rapidly. |

| | |
|---|---|
| Flaky beans | Usually very thin, light and ragged (*see also* 'drought-affected', 'lights' and 'ragged'). |
| Floats or floaters/lights | Under-developed, hollow beans – the fruit will float in water and is 'floated off' during wet processing. In washed coffee a sign of inadequate grading during wet processing. |
| Foxy beans | Rust or reddish coloured, a result either of harvesting overripe, sometimes yellow, cherries, delays in pulping, improper fermentation or faulty washing. |
| Green, water-damaged | Self-explanatory – usually brought about by dry parchment or hulled coffee becoming wet. |
| Hail-damaged beans | Show blackish circular marks on the oval side of the bean. |
| Light bean | Bean the specific weight of which is below normal – caused by drought or die-back. |
| Mottled beans | Are blotched, spotty or stained. Usually due to uneven drying. |
| Musty (mouldy) beans | Partial or wholly discoloured, whitish fur-like colour and texture (*see also* 'musty', under Liquor, below). Show mould growth visible by the naked eye or evidence of mould attack. |
| Overripe | Brownish-yellow appearance; also known as *foxy*. |
| Peaberry | A single oblong or ovaloid roundish bean – a result of only one bean developing in a cherry instead of the usual two. |
| Pulper-nipped | Bean damaged by incorrect setting of the pulping knives – can become discoloured through oxidation during fermentation and may produce off-flavours. |
| Quakers | Blighted and undeveloped beans – show up as roast defects. |
| Ragged | This description often refers to drought-affected beans – harvesting a mixture of mature and immature cherries results in beans having a ragged appearance. |
| Stinkers | Beans which are over-fermented owing to improper cleaning of pulpers, fermenting tanks and washing channels. |
| Three-cornered beans | Semi-peaberry in character. |
| Withered | Light and shrivelled beans caused by drought or poor husbandry. |

**Note**: The exporters/traders/roasters' technical vocabulary contains many more terms such as sticks, stones, pods (cherry), parchment, under-dried, under-fermented, etc. These are, however, all self-explanatory.

## Roasted coffee

| | |
|---|---|
| Brilliant, bright | Extremely bright, appears to have an oil-like surface. |
| Brokens | Self-explanatory. Presence of small elephant beans which always break apart during roasting. |
| Burnt | Over-roasted. |
| Centre cut | The dividing line of silverskin running through the flat side of the bean. |
| Chaff | Silverskin that peels off during roasting. |
| Dullish, dull | Lacking lustre. Associated with processing and age. |
| French roast | The beans are roasted high enough to bring the natural oils to the surface. |
| Hard | A desirable roast with a dark grain which, when crushed or ground, gives the full and desirable aroma of coffee. |
| Italian roast | Beans roasted a degree darker than the French roast. (This is for Europe; in the United States the French roast is darker.) |
| Mottled | Mottled beans are caused by uneven drying. They are not always too detrimental to cupping when the coffee is fresh, but coffee of this type will not keep long and deteriorates in transit. |
| Mailliard Effect | Name of the chemical transformation that takes place within the beans during roasting. |
| Open | An open bean is one in which the centre cut is inclined to split on roasting. Some open beans derive from lighter coffee; of these, some can be eliminated in the washing channel, and some by air or gravity separators at the mill. However all open beans are not necessarily light coffee. Also typical of coffee grown at lower altitudes. |
| Ordinary | Self-explanatory. |
| Pales and semi-pales | Yellow in colour, they may stink when crushed or ground. Pales come from immature or drought-affected coffee and are beans with little or no grain. These can largely be eliminated in the washing channel. Amber beans and green parchment beans also frequently cause pales in the roast. |
| Ragged or deformed | Ugly misshapen beans, semi-elephants, and drought-affected coffee. |
| Softs | Good quality coffee is often spoiled by the presence of softs. Soft beans have no grain, and are often of a dull yellowish colour. Coated raw beans often produce softs to pales. |

## Liquor

| | |
|---|---|
| Acidy | A desirable flavour that is sharp and pleasing but not biting. The term 'acid' as used by the coffee trade refers to coffee that is smooth and rich, and has verve, snap and life as against heavy, old and mellow taste notes. |
| Acrid | A burnt flavour that is sharp, bitter and perhaps irritating. |
| Astringent | A taste that causes puckering and a bitter impression. |

| | |
|---|---|
| Aftertaste | A taste that remains in the mouth longer than usual after eating or drinking. |
| Aroma | Usually, pleasant-smelling substances with the characteristic odour of coffee. Chemically, they are aldehydes, ketones, esters, volatile acids, phenols, etc. |
| Baggy | An undesirable taint, resembling the smell of a bag made from jute. Often observed in coffees that have been stored for long periods under unsuitable conditions. |
| Baked | Generally unpleasant characteristic. Sign of coffee having been over-roasted or roasted too slowly. |
| Balanced or round | Acidity and body are both present to the right extent. |
| Bitter | When strong, an unpleasant, sharp taste; biting like quinine. Similar to acidity but lacking smoothness. |
| Bland or neutral | Tasting smooth and flavourless, lacking coffee flavour and characteristics. Not necessarily always a negative comment however. |
| Body | A taste sensation or mouth feeling of more viscosity, used to describe the mouth feel of a drink corresponding to a certain consistency or an apparent viscosity but not an increase in true viscosity. Sought after in most if not all coffees. |
| Carbolic, chemical | Self-explanatory. Workers who have had wounds on legs treated with disinfectant and have then worked in tanks can cause this type of flavour. Certain emulsions in the manufacture of sacks are also a problem. |
| Carmelized | Burnt-like flavour; carmelized sugar flavour. Usually associated with spray-dried instant coffee, but sometimes found in roasted coffee. |
| Common, commonish | Poor liquor, lacking acidity but with full body. Usually associated with coated raw beans and softs and pales in roast. |
| Earthy | Self-explanatory. Not to be confused with grassy. |
| Fermented | Chemical flavor caused by enzymes on the green coffee sugars. Very unpleasant odour and taste. In its strongest form sometimes referred to as 'hidey' referring to smell of untreated animal hides. |
| Foul | Objectionable liquor often similar to rotten coffee pulp. Sometimes the most advanced stage of fruity and sour coffees. Causes: mostly bad factory preparation or the use of polluted water. It must be noted that one badly discoloured bean is sufficient to give a foul cup to an otherwise good liquor. |
| Fruity | First stage of sourness. Caused by overripe and yellow cherry or by fermentation with too many skins. |
| Grassy | A very pronounced green flavour, can be most unpleasant. |
| Green, greenish | Flavour suggestive of hay. More common in early pickings. In some coffees this flavour is lost a few weeks after curing. Seldom found in coffees which have been thoroughly dried. |

| | |
|---|---|
| Harsh | A harshness of body. Coffee of immature raw appearance (but not necessarily from green cherry) frequently has a harsh taste. Drought-stricken or over-bearing trees producing mottled cherry frequently give this flavour. |
| Musty or mouldy | Self-explanatory. Caused by piling or bagging very wet parchment or by dry parchment getting wet. (*see* 'musty', under Green or raw coffee, above). |
| Natural | Natural characteristic is the full body, slight bitterness indicative of natural processed coffee. It is a negative characteristic of a fully washed coffee. |
| Neutral | No predominant characteristics – can make a good base for blending. |
| Onion flavour | Often bordering on foul. Associated with the use of badly polluted and stagnant water. |
| Pungent | A taste sensation of overall bitterness of brew. A prickly, stinging, or piercing sensation not necessarily unpleasant. |
| Quakery | A peanutty taste, usually associated with pales in the roast. |
| Rioy or Phenolic | A taste with medicinal odour and off notes, slightly iodized phenolic or carbolic. Cannot be hidden by blending – always returns. |
| Rubbery | Odor and taste of rubber. Usually present in fresh robustas. |
| Sour, sourish | Unpleasant flavour, suggestive of rotting coffee pulp. Caused by faulty factory work, improper fermentation resulting in a continuation of the fermentation process during early stages of drying, overripe and yellow cherry, delayed drying causing a heating of the coffee, excess fermentation with many skins. Discoloured pulper-nipped beans are a frequent cause (*see* 'foxy', under Green or raw coffee, above). |
| Strong | Unbalanced liquor where body predominates to the point of being tainted. |
| Taint | A term used to denote the presence of flavours which are foreign to good clean liquor, but which cannot be clearly defined or placed in any category. It is often described as an off-taste or peculiar flavour for lack of a clear definition. Where the foreign flavour can be defined it is, of course, named accordingly. |
| Thin | Lacking body. |
| Twisty | A liquor which, although not directly unclean, is suspect and may become unclean. |
| Unclean | Self-explanatory. A coffee which has an undefined unclean taste. |
| Winey | A fruity taste similar to fresh wine. Not necessarily unpleasant when taste is in the background. |
| Woody | A coarse common flavour peculiar to old crop coffee. Coffee stored at low altitudes with high temperatures and humidity (as in many ports of shipment) tends to become woody rather quickly. Storage at higher altitudes where feasible or in temperate climates is therefore recommended for long-term warehousing. All coffees, however, become woody if stored for too long. |

# CHAPTER 12

# Marketing systems and country profiles

This chapter offers some general comments on the evolution of marketing systems and related issues, followed by brief profiles of 30 coffee producing countries.

## Historical perspective

Marketing systems in many producing countries reflect different historical, social and geographical influences, not least the desire to create a sustainable tax base. Indeed, in a number of countries, especially in Africa, former colonial powers introduced commercial coffee growing specifically for this reason. In many countries coffee became an important source of foreign exchange earnings. This in turn caused some newly independent governments to keep or take control of marketing and exports. This tendency was strengthened by the introduction in 1962 of an International Coffee Agreement (ICA), which regulated world markets, with a number of interruptions though, until 1989. It did so through a system of price-linked export quotas, administered by the International Coffee Organization (ICO) in London. ICO membership was and is restricted to national governments; the introduction of export quotas therefore effectively transferred the right to export the crop from those producing it – the growers – to those administering it – the government of the day. Chapter 1 provided a brief overview of the history of the different ICAs (for more detail go to *www.ico.org/aico/history/htm*).

The abolition of the export quota system in July 1989 more or less coincided with the 1990s wave of economic liberalization and restructuring programmes in developing countries, many of them coffee producers. Low coffee prices then caused the virtual collapse of a number of price stabilization or equalization funds because in many cases the assets of such funds were inadequate to support producer prices over any prolonged period of time. The combination of economic restructuring and low prices resulted in the transformation of most of the former closed single-channel marketing systems into totally or mostly free systems.

Usually under free marketing systems a larger proportion of the sales value (FOB price) reaches farmers than under single-channel or monopoly systems. Also, fluctuating farm gate prices transmit market signals much better, enabling growers to make more informed investment decisions. But following liberalization, coffee quality (and therefore values) deteriorated in some countries because of a decline in support and quality control services.

By the end of the twentieth century there were no marketing monopolies as such left in any coffee producing countries. Not all of today's systems are entirely free though and in a number of countries government or semi-monopolistic structures continue to play an important control role. At times this causes awkward relationships between those placing internal controls on the marketing and pricing of coffee, and exporters – who of course face an entirely free world market. By 2002 very few countries still maintained price support mechanisms such as stabilization funds, or maintained fixed producer prices.

# What controls are needed in a free market system?

## Licensing of exporters

Liberalization is not the same as anarchy or a free-for-all: there will always be rules and, to have value, these rules should be enforced. The liberalization process brought strong focus on the licensing of exporters, especially in countries where the coffee industry had previously been very tightly controlled. No one is admitted to membership of a futures market or stock exchange without satisfying certain pre-conditions. These and a system of rules ensure the public is not cheated. Producing countries may wish the same for their coffee trade – a trade that for many is of fundamental importance.

The vast majority of producing countries today have well-established professional associations of coffee growers, processors and exporters. Such associations provide government and other authorities with official counterparts. They can present industry views and they can impose a certain degree of self-discipline on their membership. Even totally free systems require a certain amount of control. Not everything can simply be left 'to the market'.

Importers and roasters need to be reasonably certain that contracts will be correctly executed whether the market rises or falls: repeated defaults or the shipment of inferior quality by some will eventually affect all the exporters and growers of an entire country. If the process is transparent and based on clear and equitable rules, the correct licensing of processors and exporters is therefore a useful disciplinary tool. Licensing is generally appreciated by coffee importers and roasters because it suggests the licensees enjoy a certain recognition from their peers.

## Quality

Ultimately a roaster somewhere will decide whether a particular coffee is acceptable or not, irrespective of what the accompanying quality certificate may say. Efficient export quality controls are important and useful tools of the trade but they can never replace the receiver's right to pass judgement on the quality of a coffee. For this reason quality certificates play *no* role in quality arbitrations, except *perhaps* (if the arbitrators agree to such a certificate being presented) to demonstrate that the defending party to a dispute may have acted in good faith.

Official quality controls can help to maintain or improve export quality, provided the target markets are convinced of their accuracy and reliability. If so, such certificates facilitate the trade in the coffee concerned; if not, it is better not to bother issuing them, or instead hand the process over to qualified private sector quality controllers as has been done in some countries. Many buyers already insist on independent quality control before shipment: without that certificate they will not take up (pay for) the shipping documents, because for a roaster to receive coffee that cannot be used is little short of disaster. Unless the contract specifically stipulates otherwise, even if the quality was passed for shipment the seller still remains responsible until the quality has been approved on arrival.

As discussed in earlier chapters, growing consumer interest in knowing how the coffee they drink is produced *and what is used to produce it* reinforces and widens the need for independent quality control and certification.

It was expected that the move to entirely free market systems would encourage *quality* because buyers would impose their own price differentials, thus improving on the old control systems that supposedly encouraged quality in the past (though in many countries it was impossible to effectively monitor the trading and weighing, let alone check the quality, of myriad small quantities of smallholder coffee in distant marketplaces or at the farm gate). In this regard liberalization has been disappointing, and many small growers argue that quality does not pay because the price for good and bad coffee is the same. If the market does not provide 'active quality control', meaning that better than average quality at the farm gate receives a premium, then all one is left with is 'passive quality control' in which people are penalized for doing something wrong. (Note that in this context 'low' quality does not mean the same as substandard, which denotes that the quality is below a given or generally accepted standard. If buyer and seller are agreed on a particular quality and the seller supplies exactly that, then the term substandard does not apply, whether the quality is low or not.)

In a number of countries export quality controls have once again been strengthened, sometimes through the use of private sector control companies such as SGS, Cornelder and others.

## Minimum export quality

Whether or not low quality coffee should be exported or not has been debated for many years and the debate has recently gained in intensity. It is not a question for this guide to answer. But any coffee that is exported must be fit for human consumption, and in terms of the trade in physical coffee *the minimum acceptable quality is the quality that was sold.*

An exporter's respect for quality must be absolute. Whether one has sold the finest exemplary coffee or a parcel of broken beans, the buyer expects to receive the quality they bought: nothing less will do. If a producing country prohibits the export of lower qualities of coffee then it is that country's responsibility to enforce that ruling.

The individual exporter's responsibility is to deliver exactly the quality that was sold and, of course, not to export anything that is prohibited. (See also ICO minimum export standards, in chapter 11, Coffee quality.)

## Export pricing

Fixed producer prices and price controls at the farm gate had virtually disappeared by the end of the 1990s with only one or two countries still retaining such arrangements. But for a variety of reasons quite a few countries continue to control export prices by limiting the freedom of exporters to set sales prices themselves. Reasons for this range from simply wishing to optimize the crop's value to wanting to prevent potential tax evasion and foreign currency export through transfer pricing. Methods range from complicated pricing formulas that, in theory, reflect the market, to simply setting minimum registration prices below which an exporter may not sell.

The wish to optimize returns is a worthy one in theory, but in practice it mostly leads to price distortion. There are examples of countries losing market share because of price or differential manipulation. Whether one likes it or not, modern roasting technology allows roasters to be ever more flexible in their purchasing and it is increasingly rare to find any large or medium-sized roaster who absolutely cannot do without a particular origin. Imposing minimum registration prices causes untold trouble when prices are as volatile as they have been since 1989, and in falling markets they have caused large and unrecoverable losses to growers and exporters alike. And yet there is no need for them. A reasonably well organized administration should be able to monitor foreign exchange receipts and other money flows, including transfer pricing if any, quite satisfactorily through customs and revenue authorities, without disrupting the free flow of business in a fast-moving trade such as coffee.

# Marketing systems

## Entirely open systems

In an entirely open system, producer prices, collection marketing and export marketing are entirely free. Such controls as may exist are managed by private industry structures or by joint government and industry structures such as coffee boards, authorities or institutes in which the private sector has a meaningful say. The impact of market liberalization has been very different in countries with a predominantly estate or commercial grower-based coffee industry, to countries where smallholders produce most of the coffee.

In the first category, commercial producers emerging from state-controlled systems were often able to organize and mobilize their resources quite quickly and many moved reasonably swiftly into exports. But for many smallholders, especially in Africa, the experience was very different. Liberalization initially brought higher farm gate prices, but access to extension services and inputs on easy or subsidized terms soon dwindled as former boards, *caisses*, authorities and the cooperative system lost income and resources, and thus gave up control. In some countries liberalization at first translated into uncontrolled change. Many unqualified newcomers entered into farm gate collection and export marketing, at times with disastrous consequences. For example, wet and substandard coffees were mixed with good quality, especially when buying competition was very fierce. Another consequence was strong growth of foreign competition that, armed with access to cheap and often plentiful credit, in many instances largely displaced local operators right down to the farm gate.

## Mixed systems

In countries with mixed systems, strong government and producer controls affect the entire production and export chain. These range from giant Colombia where the Federación Nacional dos Cafeteros de Colombia (Federacafe) has traditionally managed the coffee industry, to the small industry of Burundi where the Government traditionally sets the producer price and sells the crop in auctions to private exporters who then market the coffee overseas. In Western Africa one still encounters fairly strong government influences and successors to the old *caisses de stabilisation*. In India and Viet Nam too government influence over the marketing system remains strong although exports are entirely run by the private sector.

## Export auctions

Much of the world's tea has traditionally been sold through auctions but coffee auctions are generally found only in Africa: in Burundi, Kenya and the United Republic of Tanzania. In recent years Brazil has been selling surplus, government-held stocks by auction, and a number of countries conduct occasional small auction sales of special coffees over the Internet in order to promote the image of their specialty coffees. But in mid 2002 only these three African countries relied on auctions to market their entire crop.

Properly run auctions provide excellent price transparency but depend on competition. Without competition prices will not reflect market reality and may be open to manipulation. A first prerequisite for attracting and concentrating competition is that the entire crop is sold in this way *and buyers know this*. Any uncertainty will limit both attendance and the willingness to go 'the last cent'. A further condition is that the coffee on offer *will* be sold to the highest bidder as long as the price offered represents market value; and if it does not then the bidder will receive a realistic counteroffer.

If an auction is used for price discovery, meaning there are always counteroffers and little is directly sold 'under the hammer', then it ceases to be a genuine auction and buyers will not sell forward against it. Once the forward selling element is lost, prices will increasingly represent only spot values as the coffee on offer has to find a home on that day, and at that day's ruling price. Growers selling through auctions carry the price risk until the day of sale, of course. And as not all coffee can be sold immediately there could be long waiting periods between harvest and sale. In a rising market this is not a problem but in a falling market growers are exposed to the entire price risk because they are limited to selling spot goods. (See also chapter 10, Risk.) It is of course also possible to sell forward delivery by auction, but only if there is an agreed description for the goods and a guaranteed possibility for redress in case the actual delivery falls short of that description.

# Coffee producing countries – profiles

The countries listed here are those that traditionally export 250,000 bags or more a year. Angola is included because of its previous record and undoubted potential to be a major exporter; the Philippines because it is a substantial producer and consumes most of its output. Production figures are sourced from ICO statistics and are mostly expressed by crop years. Population figures are from the World Bank, year 2000, rounded to nearest million.

## Angola (population 13 million)

Prior to independence in 1975 Angola produced some excellent arabicas (2%–5% of total output) and was a major exporter of some of the world's best robustas (Ambriz, Amboin, Novo Redondo: all neutral liquoring coffees). The coffee industry was primarily plantation based and exports peaked at some 4 million bags in 1972/73. However, large-scale nationalization of privately held plantations in 1975, coupled with subsequent and prolonged civil war, destabilized and largely destroyed the industry.

Exports averaged just 50,000 bags in the 1990s and were only 17,000 bags in the coffee year 2000/01, all from the port of Luanda. The country's potential for the resumption of large-scale production is substantial but it can be tapped only if civil unrest subsides and the necessary incentives are put in place.

## Brazil (population 170 million)

In the 1950s Brazil accounted for more than 50% of world coffee production. The country produced a record crop of 44 million bags in 1959. Since then production has averaged around 25 million bags annually although 42 million bags were produced in 1987/88. Following two frosts and drought in 1994 output fell to just 13 million bags, only to recover again to over 29 million bags in 2000/01. Extensive planting since 1994 has given Brazil the capacity to produce significantly larger crops in the future with some forecasting crops in years to come of between 40 and 50 million bags. There are large year-on-year fluctuations in crop size mainly as a result of frosts, droughts and, more recently, low prices with consequent reduced levels of management and inputs.

In recent years the potential effect of frost on production has been reduced through the shifting of plantings from frost-prone areas such as northern Paraná, São Paolo and southern Minas Gerais, to less easily affected areas such as Espirito Santo, Bahia and Rondonia. However, as the coffee areas move and become more widespread drought may become a more critical cause of future falls in production and may accentuate a bi-annual production cycle.

Brazil is a world leader in terms of mechanization of its coffee industry, ranging from mechanized planting through to pruning and harvesting, although mechanized harvesting is not as widespread as is often suggested. Mechanization has enabled some growers at least to cap what would otherwise have become unbearable labour costs. Technology and research, together with a depreciating local currency (the *real*), put Brazilian coffee among the most competitive in the world. The coffee industry remains of great importance but many decades ago it lost the overriding importance it once held for the national economy; today its share is less than 5% of national export earnings. The area under coffee is approximately 2.5 million hectares, producing around 75% arabica and 25% robusta (known as Conillon and also exported in substantial quantities). Some quarters suggest output of Conillon may be as high as 30% of the total harvest.

The Brazilian coffee industry is highly organized although much less strictly controlled than in the past. The industry has a well functioning domestic coffee futures market, the only one with true liquidity outside the main markets of New York and London, and has a huge soluble coffee processing industry that exports all over the world (almost 2.5 million bags GBE in 2000/01), including the European Union where it has recently been granted duty free status for a substantial tonnage. Perhaps more importantly, Brazilian domestic consumption has virtually exploded in recent decades and reached over 13 million bags in 2001, making the country the world's second largest consumer market for coffee, behind the United States but ahead of Germany. Roast and ground accounts for about 95% of Brazilian domestic consumption.

In recent years Brazil has made enormous efforts to improve on its traditional image of a bulk, low quality producer. New processing methods such as the pulped method (in which cherry is pulped and the parchment is then dried with the mucilage still adhering to it, thus speeding up the drying process while retaining the body and sweetness associated with natural coffees, and also full wet processing) are increasingly providing coffees of more attractive flavour profiles that find ready acceptance in many markets.

Brazil also has a strongly growing specialty coffee sector that delivers excellent quality and serves both the international and local specialty markets. Many people have expressed surprise at the depth and variety of the flavour profiles that are now being produced. Coupled with the realization that there is a need generally to improve the quality of coffee offered to domestic consumers, this bodes well for further growth in Brazilian domestic consumption.

## Burundi (population 7 million)

Burundi, a small, landlocked and extremely hilly country in Africa's Great Lakes Region, is an entirely smallholder-based producer of mild arabica, mostly wet-processed. Land holdings are extremely small and it is not unusual to encounter coffee growers who own just 100–200 trees. There are over 800,000 coffee growers, whose production is increasingly processed by mechanized, centrally located washing stations although some is still processed manually by the use of hand pulpers. This semi-washed product was called 'washed' by the Belgian colonial administration, so coffee processed at the full-scale washing stations had to be called 'fully washed' to differentiate it.

Coffee is offered for export at the weekly Bujumbura auctions, conducted by the Office du Café du Burundi (OCIBU), where it is sold to private exporters who market abroad. Exports are through the port of Bujumbura by lake vessel to the port of Kigoma in Tanzania from where the coffee is railed to the Indian Ocean port of Dar es Salaam. Civil unrest and insurrections affected production in the 1990s. Exports fell from over 600,000 bags in 1991 and 1992 to an average of just below 400,000 bags in the five years from 1996 to 2000, and following drought conditions to just over 300,000 bags in the 2000/01 coffee year. Usually coffee provides over three-quarters of all of Burundi's export earnings.

## Cameroon (population 15 million)

Cameroon produces both arabica and robusta in the ratio of approximately 8:2. Total output peaked at 2.2 million bags in 1986/87 but has fluctuated quite considerably since then, with exports falling below 500,000 bags in 1995 and recovering to just over 1.1 million bags in 2000/01. The ICO estimates domestic consumption at approximately 100,000 bags per annum. The country is richly endowed with natural resources and benefits from a diversified production base, including mineral oil. Coffee provided just below 5% of all export revenues in the five-year period from 1996 to 2000. Production is largely smallholder based with robusta grown in the predominantly francophone areas and arabica in the predominantly anglophone areas (Northwest and Western provinces). Unlike most other robusta producing origins, Cameroon coffee farmers have always depended heavily on the use of purchased inputs, particularly (previously subsidized) fertilizers because the coffee areas are in heavy rainfall regions and nutrients are leached from the soil. But in recent years the use of fertilizer has dropped because of rising costs and falling coffee prices. In the past Cameroon operated internal pricing and price stabilization schemes but, as elsewhere, these proved unsustainable. Coffee marketing has been entirely free since 1994/95 although exporters must satisfy an impressive number of certifying agencies before export clearance is obtained. Interestingly, since about 1997 the control of export quality has been transferred entirely to the private sector and is now carried out by a number of independent, licensed companies.

## Colombia (population 42 million)

In 2000, Colombian exports were for the first time overtaken by Viet Nam. The country now ranks as the third largest exporter with exports of just below 9 million bags in the coffee year 2000/01, compared to a peak of over 16.5 million bags in 1992, an exceptional year. Colombia remains by far the world's largest producer of washed arabica and because of its production volume and the spread of its harvesting period, it is able to supply fresh green coffee all year. Currently Colombia's main exports are mineral oil and coal, but as recently as 1986 coffee still made up more than half the country's export revenues. This had fallen to 16% in the period 1996–2000, and to just 6% in the year 2001 according to USDA statistics. Compared to most coffee producing countries, Colombian domestic consumption is substantial at about 1.5 million bags, but in such a large country this still leaves plenty of scope for growth.

In spite of its sizeable output the Colombian coffee industry is essentially smallholder based, with over 500,000 farms, ranging in size from 1 hectare to more than 100 hectares but on average just 1.4 hectares, at altitudes ranging from 1,300 to 1,800 m. All coffee is wet processed, mostly on-farm. Approximately 86% of the tree park consists of high-yielding, rust-resistant Caturra and Colombia varieties, the latter resistant against the main disease affecting coffee in the world, 'roya' or coffee leaf rust. The coffee industry has developed a high degree of agricultural and technical research capacity in the Cenicafé scientific research centre, which has been responsible for innovative advances in the fields of pest and disease control, as well as coffee processing. Unfortunately low coffee prices are threatening some of these activities.

The coffee industry is very well organized. The well known National Federation of Coffee Growers of Colombia (Federacafe) has played a major role for many decades. Colombia can be said to have been the first coffee producing country to promote the 'single origin' concept by convincing roasters to offer pure Colombian brands and supporting them through advertising campaigns featuring the famous Juan Valdez and his faithful mule (steep hillsides mean much coffee is transported by mules from Colombian farms). Export marketing is divided between Federacafe and private exporters. Federacafe sets an official minimum or back-stopping price, leaving farmers free to sell to whomever they prefer. Export sales are subject to registration, so individual exporters are limited in the amount of coffee they can sell for a given period. According to Federacafe this is to limit otherwise uncontrolled selling competition between exporters and avoid possible contract defaults, thereby adding value to Colombian coffee compared to other origins. All shipments are subject to Federacafe quality control and no coffee can be exported without an export license.

## Costa Rica (population 4 million)

Costa Rica is known for producing washed arabicas of consistently high quality. Coffee is an important part of the agriculture sector and accounted for 7% of the value of all exports in the period 1996–2000. Farmers are generally very progressive and yields are high. Some 108,000 hectares are planted to coffee; a substantial number of them are owned by smallholders. Many sell their coffee as fresh cherry to large beneficios who then wet process it into parchment. The Costa Rican Coffee Institute (ICAFE) oversees the industry. By law only arabica may be planted. The usual varieties include Typica, Caturra, Catimor and Catuai. Coffee is grown throughout Costa Rica, as its volcanic soils, altitude (800 to 1,700 m) and annual rainfall of over 2,500 mm (100 inches) provide mostly optimal growing conditions. Technical standards are high, especially as regards processing techniques, and Costa Rica hosts the Central American Research Institute at Turrialba which plays an important role in research and the development of modern husbandry methods for coffee. Production has averaged just over 2.4 million bags in the period 1997–2001, with exports of around 2.1 million bags in 2000/01. Domestic consumption is among the highest per capita in producing countries but as Costa Rica is a relatively small country it only amounts to some 350,000 bags annually.

The best known coffee qualities from the Central Valley are described by altitude: Tarrazu = top quality; strictly hard bean (SHB) = grown above 1,200 m; good hard bean (GHB) = 1,100–1,200 m; and hard bean (HB) = 950–1,100 m. Coffees from the Atlantic slope (lower altitude) are classed as high grown, medium grown and low grown. Some roasted coffee is exported as well, mostly to Puerto Rico.

## Côte d'Ivoire (population 16 million)

Côte d'Ivoire was the world's largest producer of robusta and the third largest producer of coffee worldwide until the 1980s when Indonesia and Mexico overtook it. Only robusta is grown. In the five years from 1997 to 2001 production averaged about 3.9 million bags but this hides a peak of 5.9 million bags in 1999 (and 4.5 million bags in 1996). In 2000/01, green bean exports were 3.5 million bags. At just 60,000 bags annually domestic consumption is virtually negligible. Some soluble coffee is exported, totalling 163,000 bags GBE in 2000/01 (down from nearly 300,000 bags in 1996).

Traditionally Côte d'Ivoire had always operated price stabilization funds (*caisses de stabilisation*) for both coffee and its other major export, cocoa, under which the government guaranteed a minimum price for the harvest, fixed at the beginning of each season and valid for all of that season. The objective was to avoid excessive fluctuations in grower prices but the system also resulted in huge taxes being raised from coffee growers. The *caisse* negotiated export sales and allocated them for execution to registered exporters, collecting or reimbursing any difference between the cost and the export value. The 1989 abolition of ICO export quotas with its accompanying price fall resulted in the halving of the producer price in 1990 and helped set the stage for the eventual disappearance of the *caisse* system. Coffee marketing was finally fully liberalized in 1998, unfortunately just at a time when prices started collapsing once again, thereby exposing farmers directly to a world market plagued by overproduction. The low coffee prices have been exacting their toll and because the tree park is generally in need of rejuvenation, farmers also achieve relatively low yields making it difficult to afford the necessary inputs and maintenance, in turn leading to further reductions in yield and income. Growers want a return to some form of price and revenue stability and in 2001 established a new, privately run body, the Bourse du Café et du Cacao (BCC), which is expected to bring back some form of price stabilization, using contributions from grower levies, government grants and international assistance bodies.

## Democratic Republic of the Congo (population 51 million)

The Democratic Republic of the Congo, previously called Zaire, exported on average 1.8 million bags annually in the five years from 1985 to 1990, of which about 90% was robusta and the remaining 10% arabica. This had approximately halved by 1996, and in 2000/01 total recorded exports were just 214,000 bags (with an unknown amount diverted through unofficial cross-border channels). ICO statistics put domestic consumption at approximately 200,000 bags per annum. Serious and prolonged civil unrest has severely affected the coffee sector whose current status quo is therefore difficult to assess in any detail.

Coffee is grown in many different regions of this vast country with high-grown arabica in the highlands bordering Lake Kivu, and robusta in Oriental, Equateur, Bandundu and Kasai provinces. There is also a small amount of low grown Kwilu robusta from the Bas-Congo province. Commercial coffee production started primarily as a plantation crop with estates accounting for some 75% of all output in 1960; today this is estimated at less than 2% and, effectively, coffee has become a smallholder crop. There are no recent data but earlier studies suggest the average area under coffee is less than 1 hectare per family. The inherent quality potential of both robusta and arabica is excellent, as is the production potential, but until political stability returns the coffee industry will not be in a position to exploit these advantages.

## Dominican Republic (population 8 million)

The Dominican Republic occupies the eastern half of the island known as Hispaniola, part of the Greater Antilles. The other half of the island is occupied by Haiti. Whereas Haiti produces mostly natural or sun-dried arabica, the Dominican Republic production is mostly washed. Production averaged some 727,000 bags in the five years from 1997 to 2001 (with peaks of 941,000 bags in 1997 and 900,000 bags in 2001). Domestic consumption is substantial at around 340,000 bags or some 40% of production. In terms of exports the country therefore ranks amongst the smaller coffee nations.

Most coffee (75%) is produced by smallholders using relatively unsophisticated production methods and yields are generally low. Most smallholders pulp and wash their own coffee although some is also sold in cherry form to nearby estates. Coffee is grown countrywide and the best qualities originate from the higher altitude areas (up to 1,500 m). In the five years from 1996 to 2000 coffee exports provided just over 5% of all export revenues.

The Dominican Republic is the single largest producer exporter of roasted coffee, virtually all of it to Puerto Rico (about 52,000 bags GBE in 2000).

## Ecuador (population 13 million)

Like Brazil, Ecuador produces both arabica (mostly washed but also naturals) and robusta (naturals only). Arabica is grown in the highlands bordering the Andes, and robusta in the much lower-lying Amazonian regions. The coffee industry is in the main smallholder based, with an average annual production of 1.1 million bags in the period 1997–2001 (compared to about 2 million bags in earlier years). The area under coffee is said to be around 300,000 hectares. Low prices have exacted their toll but efforts are under way to rejuvenate plantings through the introduction of material that provides both better yields and higher quality. The National Coffee Council (Cofenac) brings together industry and government strategists while the National Association of Coffee Exporters (Anecafe) coordinates the industry's day-to-day affairs.

Domestic consumption accounts for some 30% of production. Substantial amounts of different types of soluble coffee are exported – some 372,000 bags GBE in 2000/01, including frozen extract. Ecuador also exports organic coffee and is attempting to diversify both its product and exports.

## El Salvador (population 6 million)

Although small in size, El Salvador is a major producer of high quality arabicas. In the five years to 2001 production averaged 2.1 million bags with a high of 2.8 million in 1998 and a low of 1.7 million in 2000 and 2001. In the late 1970s production stood at close to 3.5 million bags but subsequently output was severely affected by civil unrest. Although there are tens of thousands of coffee growers, the bulk of the production comes from estates. Domestic consumption is very respectable at about 150,000 bags annually, although it was higher in the early 1980s (about 200,000 bags). About 85% of this is roast and ground; very little soluble coffee is consumed. Over 23,000 farmers grow coffee but about 86% of these produce less than 100 bags (of 60 kgs) each. In 1996–2000 coffee accounted on average for 24% of export revenues.

The area under coffee is about 178,000 hectares. Only arabica is produced (about two-thirds Bourbon) and mostly under shade; coffee is an important component of the country's forest cover. Exports are graded according to altitude: central standard (CS) = grown at 500–900 m; high grown (HG) = 900–1,200 m; and strictly high grown (SHG) = 1,200 m and up. Specialty (gourmet) coffees are subject to stringent processing and quality requirements, including natural fermentation and 100% sun drying. Together with organic coffee they account for over 10% of total exports. The Salvadorean Coffee Council (CSC – Consejo Salvadoreno del Café) certifies the quality of both gourmet and organic coffee. The quality of regular grades is monitored and quality certificates are available upon request.

## Ethiopia (population 64 million)

Probably the oldest exporter of coffee in the world and homeland of arabica that grows wild in the forests of Kaffa, Illubabor and Gemu Goffa, Ethiopia produces some of the world's finest 'original' coffees such as Yrgacheffe, Limu and Harar. Around 4,500 different Ethiopian coffee species are preserved in a coffee field gene bank in the Kafa region, a good indication of the rich diversity of the Ethiopian coffee plant population.

ICO figures put production at close to 3.2 million bags annually in the five years from 1997 to 2001 (reaching 3.9 million in the 2001 crop year) but exports were much lower than that at about 1.8 million bags annually. Domestic consumption averages around 1.5 to 1.7 million bags a year. As might be expected from the country of origin of arabica coffee, domestic consumption in Ethiopia is huge, easily accounting for the difference between production and exports. Ethiopia is a nation of true coffee drinkers who engage in an elaborate coffee ceremony at important occasions.

Whereas previously most coffee was exported as sun-dried (natural), substantial numbers of washing stations have been built since the 1980s and the country now also exports sizeable quantities of high quality washed arabica. The famous Harar coffee is, however, always prepared and exported as sun-dried. Ethiopia has a somewhat unusual internal marketing system in which interior millers and traders bring rough hulled sun-dried or washed parchment to Addis Ababa (or Dire Dawa for Harars) where it is auctioned daily by the truckload with the selling owners sitting on one side of the auction room, and the exporters on the other. When a sale is agreed then the truck discharges at the exporter's premises and payment is made.

Since the early 1990s coffee marketing has been progressively liberalized although exporters are not permitted (mid 2002) to purchase coffee directly in the interior, being restricted to the daily auctions mentioned above. This means that, unlike most other coffee producing countries, interior millers and traders must assume the price risk from the time they purchase at the farm gate until the coffee is sold at auction, a process that can take some weeks. Coffee is the backbone of Ethiopia's economy, providing 63% of all export revenues in the period 1996–2000. This is probably the main reason why export pricing is (2002) subject to control through a coffee price differential setting committee, chaired by the

National (Central) Bank of Ethiopia. The committee sets minimum differentials that exporters must achieve for the different export qualities relating to the New York 'C' contract.

## Guatemala (population 11 million)

Guatemala is an arabica producer, although a very small amount of robusta (about 25,000 bags) is grown on the Pacific coast. The main coffee areas are spread over most of the south where several mountain ranges extend from the Andes and provide ideal ecological conditions for the production of high-grown arabica. The total area under coffee is approximately 270,000 hectares. Production averaged 4.6 million bags annually in the five years from 1997 to 2001, with a peak of 5.2 million bags in 1999. Production in 2001 was 3.9 million bags. Domestic consumption is estimated at around 300,000 bags of mostly lower quality roast and ground, plus another 20,000 bags or so of soluble. Small farmers account for approximately 30% of total output; the other 70% originates from medium and large-scale farms. There is also some unofficial cross-border importation of coffee from neighbouring Honduras.

Many years of civil conflict in Guatemala came to an end in 1996. Since then the economy has reversed earlier declines. But current low prices have caused a deep crisis in the coffee sector, requiring government to come to its assistance. The coffee industry is well organized with Anacafé, a producers' association, playing a major role in the country's coffee affairs. Anacafé provides a number of services to growers (who fund it through export levies) including the development of price protection (hedging) mechanisms whereby growers access the New York futures markets through individual exporters. Guatemala's coffee industry has always been free and competitive. The only controls were those imposed by the ICO's quota system; these were abolished as soon as that system ceased to operate.

Export classification is based on altitude: strictly hard bean (SHB) = grown at above 1,400 m; hard bean = 1,200–1,400 m; semi-hard bean = 1,100–1,200 m; extra prime washed = 900–1,100 m; prime washed = below 900 m. Anacafé also promotes Guatemalan specialty coffee abroad through a number of regional brands, each with its own distinguishable characteristics and historic reputation. Brands such as Antigua and Huehuetenango are well known. Coffee accounted on average for 24% of all export revenues in the period 1996–2000.

## Honduras (population 6 million)

Honduras is a relative newcomer to the world of large scale coffee production. In the early 1970s output was just over 500,000 bags whereas in the five years from 1997 to 2001 it averaged just over 2.5 million bags with almost 3.0 million bags in 1999 and 2.3 million bags in 2001. The main expansion came in the years immediately following the 1975 frost in Brazil whose impact at one stage catapulted coffee prices to extreme heights. Some 300,000 hectares are under coffee and smallholders account for over two-thirds of all coffee production, mostly washed arabica. Some is grown under irrigation, using canals and micro-irrigation systems.

Washed arabica is classified by altitude: central standard = grown from 700–1,000 m; high grown = 1,000–1,500 m; strictly high grown = 1,500 m and up. The Honduran Coffee Institute (IHCAFE) is the industry coordinating body and, together with the Honduran Association of Coffee Producers (AHPROCAFE), actively promotes better quality and the production of organic coffee to boost both the image and the value of Honduran coffee exports. Data on domestic consumption fluctuate but the 2001 total was put at 200,000 bags GBE by the ICO, all of it in roast and ground form. Coffee is an important export commodity, providing on average 23% of all export revenues in the period 1996–2000. There is also a certain amount of unregistered cross-border trade through neighbouring countries, particularly Guatemala.

## India (population 1,016 million)

India is the third largest Asian producer, after Viet Nam and Indonesia. It produces both arabica and robusta with an average total output of just below 5 million bags in the five years from 1997 to 2001 (with peaks of 5.5 million in 1999 and 5.3 million in 2001), compared to an average of just over 2.7 million bags in the period 1987–1991.

Domestic consumption stands at around 800,000–900,000 bags annually, a very useful tonnage but one that translates into a minuscule per capita figure in this populous nation of tea drinkers. In the mid 1980s consumption stood at well over 1 million bags but only because the cost to the consumer was subsidized; subsidies were abolished once the ICO export quota disappeared and the country could maximize its exports. India is the world's second largest exporter of soluble coffee with about 735,000 bags GBE in coffee year 2000/01; behind Brazil with exports of almost 2.5 million bags GBE.

Until the early 1990s marketing was controlled by the Coffee Board of India but the controls were gradually watered down until the board's involvement in marketing ceased altogether in 1996. Despite its relative size coffee is not a major factor in the Indian economy but the industry is of great economic importance in the main producing states of Karnataka, Kerala and Tamil Nadu.

Robusta output has risen much faster than that of arabica and currently accounts for some 65% of the total compared to about 50% in the late 1980s. Both washed and natural robusta and arabica are produced and it is noteworthy that India is the world's leading producer of the good quality washed robusta that is greatly appreciated by the fast-growing espresso industry. The famous monsooned (aged) coffees, both arabica and robusta, are another specialty. Most coffee is shade-grown, with the cropping of shade trees and pepper vines providing additional income. It is estimated that 98% of plantings are less than 10 hectares in size and that smallholders account for about 60% of total output.

Alongside Brazil, India is one of only two coffee producing countries to have established an internal coffee futures market – COFEI, or the Coffee Futures Exchange India Ltd. The contract size closely reflects the composition of the Indian coffee industry with its estimated 130,000 small growers (120,000 with less than 2 hectares, 10,000 with between 2 and 4 hectares under coffee) alongside larger growers and plantations: the contract trades arabica parchment and robusta cherry in 1,000 kg lots, or the clean coffee equivalent in units of just 600 kg. Although the market does not appear to enjoy the liquidity one would wish for, the fact that it could be established at all should be of interest to coffee producing countries generally.

## Indonesia (population 210 million)

Indonesia overtook Côte d'Ivoire in the early 1980s to become the world's largest robusta producer, only to be overtaken itself by Viet Nam in the mid 1990s. Coffee production peaked at about 8.4 million bags in the 1997/98 crop year (of which about 10% was arabica) but averaged just 6.4 million bags in the following three years. Most of the fall occurred in robusta output, thereby raising the estimated current share of arabica to about 12% (2000/01). Domestic consumption is estimated at between 1.5 million and 1.7 million bags annually, virtually all of it in roast and ground form. Exports of soluble coffee vary but were 154,000 bags GBE in 2000/01.

The area under coffee is estimated at around 1.1 million hectares. Smallholders account for over 90% of total production, scattered over many island which in turn are dispersed over a wide geographical area. Coffee is therefore exported from a great number of ecologically separate areas and from numerous large and small ports. Although important in world terms, the coffee industry is relatively insignificant in the Indonesian export economy although current low prices (2002) are, obviously, causing great hardship to those who directly depend on it. The vast majority of exports are naturals but the island of Java also produces a certain amount of plantation-grown washed robusta for which Japan and Italy have always been major markets. Wet processing was introduced into Indonesia by the Dutch from the West Indies and washed robustas were designated WIB: West Indische Bereiding (West Indian preparation).

The trade in coffee is entirely free – plantations usually process and export themselves but smallholder coffee goes through a number of intermediary stages, starting with small collectors at village levels operating on account of larger, intermediate traders who in turn sell to major merchants and so, finally, to the exporters. Exports are regulated by the Ministry of Industry and Trade and the Association of Indonesian Coffee Exporters (AEKI).

In recent years Indonesia has encountered severe competition for market share from Viet Nam where production has shown strong growth. Viet Nam's quality has not always been optimal, but that country is now making considerable efforts to boost quality, forcing Indonesia to do the same in order to remain competitive and reduce the amount of low grade coffee it exports (estimated at over 15% of total exports).

## Kenya (population 30 million)

Kenya is a leading producer of high-grown mild arabica. Production peaked at 2.15 million bags in 1987/88 but has been on the decline since then, averaging 1.1 million bags in the period 1996–2000, with yields falling from 842 kg per hectare in 1987/88 to around 400 kg at present. In the five years from 1996 to 2000 coffee exports accounted for just under 12% of all export revenues. An estimated 600,000 smallholders account for 58% of production (and 75% of national acreage), with medium to large plantations supplying the remainder. Domestic consumption is modest at about 50,000 bags.

Smallholders deliver cherry to cooperative pulping stations that are amalgamated in cooperative societies and then in unions. Plantations process their own coffee. There is no trade in fresh cherry in Kenya. Milling has been liberalized and three mills now operate alongside the Kenya Planters Co-operative Union, which previously held a monopoly. Green coffee is graded by size and density into 7 grades after which it is classified (liquored) by the Coffee Board of Kenya (CBK) into 10 classes. This intensive grading and classification system has its origins in the weekly auctions where all coffee is sold. For many decades all proceeds were pooled and all growers were paid the average price realized for each grade and class during the entire season. A first payment would be made on classification, followed by a number of interim payments and a final payment after the season had ended. Increasing payment delays, especially to smallholders, eventually caused the introduction of direct payments, giving growers the choice to receive payment directly from the auction (after statutory deductions), or to stay with the pool system. Further change is expected and the pool system is likely to disappear altogether. Coffee is auctioned in United States dollars and growers are paid in dollars.

The auction has progressed from open outcry to electronic bidding and is expected to develop into a fully fledged coffee exchange with the CBK restricting itself to the role of regulator, leaving auctioning and settlement in the hands of the exchange. At the auction, licensed exporters buy coffee in lots ranging from 40 to 100 bags, based on a catalogue, specifying the grade and the mark of the grower. Exporters receive small lot samples for every parcel which they then classify (liquor) themselves to determine its likely commercial value. After purchase, the exporters combine (blend) the individual lots into container-loads based on the grade but more especially the quality. This blending enables them to tailor coffee to the requirements of almost any market segment, including the specialty coffee industry where Kenya is a leading supplier and provides a benchmark against which many other coffees are compared.

## Madagascar (population 16 million)

Madagascar is primarily a robusta producer (around 98% of production) with some small amounts of arabica grown in the highlands. Efforts are underway to expand arabica production: the quality potential is considered excellent. There are also small pockets of low-grown arabica. The intrinsic quality of Madagascar robusta (Kouillou) is good with a neutral cup but quality is adversely affected by difficult harvesting and drying conditions. Production averaged 1.1 million bags during the 1980s but fell sharply in the 1990s with a low of between 300,000 and 400,000 bags in 2000. The last restrictions on coffee exports were removed in 1997 and the trade in coffee is entirely free.

Production and exports fluctuate sharply owing to occasional cyclone damage. The impact of individual severe cyclones is clearly visible in longer-term export statistics. Exports averaged 647,000 bags in the four years from 1995 to 1998 but were only 277,000 bags in 1999/00 and 266,000 bags in 2000/01. Coffee is almost entirely produced by smallholders, some 350,000 of whom account for 90% of the total coffee cultivated area. They are widely dispersed, often in areas that are not easily accessible. The average small farm measures 1–1.5 hectares and coffee is typically grown on just 10% to 15% of this. A number of growers exploit coffee trees that have virtually become wild (forest crop), once a year simply stripping whatever cherry has made it to that point. Agriculture is the mainstay of the economy, providing employment to some 85% of the population. In the years 1996–2000 coffee provided just under 19% of all export revenues. The Malagasy are coffee drinkers by tradition but domestic consumption growth is restricted by adverse economic conditions. Current estimates put the total at about 160,000 bags annually.

## Mexico (population 98 million)

Mexico is the fifth-largest producer in the world after Brazil, Viet Nam, Colombia and Indonesia. The industry is almost exclusively smallholder based, with most coffee grown in the states of Oaxaca, Chiapas and Veracruz. The area planted to coffee is some 730,000 hectares and production averaged 5.4 million bags during the period 1997–2001, with a peak of 6.4 million bags in 1999. Arabica is dominant although a small amount of robusta is also grown (200,000 bags in 2000). Arabica varieties include Typica, Caturra, Bourbon, Garnica and Catuai. Most arabica is washed; there is also some export of washed robusta. Exports of soluble coffee were approximately 443,000 bags GBE in 2000/01 but against this some lower grades of green coffee are also imported for processing into soluble.

Some roasted coffee (about 25,000 bags GBE in 2000/01) is exported to the United States, with whom Mexico shares a land border. Domestic consumption stands at approximately 1.25 million bags or about one-quarter of total output. Even so, annual per capita consumption remains below 1 kg.

Most exports to the United States travel by land through Laredo, making Mexico the only coffee producing country to ship a substantial portion of total exports by truck. Despite this advantage Mexican coffee farmers have also been hard hit by low coffee prices. As a result output was expected to fall, possibly quite substantially. The Mexican Coffee Council (Consejo Mexicano del Café) is responsible for quality control. Mexico is amongst the world's leading producers and exporters of organic coffee. The Finca Irlanda in Chiapas is reportedly the world's first recorded location to produce and export organic coffee: the farm was certified organic in 1967.

## Nicaragua (population 5 million)

Nicaragua is the largest of the Central American countries. Coffee was introduced into Nicaragua in the mid nineteenth century. Production reached 1 million bags in the late 1970s, declining to less than 600,000 bags in 1990. Since then production has staged a strong recovery, with an average output of 1.3 million bags in the five years 1997–2001 and a peak of 1.6 million bags in 1999/2000. Production was 1.04 million bags in 2000/01. Only arabica is produced, and all wet-processed. The area planted to coffee is estimated at about 100,000 hectares and varieties include Typica, Bourbon and Caturra. Nicaragua is considered a traditional producer of fine high washed arabicas. In recent years drought and falling world prices have however combined to create a major economic crisis as coffee revenues have plummeted.

Domestic consumption was almost 200,000 bags in 2000/01, compared to just 95,000 bags in 1995/96. A small amount of soluble coffee (36,000 bags in 2000/01) is exported.

## Papua New Guinea (population 5 million)

Papua New Guinea consists of a large mainland and some 300 islands. The coffee industry dates from the late nineteenth century. Rapid growth has been experienced since the 1960s, from less than 100,000 bags to an average output of 1.2 million bags in the five years from 1997 to 2001. All is highland-grown arabica, with the exception of 50,000–60,000 bags of robusta grown in lower-lying areas. All arabica and robusta are wet processed.

Coffee is the largest agricultural industry, with more than 270,000 growers: 80%–85% of production comes from smallholders or villagers, the majority of whom are subsistence farmers with plots averaging just half a hectare. Around 10%–15% comes from commercial plantations, some of which produce very well known brands of fine coffee. Typica is the dominant arabica variety. Smallholders either process their coffee to the parchment stage using hand pulpers, or sell fresh cherry to washing stations. Some combine their holdings into 'blocks' and sell red cherry to neighbouring plantations. Coffee accounts for between 8% and 9% of all export revenues. Domestic consumption is minimal at about 2,000 bags annually. The Coffee Industry Corporation regulates the industry, and licensed private millers and exporters handle the trade.

## Peru (population 26 million)

Peru neighbours Ecuador on the Pacific coast of South America. But, unlike Ecuador, Peru produces only arabica, most of it washed. The total area planted to coffee is about 215,000 hectares and the bulk of all coffee is produced by smallholders. The balance comes from medium and large-sized estates, some at altitudes as high as 1,700 m and upwards. Production has risen strongly from around 1.3 million bags in the late 1980s to an average output of 2.3 million bags in the five years from 1997 to 2001, with a peak of 2.7 million bags in 2001. Production costs in Peru are reportedly below those of Central American producers. The country increasingly pursues a quality-oriented production strategy to try to capitalize on this and to compensate at least partly for the price falls of recent years.

Green coffee exports were 2.4 million bags in 2000/01. Coffee accounts for approximately half of all agricultural exports. Domestic consumption is more or less stable at around 120,000 bags per annum with an increasing proportion of soluble (now as high as 75% according to some).

## Philippines (population 76 million)

With an average annual output of about 780,000 bags in the period 1997–2001, mostly robusta but also a small amount of arabica, the Philippines is not an inconsequential producer. What sets the country apart though is that virtually all this coffee is consumed locally and the country exports almost none at all (just 3,000 bags in 2000/01 down from an average of 450,000 bags in 1985–1989). The local market is very well developed with many roasters and large manufacturers of soluble coffee (although soluble exports too are minimal). Fluctuations in exports are directly linked to external coffee prices: it makes sense to export only when external prices exceed those offered domestically. In recent years production has not kept up with demand and substantial quantities have been imported (255,000 bags in 2000, mostly from Indonesia and Viet Nam).

Interestingly, the Philippines produces all four commercial varieties of coffee: arabica, robusta, liberica and excelsa: small quantities of the latter two are exported to the Middle East, often through Singapore, and probably account for the 3,000 bags exported in 2000/01.

## Rwanda (population 9 million)

Like its immediate neighbour Burundi, Rwanda too is a small, landlocked and extremely hilly country in Africa's Great Lakes region. While Burundi borders onto Lake Tanganyika, Rwanda borders onto Lake Kivu. Its formerly flourishing coffee industry was devastated by the human tragedies that befell the country in the 1990s and has only recently starting showing signs of recovery. From an average of 650,000 bags annually in the period 1986–1990 (this may however have included some coffee from neighbouring Zaire, as it was then), production fell to just over 250,000 bags in 1997–2001. However the 2000/01 output was approximately 300,000 bags. Even at these sharply reduced levels, coffee revenues still account for well over half of Rwanda's total export earnings. Domestic coffee consumption is negligible.

Most production is of the semi-washed type but recently a number of washing stations have been established and the export of washed arabica is expected to increase. Exports have to travel a long way to the Indian Ocean port of Mombasa (Kenya), all of it by road.

## Thailand (population 61 million)

Coffee production in Thailand reached 1.0 million bags for the first time in 1989. In the five years from 1997 to 2001 output has averaged 1.3 million bags; a peak of nearly 1.7 million bags in 2000 shows that the country does not lack potential and if coffee prices had not collapsed as they did, perhaps production would have continued to grow.

The Thai government had in earlier years tried to slow the expansion of the coffee sector. Lately it has found itself in the position of having to support prices to prevent the wholesale ruination of coffee farmers. Only robusta is grown. Although production will continue to be stifled as long as low prices persist, it is entirely possible that, like Viet Nam, Thailand too is a future source of growth in Asian production. The country has a strong domestic market, taking some 500,000 bags annually, much of it in the form of soluble coffee. A small amount of soluble is also exported (2,000 bags GBE in 2000/01).

## Togo (population 5 million)

Togo is a small producer of good quality sun-dried robusta, mostly grown by an estimated 40,000 smallholders (who also grow cocoa) in the southwestern part of the country, along the border with Ghana. Production reached 320,000 bags in 1989, fell to just 120,000 bags in 1993 and averaged 285,000 bags in the five years from 1997 to 2001 with a peak of 334,000 bags in 1999/00. In 2000/01 output was 285,000 bags. Domestic consumption is negligible. Like some other West African countries, Togo too operated a *caisse* system for many years but, following the disappearance of the ICO quota system, increasing levels of debt rendered the system increasingly untenable and the coffee and cocoa trade was fully liberalized in 1996.

## Uganda (population 22 million)

Uganda is one of the world's major robusta producers, with some arabica also grown in different highland areas, most notably on the slopes of Mount Elgon on the border with Kenya, and on the slopes of the Rwenzori Mountain Range (known as the Mountains of the Moon) on the border with the Democratic Republic of the Congo. While the economy as a whole has expanded and improved in recent years, coffee remains of vital importance, earning on average just under 60% of annual export revenues during the period 1996–2000.

It is estimated that as many as one-fifth of the population earn all or a large part of their cash income from coffee. Following decades of total state control of the sector, the coffee industry is once again fully liberalized and entirely in private hands although export quality control remains the responsibility of the Uganda Coffee Development Authority (UCDA), which liquors and classifies all export shipments.

Production averaged almost 3.3 million bags in the six years from 1996 to 2001, with a peak of 4.3 million bags in 1996 (a total last seen in 1972) and a low of 2.5 million in 1997. The proportion of arabica fluctuates from around 8% to 10% of the total. Local consumption is limited at around 3% of production. Most robusta is sun-dried although in recent years there have been modest attempts to reintroduce wet processing. These attempts are ongoing, with the support of the Uganda Coffee Development Authority. In the early 1960s the Uganda coffee industry produced close to 25,000 tons of good quality pulped and washed robusta but this segment vanished entirely during the monopoly years, together with the plantation sector that supported it. It is estimated that today (2002) there are about 500,000 small farms of varying sizes that grow at least some coffee.

Robusta is native to Uganda. Two types are grown: Nganda and Erecta. An extensive clonal replanting programme combines high yielding clones of both varieties that are vegetatively propagated and self sterile. The progenies are true to type and retain their parental characteristics: they are high yielding, mature faster and produce a bigger bean with improved liquor characteristics. Reportedly they also show resistance to coffee leaf rust disease. The intrinsic quality of Uganda robusta has always been excellent and the ongoing replanting programme using this locally developed clonal material is likely to result in a general revival of the country's ability to supply good, neutral liquoring coffee. Robusta in Uganda is grown at relatively high altitudes, some as high as 1,500 m, making these coffees especially attractive for the fast growing espresso industry. Most arabica is processed with the use of hand pulpers. Here too attempts are underway to upgrade processing through the introduction of eco-friendly integrated pulping systems that simultaneously remove both pulp and mucilage while using only small amounts of water, making them particularly suitable for use by smallholders.

## United Republic of Tanzania (population 34 million)

Tanzania produces both arabica and robusta: arabica on the slopes of the world-famous Mount Kilimanjaro and surrounding areas, as well as in the Southern Highlands, and robusta in the Bukoba area west of the equally famous Lake Victoria (where a small amount of low-grown natural arabica is also found). Total production averaged around 750,000 bags annually in the period 1996–2001, ranging from a low of 670,000 in 1997/98 to just below 850,000 bags in 2000/01 (of which about 170,000 bags robusta). Coffee remains an important crop in Tanzania but accounted for only 15% of total export revenues in the period 1996–2000. Domestic consumption is negligible. Arabica is both washed and semi-washed while all robusta is dry processed. The Mount Kilimanjaro area is particularly known for the production of some exceptionally fine coffees, combining altitude with deep volcanic soils and abundant rainfall. Originally the industry was estate-oriented, but it is now dominated by smallholders following the demise of large parts of the estate sector through nationalization in 1973. In recent years, following liberalization of the coffee sector, the estate sector has however made something of a comeback. Smallholder production in the Southern Highlands (bordering Zambia and Malawi) has expanded considerably as one of the spin-offs of the construction of the Tazara railway (which connects Zambia with the Indian Ocean port of Dar es Salaam). Increasing numbers of washing stations are being built and, subject to the recovery of world market prices, the outlook for expansion is considered quite positive.

Like Kenya and Burundi, Tanzania uses the auction system to market its coffee.

## Venezuela (population 24 million)

Coffee production has stood at around 1 million bags of mostly wet processed (80%) arabica since the 1970s, occasionally falling to around 700,000–800,000 bags. The area planted to coffee is about 315,000 hectares and annual output averaged approximately 1 million bags in 1997–2000. In 2000/01 production was 1.1 million bags. The domestic market is well developed and accounts on average for about 70% of production but has declined in recent years from 2.5 kg per capita to just 1.5 kg (from 1 million bags in the 1996 crop year to 690,000 bags in 2000). There is some modest export of soluble coffee but green coffee exports virtually collapsed in 2000 because of artificially high domestic prices that in turn led to stockpiling of coffee at a time when external prices were falling sharply. At one stage Venezuela exported some of the world's best 'fine washed' arabica but as a relatively high-cost producer the country has found the going difficult in recent years and the recent price manipulation has made green exports uncompetitive.

At one time coffee was fairly important in terms of agricultural exports but now it is insignificant in relation to total export revenues. The recovery of coffee's importance will require the reactivation of exports and a reversal of the decline in domestic consumption.

## Viet Nam (population 79 million)

From modest beginnings the growth of the Vietnamese coffee industry has been nothing short of spectacular. Exports rose from 1.2 million bags in 1990/91 to 14.4 million bags in the 2000/01 coffee year, and coffee has become one of the country's key agricultural products, alongside rice. Some 500,000 hectares are under coffee, of which between 10% and 15% are state farms. The remainder (or about 85%) are small individual household farms, usually with just 2–5 hectares under coffee although some may have 30–50 hectares. Robusta accounts for some 480,000 hectares at an average density of about 1,300 trees per hectare; the remaining 20,000 hectares are arabica planted at about 4,000 trees per hectare. Robusta is grown in the south, mostly in Dak Lak province, and harvested in November–March. Arabica is grown in the north and is harvested during October–November.

Production has risen sharply not just because of additional plantings but also because of intensive cultivation practices including the use of fertilizers and irrigation. Viet Nam's cost of production is reportedly extremely competitive but Vietnamese farmers were losing money at the prices prevailing in 2001/02. Despite the huge population domestic consumption is still relatively modest at around 500,000 bags annually; it is however growing slowly at the rate of about 3%. Only a minimum amount of soluble coffee is exported (12,000 bags in 2000/01) but exports of roasted coffee were 170,000 bags GBE in the same coffee year.

Small growers, who constitute the vast majority, mostly use the dry process and produce naturals. The rain that occurs during the harvest season complicates drying. State farms tend to use an abbreviated wet process (for both robusta and arabica) with mechanical stripping of the mucilage. State-owned enterprises, at both national and provincial level, account for 10%–15% of the total area under coffee. The largest and best known is VINACAFE, which also engages in coffee export. Interestingly, land owned by state enterprises is being transferred to the workforce with the organizations retaining responsibility for providing inputs, social services and technical assistance. The Viet Nam Coffee and Cocoa Association (VICOFA) groups and represents all those engaged in coffee production, processing, export and research.

Viet Nam is a typical example of a producing country that has achieved market share by competing on price: quality has tended to be variable but without direct and visible incentives to growers it was difficult to ratchet this now very large industry to higher quality levels. Even so, Viet Nam has become a permanent feature in the purchasing strategy of many leading roasters who appear to welcome the country's coffee and who consider that the quality is showing signs of improvement. Strongly growing exports to Germany (almost 14% of green coffee imports in 2001) are but one example of this. The Vietnamese industry is aware of the need to improve quality and is actively engaging the issue by increasingly stressing quality over quantity to its growers in order to improve prices. The country also plans to increase the area under arabica to reach about 25% of total production, and to reduce that under robusta by removing aged and unsuitably located plantations.

# Appendix

# Useful websites

These website addresses make up only a small sample of the vast and growing number of Internet sites providing useful information on coffee. The inclusion of a name on the list does not imply endorsement by ITC.

Many websites cover several categories of activities. The category under which they are listed here does not necessarily reflect their main line of activity.

| Associations and organizations | | |
|---|---|---|
| www.ico.org | ICO | International Coffee Organization |
| www.ncausa.org | NCA | National Coffee Association |
| www.green-coffee-assoc.org | GCA | Green Coffee Association |
| www.scaa.org | SCAA | Specialty Coffee Association of America |
| www.ecf-coffee.org | ECF | European Coffee Federation |
| www.scae.com | SCAE | Specialty Coffee Association of Europe |
| www.oiac-iaco.org | IACO | Interafrican Coffee Organisation |
| www.eafca.org | EAFCA | Eastern African Fine Coffees Association |
| www.bsca.com.br | BSCA | Brazil Specialty Coffee Association |
| www.fao.org | FAO | Food and Agriculture Organization of the United Nations |
| www.common-fund.org | CFC | Common Fund for Commodities |
| www.worldbank.org | WB | World Bank |
| www.wto.org | WTO | World Trade Organization |
| www.imo.org | IMO | International Maritime Organization |
| www.intracen.org | ITC | International Trade Centre UNCTAD/WTO |
| **Trading and prices** | | |
| www.nybot.com | NYBOT | New York Board of Trade |
| www.liffe.com | LIFFE | London International Financial Futures and Options Exchange |
| www.bmf.com.br | BM&F | Bolsa de Mercadorias & Futuros (Brazilian Mercantile & Futures Exchange) |
| www.cofei.com | COFEI | Coffee Futures Exchange India Ltd |
| www.tge.or.jp | TGE | Tokyo Grain Exchange |
| www.iccwbo.org | ICC | International Chamber of Commerce; Incoterms |
| www.cftc.gov | CFTC | Commodity Futures Trading Commission |
| www.bolero.net | | Bolero International (e-commerce) |
| www.intercommercial.com | | InterCommercial Markets Corp. (e-commerce) |
| www.identrus.com | | Identrus (e-commerce) |
| www.coffee-exchange.com | | Coffee Trading & Information Services |
| www.futures.tradingcharts.com | TFC | International TradingCharts.com, Inc. |
| www.coffeenetwork.com | | CoffeeNetwork |

| Research and pest/disease management | | |
|---|---|---|
| www.cabi.org | CABI | CAB International |
| www.fao.org | FAO | Food and Agriculture Organization |
| www.pestmanagement.co.uk | IPMRC | Integrated Pest Management Resource Centre |
| www.codexalimentarius.net | | FAO/WHO Codex Alimentarius Commission |
| www.cirad.fr | CIRAD | Centre de coopération internationale en recherche agronomique pour le développement |
| www.catie.ac.cr | CATIE | Centro Agronómico Tropical de Investigación y Enseñanza – Tropical Agricultural Research and Higher Education Center |
| www.coffeeresearch.org | | Coffee Research Institute |
| www.asic-cafe.org | ASIC | Association scientifique internationale du café |
| www.coffeeinstitute.org | CQI | Coffee Quality Institute |
| **Sustainability and environment** | | |
| www.ifoam.org | IFOAM | International Federation of Organic Agriculture Movements |
| www.fairtrade.net | FLO | Fairtrade Labelling Organizations International |
| www.maxhavelaar.org | | Max Havelaar Foundation (fair trade) |
| www.transfairusa.org | | TransFair USA (fair trade) |
| www.rainforest-alliance.org | | The Rainforest Alliance |
| www.ioia.net | IOIA | Independent Organic Inspectors Association |
| www.natzoo.si.edu.smbc | | Smithsonian Migratory Bird Center |
| www.technoserve.org | | TechnoServe |
| www.coffeekids.org | | Coffee Kids |
| www.utzkapeh.org | | Utz Kapeh |
| www.gtz.de | GTZ | Deutsche Gesellschaft für Technische Zusammenarbeit (GTZ) GmbH |
| **Health** | | |
| www.cosic.org | CoSIC | Coffee Science Information Centre |
| www.mc.vanderbilt.edu/coffee | ICS | Institute for Coffee Studies, Vanderbilt University Medical Center |
| www.coffeescience.org | CSS | Coffee Science Source |
| www.codexalimentarius.net | | FAO/WHO Codex Alimentarius Commission |
| www.fda.gov | FDA | United States Food and Drug Administration |
| **Other useful information** | | |
| www.p-maps.org | ITC | ITC's Coffee Product Map |
| www.fas.usda.gov | USDA | United States Department of Agriculture, Foreign Agricultural Service |
| www.europa.eu.int | EU | The European Union |
| www.iso.org | ISO | International Organization for Standardization |
| www.supremo.be | | Coffee Origins' Encyclopedia |
| www.jobin.fr | | P. Jobin & Cie |
| www.tis-gdv.de | TIS-GDV | Transport Information Service, German Insurance Association |
| www.inttra.com | INTTRA | INTTRA (ocean freight services) |
| www.xrefer.com | | Xrefer (reference library) |
| www.dmgworldmedia.com | | Coffee & Cocoa International (magazine) |
| **ITC's Coffee Product Map** | | |

ITC's Coffee and Coffee Product Market Analysis Portal (*www.p-maps.org*) is a platform designed for the coffee industry to easily access international coffee trade data and market intelligence and gain visibility through networking facilities. Two freely accessible modules – Business Contacts and Smart Links – provide classified links to information available on the web.